image COMICS PRESENTS

GUARDING THE GLOBE ™
UNDER SIEGE

D1288404

CREATED BY
ROBERT KIRKMAN
CORY WALKER
& RYAN OTTLEY

image®

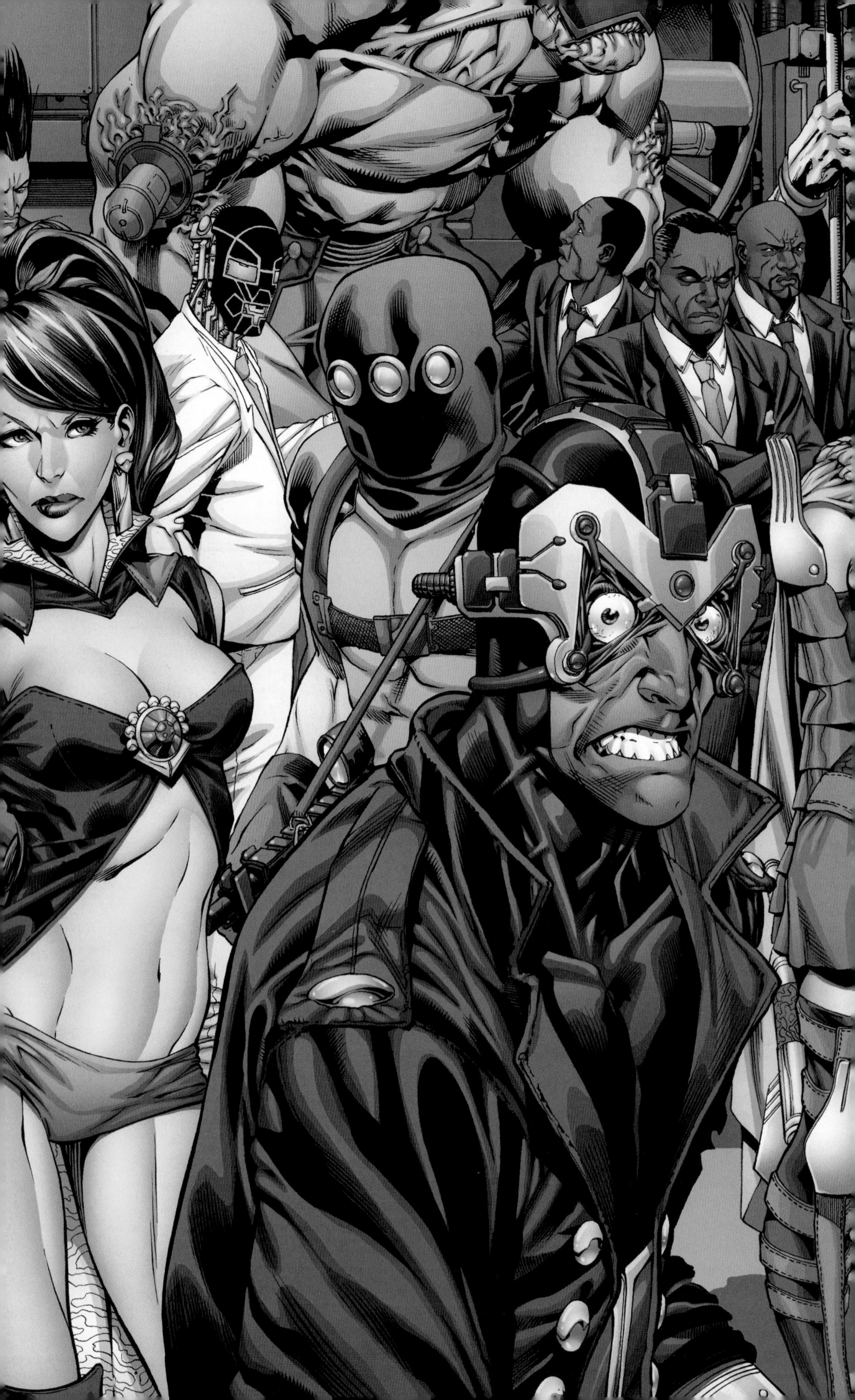

writers
ROBERT KIRKMAN
BENITO CERENO

pencilers
RANSOM GETTY [chaps 1-5]
KRIS ANKA [chap 6]

inkers
RANSOM GETTY
[chap 1, pgs 1-20; chap 3, pgs 2, 14, 16, 18-20;
chap 5, pgs 3, 5, 7, 18-20]

CLIFF RATHBURN
[chap 1, pgs 21-22; chap 2]

JONATHAN GLAPION
[chap 3, pgs 1, 3, 4, 6, 12]

RUSSELL JACKSON
[chap 3, pgs 5, 7-11, 13, 15, 17; chap 4;
chap 5, pgs 1, 2, 4, 6, 8-17]

KRIS ANKA [chap 6]

colorists
FCO PLASCENCIA [chap 1, pgs 1, 8-10]
RON RILEY [chap 1, pgs 2-7, 11, 16-20]
THOMAS MASON
[chap 1, pgs 12-15, 21, 22; chap 2-6]

color assists
REX STABBS [chaps 2-6]

letterer
RUS WOOTON

editor
SINA GRACE

cover
TODD NAUCK & JOHN RAUCH

GUARDING THE GLOBE, VOL. 1: UNDER SIEGE
ISBN: 978-1-60706-356-8
First Printing

Published by Image Comics, Inc. Office of publication: 2134 Allston Way, 2nd Floor, Berkeley, California 94704. Image and its logos are ® and © 2012 Image Comics Inc. All rights reserved. Originally published in single magazine form as GUARDING THE GLOBE #1-6. GUARDING THE GLOBE and all character likenesses are ™ and © 2012, Robert Kirkman, LLC, Cory Walker, and Ryan Ottley. All rights reserved. All names, characters, events and locales in this publication are entirely fictional. Any resemblance to actual persons (living or dead), events or places, without satiric intent, is coincidental. No part of this publication may be reproduced or transmitted, in any form or by any means (except for short excerpts for review purposes) without the express written permission of the copyright holder.

PRINTED IN U.S.A.

For information regarding the CPSIA on this printed material call: 203-595-3636 and provide reference # RICH – 447731.

SKYBOUND ENTERTAINMENT
www.skybound.com

Robert Kirkman - *CEO*
J.J. Didde - *President*
Sean Mackiewicz - *Editorial Director*
Shawn Kirkham - *Director of Business Development*
Tim Daniel - *Digital Content Manager*
Chad Manion - *Assistant to Mr. Grace*
Sydney Pennington - *Assistant to Mr. Kirkham*
Feldman Public Relations LA - *Public Relations*
For international rights inquiries, please contact: foreign@skybound.com

IMAGE COMICS, INC.
www.imagecomics.com

Robert Kirkman - *Chief Operating Officer*
Erik Larsen - *Chief Financial Officer*
Todd McFarlane - *President*
Marc Silvestri - *CEO*
Jim Valentino - *Vice-President*

Eric Stephenson - *Publisher*
Todd Martinez - *Sales & Licensing Coordinator*
Jennifer de Guzman - *PR & Marketing Director*
Branwyn Bigglestone - *Accounts Manager*
Emily Miller - *Administrative Assistant*
Jamie Parreno - *Marketing Assistant*
Sarah deLaine - *Events Coordinator*
Kevin Yuen - *Digital Rights Coordinator*
Tyler Shainline - *Traffic Manager*
Drew Gill - *Art Director*
Jonathan Chan - *Design Director*
Monica Garcia - *Production Artist*
Vincent Kukua - *Production Artist*
Jana Cook - *Production Artist*

CHAPTER ONE

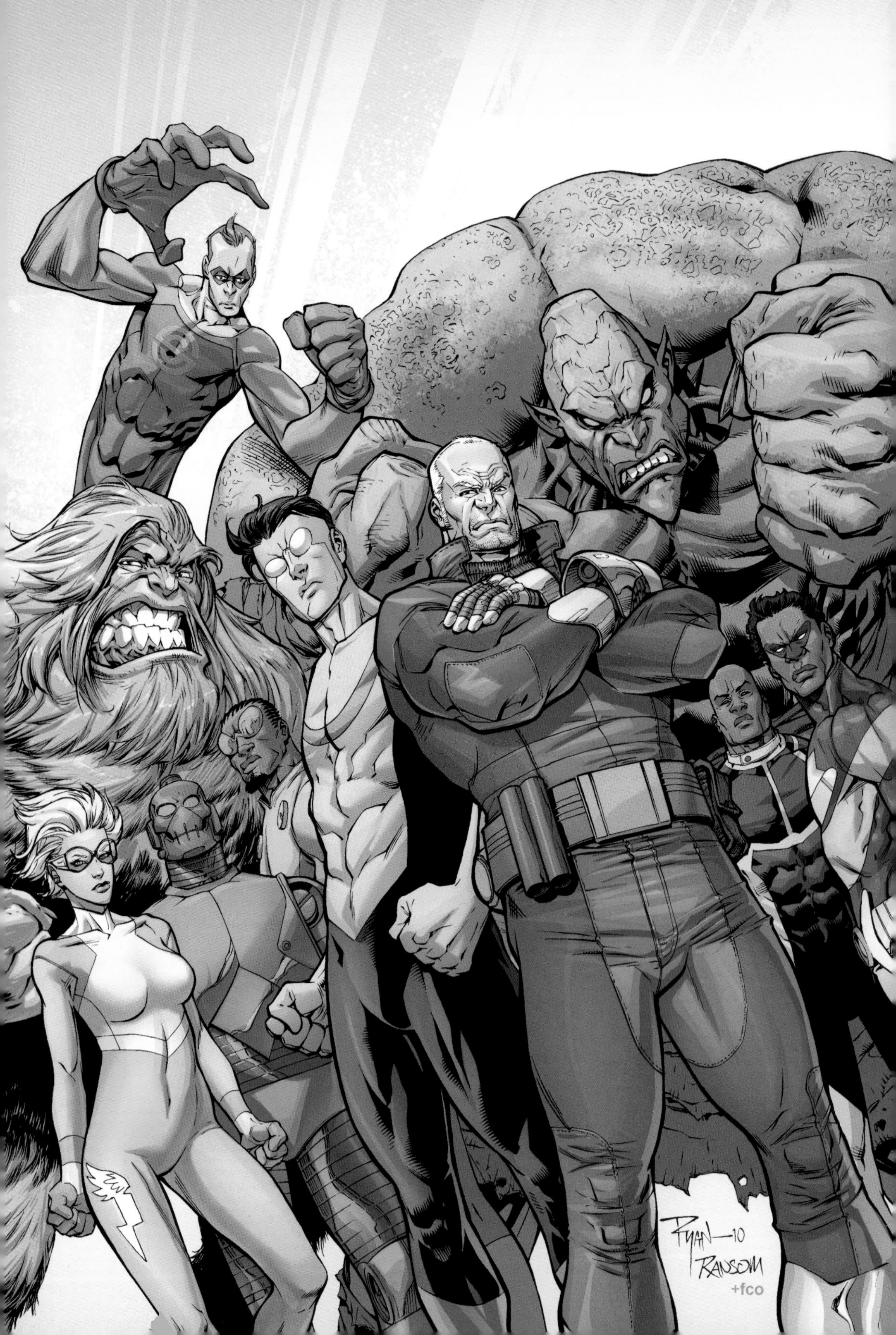
RYAN —10
RANSOM
+fco

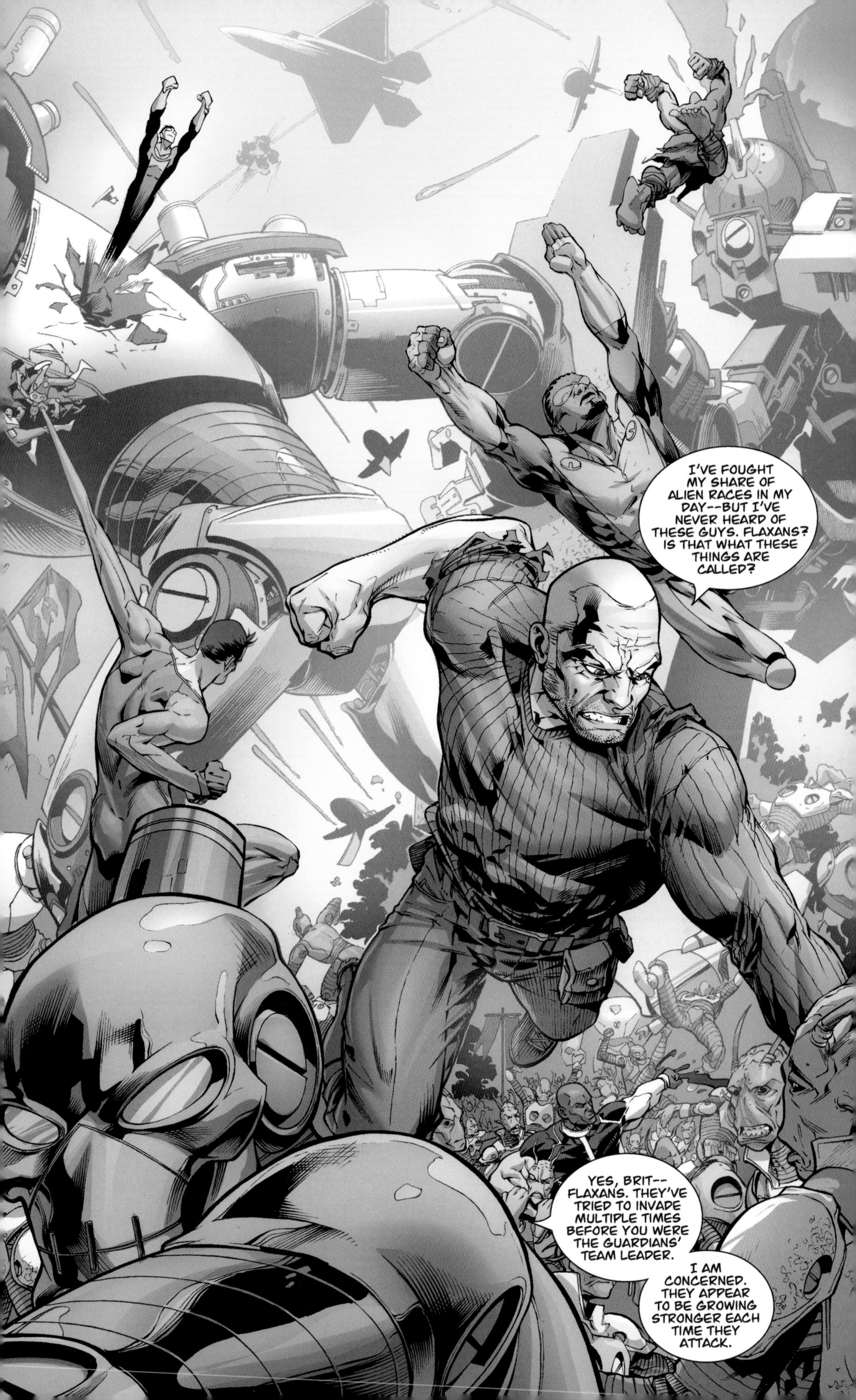
I'VE FOUGHT MY SHARE OF ALIEN RACES IN MY DAY--BUT I'VE NEVER HEARD OF THESE GUYS. FLAXANS? IS THAT WHAT THESE THINGS ARE CALLED?
YES, BRIT--FLAXANS. THEY'VE TRIED TO INVADE MULTIPLE TIMES BEFORE YOU WERE THE GUARDIANS' TEAM LEADER.
I AM CONCERNED. THEY APPEAR TO BE GROWING STRONGER EACH TIME THEY ATTACK.

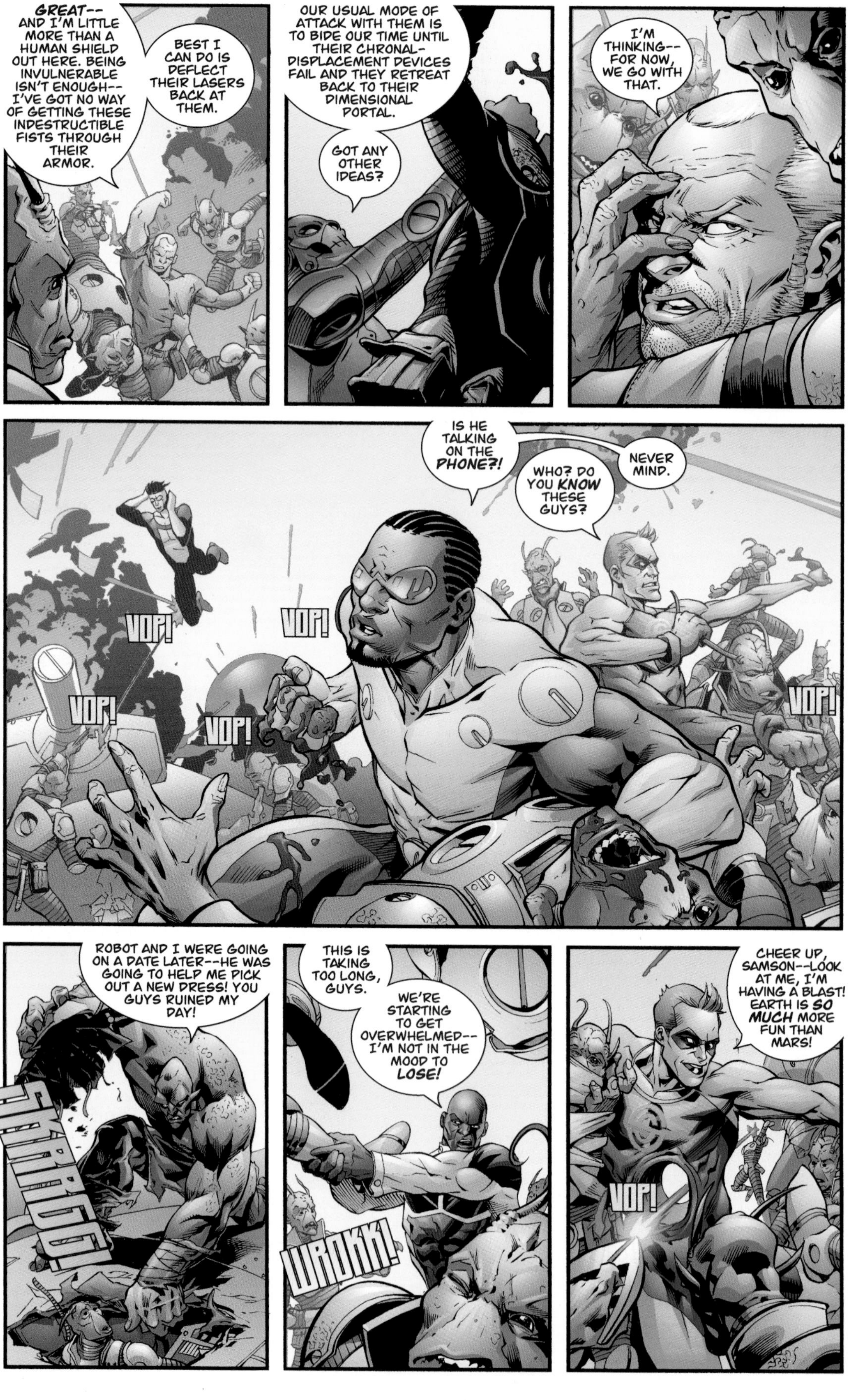
GREAT-- AND I'M LITTLE MORE THAN A HUMAN SHIELD OUT HERE. BEING INVULNERABLE ISN'T ENOUGH-- I'VE GOT NO WAY OF GETTING THESE INDESTRUCTIBLE FISTS THROUGH THEIR ARMOR.
BEST I CAN DO IS DEFLECT THEIR LASERS BACK AT THEM.
OUR USUAL MODE OF ATTACK WITH THEM IS TO BIDE OUR TIME UNTIL THEIR CHRONAL-DISPLACEMENT DEVICES FAIL AND THEY RETREAT BACK TO THEIR DIMENSIONAL PORTAL.
GOT ANY OTHER IDEAS?
I'M THINKING-- FOR NOW, WE GO WITH THAT.
IS HE TALKING ON THE PHONE?!
WHO? DO YOU KNOW THESE GUYS?
NEVER MIND.
VOP!
VOP!
VOP!
VOP!
VOP!
ROBOT AND I WERE GOING ON A DATE LATER--HE WAS GOING TO HELP ME PICK OUT A NEW DRESS! YOU GUYS RUINED MY DAY!
SKRADOOM!
THIS IS TAKING TOO LONG, GUYS.
WE'RE STARTING TO GET OVERWHELMED-- I'M NOT IN THE MOOD TO LOSE!
UROKK!
CHEER UP, SAMSON--LOOK AT ME, I'M HAVING A BLAST! EARTH IS SO MUCH MORE FUN THAN MARS!
VOP!

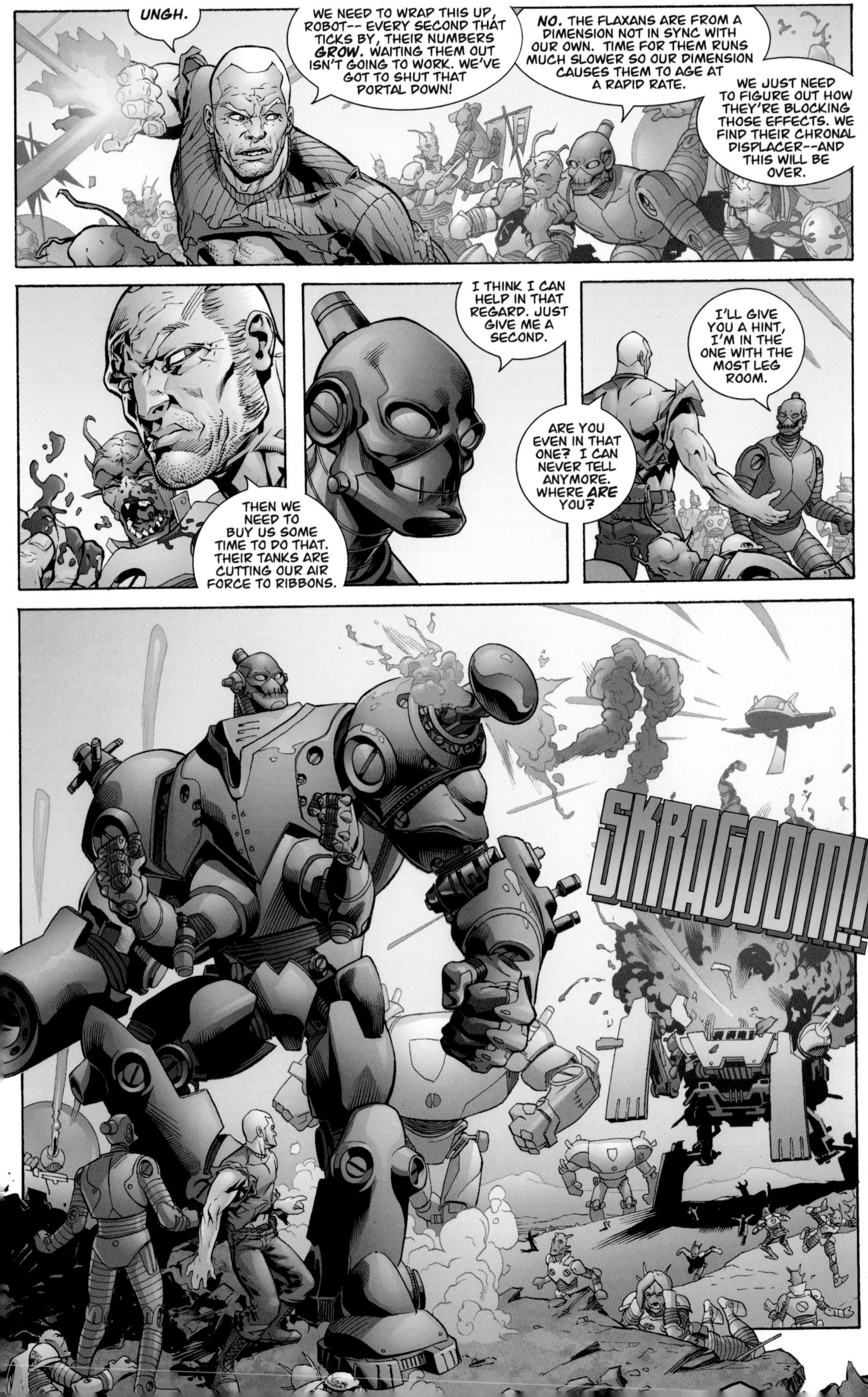
UNGH.
WE NEED TO WRAP THIS UP, ROBOT-- EVERY SECOND THAT TICKS BY, THEIR NUMBERS GROW. WAITING THEM OUT ISN'T GOING TO WORK. WE'VE GOT TO SHUT THAT PORTAL DOWN!
NO. THE FLAXANS ARE FROM A DIMENSION NOT IN SYNC WITH OUR OWN. TIME FOR THEM RUNS MUCH SLOWER SO OUR DIMENSION CAUSES THEM TO AGE AT A RAPID RATE.
WE JUST NEED TO FIGURE OUT HOW THEY'RE BLOCKING THOSE EFFECTS. WE FIND THEIR CHRONAL DISPLACER--AND THIS WILL BE OVER.
THEN WE NEED TO BUY US SOME TIME TO DO THAT. THEIR TANKS ARE CUTTING OUR AIR FORCE TO RIBBONS.
I THINK I CAN HELP IN THAT REGARD. JUST GIVE ME A SECOND.
ARE YOU EVEN IN THAT ONE? I CAN NEVER TELL ANYMORE. WHERE ARE YOU?
I'LL GIVE YOU A HINT, I'M IN THE ONE WITH THE MOST LEG ROOM.
SKRADOOM!!

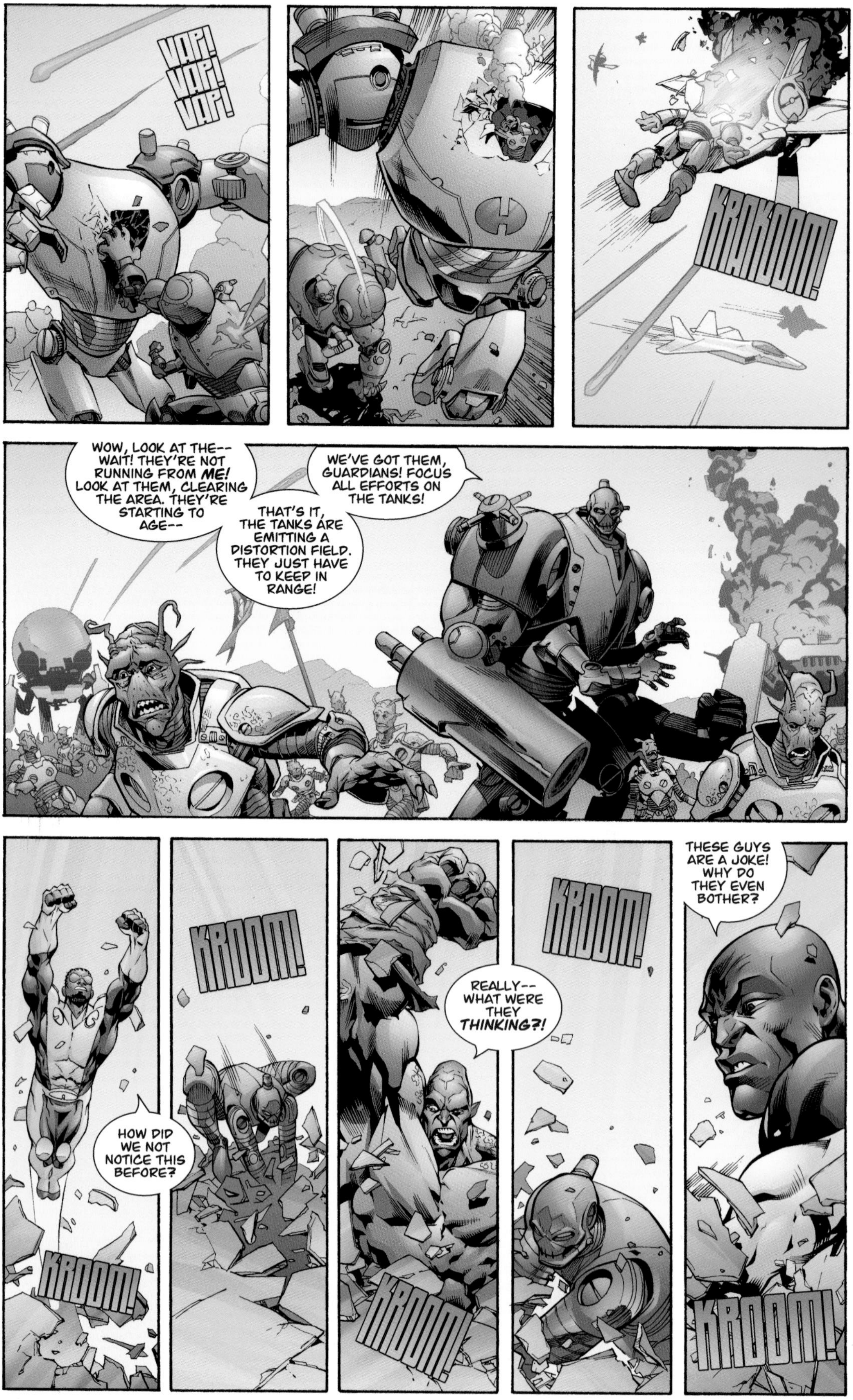
VAP! VAP! VAP!
KRAKOOM!
WOW, LOOK AT THE-- WAIT! THEY'RE NOT RUNNING FROM ME! LOOK AT THEM, CLEARING THE AREA. THEY'RE STARTING TO AGE--
WE'VE GOT THEM, GUARDIANS! FOCUS ALL EFFORTS ON THE TANKS!
THAT'S IT, THE TANKS ARE EMITTING A DISTORTION FIELD. THEY JUST HAVE TO KEEP IN RANGE!
HOW DID WE NOT NOTICE THIS BEFORE?
KROOM!
KROOM!
REALLY-- WHAT WERE THEY THINKING?!
KROOM!
KROOM!
THESE GUYS ARE A JOKE! WHY DO THEY EVEN BOTHER?
KROOM!

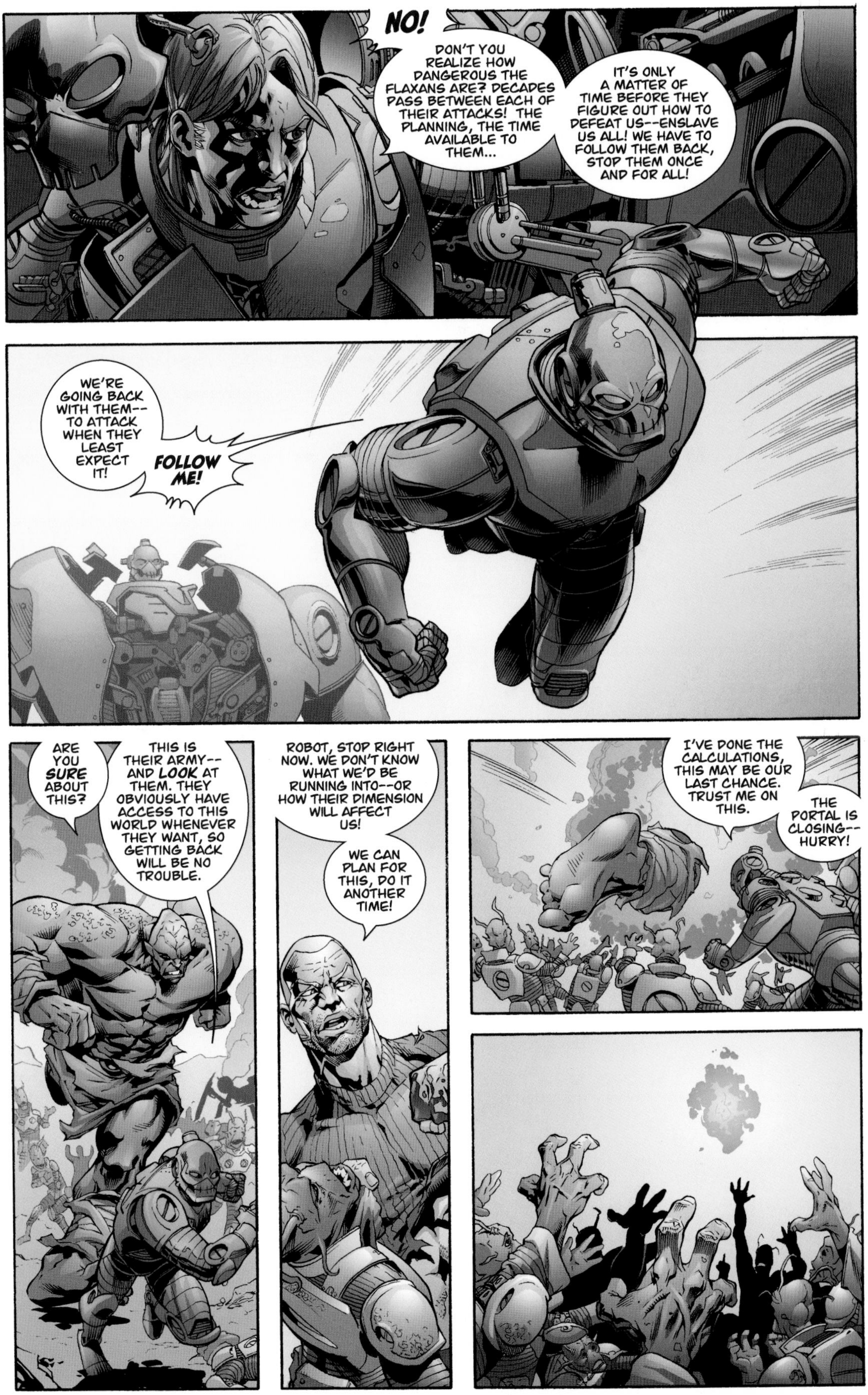
NO!
DON'T YOU REALIZE HOW DANGEROUS THE FLAXANS ARE? DECADES PASS BETWEEN EACH OF THEIR ATTACKS! THE PLANNING, THE TIME AVAILABLE TO THEM...
IT'S ONLY A MATTER OF TIME BEFORE THEY FIGURE OUT HOW TO DEFEAT US--ENSLAVE US ALL! WE HAVE TO FOLLOW THEM BACK, STOP THEM ONCE AND FOR ALL!
WE'RE GOING BACK WITH THEM--TO ATTACK WHEN THEY LEAST EXPECT IT!
FOLLOW ME!
ARE YOU SURE ABOUT THIS?
THIS IS THEIR ARMY--AND LOOK AT THEM. THEY OBVIOUSLY HAVE ACCESS TO THIS WORLD WHENEVER THEY WANT, SO GETTING BACK WILL BE NO TROUBLE.
ROBOT, STOP RIGHT NOW. WE DON'T KNOW WHAT WE'D BE RUNNING INTO--OR HOW THEIR DIMENSION WILL AFFECT US!
WE CAN PLAN FOR THIS, DO IT ANOTHER TIME!
I'VE DONE THE CALCULATIONS, THIS MAY BE OUR LAST CHANCE. TRUST ME ON THIS.
THE PORTAL IS CLOSING--HURRY!

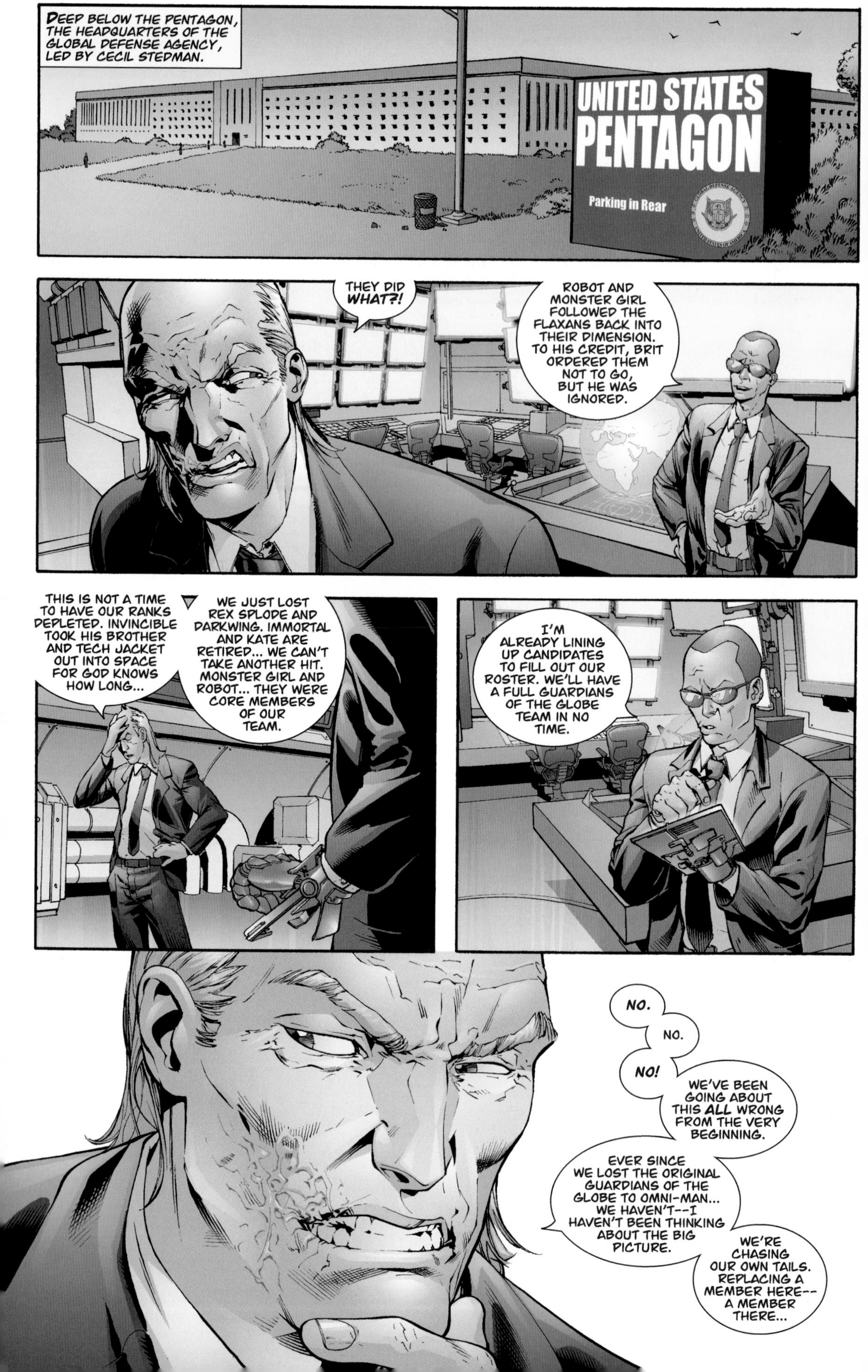
DEEP BELOW THE PENTAGON, THE HEADQUARTERS OF THE GLOBAL DEFENSE AGENCY, LED BY CECIL STEDMAN.
UNITED STATES PENTAGON
Parking in Rear
THEY DID WHAT?!
ROBOT AND MONSTER GIRL FOLLOWED THE FLAXANS BACK INTO THEIR DIMENSION. TO HIS CREDIT, BRIT ORDERED THEM NOT TO GO, BUT HE WAS IGNORED.
THIS IS NOT A TIME TO HAVE OUR RANKS DEPLETED. INVINCIBLE TOOK HIS BROTHER AND TECH JACKET OUT INTO SPACE FOR GOD KNOWS HOW LONG...
WE JUST LOST REX SPLODE AND DARKWING. IMMORTAL AND KATE ARE RETIRED... WE CAN'T TAKE ANOTHER HIT. MONSTER GIRL AND ROBOT... THEY WERE CORE MEMBERS OF OUR TEAM.
I'M ALREADY LINING UP CANDIDATES TO FILL OUT OUR ROSTER. WE'LL HAVE A FULL GUARDIANS OF THE GLOBE TEAM IN NO TIME.
NO.
NO.
NO!
WE'VE BEEN GOING ABOUT THIS ALL WRONG FROM THE VERY BEGINNING.
EVER SINCE WE LOST THE ORIGINAL GUARDIANS OF THE GLOBE TO OMNI-MAN... WE HAVEN'T--I HAVEN'T BEEN THINKING ABOUT THE BIG PICTURE.
WE'RE CHASING OUR OWN TAILS. REPLACING A MEMBER HERE-- A MEMBER THERE...

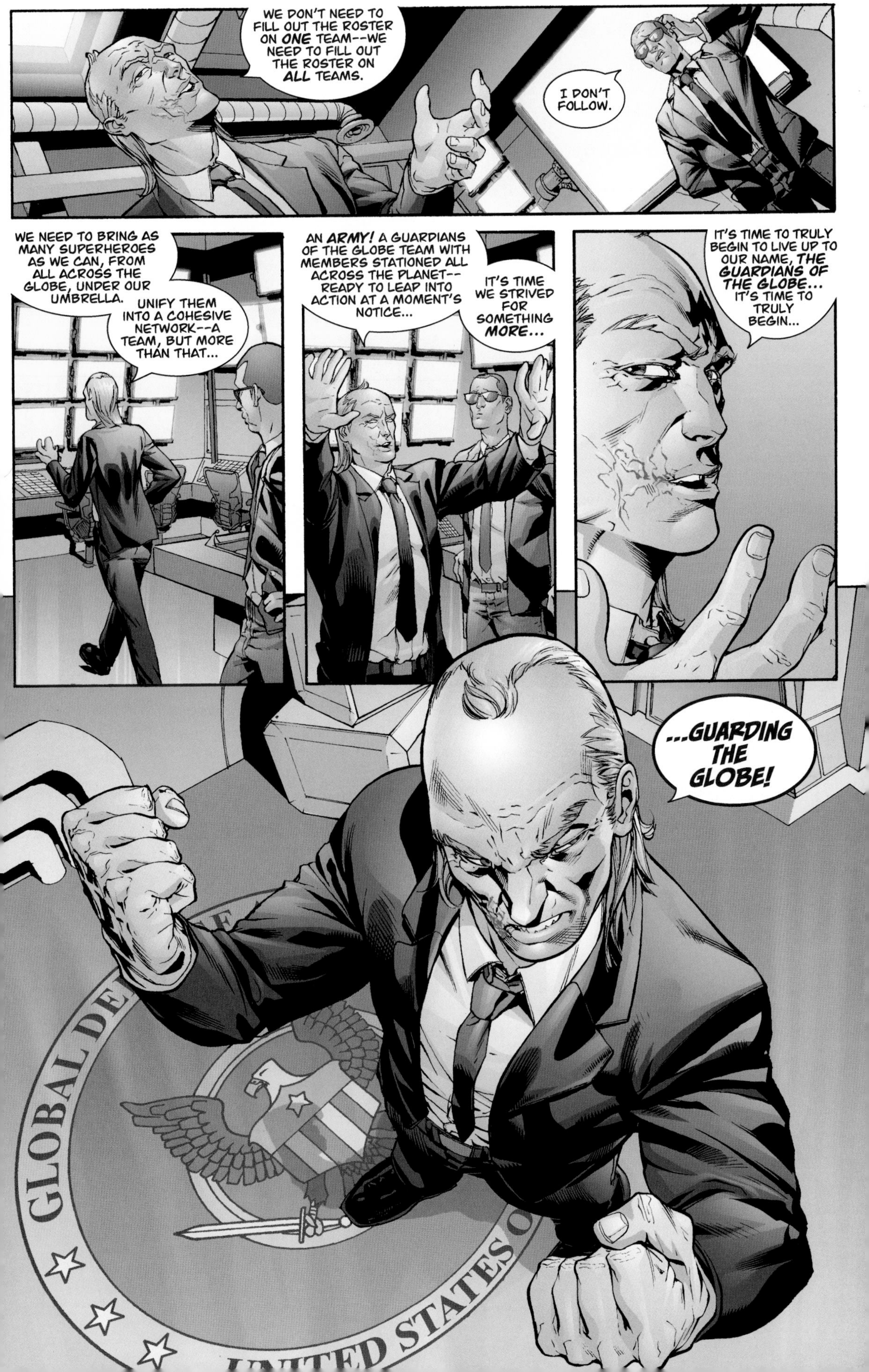

WE DON'T NEED TO FILL OUT THE ROSTER ON ONE TEAM--WE NEED TO FILL OUT THE ROSTER ON ALL TEAMS.
I DON'T FOLLOW.
WE NEED TO BRING AS MANY SUPERHEROES AS WE CAN, FROM ALL ACROSS THE GLOBE, UNDER OUR UMBRELLA.
UNIFY THEM INTO A COHESIVE NETWORK--A TEAM, BUT MORE THAN THAT...
AN ARMY! A GUARDIANS OF THE GLOBE TEAM WITH MEMBERS STATIONED ALL ACROSS THE PLANET--READY TO LEAP INTO ACTION AT A MOMENT'S NOTICE...
IT'S TIME WE STRIVED FOR SOMETHING MORE...
IT'S TIME TO TRULY BEGIN TO LIVE UP TO OUR NAME, THE GUARDIANS OF THE GLOBE... IT'S TIME TO TRULY BEGIN...
...GUARDING THE GLOBE!
GLOBAL DE
UNITED STATES O

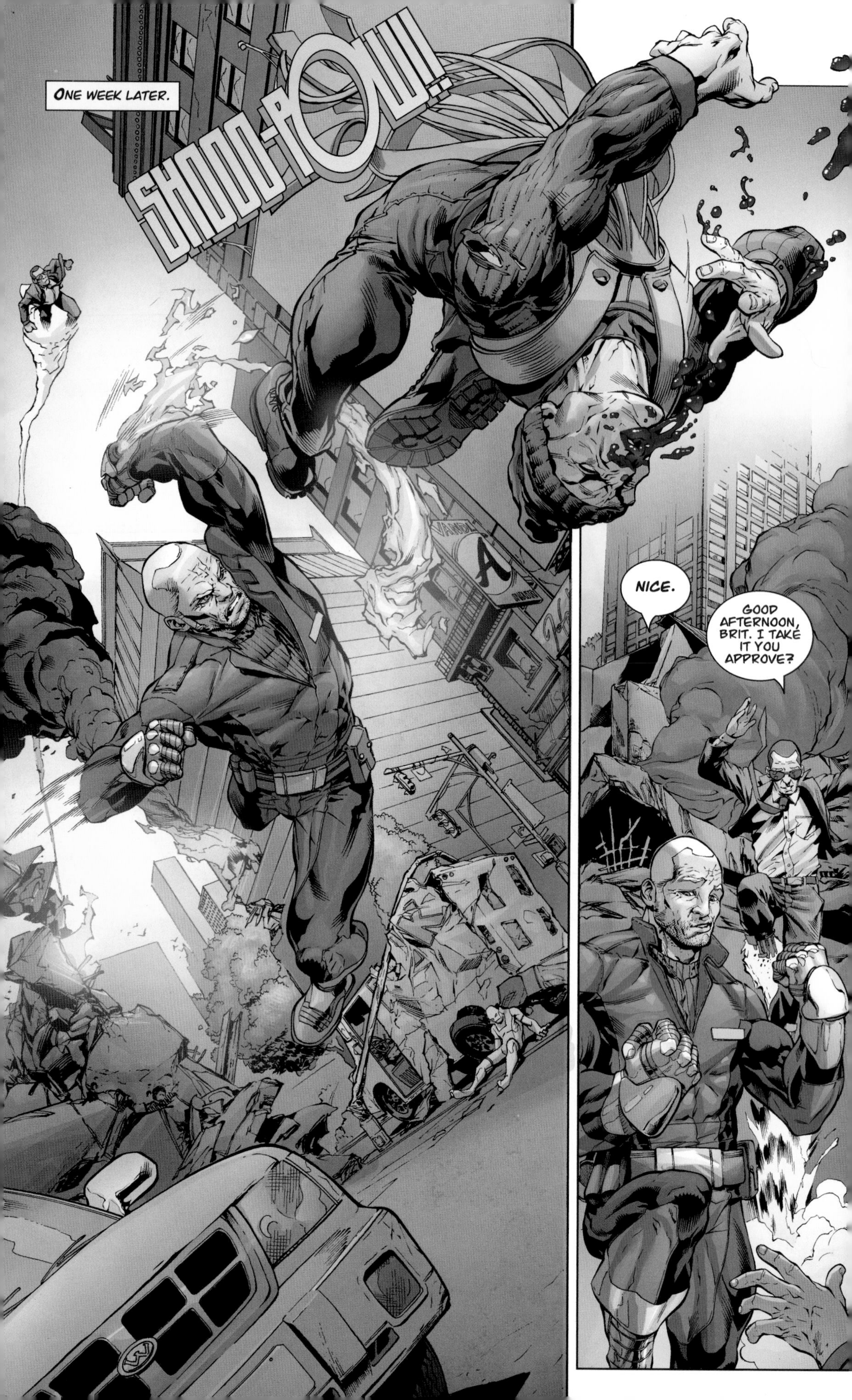
ONE WEEK LATER.
SHOOO-POW!!
NICE.
GOOD AFTERNOON, BRIT. I TAKE IT YOU APPROVE?

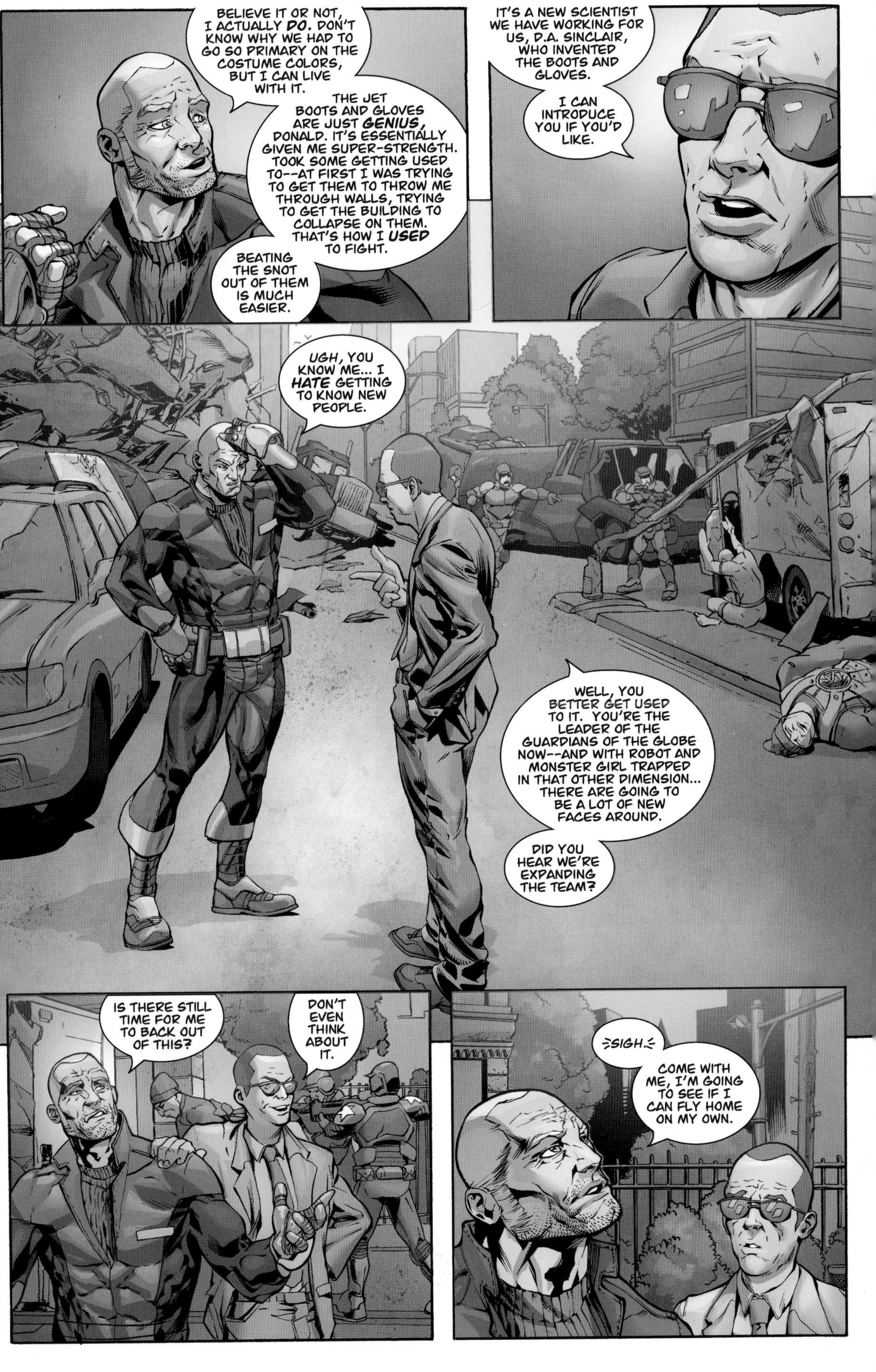
BELIEVE IT OR NOT, I ACTUALLY DO. DON'T KNOW WHY WE HAD TO GO SO PRIMARY ON THE COSTUME COLORS, BUT I CAN LIVE WITH IT.
THE JET BOOTS AND GLOVES ARE JUST GENIUS, DONALD. IT'S ESSENTIALLY GIVEN ME SUPER-STRENGTH. TOOK SOME GETTING USED TO--AT FIRST I WAS TRYING TO GET THEM TO THROW ME THROUGH WALLS, TRYING TO GET THE BUILDING TO COLLAPSE ON THEM. THAT'S HOW I USED TO FIGHT.
BEATING THE SNOT OUT OF THEM IS MUCH EASIER.
IT'S A NEW SCIENTIST WE HAVE WORKING FOR US, D.A. SINCLAIR, WHO INVENTED THE BOOTS AND GLOVES.
I CAN INTRODUCE YOU IF YOU'D LIKE.
UGH, YOU KNOW ME... I HATE GETTING TO KNOW NEW PEOPLE.
WELL, YOU BETTER GET USED TO IT. YOU'RE THE LEADER OF THE GUARDIANS OF THE GLOBE NOW--AND WITH ROBOT AND MONSTER GIRL TRAPPED IN THAT OTHER DIMENSION... THERE ARE GOING TO BE A LOT OF NEW FACES AROUND.
DID YOU HEAR WE'RE EXPANDING THE TEAM?
IS THERE STILL TIME FOR ME TO BACK OUT OF THIS?
DON'T EVEN THINK ABOUT IT.
SIGH.
COME WITH ME, I'M GOING TO SEE IF I CAN FLY HOME ON MY OWN.

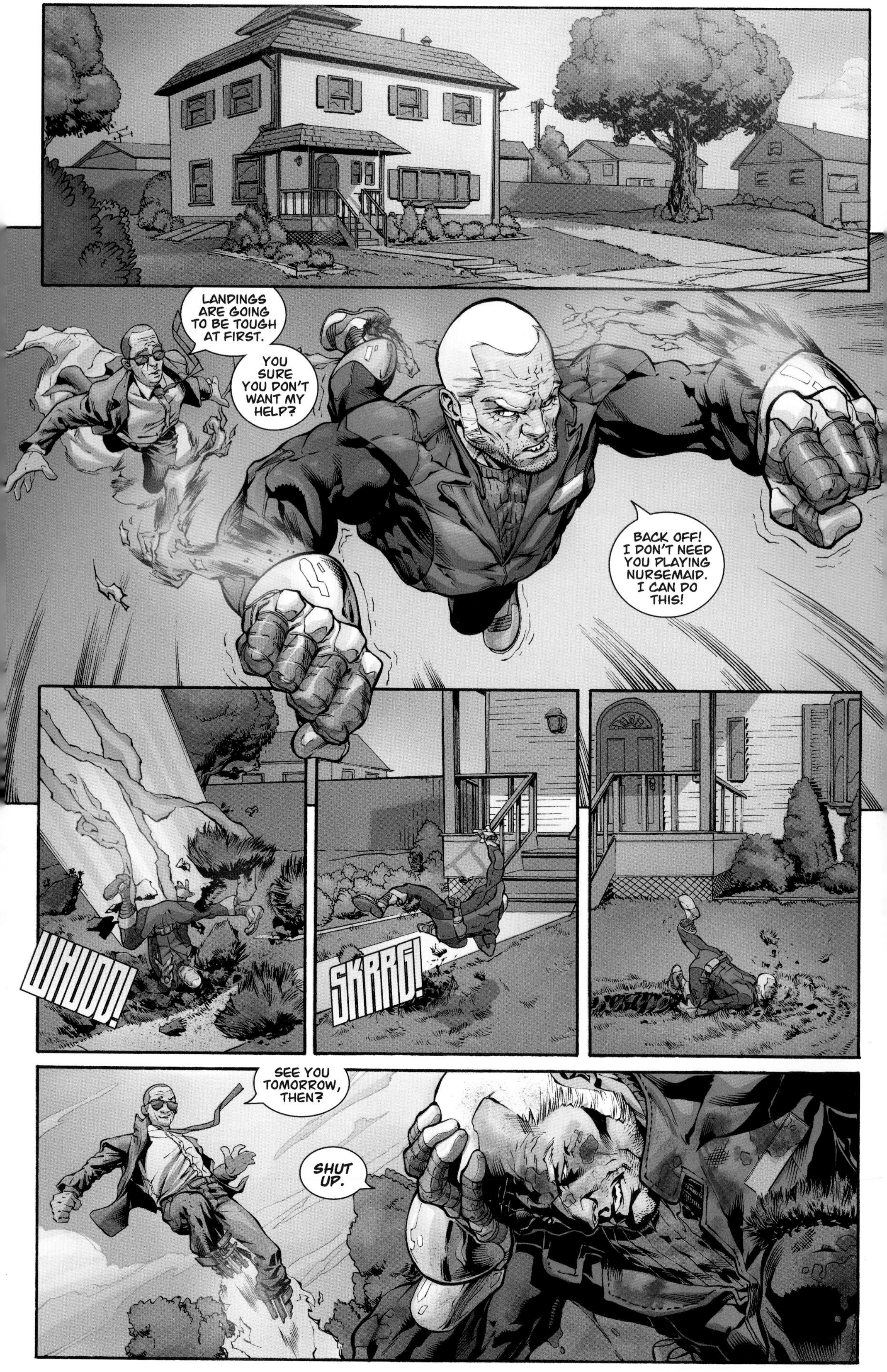
LANDINGS ARE GOING TO BE TOUGH AT FIRST.
YOU SURE YOU DON'T WANT MY HELP?
BACK OFF! I DON'T NEED YOU PLAYING NURSEMAID. I CAN DO THIS!
WHUDD!
SKRRG!
SEE YOU TOMORROW, THEN?
SHUT UP.

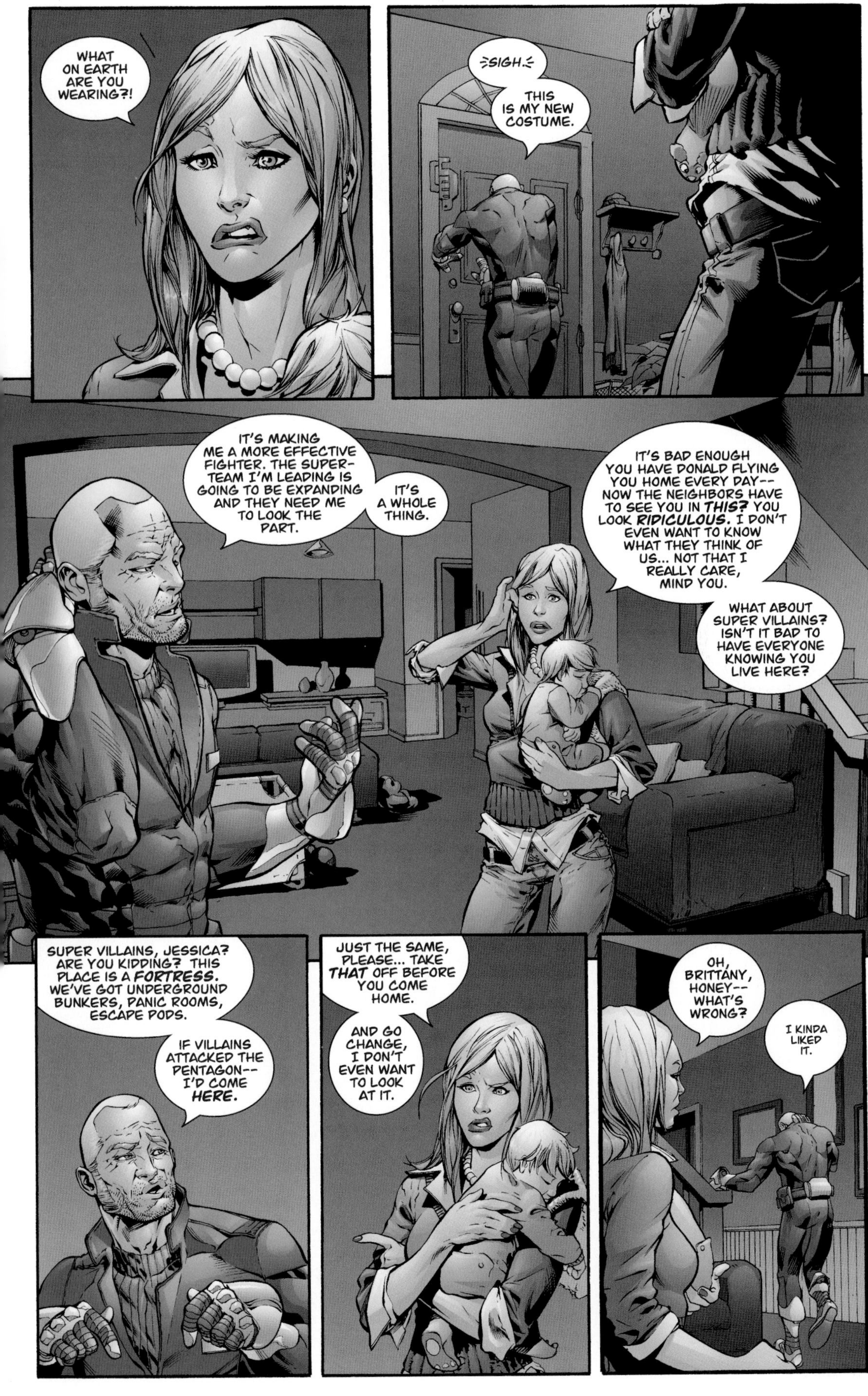
WHAT ON EARTH ARE YOU WEARING?!
SIGH.
THIS IS MY NEW COSTUME.
IT'S MAKING ME A MORE EFFECTIVE FIGHTER. THE SUPER-TEAM I'M LEADING IS GOING TO BE EXPANDING AND THEY NEED ME TO LOOK THE PART.
IT'S A WHOLE THING.
IT'S BAD ENOUGH YOU HAVE DONALD FLYING YOU HOME EVERY DAY--NOW THE NEIGHBORS HAVE TO SEE YOU IN THIS? YOU LOOK RIDICULOUS. I DON'T EVEN WANT TO KNOW WHAT THEY THINK OF US... NOT THAT I REALLY CARE, MIND YOU.
WHAT ABOUT SUPER VILLAINS? ISN'T IT BAD TO HAVE EVERYONE KNOWING YOU LIVE HERE?
SUPER VILLAINS, JESSICA? ARE YOU KIDDING? THIS PLACE IS A FORTRESS. WE'VE GOT UNDERGROUND BUNKERS, PANIC ROOMS, ESCAPE PODS.
IF VILLAINS ATTACKED THE PENTAGON--I'D COME HERE.
JUST THE SAME, PLEASE... TAKE THAT OFF BEFORE YOU COME HOME.
AND GO CHANGE, I DON'T EVEN WANT TO LOOK AT IT.
OH, BRITTANY, HONEY--WHAT'S WRONG?
I KINDA LIKED IT.

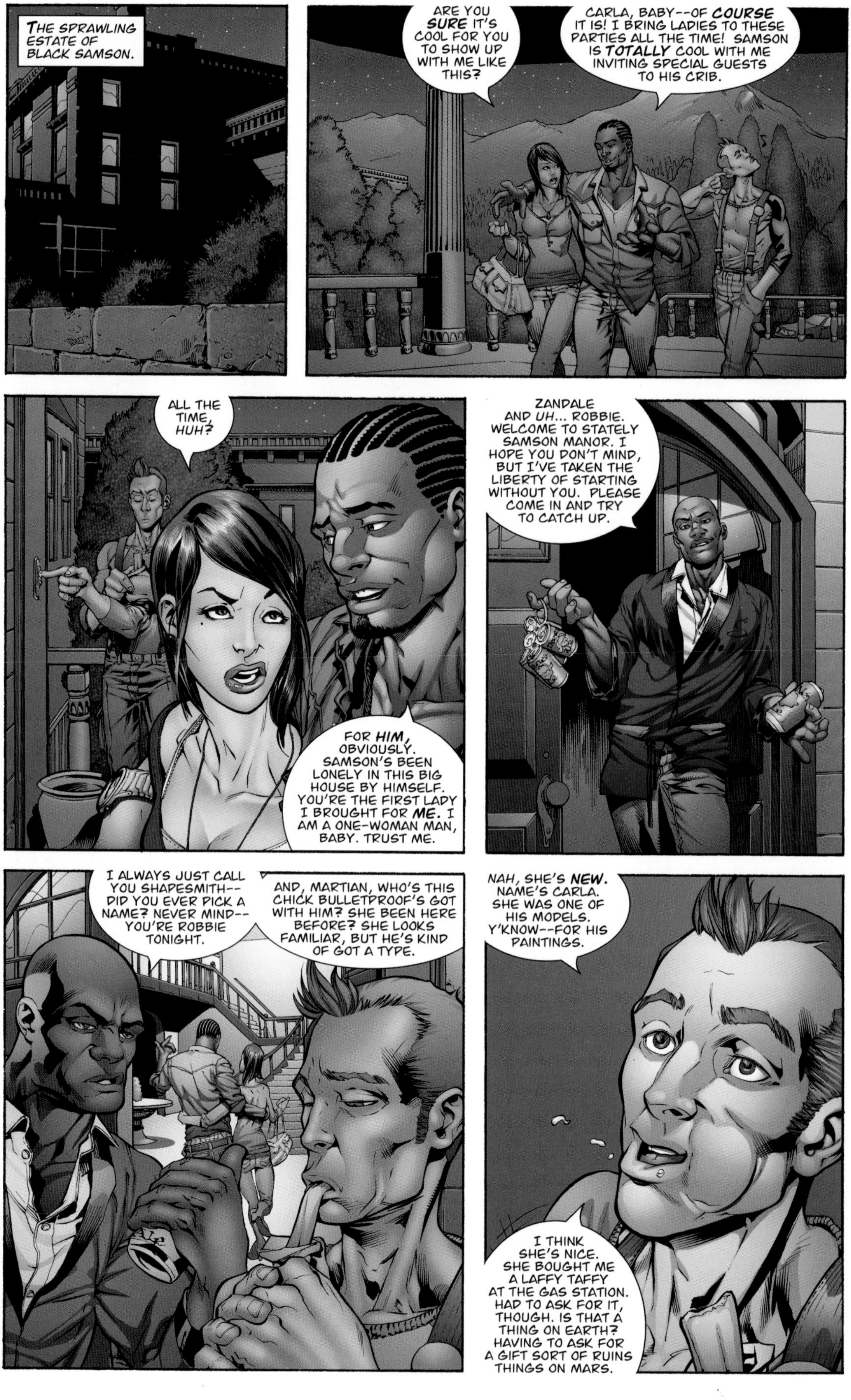
THE SPRAWLING ESTATE OF BLACK SAMSON.
ARE YOU SURE IT'S COOL FOR YOU TO SHOW UP WITH ME LIKE THIS?
CARLA, BABY--OF COURSE IT IS! I BRING LADIES TO THESE PARTIES ALL THE TIME! SAMSON IS TOTALLY COOL WITH ME INVITING SPECIAL GUESTS TO HIS CRIB.
ALL THE TIME, HUH?
FOR HIM, OBVIOUSLY. SAMSON'S BEEN LONELY IN THIS BIG HOUSE BY HIMSELF. YOU'RE THE FIRST LADY I BROUGHT FOR ME. I AM A ONE-WOMAN MAN, BABY. TRUST ME.
ZANDALE AND UH... ROBBIE. WELCOME TO STATELY SAMSON MANOR. I HOPE YOU DON'T MIND, BUT I'VE TAKEN THE LIBERTY OF STARTING WITHOUT YOU. PLEASE COME IN AND TRY TO CATCH UP.
I ALWAYS JUST CALL YOU SHAPESMITH-- DID YOU EVER PICK A NAME? NEVER MIND-- YOU'RE ROBBIE TONIGHT.
AND, MARTIAN, WHO'S THIS CHICK BULLETPROOF'S GOT WITH HIM? SHE BEEN HERE BEFORE? SHE LOOKS FAMILIAR, BUT HE'S KIND OF GOT A TYPE.
NAH, SHE'S NEW. NAME'S CARLA. SHE WAS ONE OF HIS MODELS. Y'KNOW--FOR HIS PAINTINGS.
I THINK SHE'S NICE. SHE BOUGHT ME A LAFFY TAFFY AT THE GAS STATION. HAD TO ASK FOR IT, THOUGH. IS THAT A THING ON EARTH? HAVING TO ASK FOR A GIFT SORT OF RUINS THINGS ON MARS.

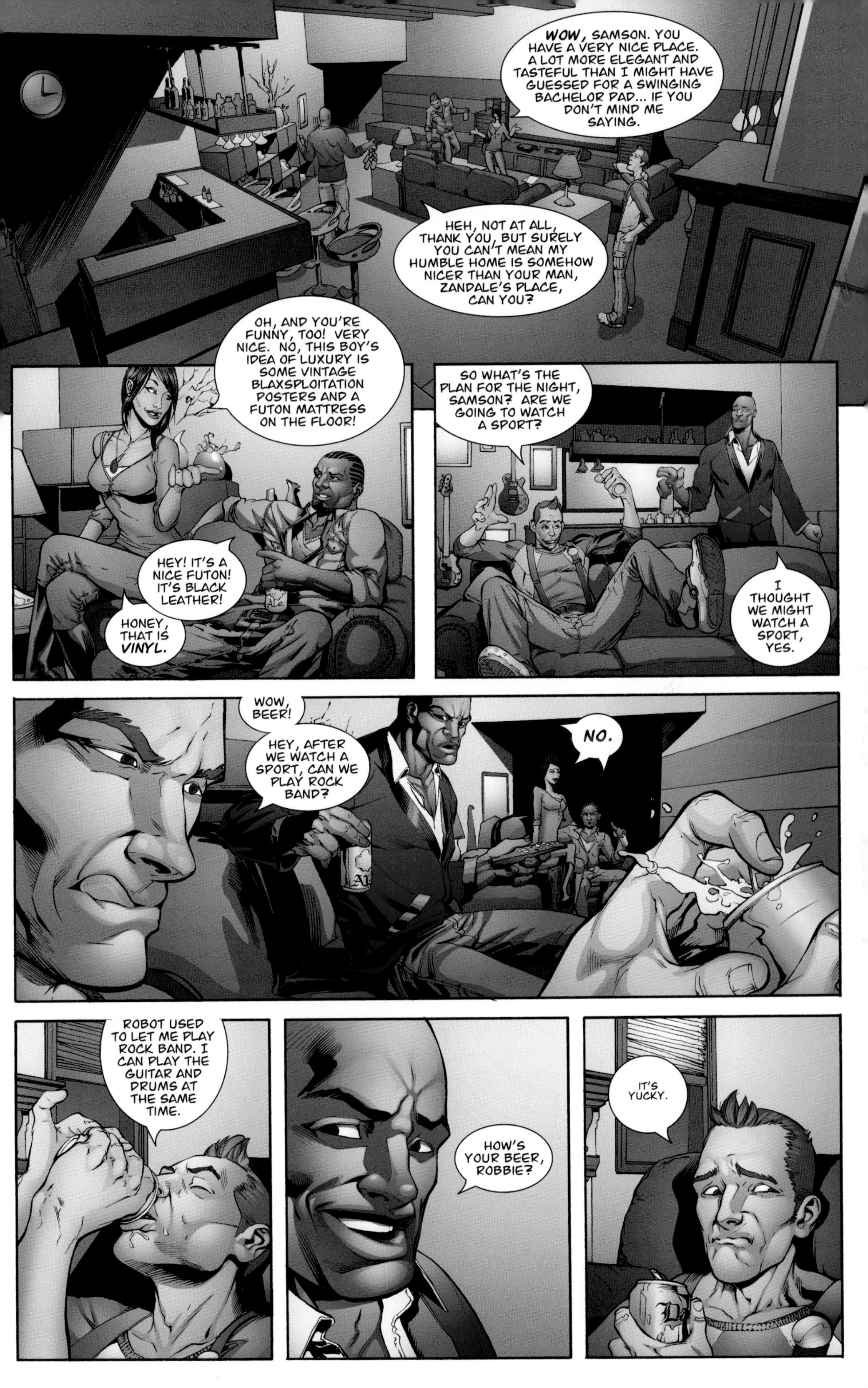
WOW, SAMSON. YOU HAVE A VERY NICE PLACE. A LOT MORE ELEGANT AND TASTEFUL THAN I MIGHT HAVE GUESSED FOR A SWINGING BACHELOR PAD... IF YOU DON'T MIND ME SAYING.
HEH, NOT AT ALL, THANK YOU, BUT SURELY YOU CAN'T MEAN MY HUMBLE HOME IS SOMEHOW NICER THAN YOUR MAN, ZANDALE'S PLACE, CAN YOU?
OH, AND YOU'RE FUNNY, TOO! VERY NICE. NO, THIS BOY'S IDEA OF LUXURY IS SOME VINTAGE BLAXSPLOITATION POSTERS AND A FUTON MATTRESS ON THE FLOOR!
HEY! IT'S A NICE FUTON! IT'S BLACK LEATHER!
HONEY, THAT IS VINYL.
SO WHAT'S THE PLAN FOR THE NIGHT, SAMSON? ARE WE GOING TO WATCH A SPORT?
I THOUGHT WE MIGHT WATCH A SPORT, YES.
WOW, BEER!
HEY, AFTER WE WATCH A SPORT, CAN WE PLAY ROCK BAND?
NO.
ROBOT USED TO LET ME PLAY ROCK BAND. I CAN PLAY THE GUITAR AND DRUMS AT THE SAME TIME.
HOW'S YOUR BEER, ROBBIE?
IT'S YUCKY.

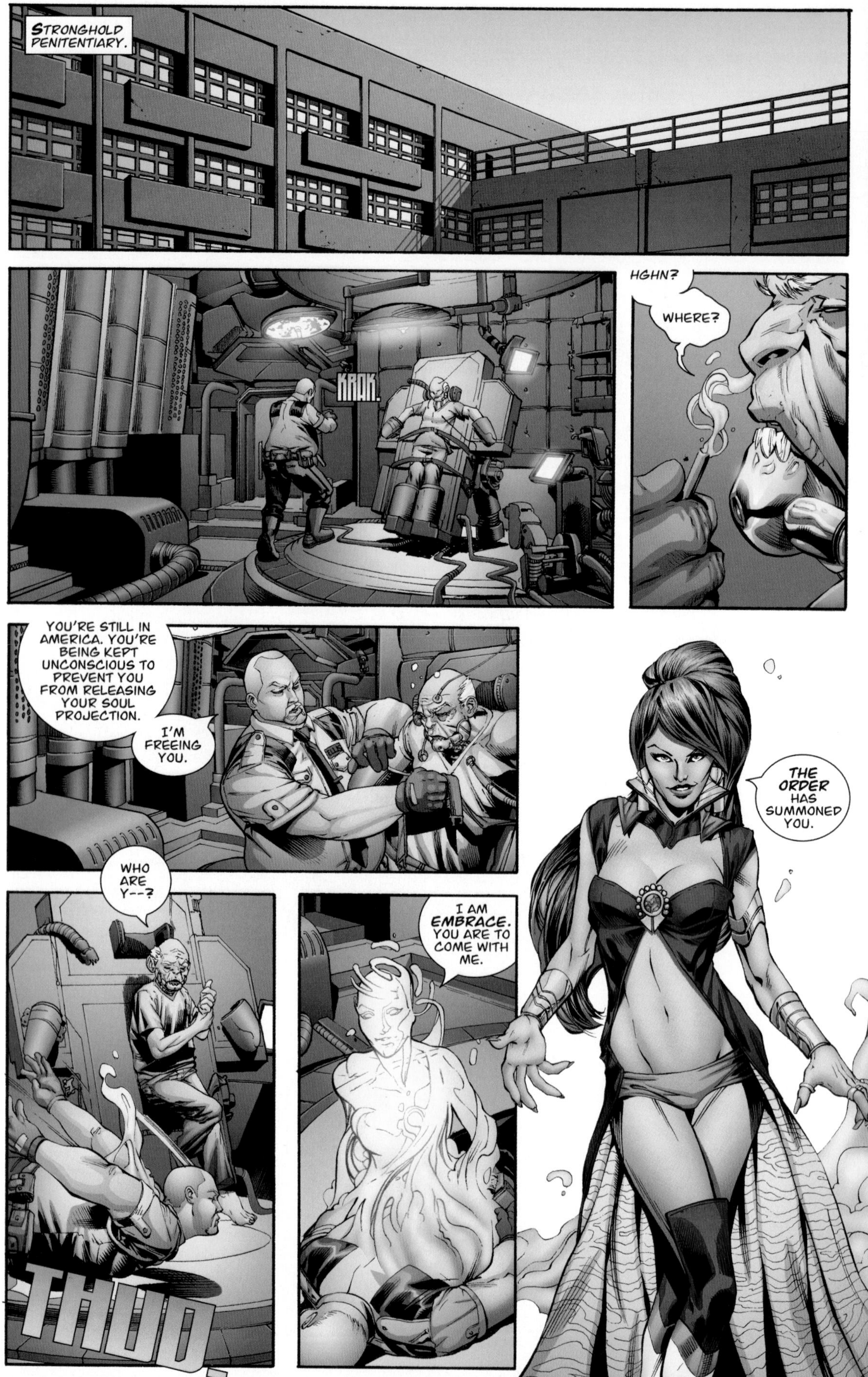
STRONGHOLD PENITENTIARY.
KRAK.
HGHN?
WHERE?
YOU'RE STILL IN AMERICA. YOU'RE BEING KEPT UNCONSCIOUS TO PREVENT YOU FROM RELEASING YOUR SOUL PROJECTION.
I'M FREEING YOU.
WHO ARE Y--?
THUD.
I AM EMBRACE. YOU ARE TO COME WITH ME.
THE ORDER HAS SUMMONED YOU.

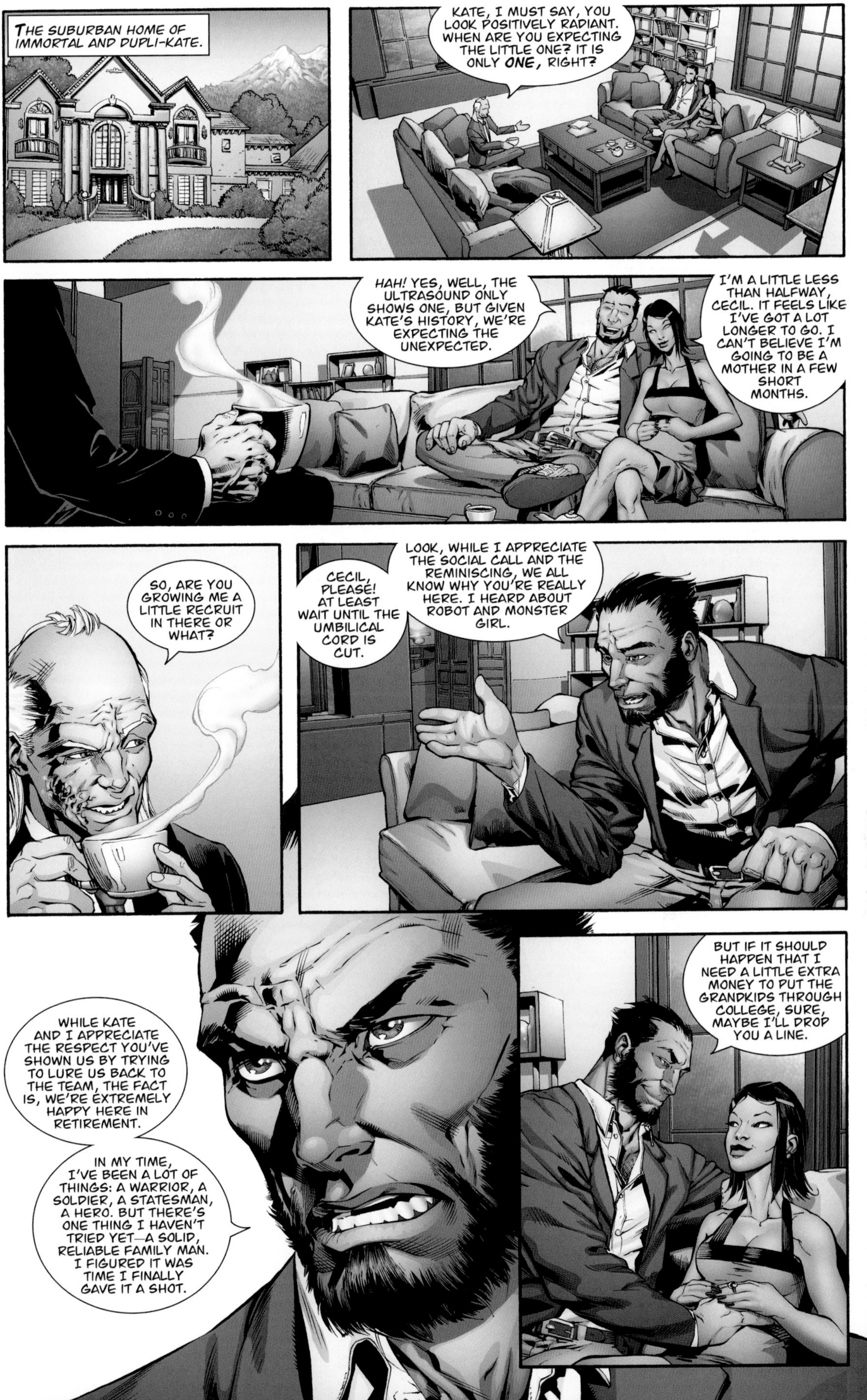
THE SUBURBAN HOME OF IMMORTAL AND DUPLI-KATE.
KATE, I MUST SAY, YOU LOOK POSITIVELY RADIANT. WHEN ARE YOU EXPECTING THE LITTLE ONE? IT IS ONLY ONE, RIGHT?
HAH! YES, WELL, THE ULTRASOUND ONLY SHOWS ONE, BUT GIVEN KATE'S HISTORY, WE'RE EXPECTING THE UNEXPECTED.
I'M A LITTLE LESS THAN HALFWAY, CECIL. IT FEELS LIKE I'VE GOT A LOT LONGER TO GO. I CAN'T BELIEVE I'M GOING TO BE A MOTHER IN A FEW SHORT MONTHS.
SO, ARE YOU GROWING ME A LITTLE RECRUIT IN THERE OR WHAT?
CECIL, PLEASE! AT LEAST WAIT UNTIL THE UMBILICAL CORD IS CUT.
LOOK, WHILE I APPRECIATE THE SOCIAL CALL AND THE REMINISCING, WE ALL KNOW WHY YOU'RE REALLY HERE. I HEARD ABOUT ROBOT AND MONSTER GIRL.
WHILE KATE AND I APPRECIATE THE RESPECT YOU'VE SHOWN US BY TRYING TO LURE US BACK TO THE TEAM, THE FACT IS, WE'RE EXTREMELY HAPPY HERE IN RETIREMENT.
IN MY TIME, I'VE BEEN A LOT OF THINGS: A WARRIOR, A SOLDIER, A STATESMAN, A HERO. BUT THERE'S ONE THING I HAVEN'T TRIED YET—A SOLID, RELIABLE FAMILY MAN. I FIGURED IT WAS TIME I FINALLY GAVE IT A SHOT.
BUT IF IT SHOULD HAPPEN THAT I NEED A LITTLE EXTRA MONEY TO PUT THE GRANDKIDS THROUGH COLLEGE, SURE, MAYBE I'LL DROP YOU A LINE.

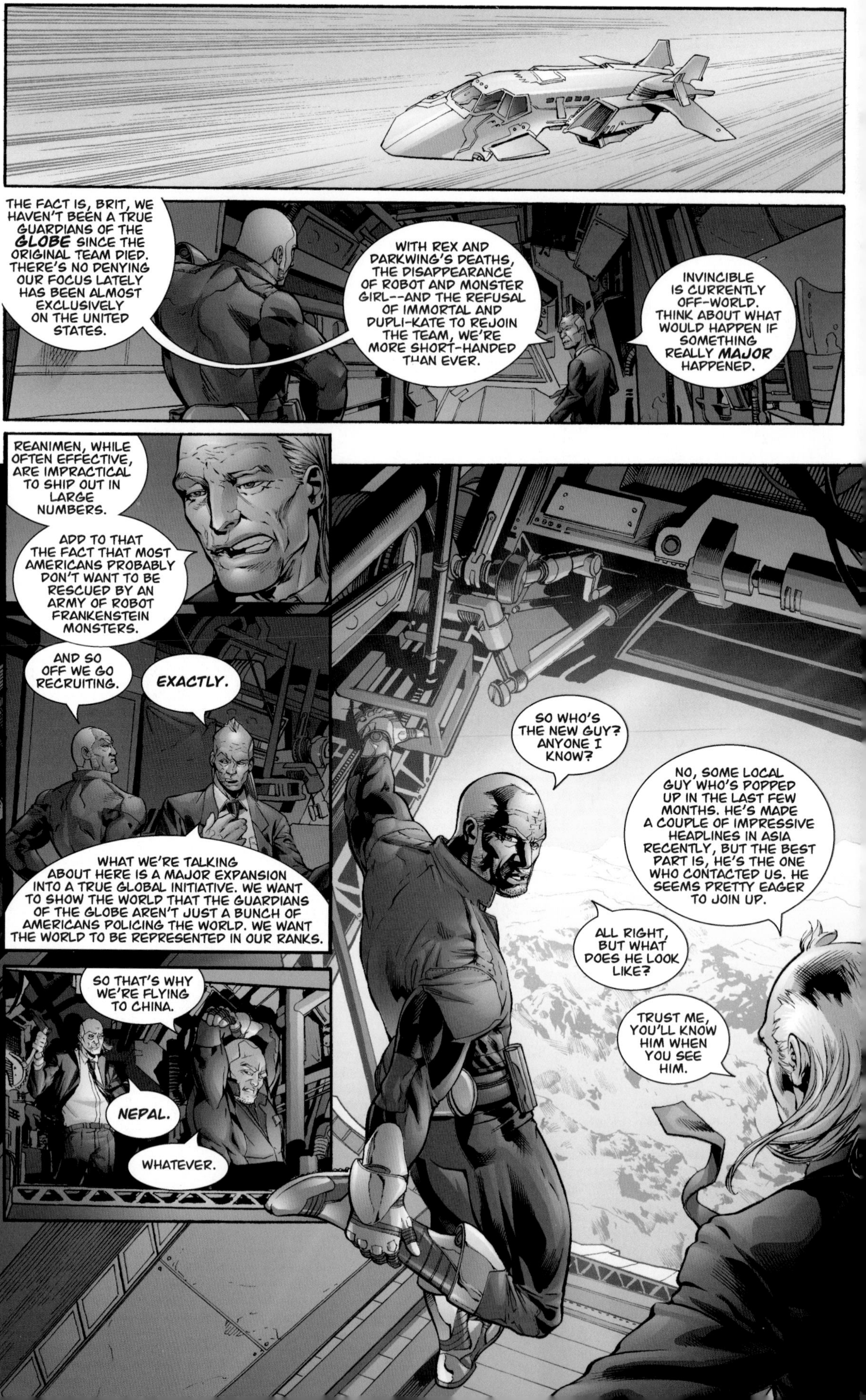

THE FACT IS, BRIT, WE HAVEN'T BEEN A TRUE GUARDIANS OF THE GLOBE SINCE THE ORIGINAL TEAM DIED. THERE'S NO DENYING OUR FOCUS LATELY HAS BEEN ALMOST EXCLUSIVELY ON THE UNITED STATES.
WITH REX AND DARKWING'S DEATHS, THE DISAPPEARANCE OF ROBOT AND MONSTER GIRL--AND THE REFUSAL OF IMMORTAL AND DUPLI-KATE TO REJOIN THE TEAM, WE'RE MORE SHORT-HANDED THAN EVER.
INVINCIBLE IS CURRENTLY OFF-WORLD. THINK ABOUT WHAT WOULD HAPPEN IF SOMETHING REALLY MAJOR HAPPENED.
REANIMEN, WHILE OFTEN EFFECTIVE, ARE IMPRACTICAL TO SHIP OUT IN LARGE NUMBERS.
ADD TO THAT THE FACT THAT MOST AMERICANS PROBABLY DON'T WANT TO BE RESCUED BY AN ARMY OF ROBOT FRANKENSTEIN MONSTERS.
AND SO OFF WE GO RECRUITING.
EXACTLY.
WHAT WE'RE TALKING ABOUT HERE IS A MAJOR EXPANSION INTO A TRUE GLOBAL INITIATIVE. WE WANT TO SHOW THE WORLD THAT THE GUARDIANS OF THE GLOBE AREN'T JUST A BUNCH OF AMERICANS POLICING THE WORLD. WE WANT THE WORLD TO BE REPRESENTED IN OUR RANKS.
SO THAT'S WHY WE'RE FLYING TO CHINA.
NEPAL.
WHATEVER.
SO WHO'S THE NEW GUY? ANYONE I KNOW?
NO, SOME LOCAL GUY WHO'S POPPED UP IN THE LAST FEW MONTHS. HE'S MADE A COUPLE OF IMPRESSIVE HEADLINES IN ASIA RECENTLY, BUT THE BEST PART IS, HE'S THE ONE WHO CONTACTED US. HE SEEMS PRETTY EAGER TO JOIN UP.
ALL RIGHT, BUT WHAT DOES HE LOOK LIKE?
TRUST ME, YOU'LL KNOW HIM WHEN YOU SEE HIM.

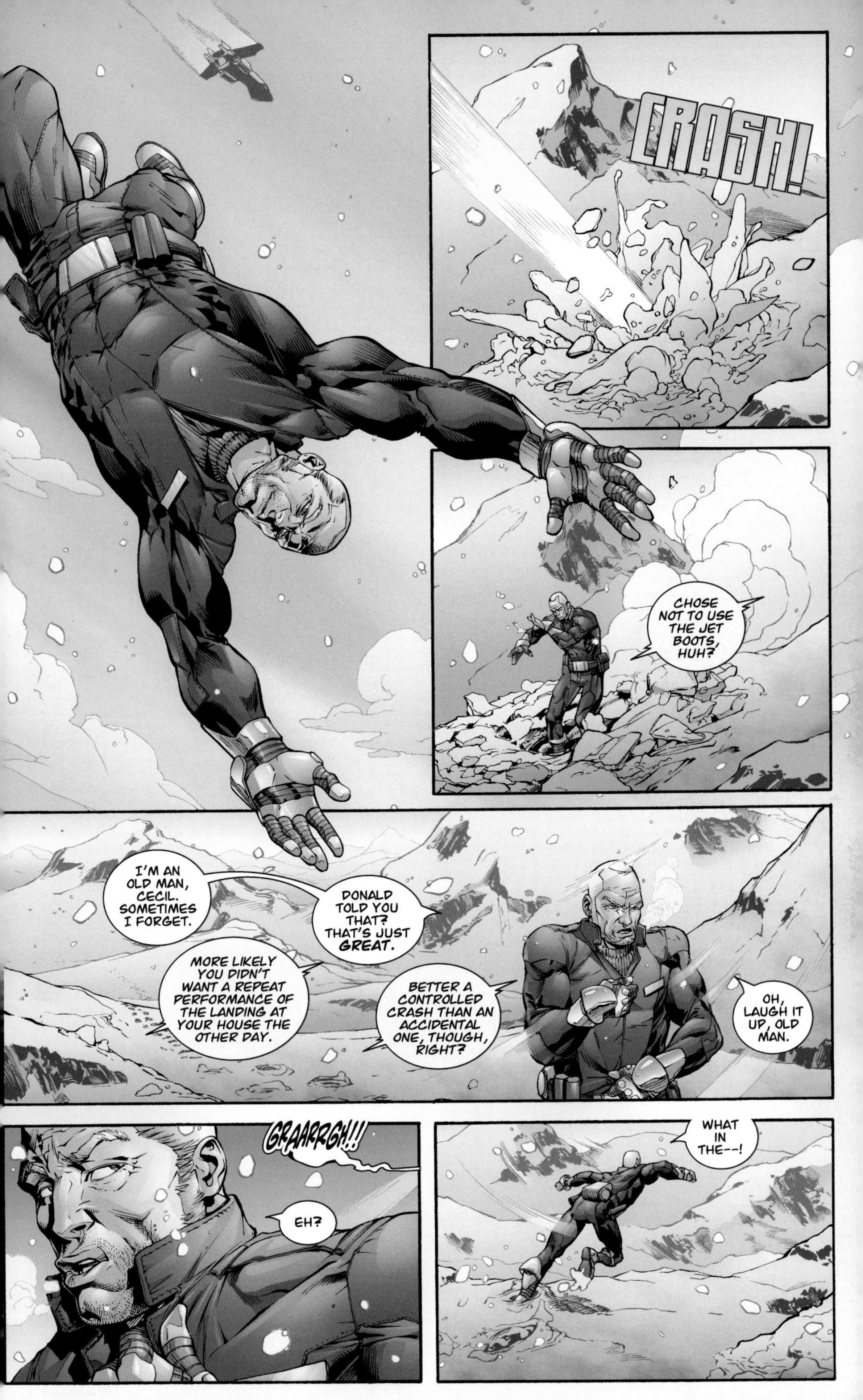
CRASH!
CHOSE NOT TO USE THE JET BOOTS, HUH?
I'M AN OLD MAN, CECIL. SOMETIMES I FORGET.
DONALD TOLD YOU THAT? THAT'S JUST GREAT.
MORE LIKELY YOU DIDN'T WANT A REPEAT PERFORMANCE OF THE LANDING AT YOUR HOUSE THE OTHER DAY.
BETTER A CONTROLLED CRASH THAN AN ACCIDENTAL ONE, THOUGH, RIGHT?
OH, LAUGH IT UP, OLD MAN.
GRAARRGH!!!
EH?
WHAT IN THE--!

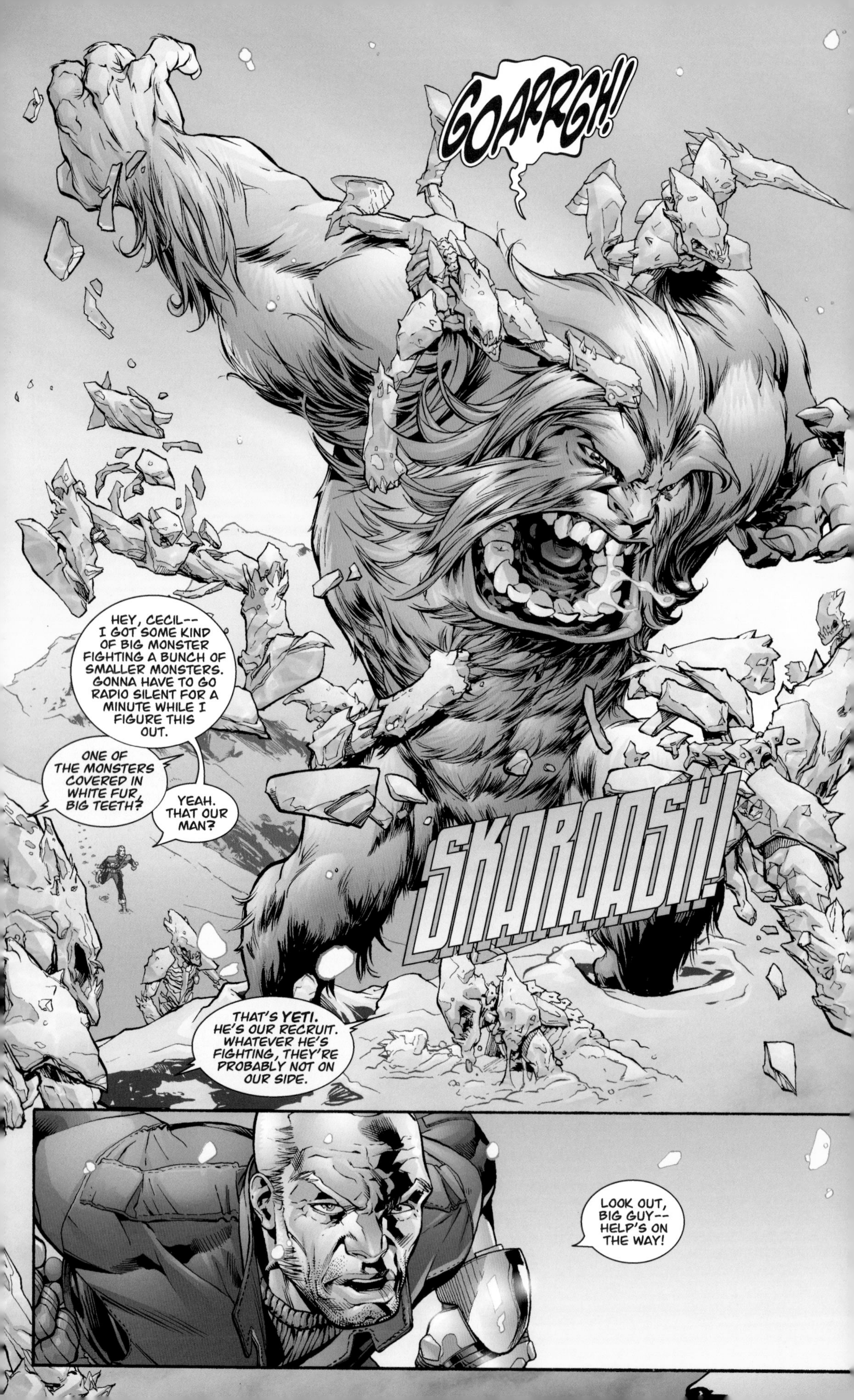
GOARRGH!
HEY, CECIL-- I GOT SOME KIND OF BIG MONSTER FIGHTING A BUNCH OF SMALLER MONSTERS. GONNA HAVE TO GO RADIO SILENT FOR A MINUTE WHILE I FIGURE THIS OUT.
ONE OF THE MONSTERS COVERED IN WHITE FUR, BIG TEETH?
YEAH. THAT OUR MAN?
SKROOSH!
THAT'S YETI. HE'S OUR RECRUIT. WHATEVER HE'S FIGHTING, THEY'RE PROBABLY NOT ON OUR SIDE.
LOOK OUT, BIG GUY-- HELP'S ON THE WAY!

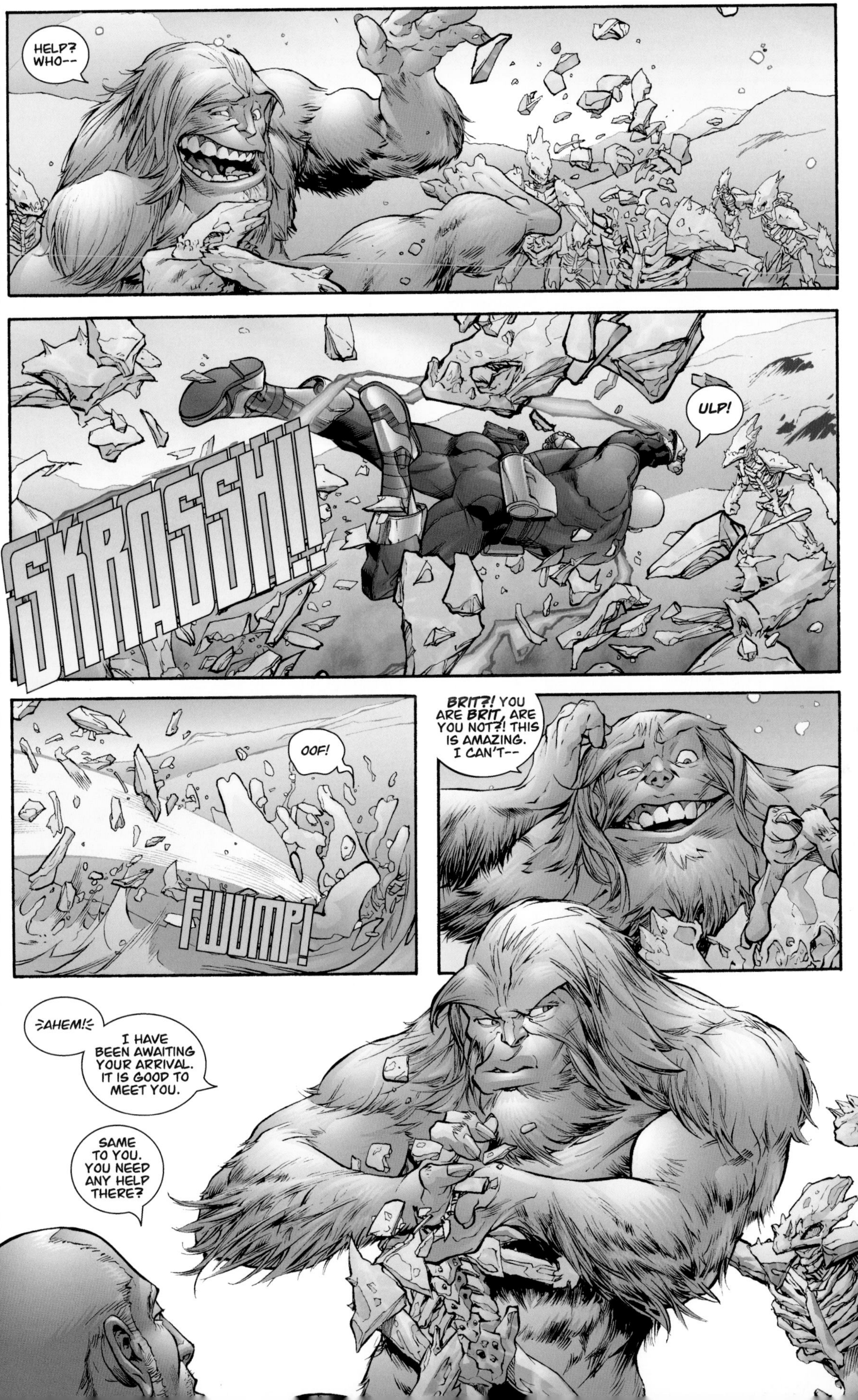
HELP? WHO--
SKRASSH!!
ULP!
OOF!
FWUMP!
BRIT?! YOU ARE BRIT, ARE YOU NOT?! THIS IS AMAZING. I CAN'T--
AHEM!
I HAVE BEEN AWAITING YOUR ARRIVAL. IT IS GOOD TO MEET YOU.
SAME TO YOU. YOU NEED ANY HELP THERE?

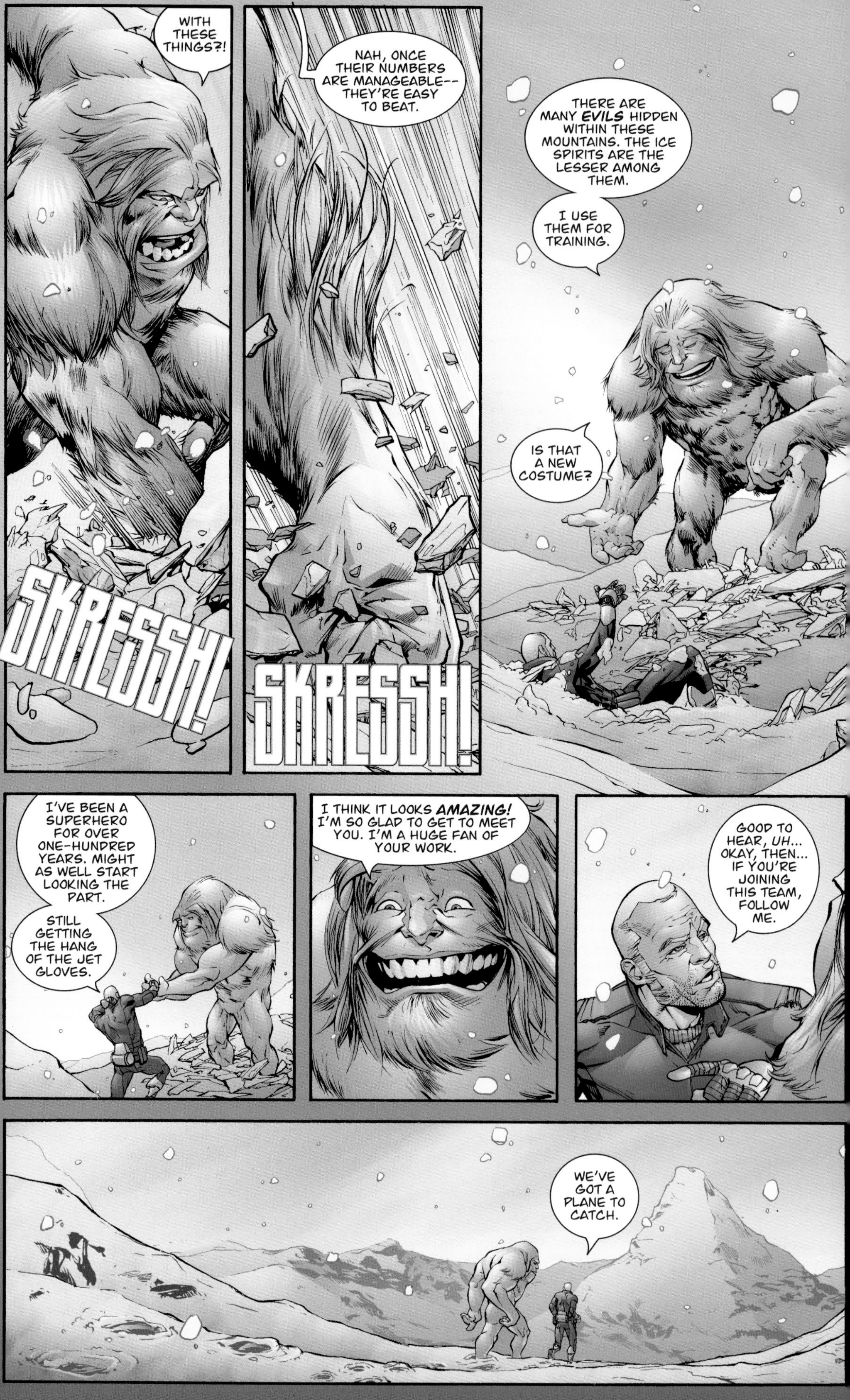
WITH THESE THINGS?!
NAH, ONCE THEIR NUMBERS ARE MANAGEABLE-- THEY'RE EASY TO BEAT.
SKRESSH!
SKRESSH!
THERE ARE MANY EVILS HIDDEN WITHIN THESE MOUNTAINS. THE ICE SPIRITS ARE THE LESSER AMONG THEM.
I USE THEM FOR TRAINING.
IS THAT A NEW COSTUME?
I'VE BEEN A SUPERHERO FOR OVER ONE-HUNDRED YEARS. MIGHT AS WELL START LOOKING THE PART.
STILL GETTING THE HANG OF THE JET GLOVES.
I THINK IT LOOKS AMAZING! I'M SO GLAD TO GET TO MEET YOU. I'M A HUGE FAN OF YOUR WORK.
GOOD TO HEAR, UH... OKAY, THEN... IF YOU'RE JOINING THIS TEAM, FOLLOW ME.
WE'VE GOT A PLANE TO CATCH.

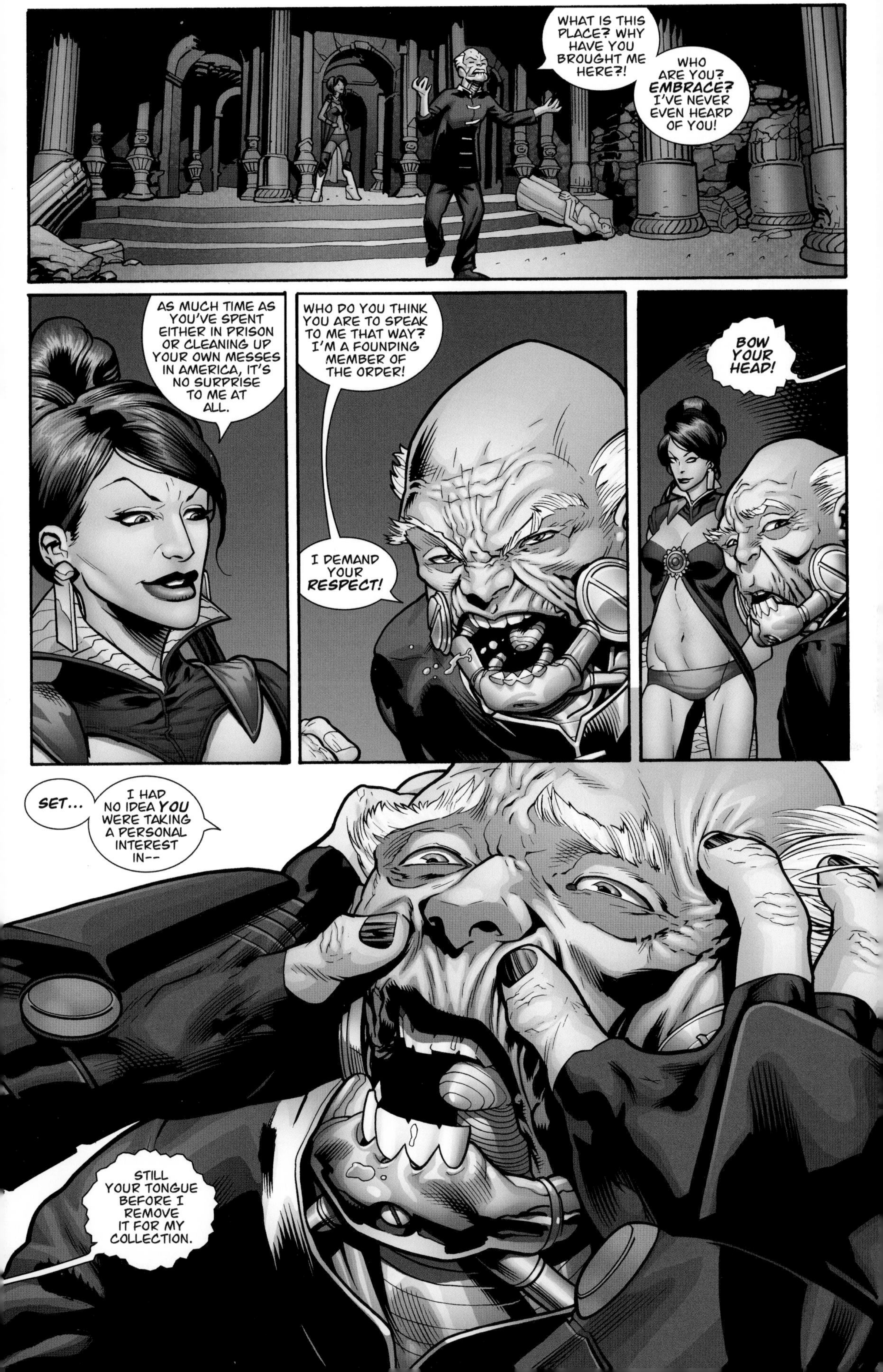
WHAT IS THIS PLACE? WHY HAVE YOU BROUGHT ME HERE?!
WHO ARE YOU? EMBRACE? I'VE NEVER EVEN HEARD OF YOU!
AS MUCH TIME AS YOU'VE SPENT EITHER IN PRISON OR CLEANING UP YOUR OWN MESSES IN AMERICA, IT'S NO SURPRISE TO ME AT ALL.
WHO DO YOU THINK YOU ARE TO SPEAK TO ME THAT WAY? I'M A FOUNDING MEMBER OF THE ORDER!
I DEMAND YOUR RESPECT!
BOW YOUR HEAD!
SET...
I HAD NO IDEA YOU WERE TAKING A PERSONAL INTEREST IN--
STILL YOUR TONGUE BEFORE I REMOVE IT FOR MY COLLECTION.

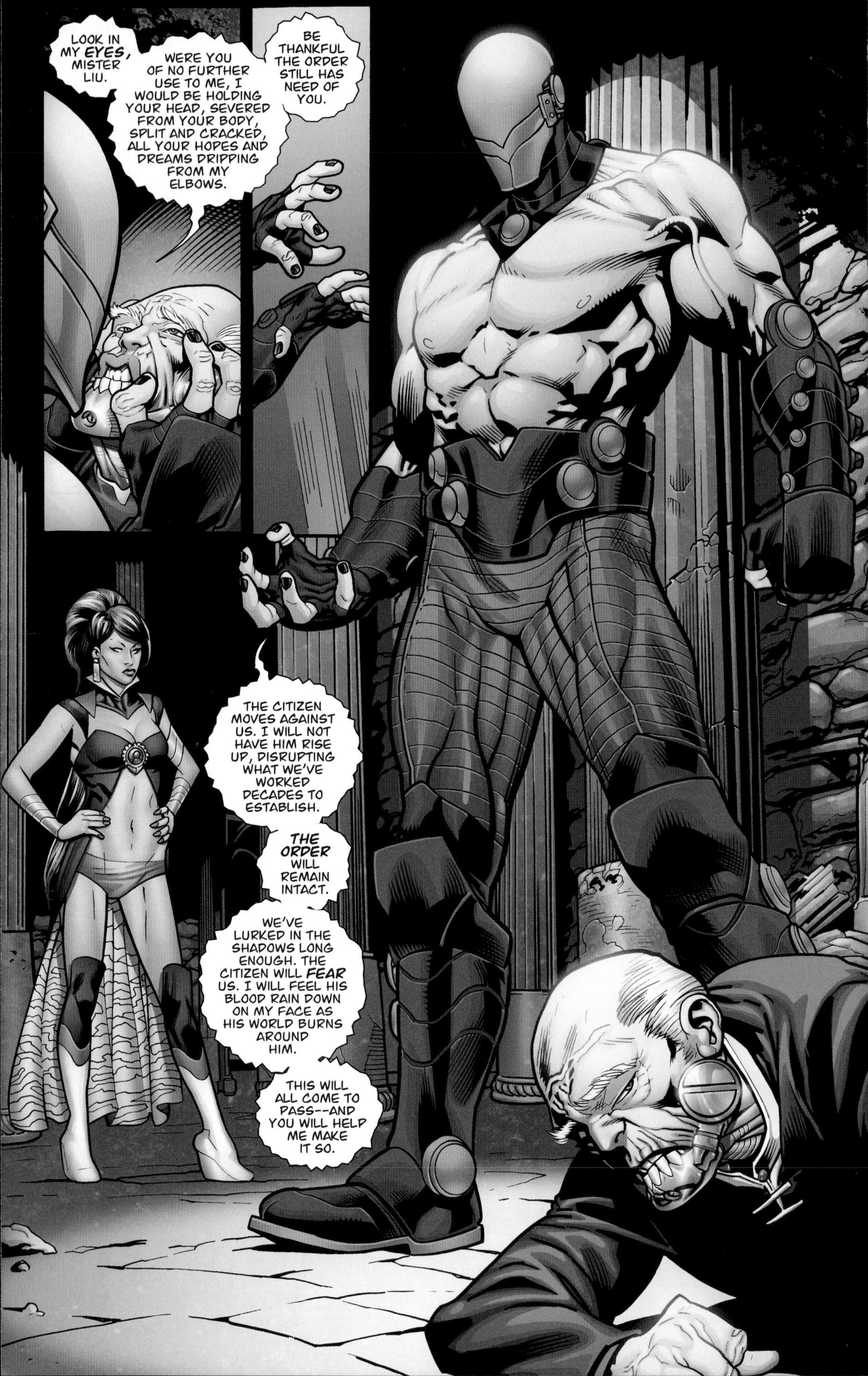
LOOK IN MY EYES, MISTER LIU.
WERE YOU OF NO FURTHER USE TO ME, I WOULD BE HOLDING YOUR HEAD, SEVERED FROM YOUR BODY, SPLIT AND CRACKED, ALL YOUR HOPES AND DREAMS DRIPPING FROM MY ELBOWS.
BE THANKFUL THE ORDER STILL HAS NEED OF YOU.
THE CITIZEN MOVES AGAINST US. I WILL NOT HAVE HIM RISE UP, DISRUPTING WHAT WE'VE WORKED DECADES TO ESTABLISH.
THE ORDER WILL REMAIN INTACT.
WE'VE LURKED IN THE SHADOWS LONG ENOUGH. THE CITIZEN WILL FEAR US. I WILL FEEL HIS BLOOD RAIN DOWN ON MY FACE AS HIS WORLD BURNS AROUND HIM.
THIS WILL ALL COME TO PASS--AND YOU WILL HELP ME MAKE IT SO.

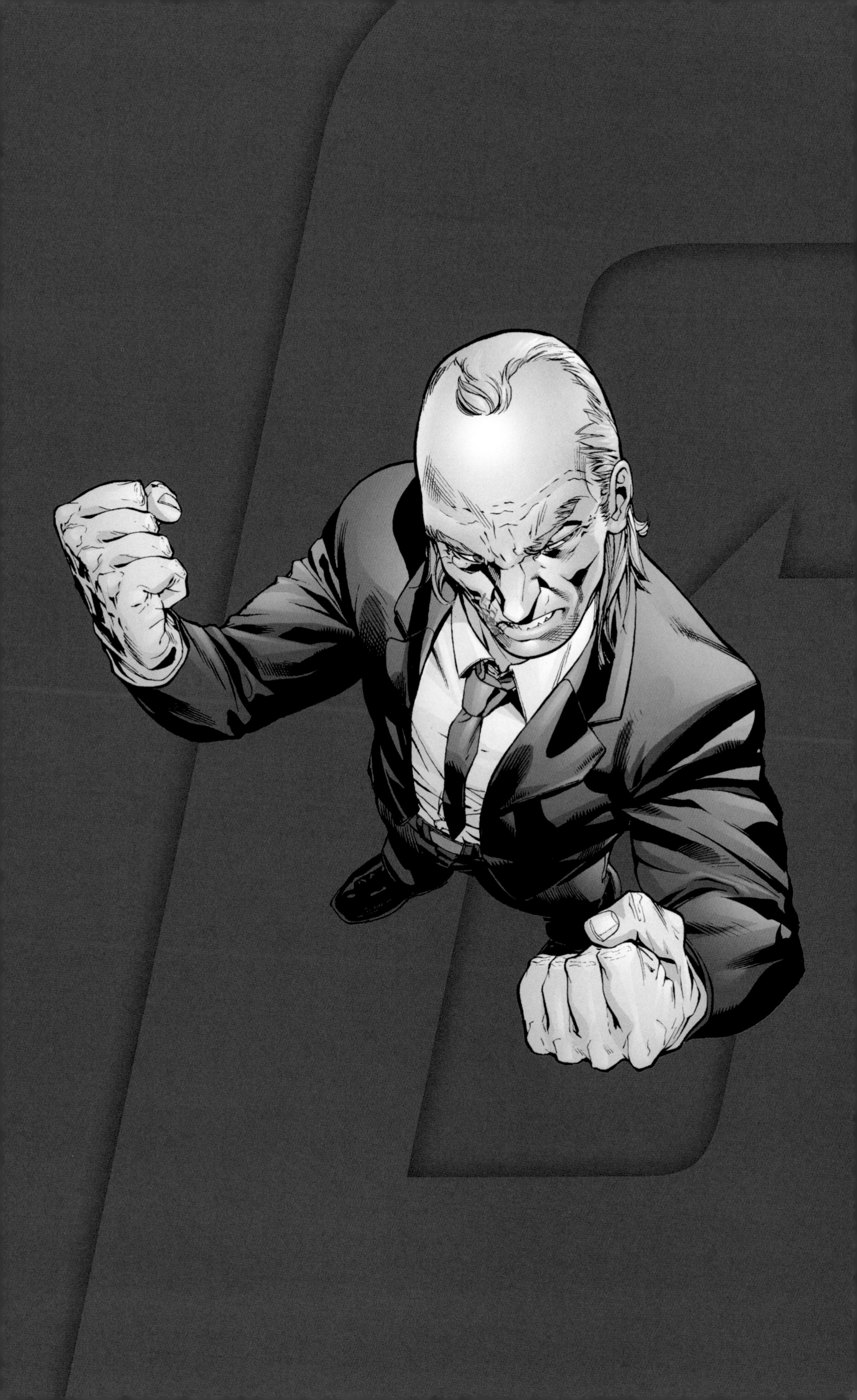

CHAPTER TWO

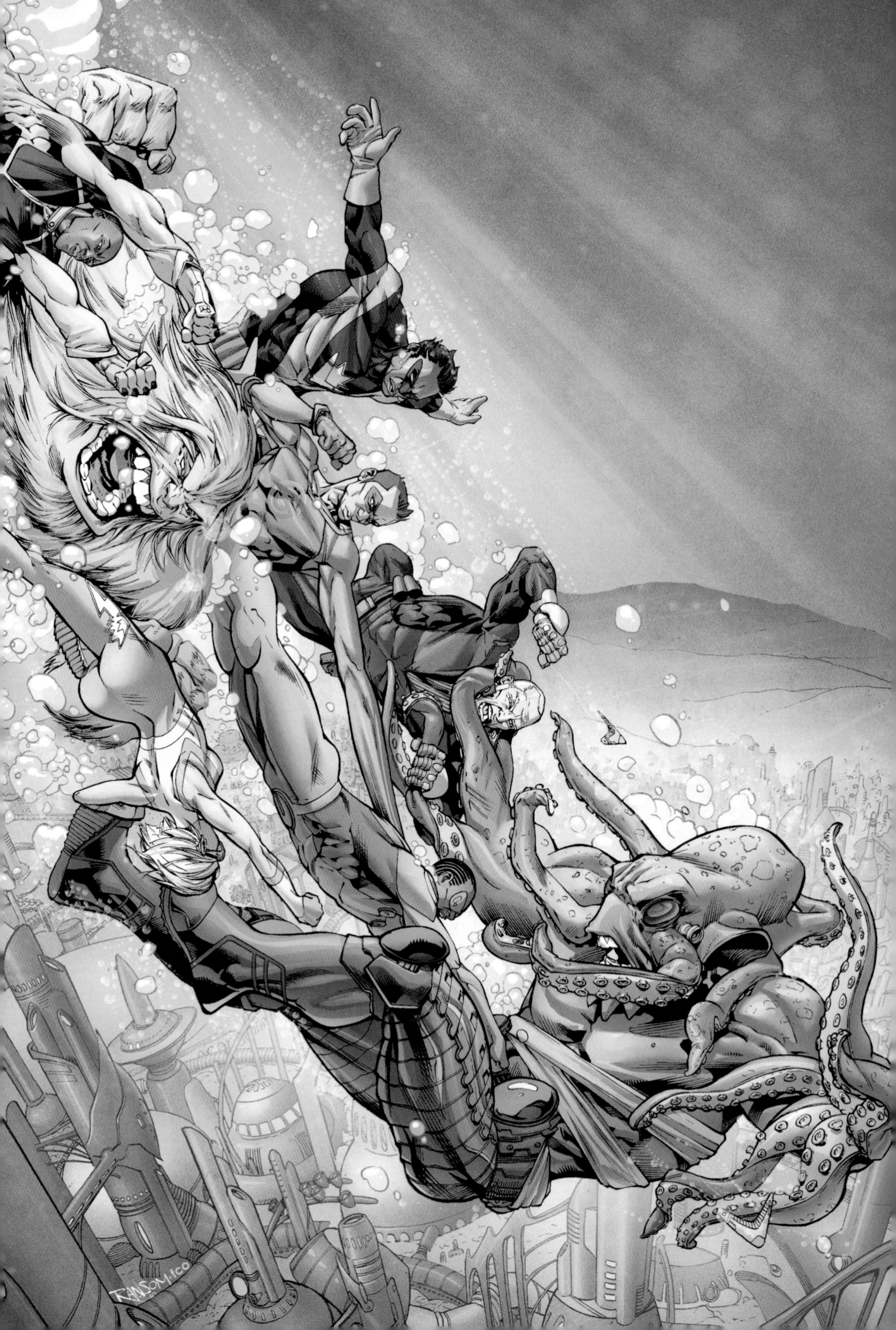

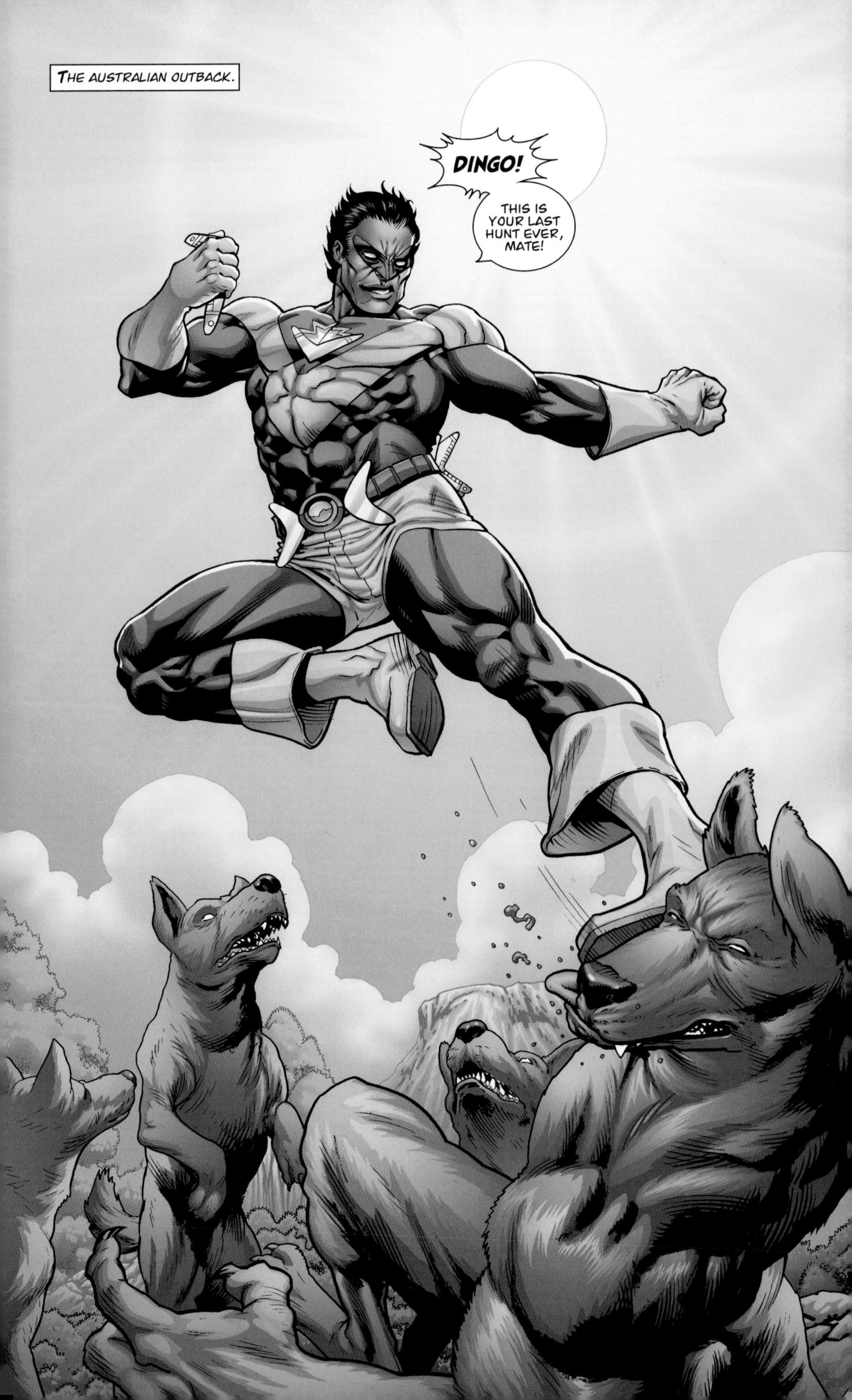
THE AUSTRALIAN OUTBACK.
DINGO!
THIS IS YOUR LAST HUNT EVER, MATE!

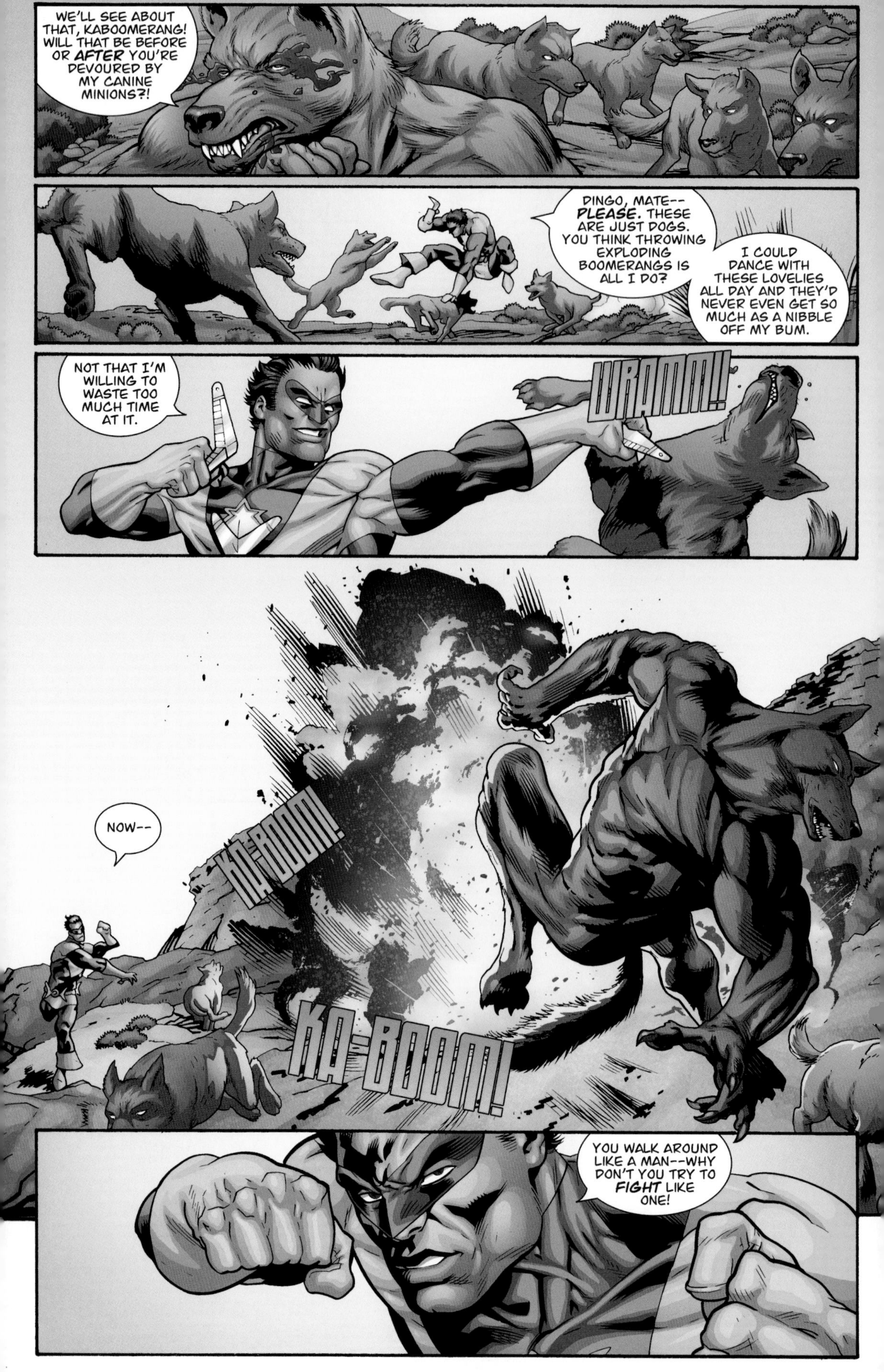
WE'LL SEE ABOUT THAT, KABOOMERANG! WILL THAT BE BEFORE OR AFTER YOU'RE DEVOURED BY MY CANINE MINIONS?!
DINGO, MATE-- PLEASE. THESE ARE JUST DOGS. YOU THINK THROWING EXPLODING BOOMERANGS IS ALL I DO?
I COULD DANCE WITH THESE LOVELIES ALL DAY AND THEY'D NEVER EVEN GET SO MUCH AS A NIBBLE OFF MY BUM.
NOT THAT I'M WILLING TO WASTE TOO MUCH TIME AT IT.
WRAMM!!
NOW--
KA-BOOM!
KA-BOOM!
YOU WALK AROUND LIKE A MAN--WHY DON'T YOU TRY TO FIGHT LIKE ONE!

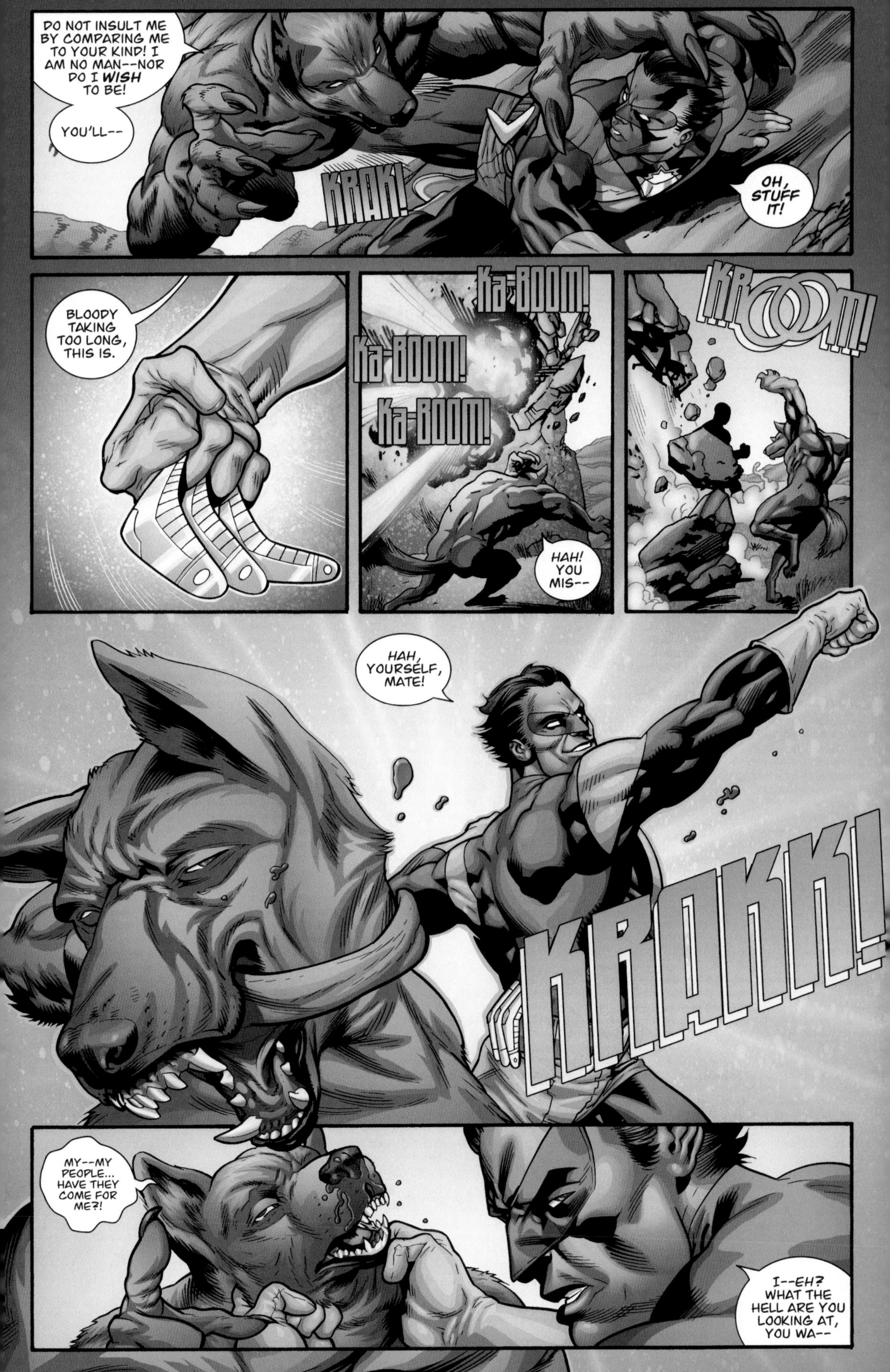

DO NOT INSULT ME BY COMPARING ME TO YOUR KIND! I AM NO MAN--NOR DO I WISH TO BE!
YOU'LL--
KRAK!
OH, STUFF IT!
BLOODY TAKING TOO LONG, THIS IS.
Ka-BOOM!
Ka-BOOM!
Ka-BOOM!
HAH! YOU MIS--
KROOOM!
HAH, YOURSELF, MATE!
KRAKK!
MY--MY PEOPLE... HAVE THEY COME FOR ME?!
I--EH? WHAT THE HELL ARE YOU LOOKING AT, YOU WA--

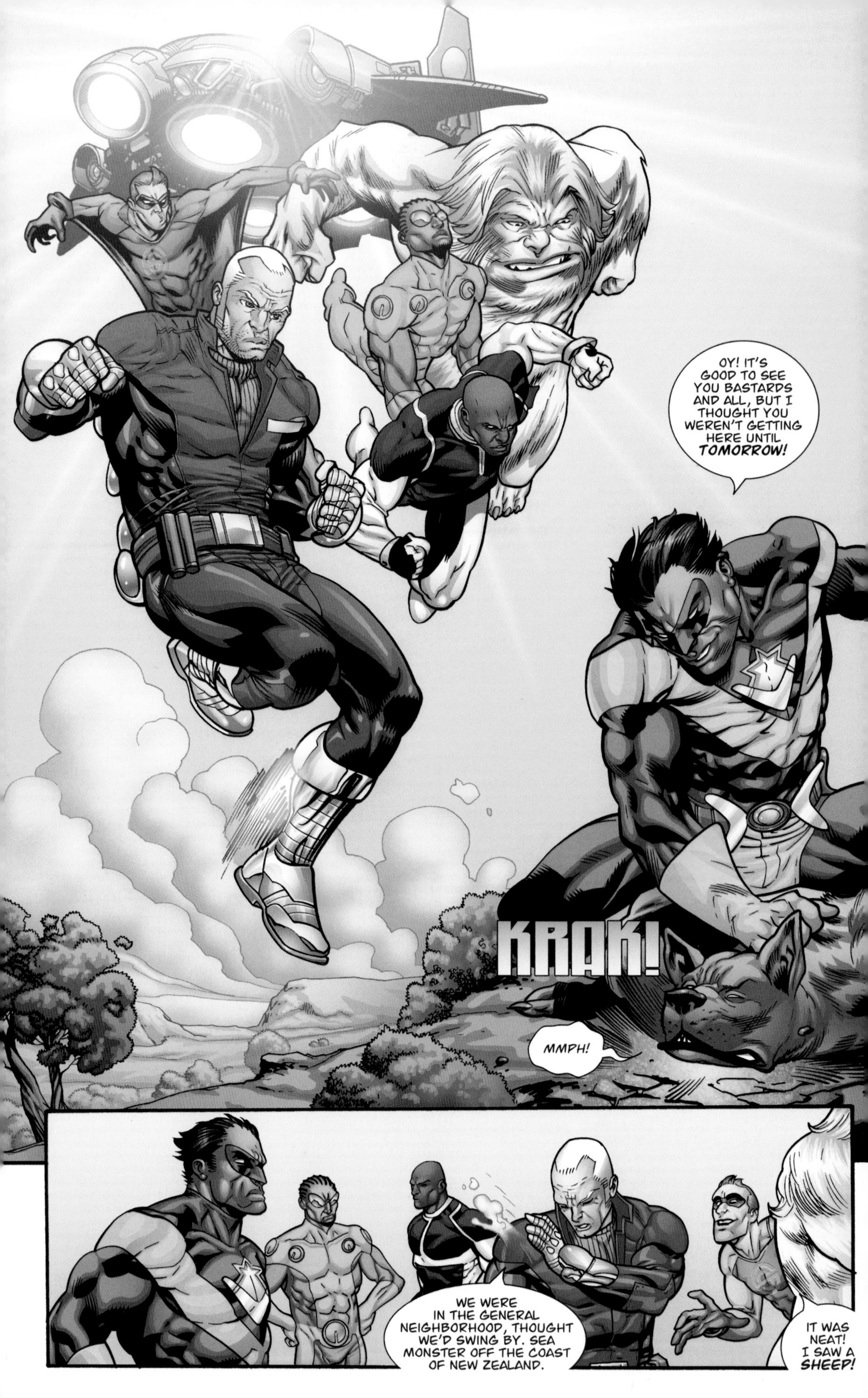
OY! IT'S GOOD TO SEE YOU BASTARDS AND ALL, BUT I THOUGHT YOU WEREN'T GETTING HERE UNTIL *TOMORROW!*
KRAK!
MMPH!
WE WERE IN THE GENERAL NEIGHBORHOOD, THOUGHT WE'D SWING BY. SEA MONSTER OFF THE COAST OF NEW ZEALAND.
IT WAS NEAT! I SAW A *SHEEP!*

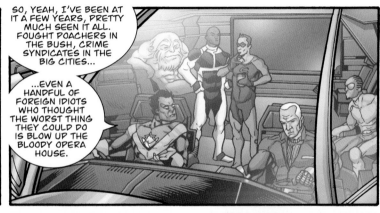

SO, YEAH, I'VE BEEN AT IT A FEW YEARS, PRETTY MUCH SEEN IT ALL. FOUGHT POACHERS IN THE BUSH, CRIME SYNDICATES IN THE BIG CITIES...

...EVEN A HANDFUL OF FOREIGN IDIOTS WHO THOUGHT THE WORST THING THEY COULD DO IS BLOW UP THE BLOODY OPERA HOUSE.

DO YOU THINK YOU WILL HAVE A HARD TIME ADJUSTING TO HAVING TO LIVE RIGHT SIDE UP?

ER, NO, MATE-- I DON'T.

HOW CAN YOU EAT THAT STUFF? IT SMELLS LIKE DIRT HAD A BABY IN THERE.

I DUNNO. IT REMINDS ME OF HOME.

SO WHAT IS IT THAT MADE YOU DECIDE TO JOIN UP WITH OUR OUTFIT?

WELL, MATE, I DON'T WANT TO BIG-NOTE MYSELF, BUT I'VE DONE ALL AN AUSSIE SUPER CAN. I'LL NEVER GET ANYWHERE JUST BUSTING HEADS OUT IN THE BLOODY SAND, YOU GET ME?

I THOUGHT THE BEST WAY TO MAKE A NAME FOR MYSELF, AND MAYBE MAKE A BUCK, YOU KNOW, WAS TO GO O.S. AND JOIN UP WITH YOU SEPPOS.

ERM, NO OFFENSE, MATE.

UH, NONE COMPREHENDED.

OY, I WANT TO THANK YOU BLOKES FOR INVITING ME TO THIS HERE SAUSAGE PARTY... BUT, MATE, WHERE ARE ALL THE BLOODY CHICKS?

TRUST ME, WE'RE WORKING ON IT.

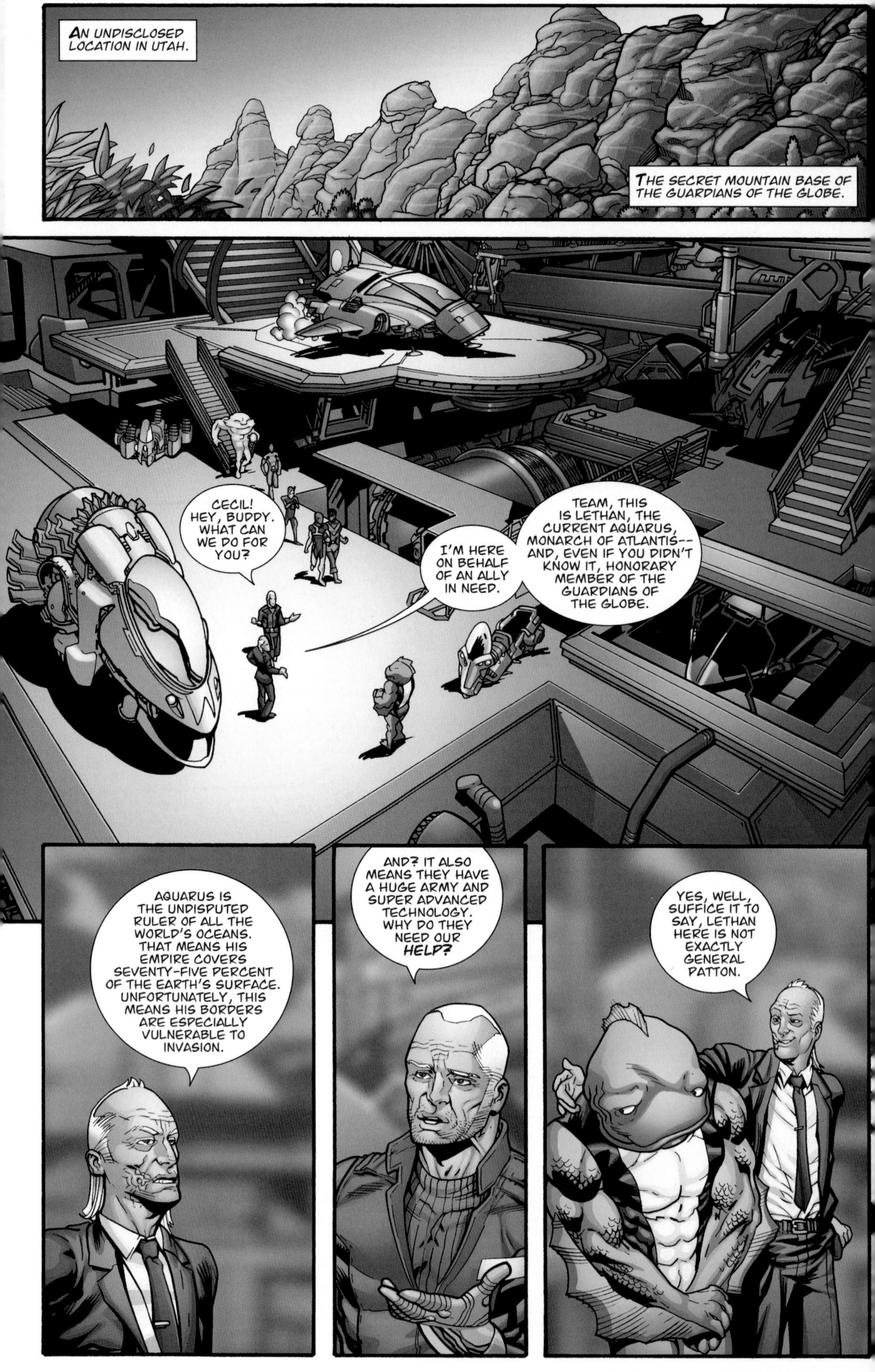
AN UNDISCLOSED LOCATION IN UTAH.
THE SECRET MOUNTAIN BASE OF THE GUARDIANS OF THE GLOBE.
CECIL! HEY, BUDDY. WHAT CAN WE DO FOR YOU?
I'M HERE ON BEHALF OF AN ALLY IN NEED.
TEAM, THIS IS LETHAN, THE CURRENT AQUARUS, MONARCH OF ATLANTIS-- AND, EVEN IF YOU DIDN'T KNOW IT, HONORARY MEMBER OF THE GUARDIANS OF THE GLOBE.
AQUARUS IS THE UNDISPUTED RULER OF ALL THE WORLD'S OCEANS. THAT MEANS HIS EMPIRE COVERS SEVENTY-FIVE PERCENT OF THE EARTH'S SURFACE. UNFORTUNATELY, THIS MEANS HIS BORDERS ARE ESPECIALLY VULNERABLE TO INVASION.
AND? IT ALSO MEANS THEY HAVE A HUGE ARMY AND SUPER ADVANCED TECHNOLOGY. WHY DO THEY NEED OUR HELP?
YES, WELL, SUFFICE IT TO SAY, LETHAN HERE IS NOT EXACTLY GENERAL PATTON.

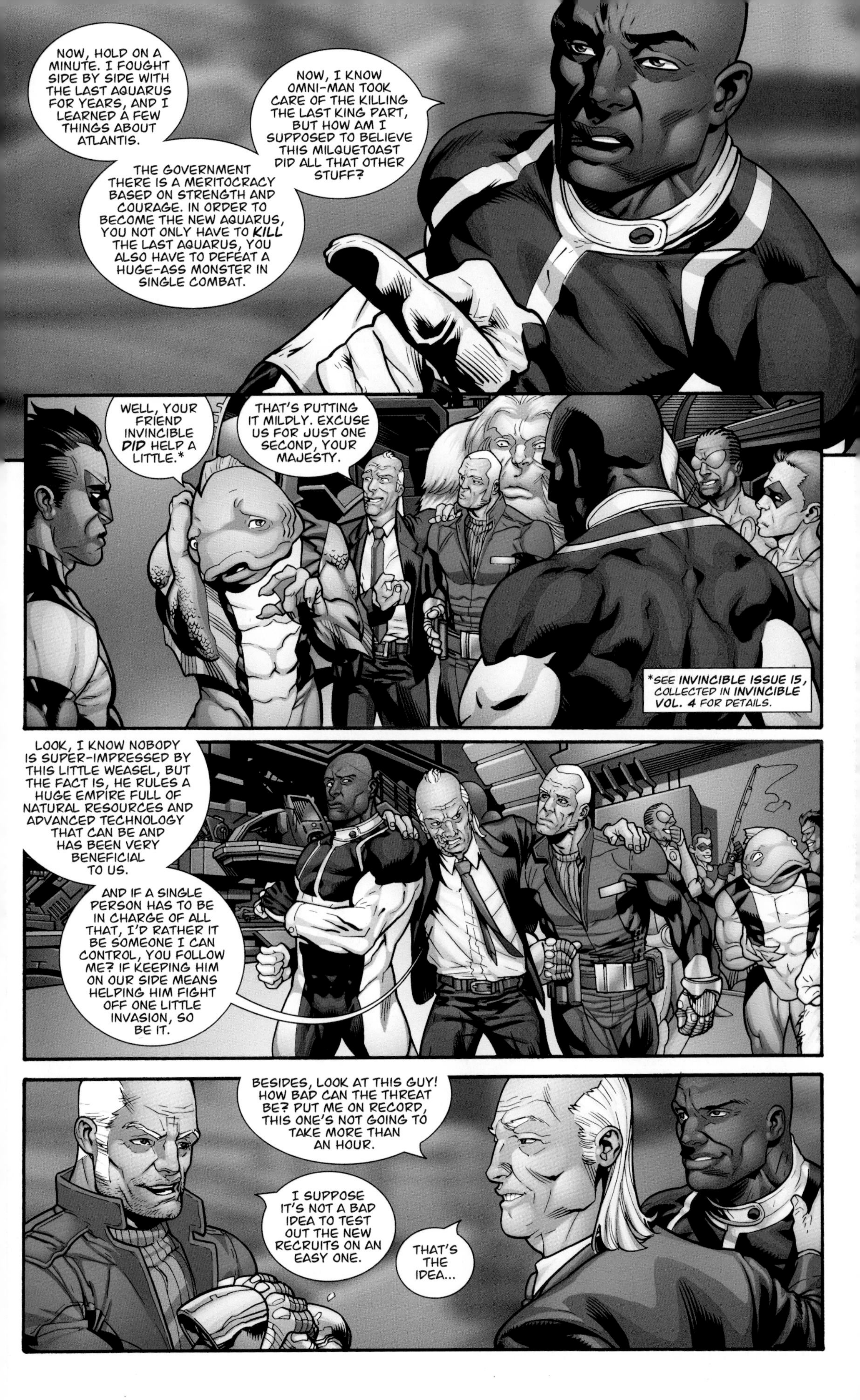
NOW, HOLD ON A MINUTE. I FOUGHT SIDE BY SIDE WITH THE LAST AQUARUS FOR YEARS, AND I LEARNED A FEW THINGS ABOUT ATLANTIS.
THE GOVERNMENT THERE IS A MERITOCRACY BASED ON STRENGTH AND COURAGE. IN ORDER TO BECOME THE NEW AQUARUS, YOU NOT ONLY HAVE TO KILL THE LAST AQUARUS, YOU ALSO HAVE TO DEFEAT A HUGE-ASS MONSTER IN SINGLE COMBAT.
NOW, I KNOW OMNI-MAN TOOK CARE OF THE KILLING THE LAST KING PART, BUT HOW AM I SUPPOSED TO BELIEVE THIS MILQUETOAST DID ALL THAT OTHER STUFF?
WELL, YOUR FRIEND INVINCIBLE DID HELP A LITTLE.*
THAT'S PUTTING IT MILDLY. EXCUSE US FOR JUST ONE SECOND, YOUR MAJESTY.
*SEE INVINCIBLE ISSUE 15, COLLECTED IN INVINCIBLE VOL. 4 FOR DETAILS.
LOOK, I KNOW NOBODY IS SUPER-IMPRESSED BY THIS LITTLE WEASEL, BUT THE FACT IS, HE RULES A HUGE EMPIRE FULL OF NATURAL RESOURCES AND ADVANCED TECHNOLOGY THAT CAN BE AND HAS BEEN VERY BENEFICIAL TO US.
AND IF A SINGLE PERSON HAS TO BE IN CHARGE OF ALL THAT, I'D RATHER IT BE SOMEONE I CAN CONTROL, YOU FOLLOW ME? IF KEEPING HIM ON OUR SIDE MEANS HELPING HIM FIGHT OFF ONE LITTLE INVASION, SO BE IT.
BESIDES, LOOK AT THIS GUY! HOW BAD CAN THE THREAT BE? PUT ME ON RECORD, THIS ONE'S NOT GOING TO TAKE MORE THAN AN HOUR.
I SUPPOSE IT'S NOT A BAD IDEA TO TEST OUT THE NEW RECRUITS ON AN EASY ONE.
THAT'S THE IDEA...

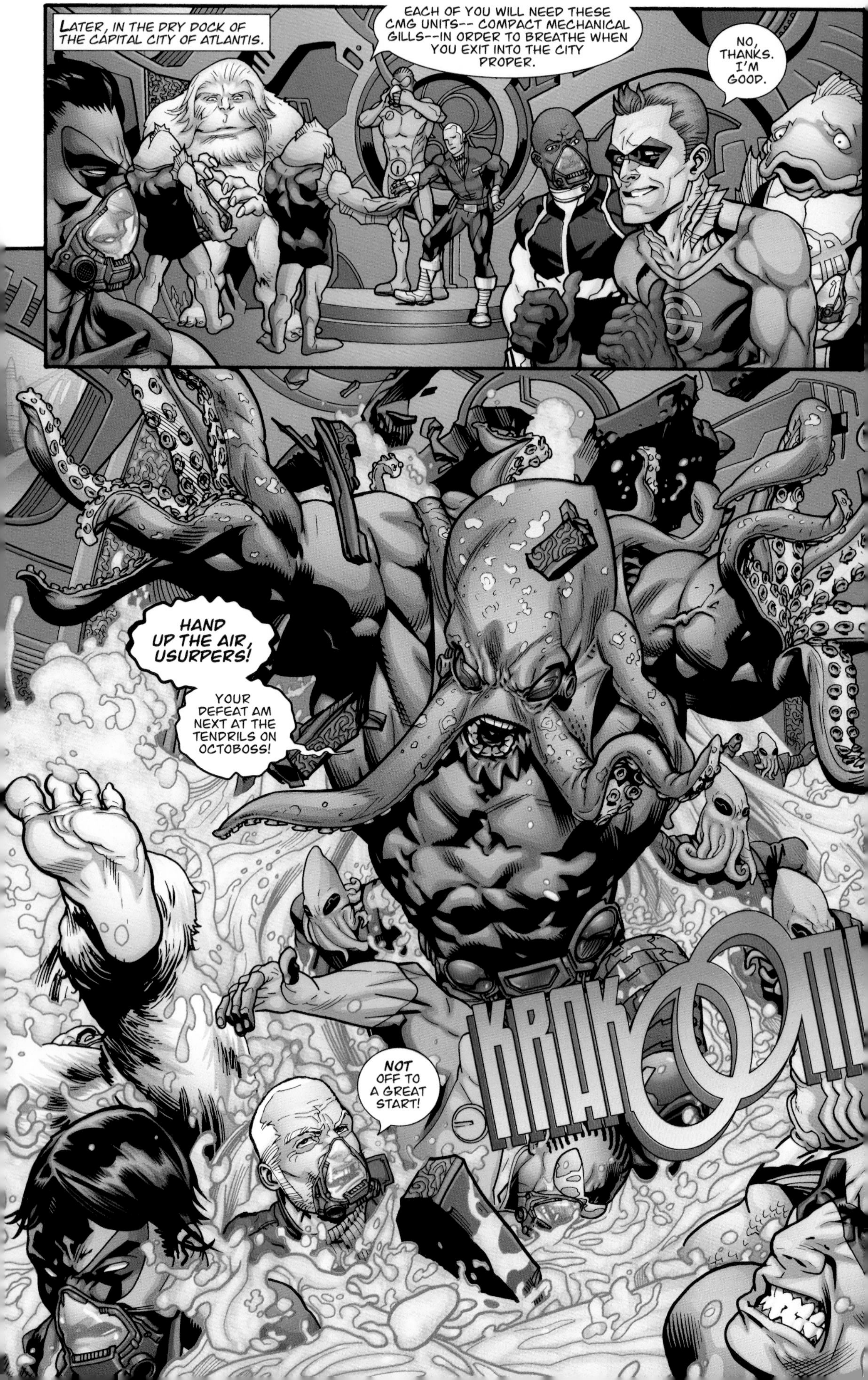
LATER, IN THE DRY DOCK OF THE CAPITAL CITY OF ATLANTIS.
EACH OF YOU WILL NEED THESE CMG UNITS-- COMPACT MECHANICAL GILLS--IN ORDER TO BREATHE WHEN YOU EXIT INTO THE CITY PROPER.
NO, THANKS. I'M GOOD.
HAND UP THE AIR, USURPERS!
YOUR DEFEAT AM NEXT AT THE TENDRILS ON OCTOBOSS!
KRAKOOM
NOT OFF TO A GREAT START!

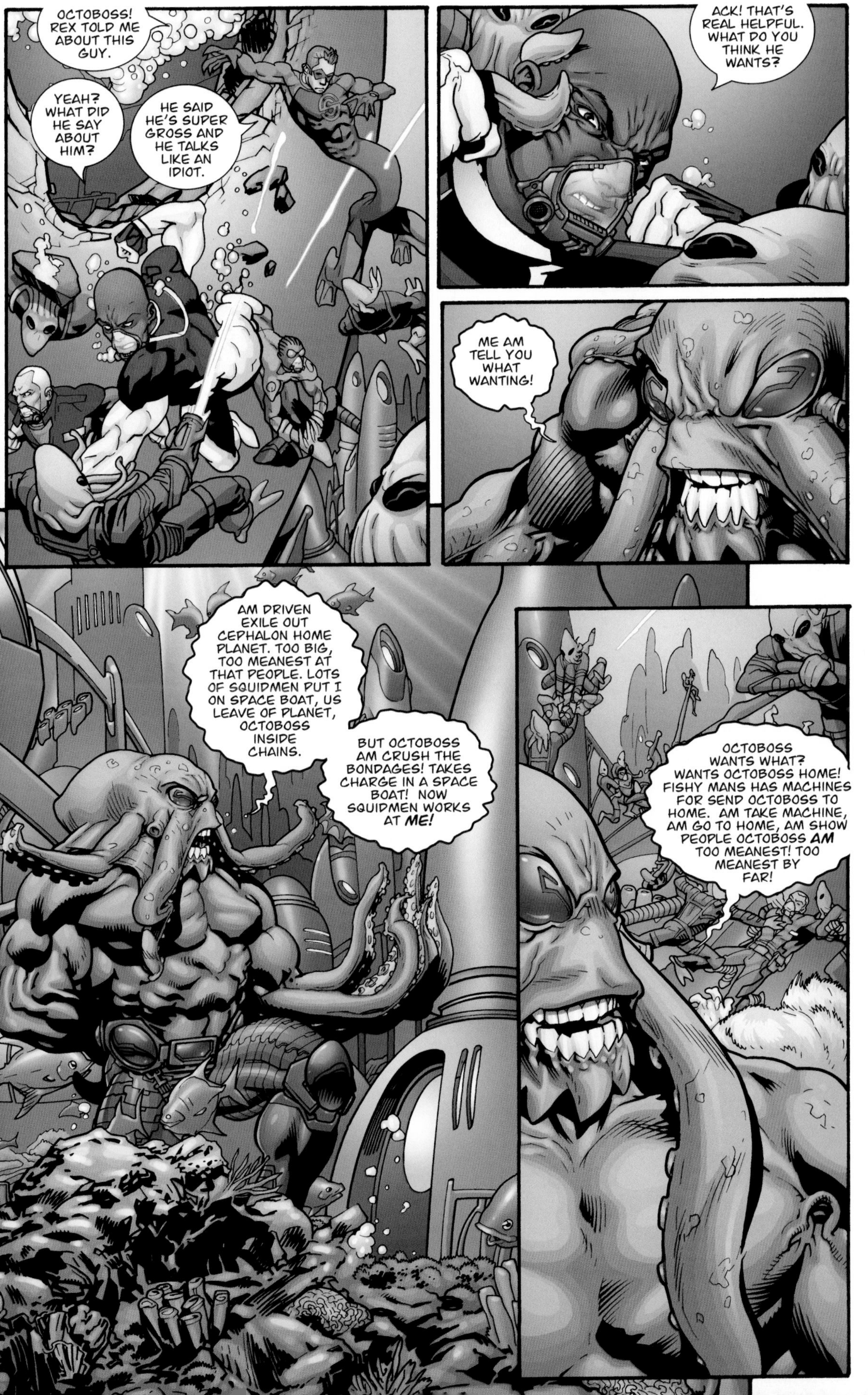
OCTOBOSS! REX TOLD ME ABOUT THIS GUY.
YEAH? WHAT DID HE SAY ABOUT HIM?
HE SAID HE'S SUPER GROSS AND HE TALKS LIKE AN IDIOT.
ACK! THAT'S REAL HELPFUL. WHAT DO YOU THINK HE WANTS?
ME AM TELL YOU WHAT WANTING!
AM DRIVEN EXILE OUT CEPHALON HOME PLANET. TOO BIG, TOO MEANEST AT THAT PEOPLE. LOTS OF SQUIDMEN PUT I ON SPACE BOAT, US LEAVE OF PLANET, OCTOBOSS INSIDE CHAINS.
BUT OCTOBOSS AM CRUSH THE BONDAGES! TAKES CHARGE IN A SPACE BOAT! NOW SQUIDMEN WORKS AT ME!
OCTOBOSS WANTS WHAT? WANTS OCTOBOSS HOME! FISHY MANS HAS MACHINES FOR SEND OCTOBOSS TO HOME. AM TAKE MACHINE, AM GO TO HOME, AM SHOW PEOPLE OCTOBOSS AM TOO MEANEST! TOO MEANEST BY FAR!

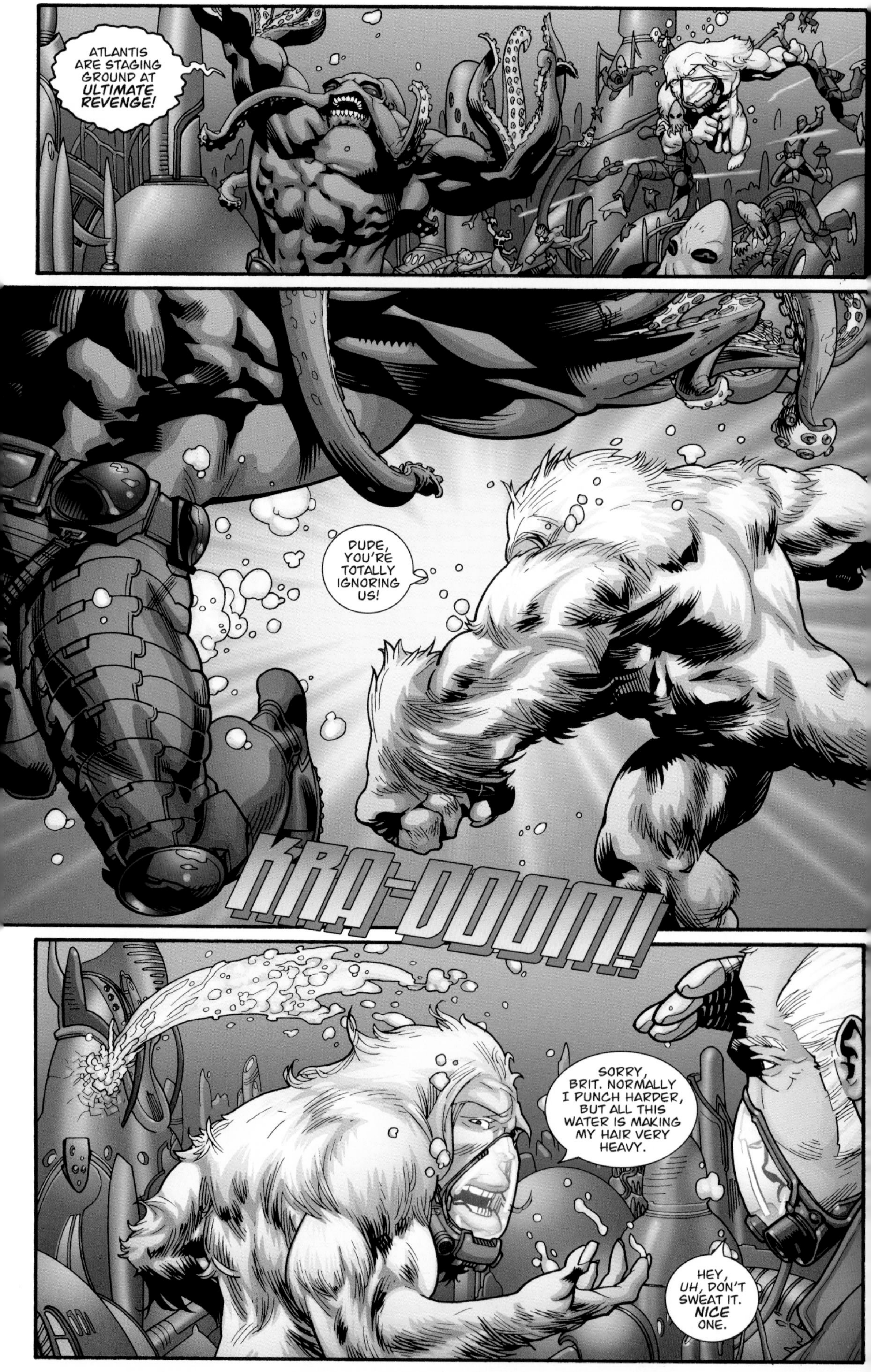
ATLANTIS ARE STAGING GROUND AT ULTIMATE REVENGE!
DUDE, YOU'RE TOTALLY IGNORING US!
KRA-DOOOM!
SORRY, BRIT. NORMALLY I PUNCH HARDER, BUT ALL THIS WATER IS MAKING MY HAIR VERY HEAVY.
HEY, UH, DON'T SWEAT IT. NICE ONE.

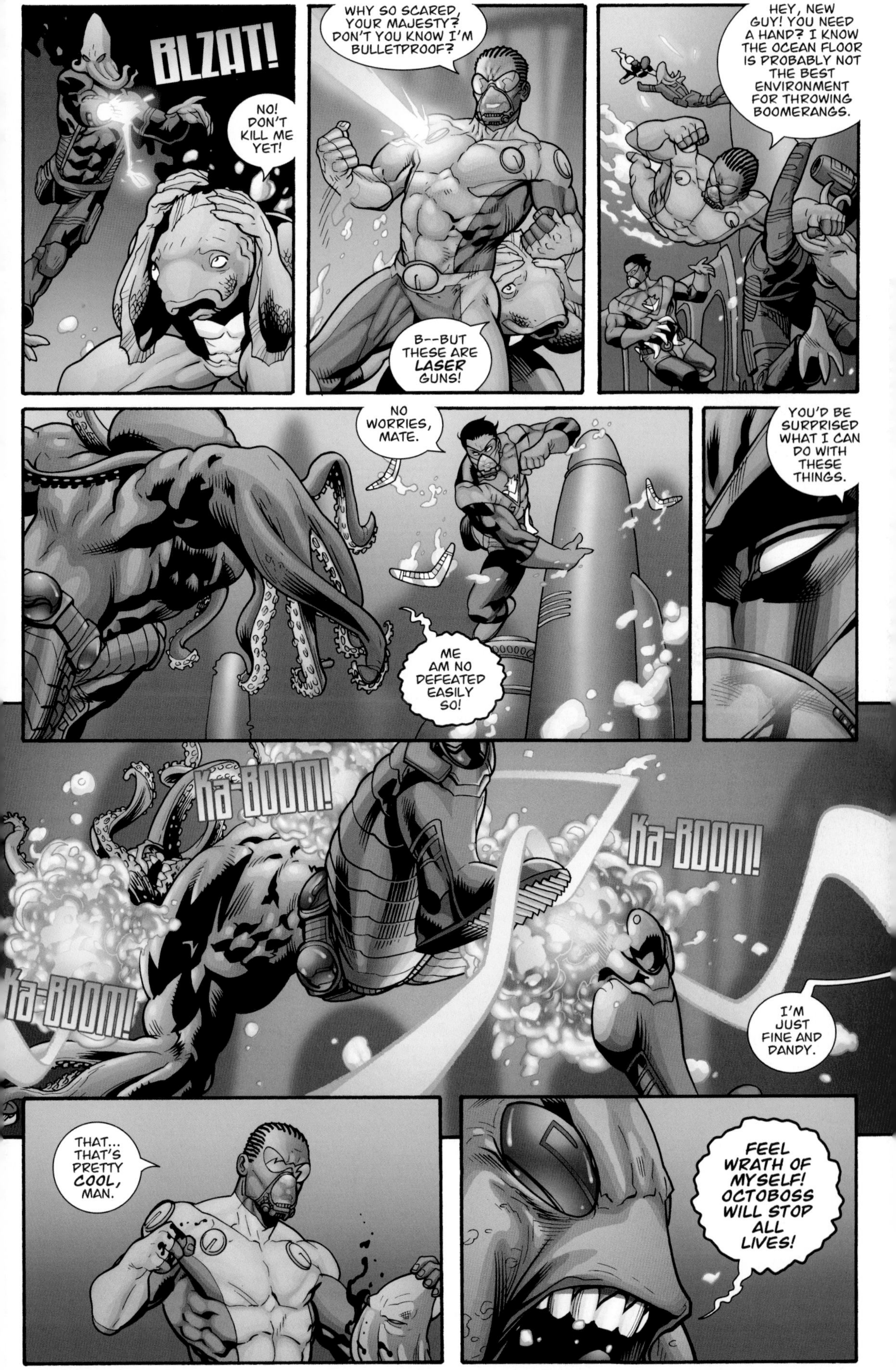
BLZAT!
NO! DON'T KILL ME YET!
WHY SO SCARED, YOUR MAJESTY? DON'T YOU KNOW I'M BULLETPROOF?
B--BUT THESE ARE LASER GUNS!
HEY, NEW GUY! YOU NEED A HAND? I KNOW THE OCEAN FLOOR IS PROBABLY NOT THE BEST ENVIRONMENT FOR THROWING BOOMERANGS.
NO WORRIES, MATE.
ME AM NO DEFEATED EASILY SO!
YOU'D BE SURPRISED WHAT I CAN DO WITH THESE THINGS.
KA-BOOM!
KA-BOOM!
KA-BOOM!
I'M JUST FINE AND DANDY.
THAT... THAT'S PRETTY COOL, MAN.
FEEL WRATH OF MYSELF! OCTOBOSS WILL STOP ALL LIVES!

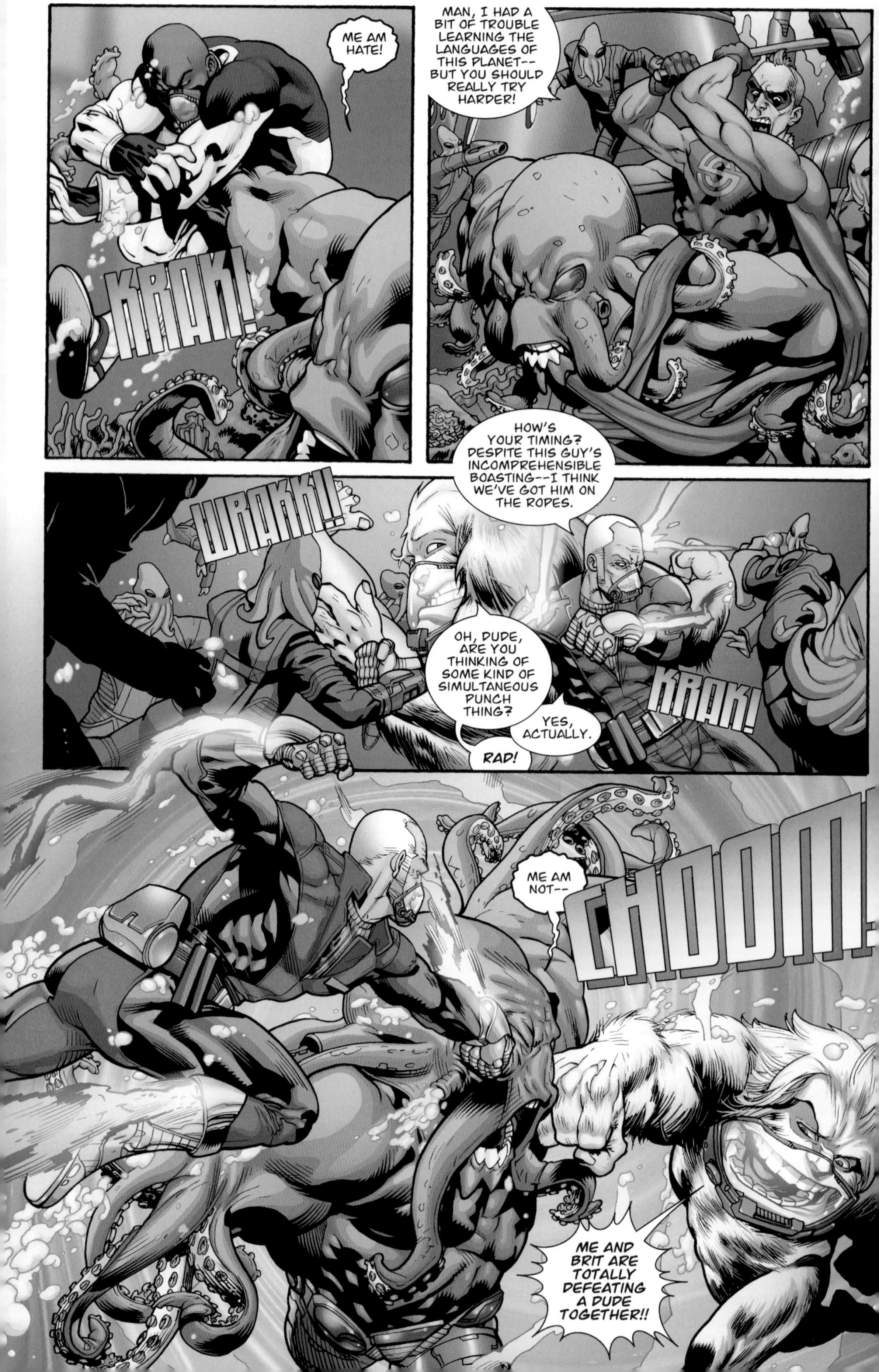
ME AM HATE!
KRAK!
MAN, I HAD A BIT OF TROUBLE LEARNING THE LANGUAGES OF THIS PLANET-- BUT YOU SHOULD REALLY TRY HARDER!
HOW'S YOUR TIMING? DESPITE THIS GUY'S INCOMPREHENSIBLE BOASTING--I THINK WE'VE GOT HIM ON THE ROPES.
WRAKK!!
OH, DUDE, ARE YOU THINKING OF SOME KIND OF SIMULTANEOUS PUNCH THING?
KRAK!
YES, ACTUALLY.
RAD!
ME AM NOT--
CHOOM!
ME AND BRIT ARE TOTALLY DEFEATING A DUDE TOGETHER!!

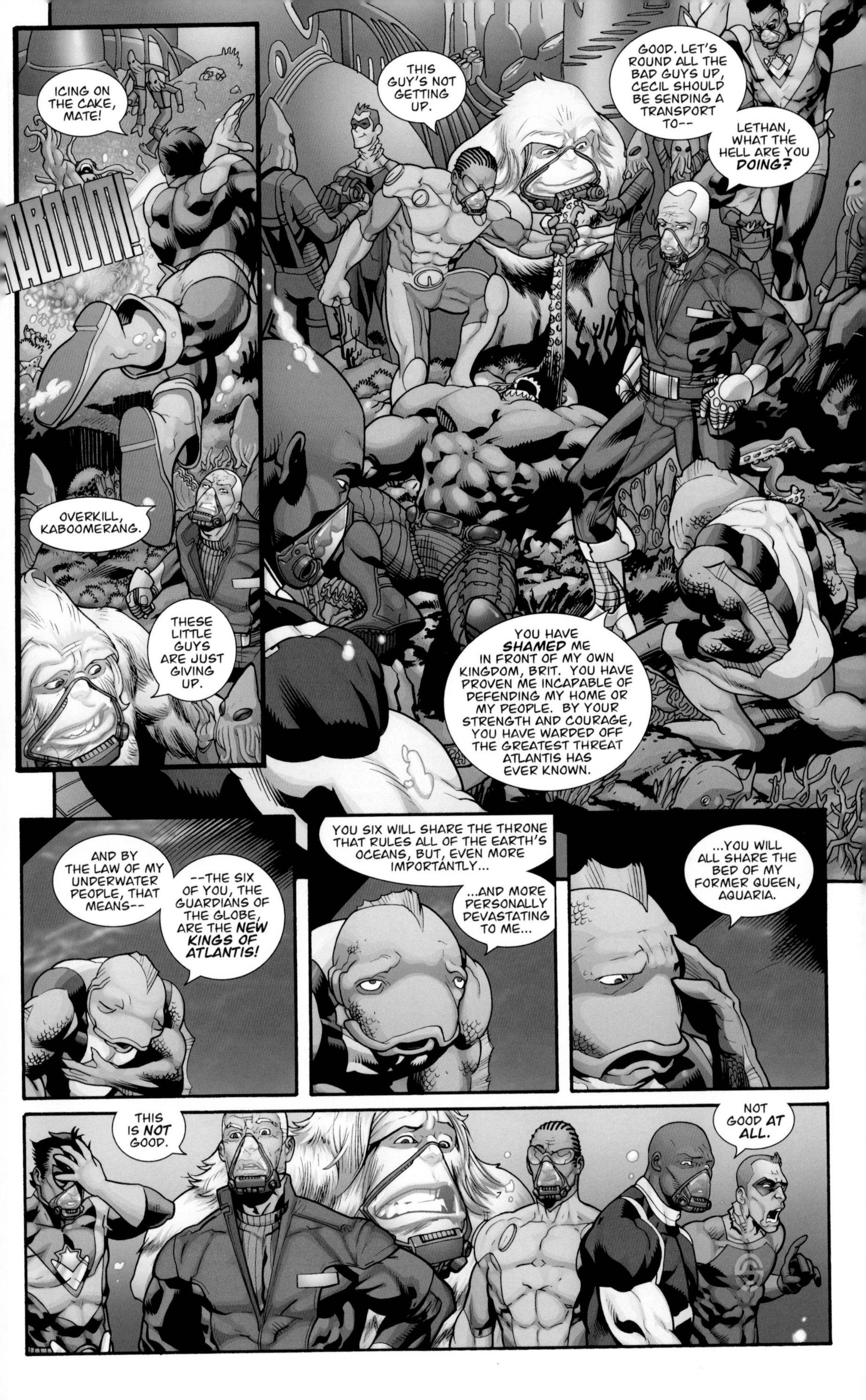
ICING ON THE CAKE, MATE!
KABOOOM!
OVERKILL, KABOOMERANG.
THESE LITTLE GUYS ARE JUST GIVING UP.
THIS GUY'S NOT GETTING UP.
GOOD. LET'S ROUND ALL THE BAD GUYS UP, CECIL SHOULD BE SENDING A TRANSPORT TO--
LETHAN, WHAT THE HELL ARE YOU **DOING?**
YOU HAVE **SHAMED** ME IN FRONT OF MY OWN KINGDOM, BRIT. YOU HAVE PROVEN ME INCAPABLE OF DEFENDING MY HOME OR MY PEOPLE. BY YOUR STRENGTH AND COURAGE, YOU HAVE WARDED OFF THE GREATEST THREAT ATLANTIS HAS EVER KNOWN.
AND BY THE LAW OF MY UNDERWATER PEOPLE, THAT MEANS--
--THE SIX OF YOU, THE GUARDIANS OF THE GLOBE, ARE THE **NEW KINGS OF ATLANTIS!**
YOU SIX WILL SHARE THE THRONE THAT RULES ALL OF THE EARTH'S OCEANS, BUT, EVEN MORE IMPORTANTLY...
...AND MORE PERSONALLY DEVASTATING TO ME...
...YOU WILL ALL SHARE THE BED OF MY FORMER QUEEN, AQUARIA.
THIS IS **NOT** GOOD.
NOT GOOD **AT ALL.**

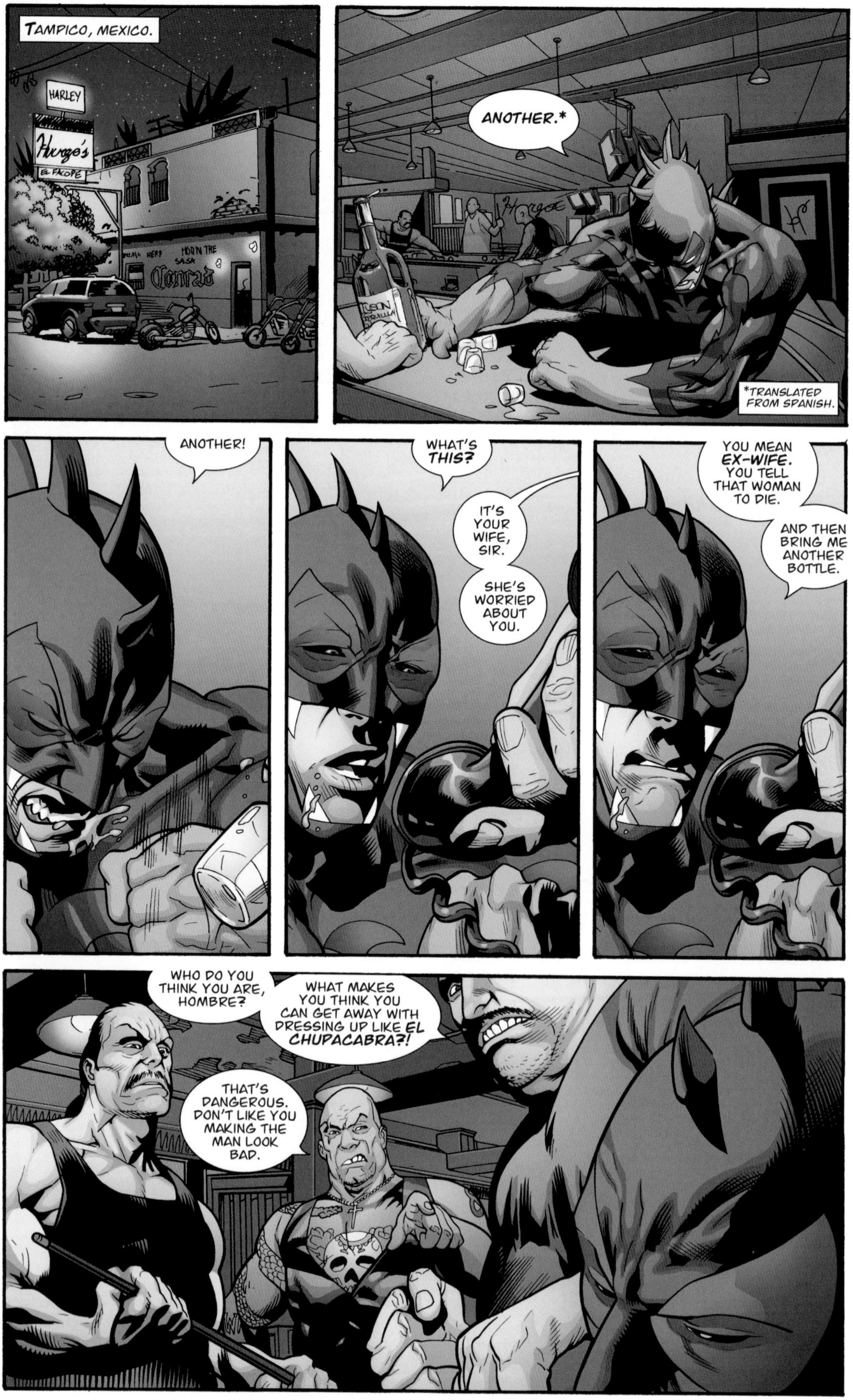
TAMPICO, MEXICO.
HARLEY
ANOTHER.*
*TRANSLATED FROM SPANISH.
ANOTHER!
WHAT'S THIS?
IT'S YOUR WIFE, SIR.
SHE'S WORRIED ABOUT YOU.
YOU MEAN EX-WIFE. YOU TELL THAT WOMAN TO DIE.
AND THEN BRING ME ANOTHER BOTTLE.
WHO DO YOU THINK YOU ARE, HOMBRE?
WHAT MAKES YOU THINK YOU CAN GET AWAY WITH DRESSING UP LIKE EL CHUPACABRA?!
THAT'S DANGEROUS. DON'T LIKE YOU MAKING THE MAN LOOK BAD.

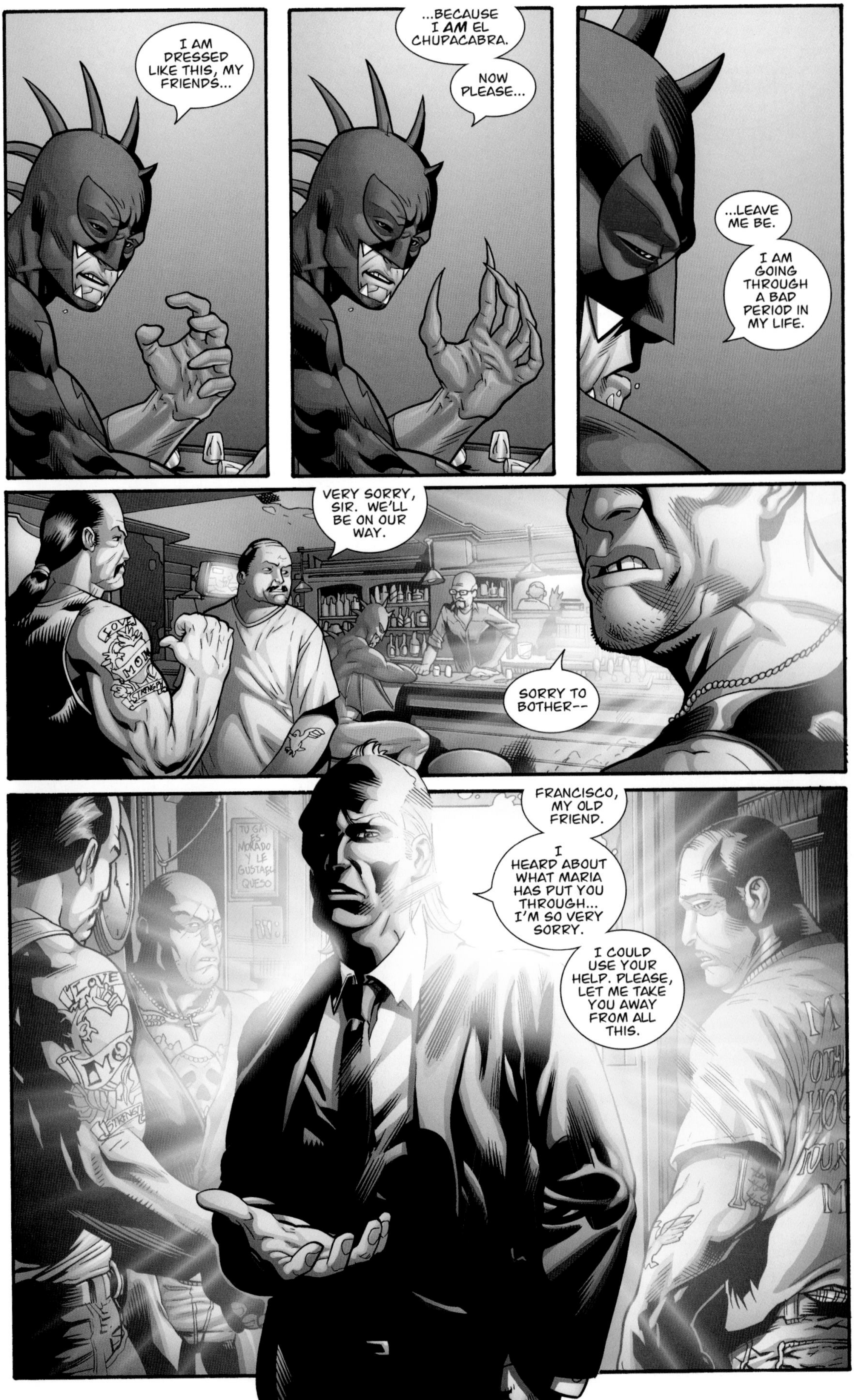
I AM DRESSED LIKE THIS, MY FRIENDS...
...BECAUSE I AM EL CHUPACABRA.
NOW PLEASE...
...LEAVE ME BE.
I AM GOING THROUGH A BAD PERIOD IN MY LIFE.
VERY SORRY, SIR. WE'LL BE ON OUR WAY.
SORRY TO BOTHER--
FRANCISCO, MY OLD FRIEND.
I HEARD ABOUT WHAT MARIA HAS PUT YOU THROUGH... I'M SO VERY SORRY.
I COULD USE YOUR HELP. PLEASE, LET ME TAKE YOU AWAY FROM ALL THIS.

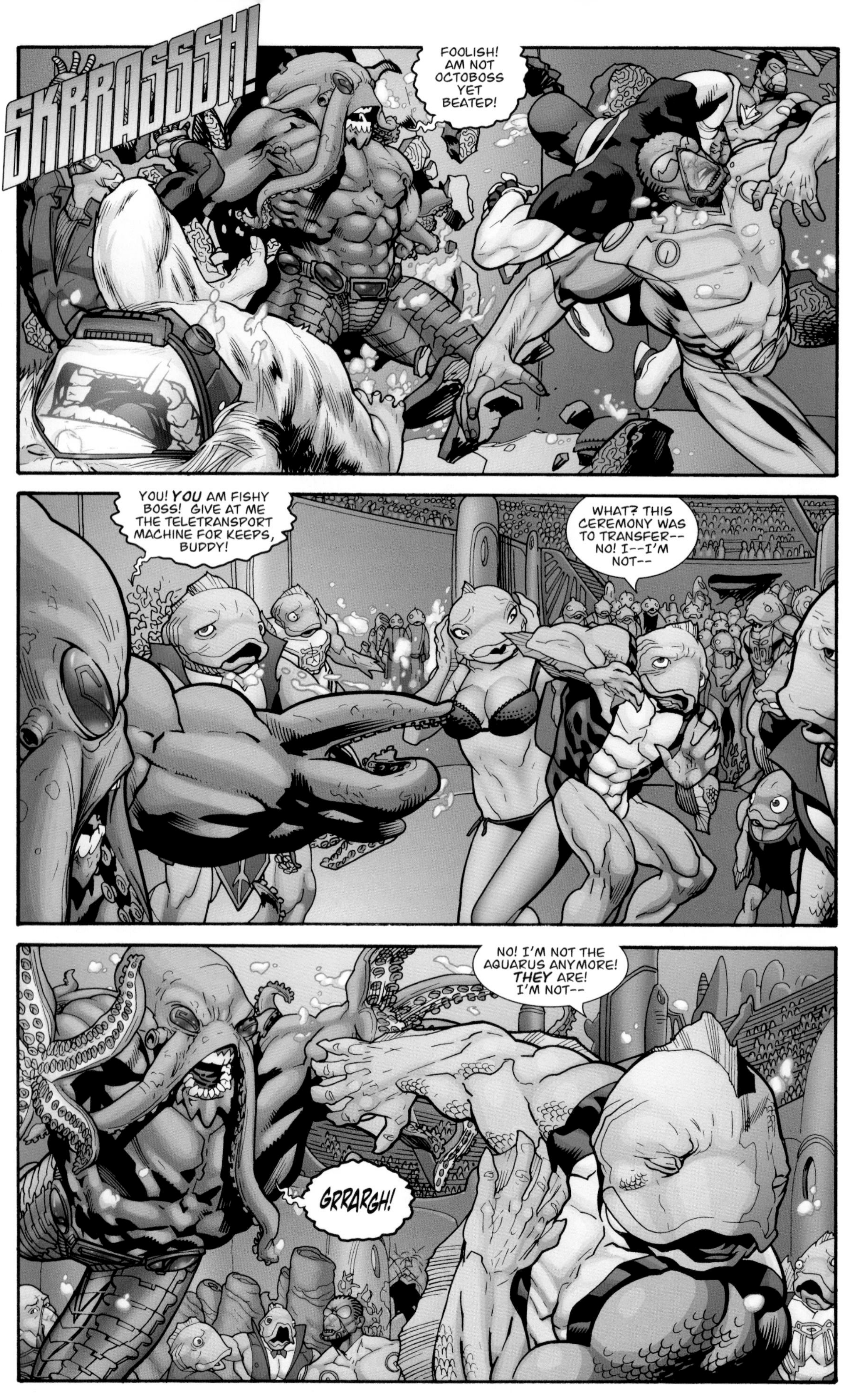
SKRASSSH!
FOOLISH! AM NOT OCTOBOSS YET BEATED!
YOU! YOU AM FISHY BOSS! GIVE AT ME THE TELETRANSPORT MACHINE FOR KEEPS, BUDDY!
WHAT? THIS CEREMONY WAS TO TRANSFER-- NO! I--I'M NOT--
NO! I'M NOT THE AQUARUS ANYMORE! THEY ARE! I'M NOT--
GRRARGH!

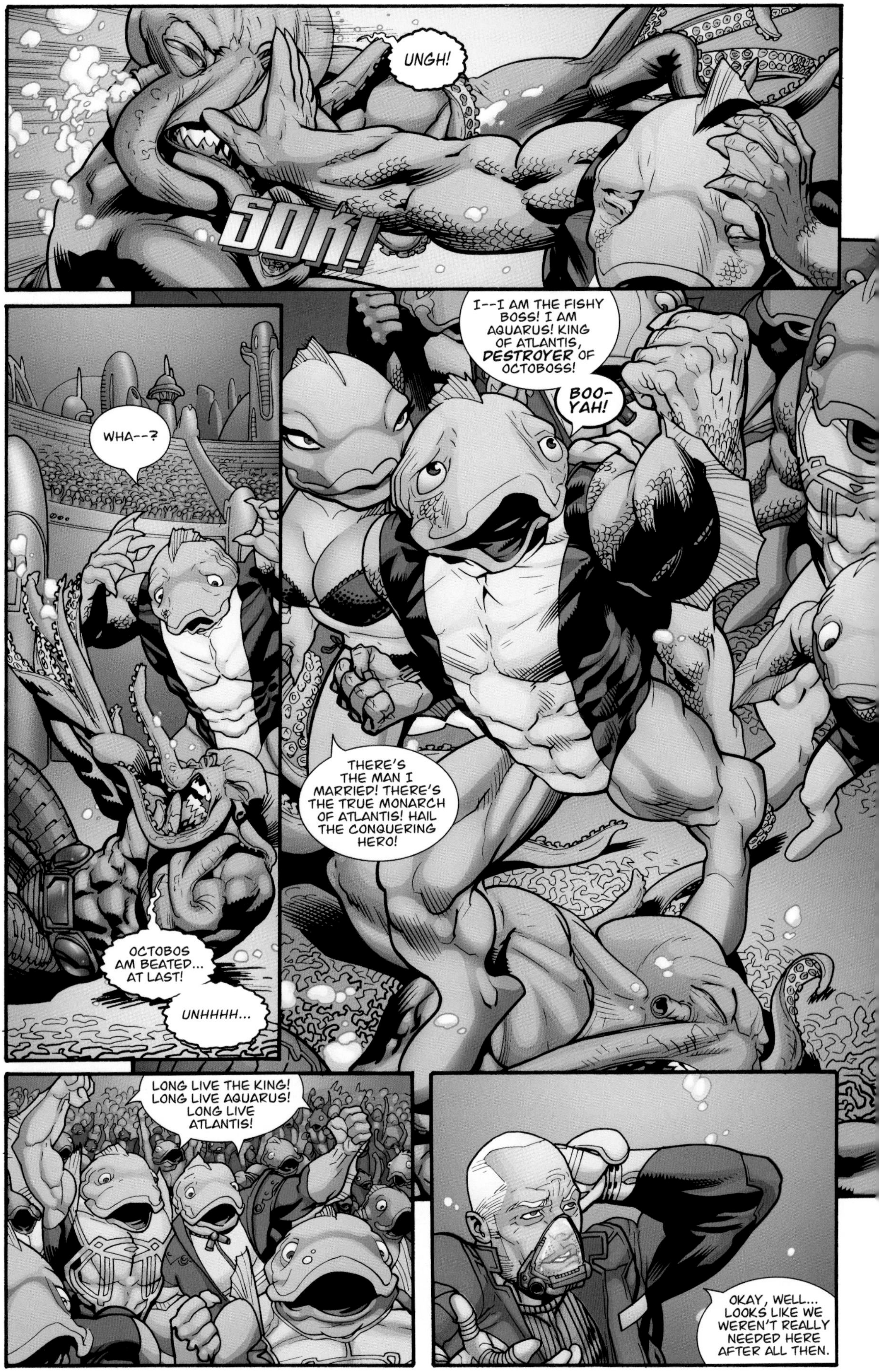
UNGH!
SOK!
WHA--?
I--I AM THE FISHY BOSS! I AM AQUARUS! KING OF ATLANTIS, DESTROYER OF OCTOBOSS!
BOO-YAH!
THERE'S THE MAN I MARRIED! THERE'S THE TRUE MONARCH OF ATLANTIS! HAIL THE CONQUERING HERO!
OCTOBOS AM BEATED... AT LAST!
UNHHHH...
LONG LIVE THE KING! LONG LIVE AQUARUS! LONG LIVE ATLANTIS!
OKAY, WELL... LOOKS LIKE WE WEREN'T REALLY NEEDED HERE AFTER ALL THEN.

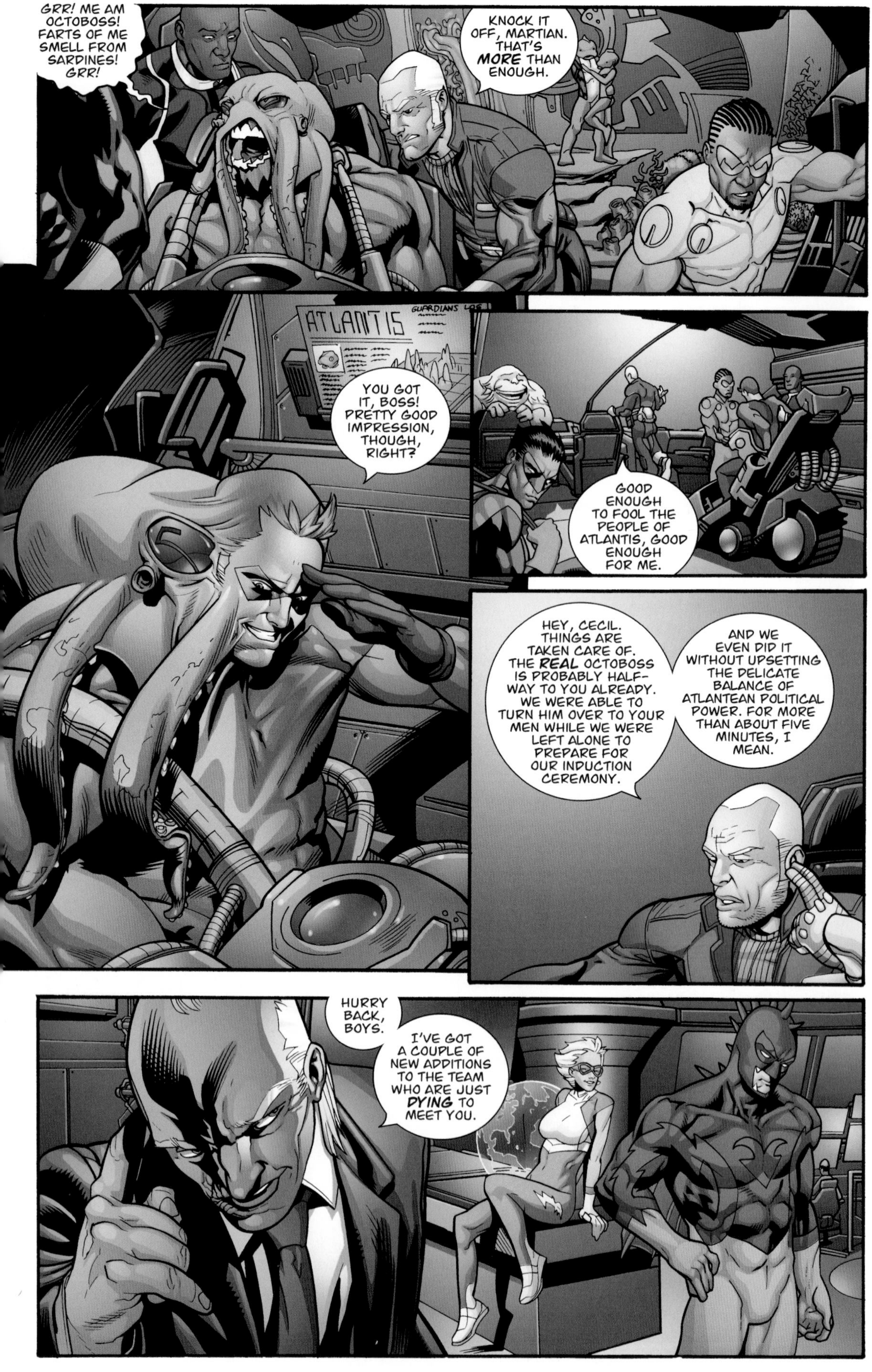
GRR! ME AM OCTOBOSS! FARTS OF ME SMELL FROM SARDINES! GRR!
KNOCK IT OFF, MARTIAN. THAT'S MORE THAN ENOUGH.
ATLANTIS
GUARDIANS LOG
YOU GOT IT, BOSS! PRETTY GOOD IMPRESSION, THOUGH, RIGHT?
GOOD ENOUGH TO FOOL THE PEOPLE OF ATLANTIS, GOOD ENOUGH FOR ME.
HEY, CECIL. THINGS ARE TAKEN CARE OF. THE REAL OCTOBOSS IS PROBABLY HALF-WAY TO YOU ALREADY. WE WERE ABLE TO TURN HIM OVER TO YOUR MEN WHILE WE WERE LEFT ALONE TO PREPARE FOR OUR INDUCTION CEREMONY.
AND WE EVEN DID IT WITHOUT UPSETTING THE DELICATE BALANCE OF ATLANTEAN POLITICAL POWER. FOR MORE THAN ABOUT FIVE MINUTES, I MEAN.
HURRY BACK, BOYS.
I'VE GOT A COUPLE OF NEW ADDITIONS TO THE TEAM WHO ARE JUST DYING TO MEET YOU.

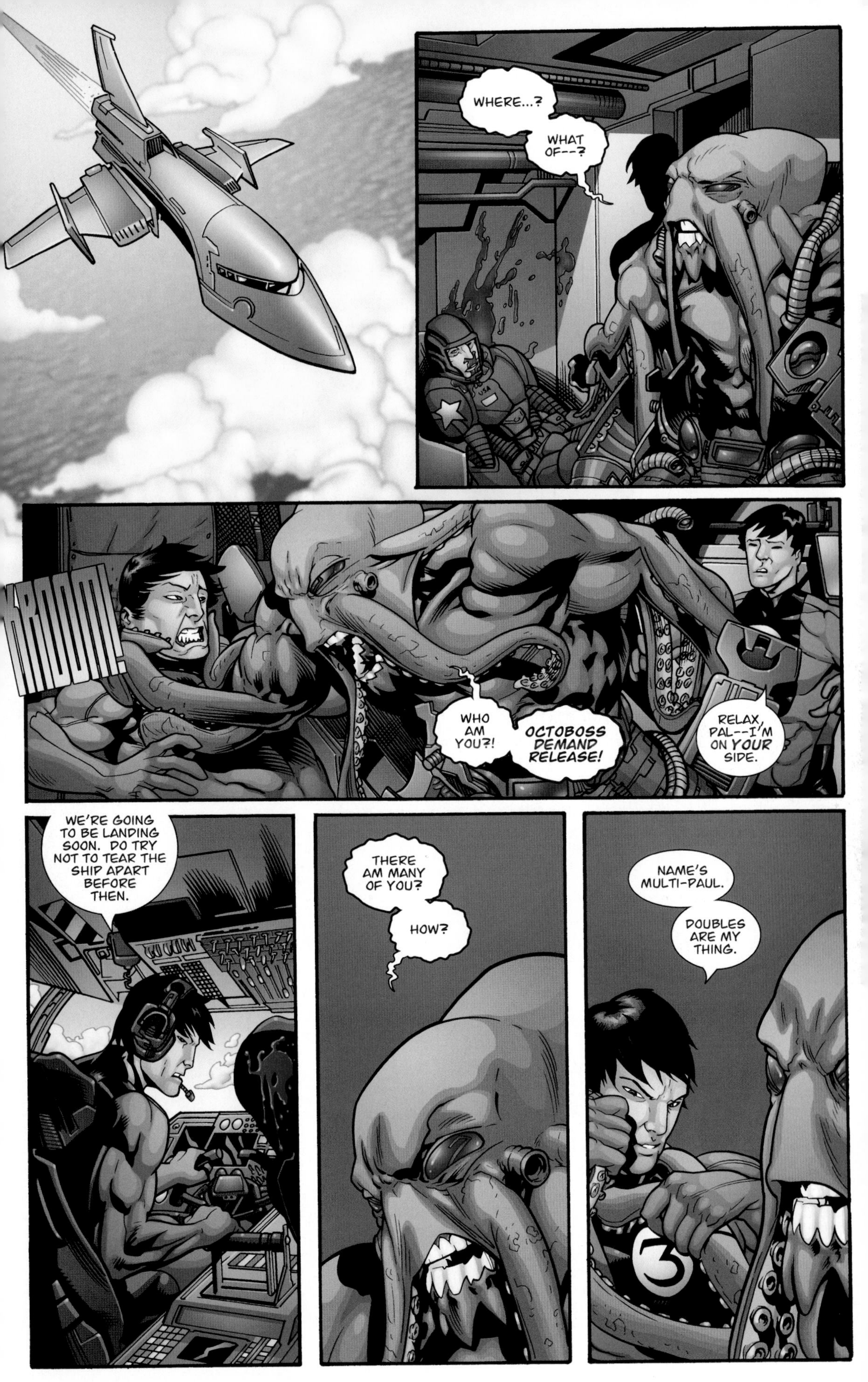
WHERE...?
WHAT OF--?
KROOM!
WHO AM YOU?!
OCTOBOSS DEMAND RELEASE!
RELAX, PAL--I'M ON YOUR SIDE.
WE'RE GOING TO BE LANDING SOON. DO TRY NOT TO TEAR THE SHIP APART BEFORE THEN.
THERE AM MANY OF YOU?
HOW?
NAME'S MULTI-PAUL.
DOUBLES ARE MY THING.

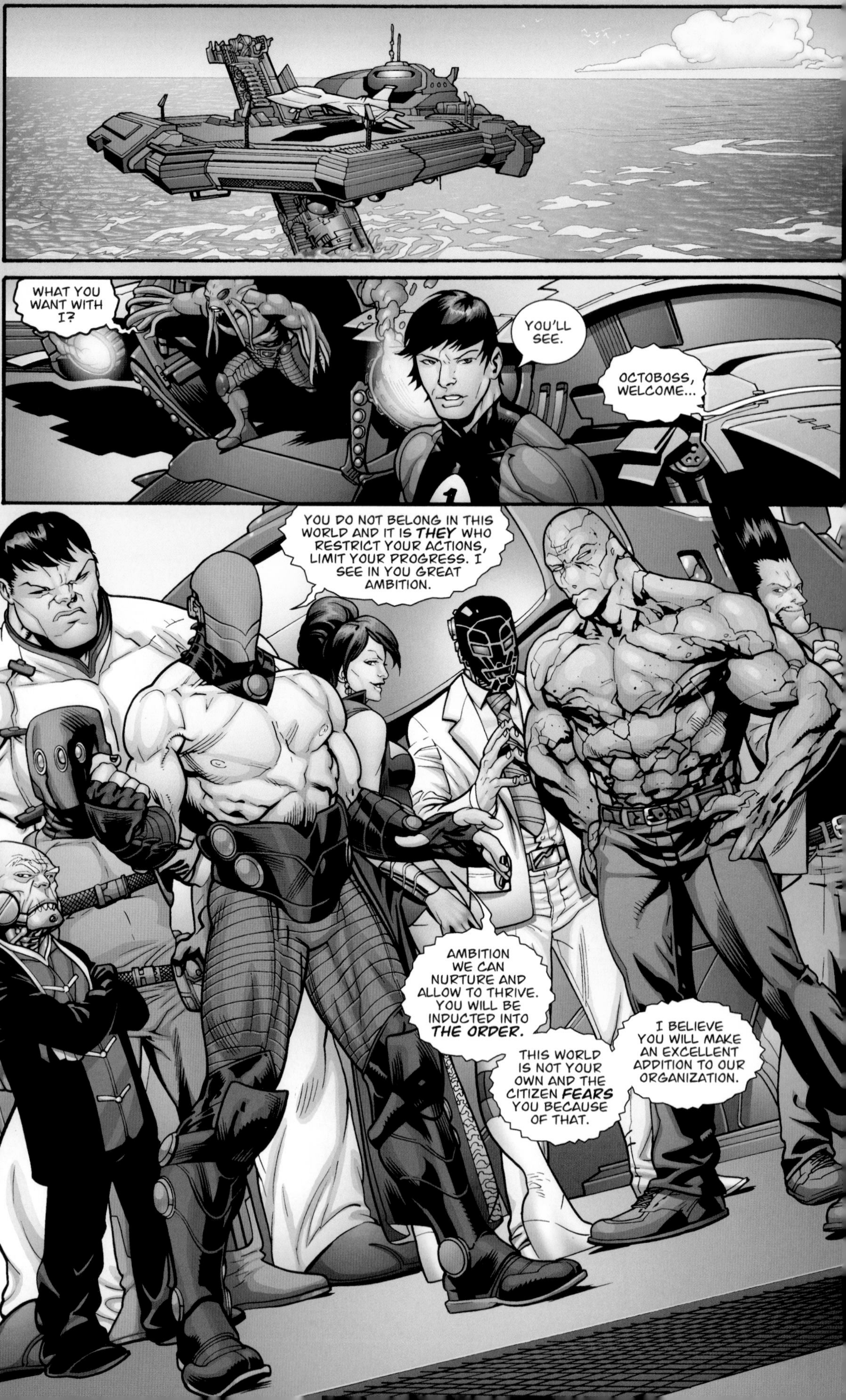
WHAT YOU WANT WITH I?
YOU'LL SEE.
OCTOBOSS, WELCOME...
YOU DO NOT BELONG IN THIS WORLD AND IT IS THEY WHO RESTRICT YOUR ACTIONS, LIMIT YOUR PROGRESS. I SEE IN YOU GREAT AMBITION.
AMBITION WE CAN NURTURE AND ALLOW TO THRIVE. YOU WILL BE INDUCTED INTO THE ORDER.
THIS WORLD IS NOT YOUR OWN AND THE CITIZEN FEARS YOU BECAUSE OF THAT.
I BELIEVE YOU WILL MAKE AN EXCELLENT ADDITION TO OUR ORGANIZATION.

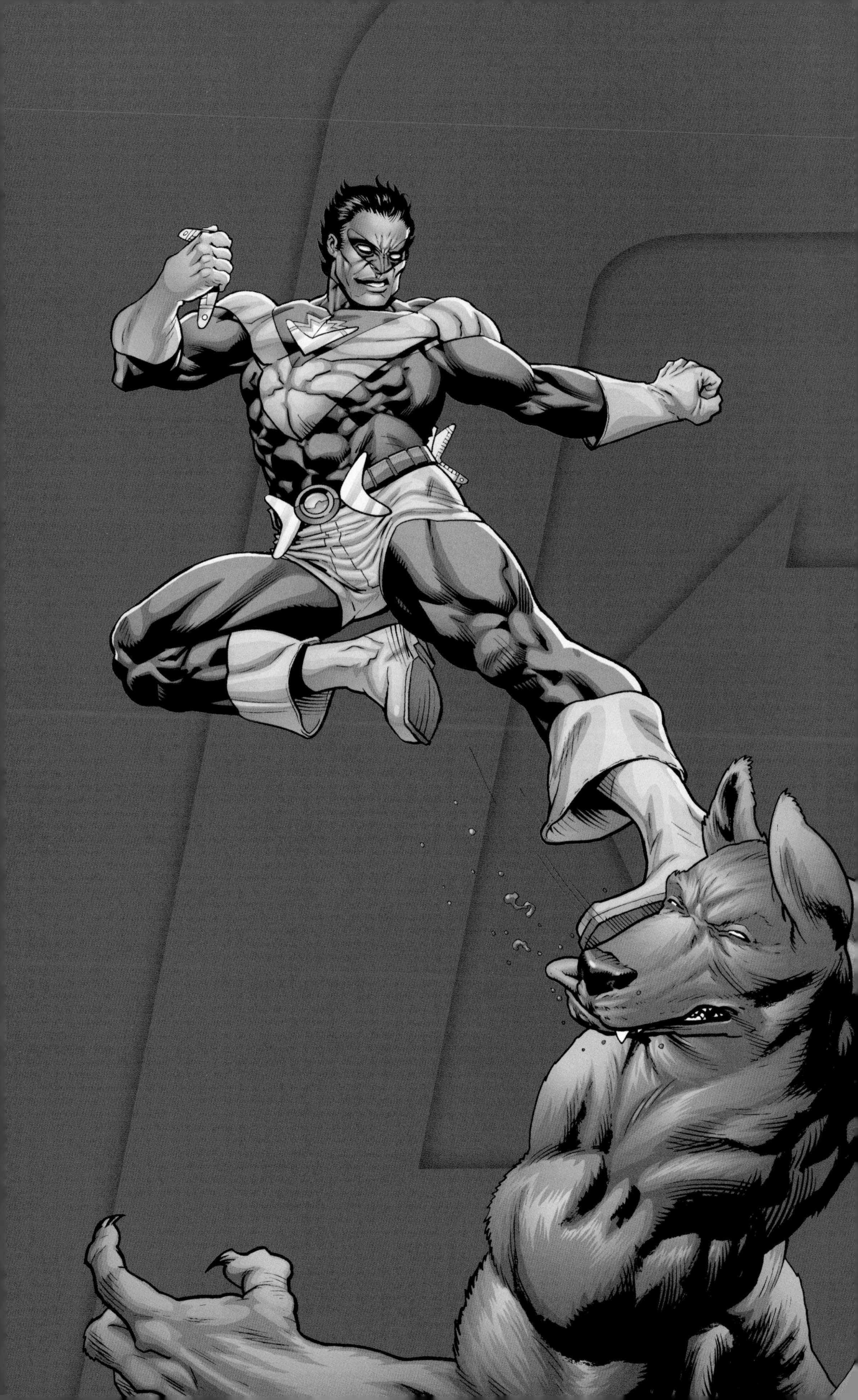

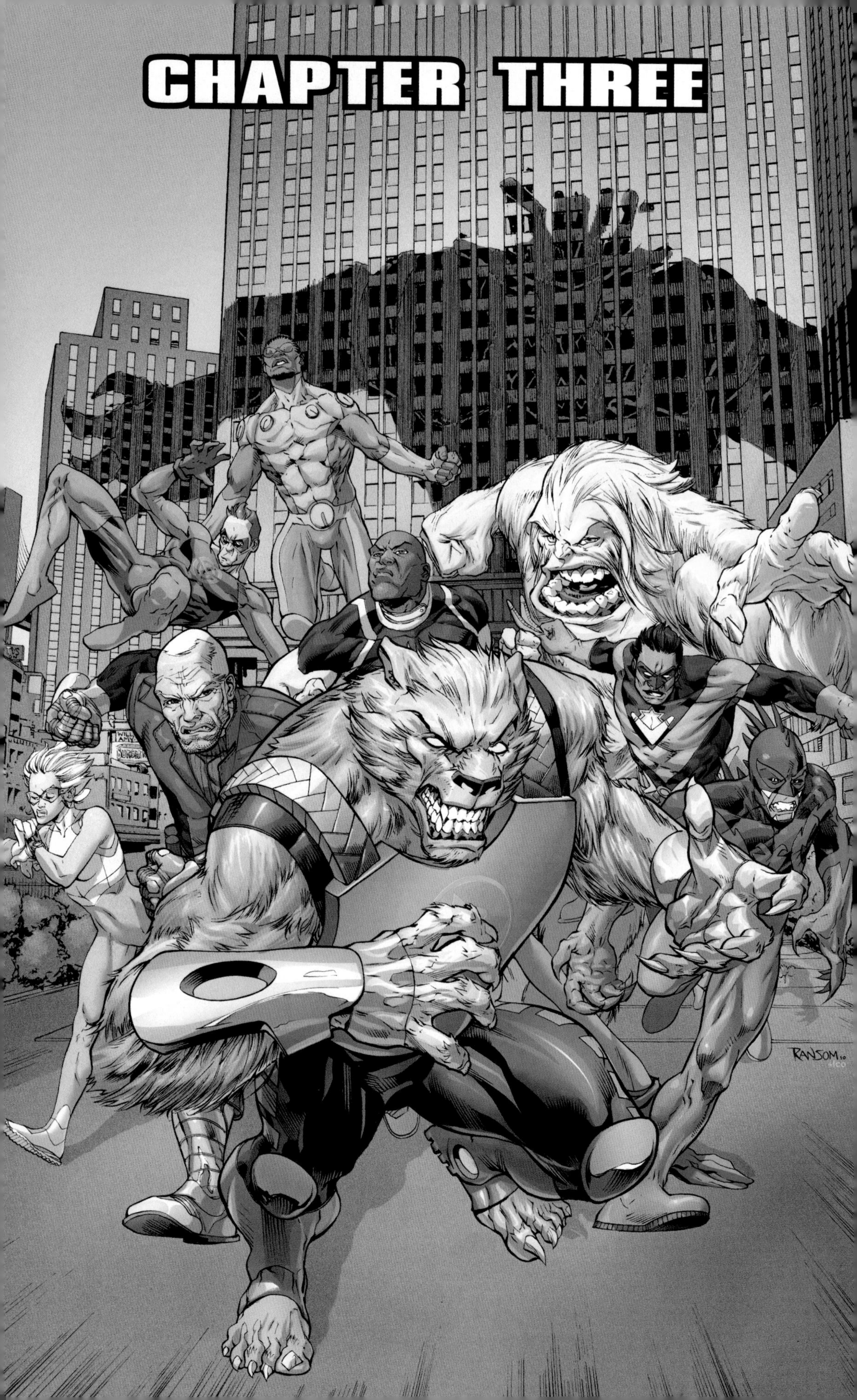
CHAPTER THREE
RANSOM

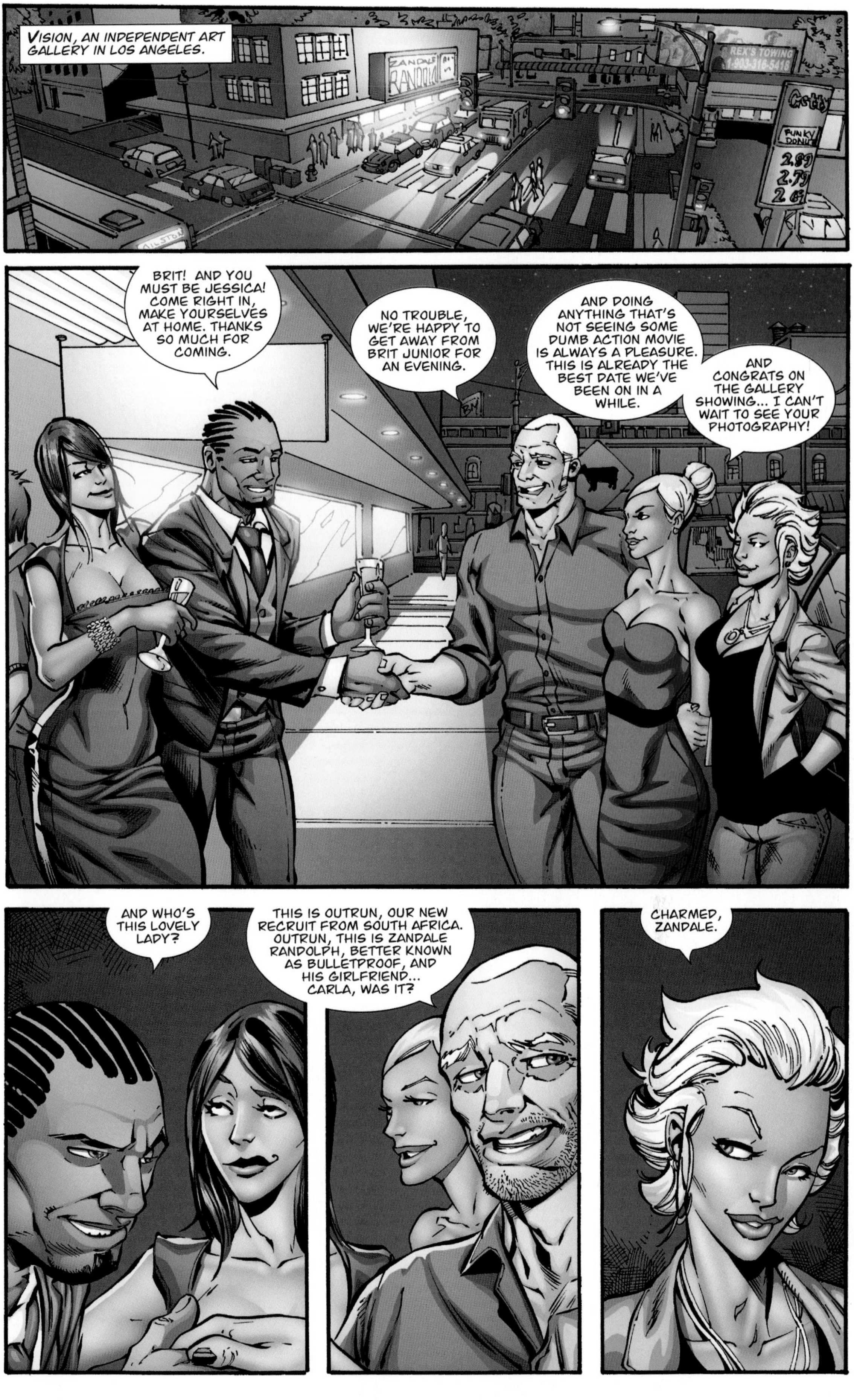
VISION, AN INDEPENDENT ART GALLERY IN LOS ANGELES.
REX'S TOWING
1-903-316-5418
BRIT! AND YOU MUST BE JESSICA! COME RIGHT IN, MAKE YOURSELVES AT HOME. THANKS SO MUCH FOR COMING.
NO TROUBLE, WE'RE HAPPY TO GET AWAY FROM BRIT JUNIOR FOR AN EVENING.
AND DOING ANYTHING THAT'S NOT SEEING SOME DUMB ACTION MOVIE IS ALWAYS A PLEASURE. THIS IS ALREADY THE BEST DATE WE'VE BEEN ON IN A WHILE.
AND CONGRATS ON THE GALLERY SHOWING... I CAN'T WAIT TO SEE YOUR PHOTOGRAPHY!
AND WHO'S THIS LOVELY LADY?
THIS IS OUTRUN, OUR NEW RECRUIT FROM SOUTH AFRICA. OUTRUN, THIS IS ZANDALE RANDOLPH, BETTER KNOWN AS BULLETPROOF, AND HIS GIRLFRIEND... CARLA, WAS IT?
CHARMED, ZANDALE.

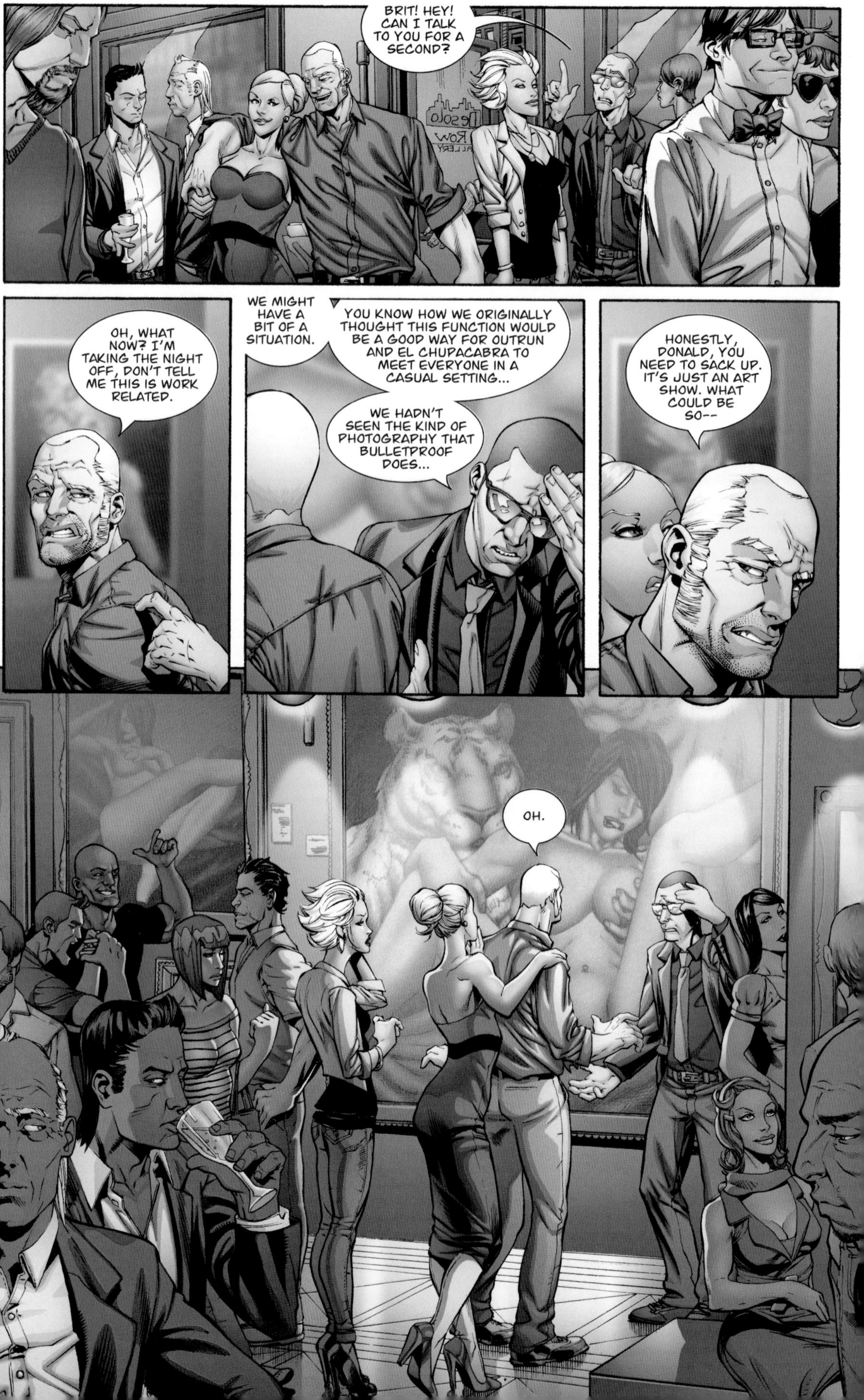
BRIT! HEY! CAN I TALK TO YOU FOR A SECOND?
OH, WHAT NOW? I'M TAKING THE NIGHT OFF, DON'T TELL ME THIS IS WORK RELATED.
WE MIGHT HAVE A BIT OF A SITUATION.
YOU KNOW HOW WE ORIGINALLY THOUGHT THIS FUNCTION WOULD BE A GOOD WAY FOR OUTRUN AND EL CHUPACABRA TO MEET EVERYONE IN A CASUAL SETTING...
WE HADN'T SEEN THE KIND OF PHOTOGRAPHY THAT BULLETPROOF DOES...
HONESTLY, DONALD, YOU NEED TO SACK UP. IT'S JUST AN ART SHOW. WHAT COULD BE SO--
OH.

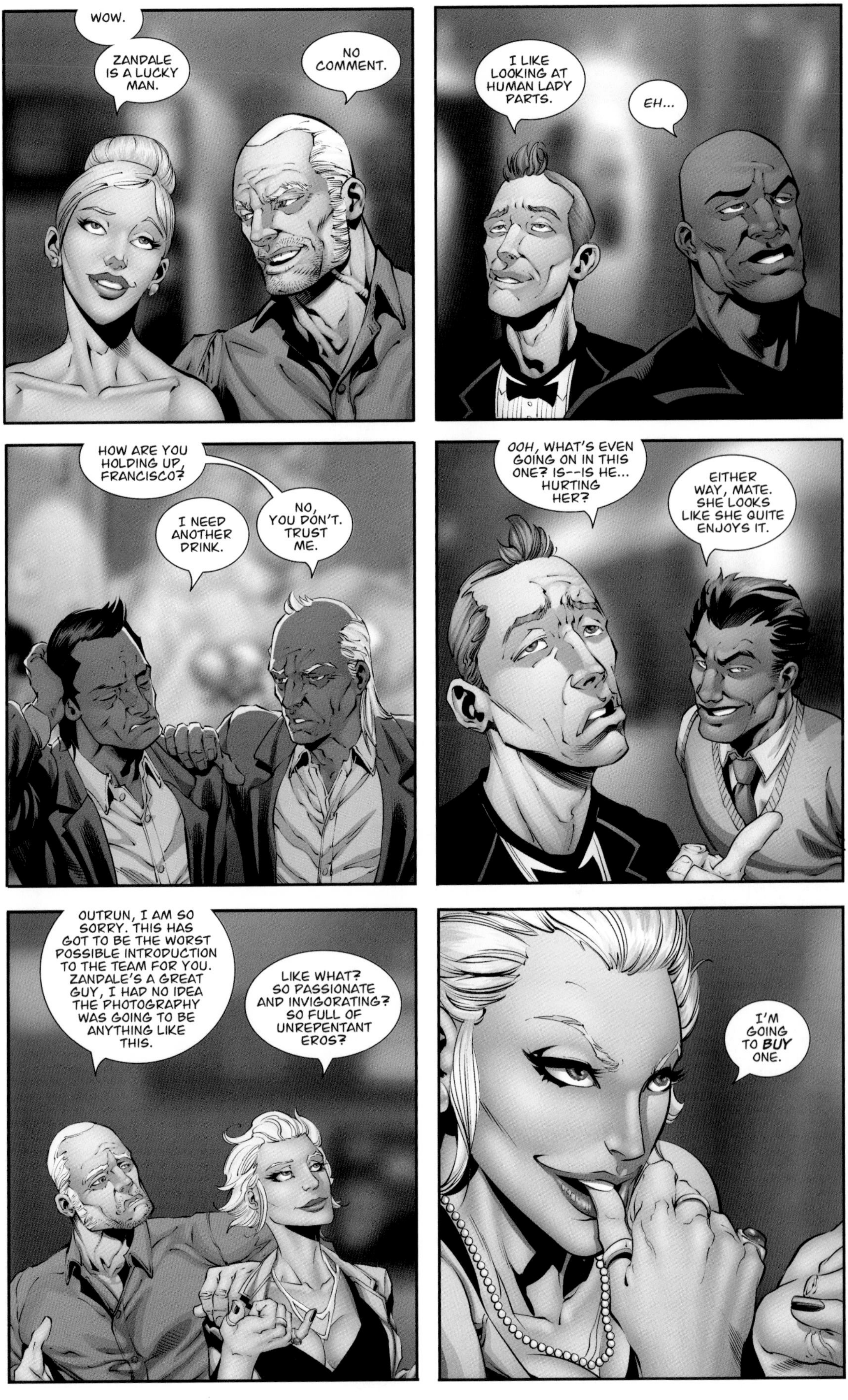
WOW.
ZANDALE IS A LUCKY MAN.
NO COMMENT.
I LIKE LOOKING AT HUMAN LADY PARTS.
EH...
HOW ARE YOU HOLDING UP, FRANCISCO?
I NEED ANOTHER DRINK.
NO, YOU DON'T. TRUST ME.
OOH, WHAT'S EVEN GOING ON IN THIS ONE? IS--IS HE... HURTING HER?
EITHER WAY, MATE. SHE LOOKS LIKE SHE QUITE ENJOYS IT.
OUTRUN, I AM SO SORRY. THIS HAS GOT TO BE THE WORST POSSIBLE INTRODUCTION TO THE TEAM FOR YOU. ZANDALE'S A GREAT GUY, I HAD NO IDEA THE PHOTOGRAPHY WAS GOING TO BE ANYTHING LIKE THIS.
LIKE WHAT? SO PASSIONATE AND INVIGORATING? SO FULL OF UNREPENTANT EROS?
I'M GOING TO **BUY** ONE.

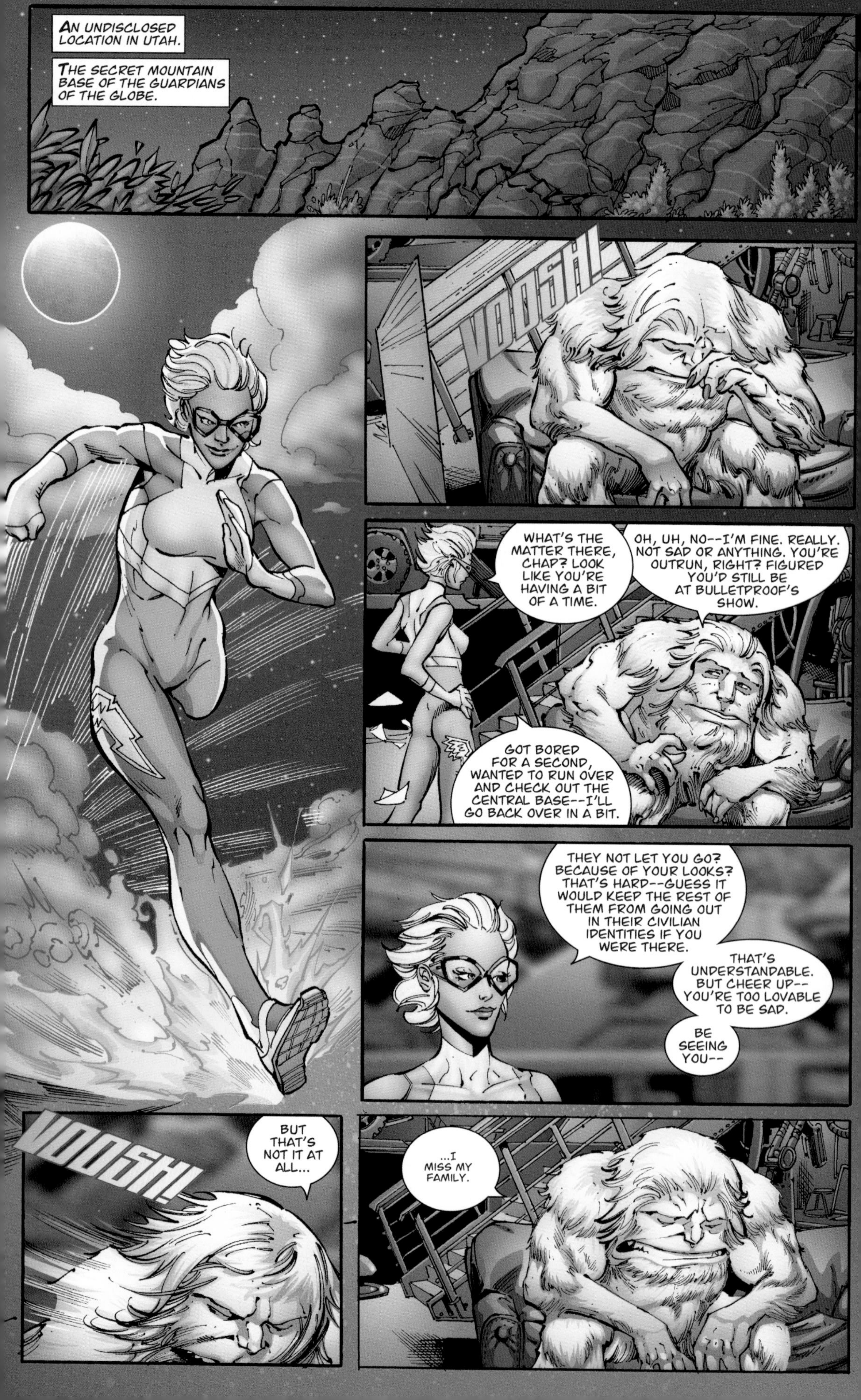
AN UNDISCLOSED LOCATION IN UTAH.
THE SECRET MOUNTAIN BASE OF THE GUARDIANS OF THE GLOBE.
VOOSH!
WHAT'S THE MATTER THERE, CHAP? LOOK LIKE YOU'RE HAVING A BIT OF A TIME.
OH, UH, NO--I'M FINE. REALLY. NOT SAD OR ANYTHING. YOU'RE OUTRUN, RIGHT? FIGURED YOU'D STILL BE AT BULLETPROOF'S SHOW.
GOT BORED FOR A SECOND, WANTED TO RUN OVER AND CHECK OUT THE CENTRAL BASE--I'LL GO BACK OVER IN A BIT.
THEY NOT LET YOU GO? BECAUSE OF YOUR LOOKS? THAT'S HARD--GUESS IT WOULD KEEP THE REST OF THEM FROM GOING OUT IN THEIR CIVILIAN IDENTITIES IF YOU WERE THERE.
THAT'S UNDERSTANDABLE. BUT CHEER UP--YOU'RE TOO LOVABLE TO BE SAD.
BE SEEING YOU--
VOOSH!
BUT THAT'S NOT IT AT ALL...
...I MISS MY FAMILY.

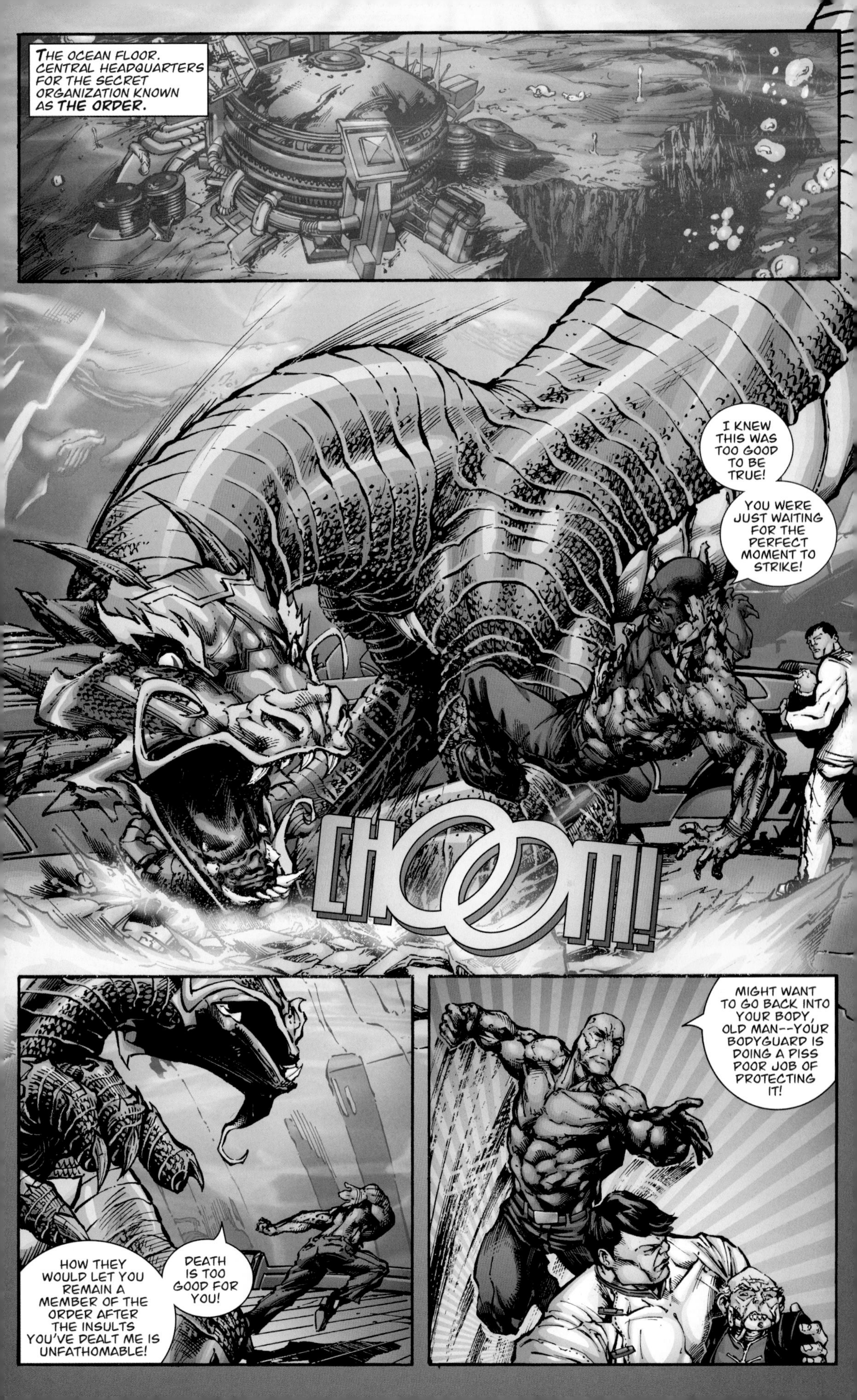

THE OCEAN FLOOR. CENTRAL HEADQUARTERS FOR THE SECRET ORGANIZATION KNOWN AS THE ORDER.
I KNEW THIS WAS TOO GOOD TO BE TRUE!
YOU WERE JUST WAITING FOR THE PERFECT MOMENT TO STRIKE!
CHOOM!
HOW THEY WOULD LET YOU REMAIN A MEMBER OF THE ORDER AFTER THE INSULTS YOU'VE DEALT ME IS UNFATHOMABLE!
DEATH IS TOO GOOD FOR YOU!
MIGHT WANT TO GO BACK INTO YOUR BODY, OLD MAN--YOUR BODYGUARD IS DOING A PISS POOR JOB OF PROTECTING IT!

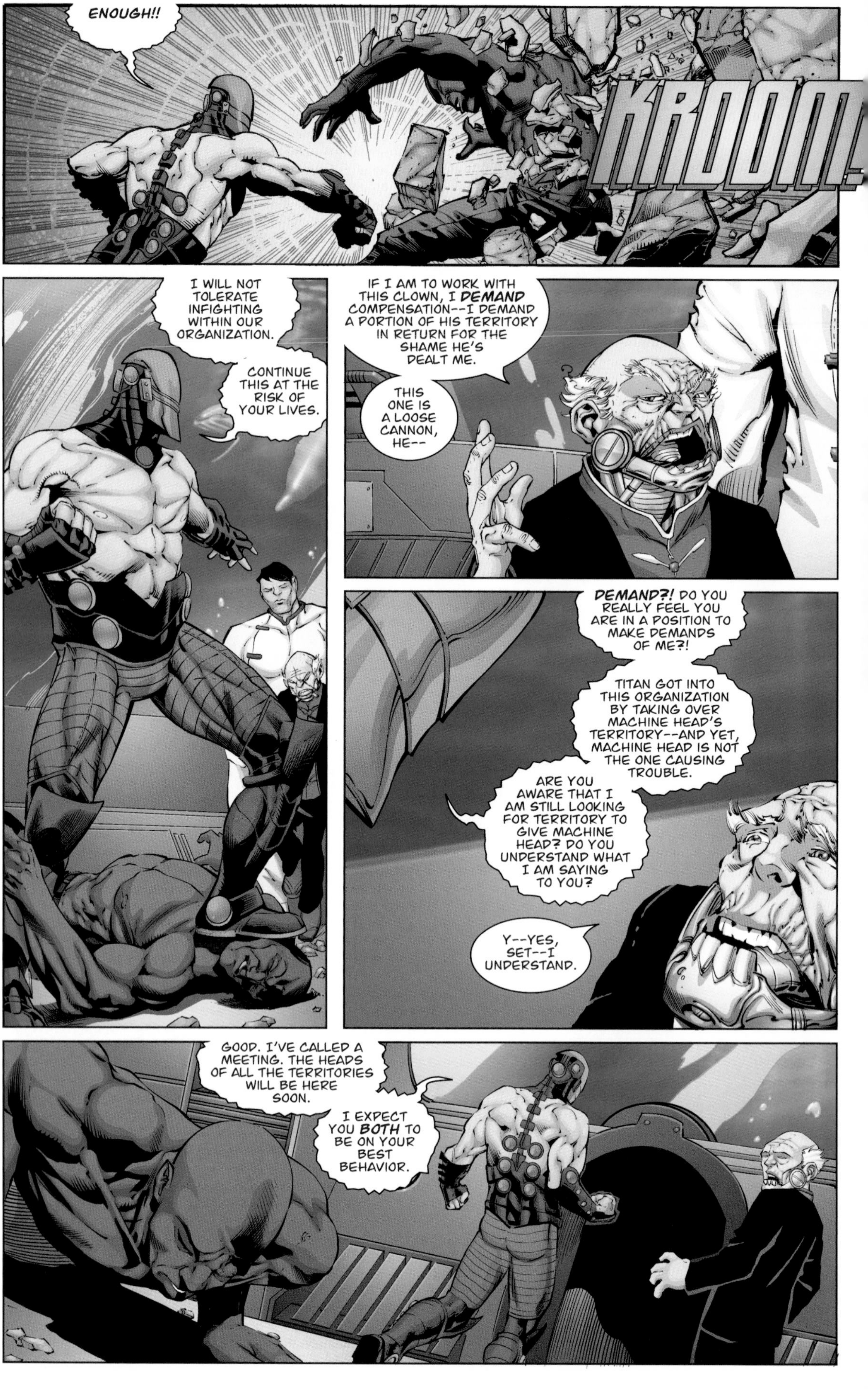
ENOUGH!!
KROOM!
I WILL NOT TOLERATE INFIGHTING WITHIN OUR ORGANIZATION.
CONTINUE THIS AT THE RISK OF YOUR LIVES.
IF I AM TO WORK WITH THIS CLOWN, I DEMAND COMPENSATION--I DEMAND A PORTION OF HIS TERRITORY IN RETURN FOR THE SHAME HE'S DEALT ME.
THIS ONE IS A LOOSE CANNON, HE--
DEMAND?! DO YOU REALLY FEEL YOU ARE IN A POSITION TO MAKE DEMANDS OF ME?!
TITAN GOT INTO THIS ORGANIZATION BY TAKING OVER MACHINE HEAD'S TERRITORY--AND YET, MACHINE HEAD IS NOT THE ONE CAUSING TROUBLE.
ARE YOU AWARE THAT I AM STILL LOOKING FOR TERRITORY TO GIVE MACHINE HEAD? DO YOU UNDERSTAND WHAT I AM SAYING TO YOU?
Y--YES, SET--I UNDERSTAND.
GOOD. I'VE CALLED A MEETING. THE HEADS OF ALL THE TERRITORIES WILL BE HERE SOON.
I EXPECT YOU BOTH TO BE ON YOUR BEST BEHAVIOR.

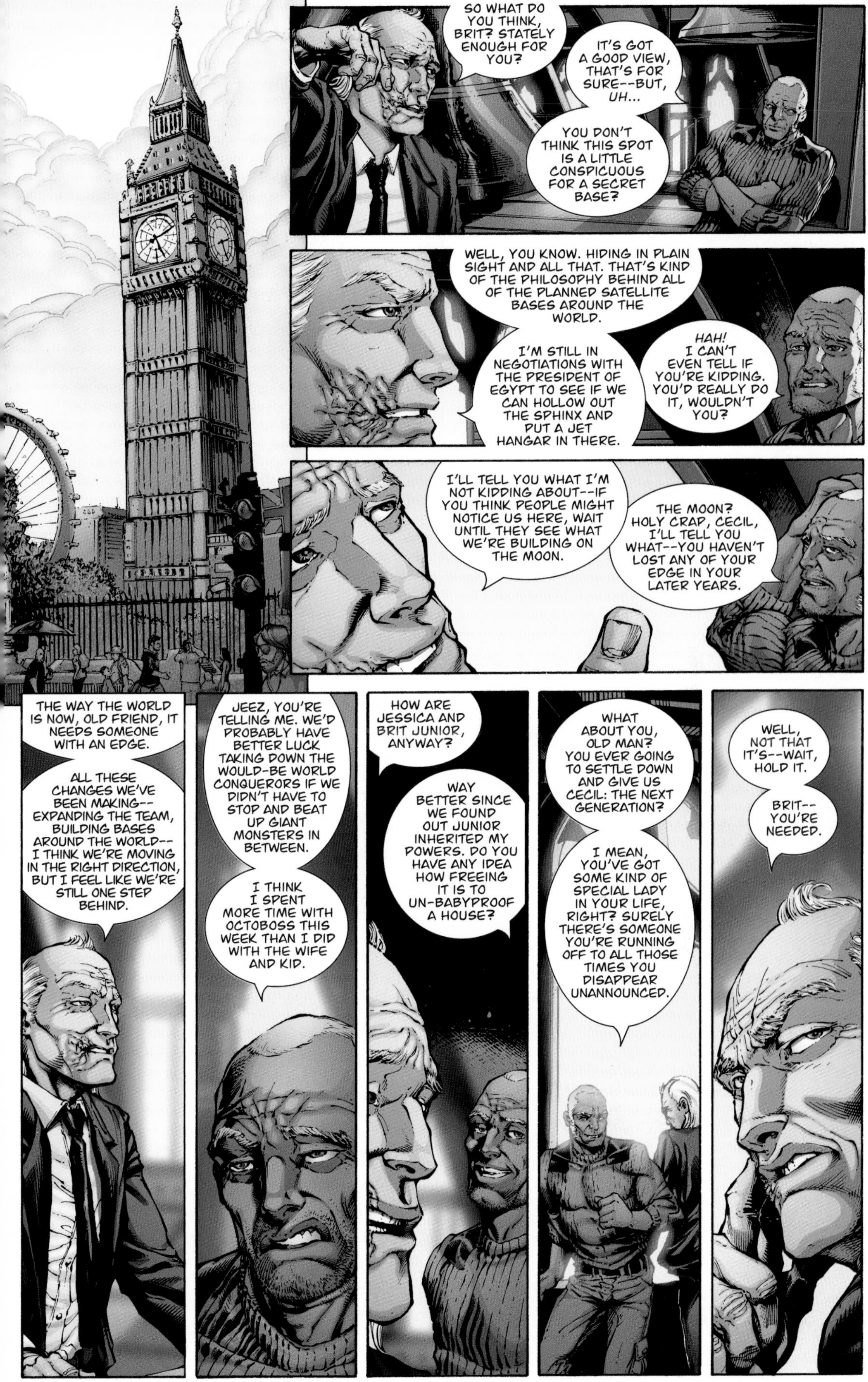
SO WHAT DO YOU THINK, BRIT? STATELY ENOUGH FOR YOU?
IT'S GOT A GOOD VIEW, THAT'S FOR SURE--BUT, UH...
YOU DON'T THINK THIS SPOT IS A LITTLE CONSPICUOUS FOR A SECRET BASE?
WELL, YOU KNOW. HIDING IN PLAIN SIGHT AND ALL THAT. THAT'S KIND OF THE PHILOSOPHY BEHIND ALL OF THE PLANNED SATELLITE BASES AROUND THE WORLD.
I'M STILL IN NEGOTIATIONS WITH THE PRESIDENT OF EGYPT TO SEE IF WE CAN HOLLOW OUT THE SPHINX AND PUT A JET HANGAR IN THERE.
HAH! I CAN'T EVEN TELL IF YOU'RE KIDDING. YOU'D REALLY DO IT, WOULDN'T YOU?
I'LL TELL YOU WHAT I'M NOT KIDDING ABOUT--IF YOU THINK PEOPLE MIGHT NOTICE US HERE, WAIT UNTIL THEY SEE WHAT WE'RE BUILDING ON THE MOON.
THE MOON? HOLY CRAP, CECIL, I'LL TELL YOU WHAT--YOU HAVEN'T LOST ANY OF YOUR EDGE IN YOUR LATER YEARS.
THE WAY THE WORLD IS NOW, OLD FRIEND, IT NEEDS SOMEONE WITH AN EDGE.
ALL THESE CHANGES WE'VE BEEN MAKING-- EXPANDING THE TEAM, BUILDING BASES AROUND THE WORLD-- I THINK WE'RE MOVING IN THE RIGHT DIRECTION, BUT I FEEL LIKE WE'RE STILL ONE STEP BEHIND.
JEEZ, YOU'RE TELLING ME. WE'D PROBABLY HAVE BETTER LUCK TAKING DOWN THE WOULD-BE WORLD CONQUERORS IF WE DIDN'T HAVE TO STOP AND BEAT UP GIANT MONSTERS IN BETWEEN.
I THINK I SPENT MORE TIME WITH OCTOBOSS THIS WEEK THAN I DID WITH THE WIFE AND KID.
HOW ARE JESSICA AND BRIT JUNIOR, ANYWAY?
WAY BETTER SINCE WE FOUND OUT JUNIOR INHERITED MY POWERS. DO YOU HAVE ANY IDEA HOW FREEING IT IS TO UN-BABYPROOF A HOUSE?
WHAT ABOUT YOU, OLD MAN? YOU EVER GOING TO SETTLE DOWN AND GIVE US CECIL: THE NEXT GENERATION?
I MEAN, YOU'VE GOT SOME KIND OF SPECIAL LADY IN YOUR LIFE, RIGHT? SURELY THERE'S SOMEONE YOU'RE RUNNING OFF TO ALL THOSE TIMES YOU DISAPPEAR UNANNOUNCED.
WELL, NOT THAT IT'S--WAIT, HOLD IT.
BRIT-- YOU'RE NEEDED.

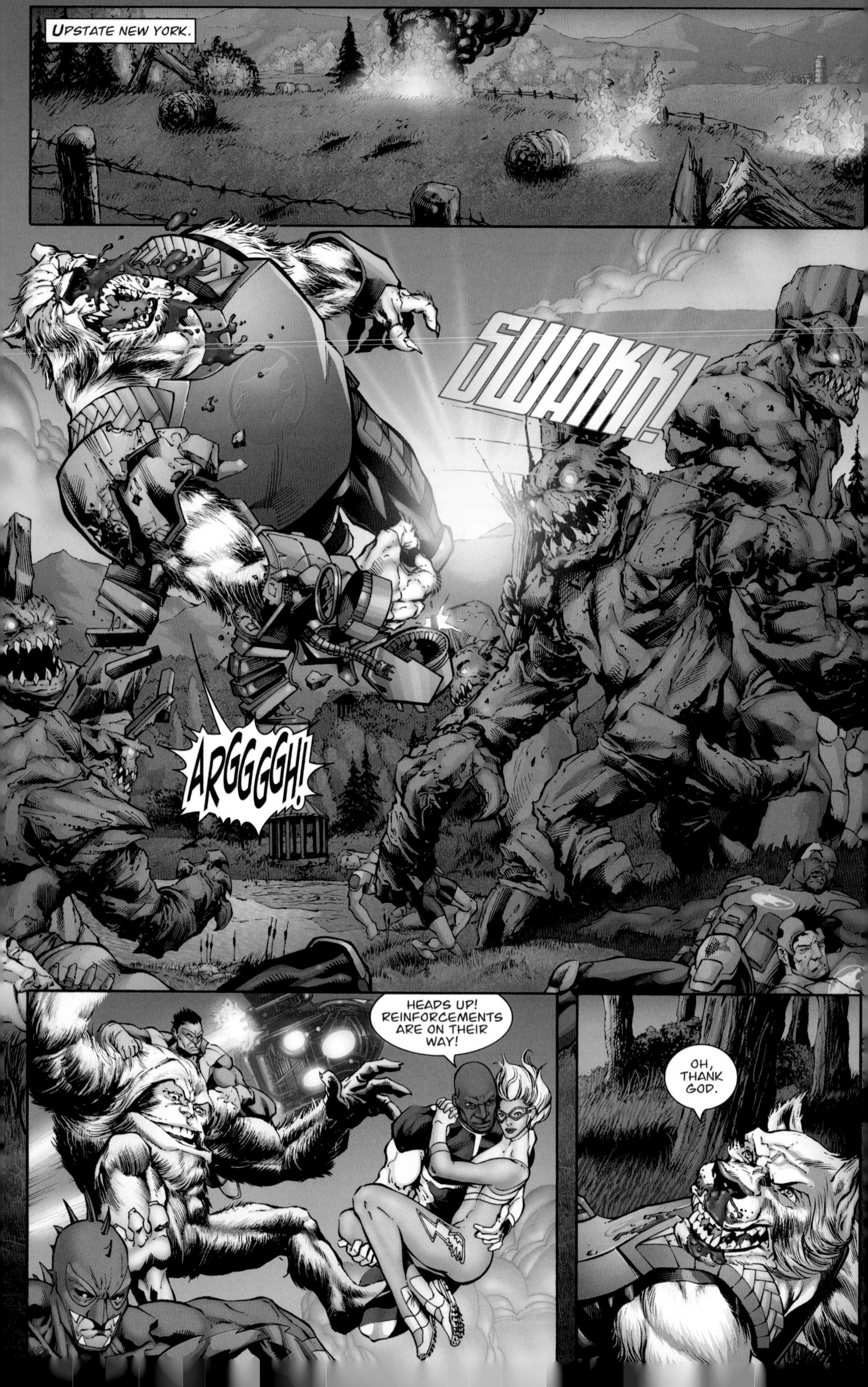
UPSTATE NEW YORK.
SWOKK!
ARGGGGH!
HEADS UP! REINFORCEMENTS ARE ON THEIR WAY!
OH, THANK GOD.

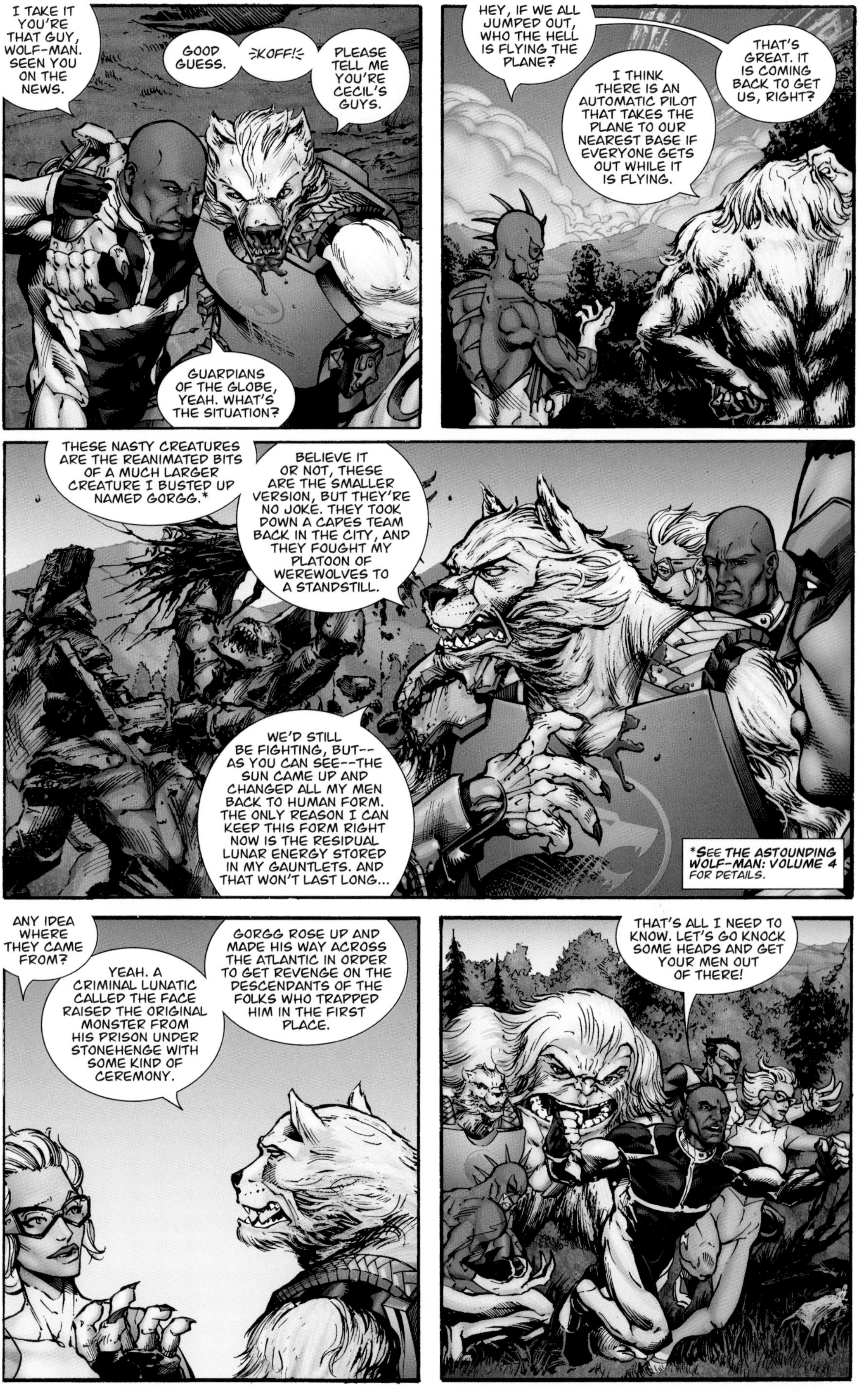
I TAKE IT YOU'RE THAT GUY, WOLF-MAN. SEEN YOU ON THE NEWS.
GOOD GUESS.
KOFF!
PLEASE TELL ME YOU'RE CECIL'S GUYS.
GUARDIANS OF THE GLOBE, YEAH. WHAT'S THE SITUATION?
HEY, IF WE ALL JUMPED OUT, WHO THE HELL IS FLYING THE PLANE?
I THINK THERE IS AN AUTOMATIC PILOT THAT TAKES THE PLANE TO OUR NEAREST BASE IF EVERYONE GETS OUT WHILE IT IS FLYING.
THAT'S GREAT. IT IS COMING BACK TO GET US, RIGHT?
THESE NASTY CREATURES ARE THE REANIMATED BITS OF A MUCH LARGER CREATURE I BUSTED UP NAMED GORGG.*
BELIEVE IT OR NOT, THESE ARE THE SMALLER VERSION, BUT THEY'RE NO JOKE. THEY TOOK DOWN A CAPES TEAM BACK IN THE CITY, AND THEY FOUGHT MY PLATOON OF WEREWOLVES TO A STANDSTILL.
WE'D STILL BE FIGHTING, BUT-- AS YOU CAN SEE--THE SUN CAME UP AND CHANGED ALL MY MEN BACK TO HUMAN FORM. THE ONLY REASON I CAN KEEP THIS FORM RIGHT NOW IS THE RESIDUAL LUNAR ENERGY STORED IN MY GAUNTLETS. AND THAT WON'T LAST LONG...
*SEE THE ASTOUNDING WOLF-MAN: VOLUME 4 FOR DETAILS.
ANY IDEA WHERE THEY CAME FROM?
YEAH. A CRIMINAL LUNATIC CALLED THE FACE RAISED THE ORIGINAL MONSTER FROM HIS PRISON UNDER STONEHENGE WITH SOME KIND OF CEREMONY.
GORGG ROSE UP AND MADE HIS WAY ACROSS THE ATLANTIC IN ORDER TO GET REVENGE ON THE DESCENDANTS OF THE FOLKS WHO TRAPPED HIM IN THE FIRST PLACE.
THAT'S ALL I NEED TO KNOW. LET'S GO KNOCK SOME HEADS AND GET YOUR MEN OUT OF THERE!

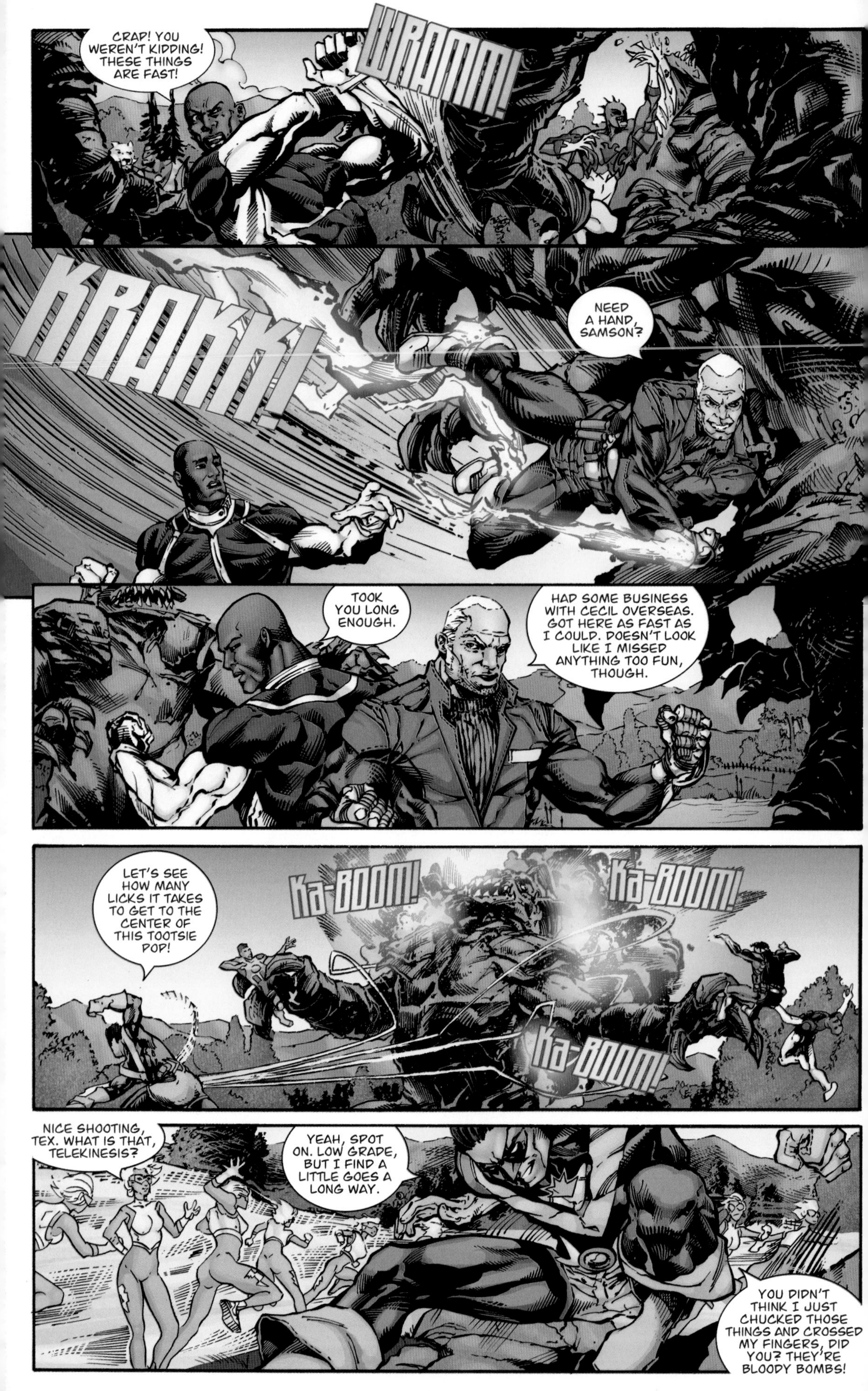
CRAP! YOU WEREN'T KIDDING! THESE THINGS ARE FAST!
WROMM!
KRAKK!
NEED A HAND, SAMSON?
TOOK YOU LONG ENOUGH.
HAD SOME BUSINESS WITH CECIL OVERSEAS. GOT HERE AS FAST AS I COULD. DOESN'T LOOK LIKE I MISSED ANYTHING TOO FUN, THOUGH.
LET'S SEE HOW MANY LICKS IT TAKES TO GET TO THE CENTER OF THIS TOOTSIE POP!
Ka-BOOM!
Ka-BOOM!
Ka-BOOM!
NICE SHOOTING, TEX. WHAT IS THAT, TELEKINESIS?
YEAH, SPOT ON. LOW GRADE, BUT I FIND A LITTLE GOES A LONG WAY.
YOU DIDN'T THINK I JUST CHUCKED THOSE THINGS AND CROSSED MY FINGERS, DID YOU? THEY'RE BLOODY BOMBS!

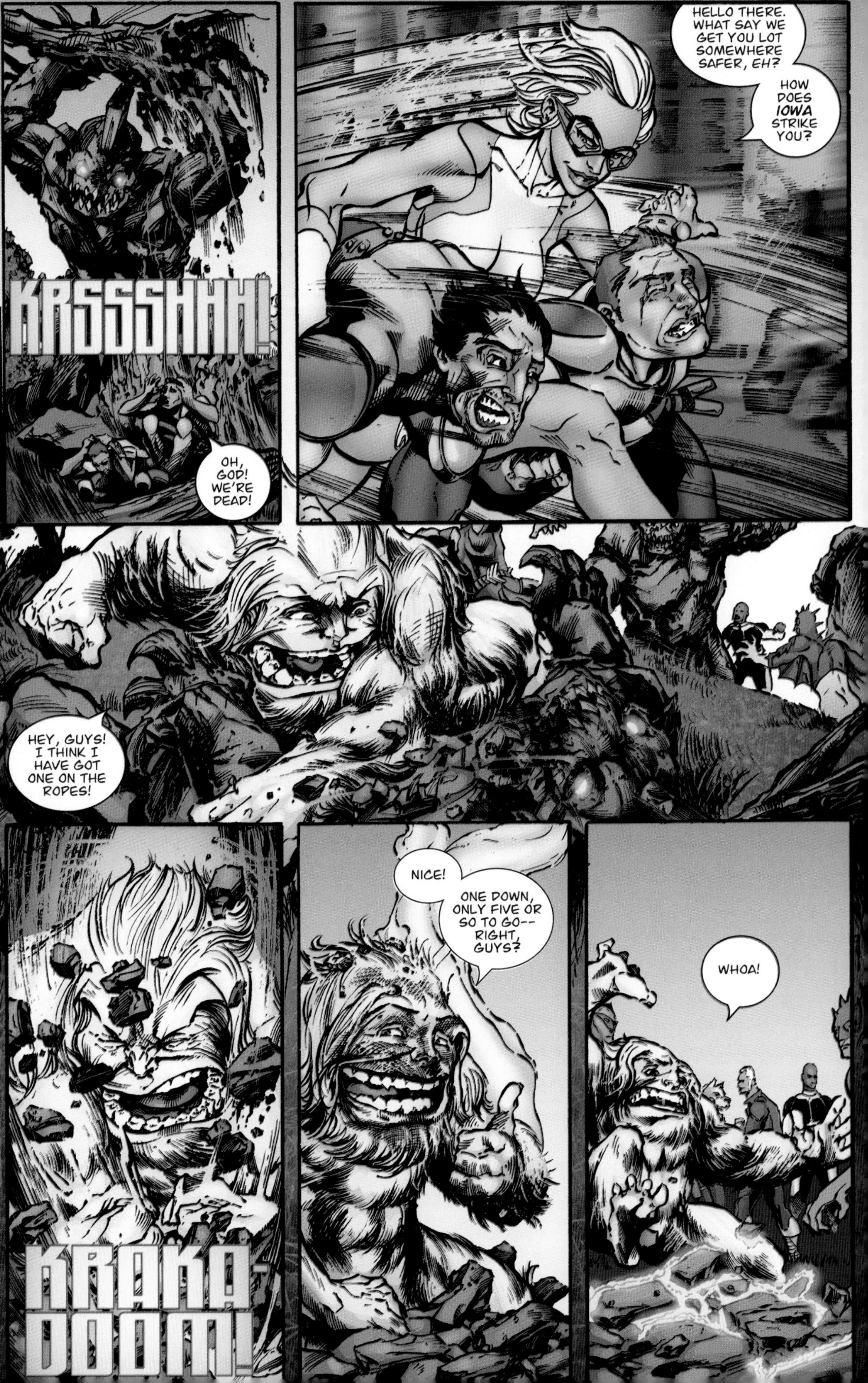
KRSSSHHH!
OH, GOD! WE'RE DEAD!
HELLO THERE. WHAT SAY WE GET YOU LOT SOMEWHERE SAFER, EH?
HOW DOES IOWA STRIKE YOU?
HEY, GUYS! I THINK I HAVE GOT ONE ON THE ROPES!
KRAKA-DOOM!
NICE!
ONE DOWN, ONLY FIVE OR SO TO GO-- RIGHT, GUYS?
WHOA!

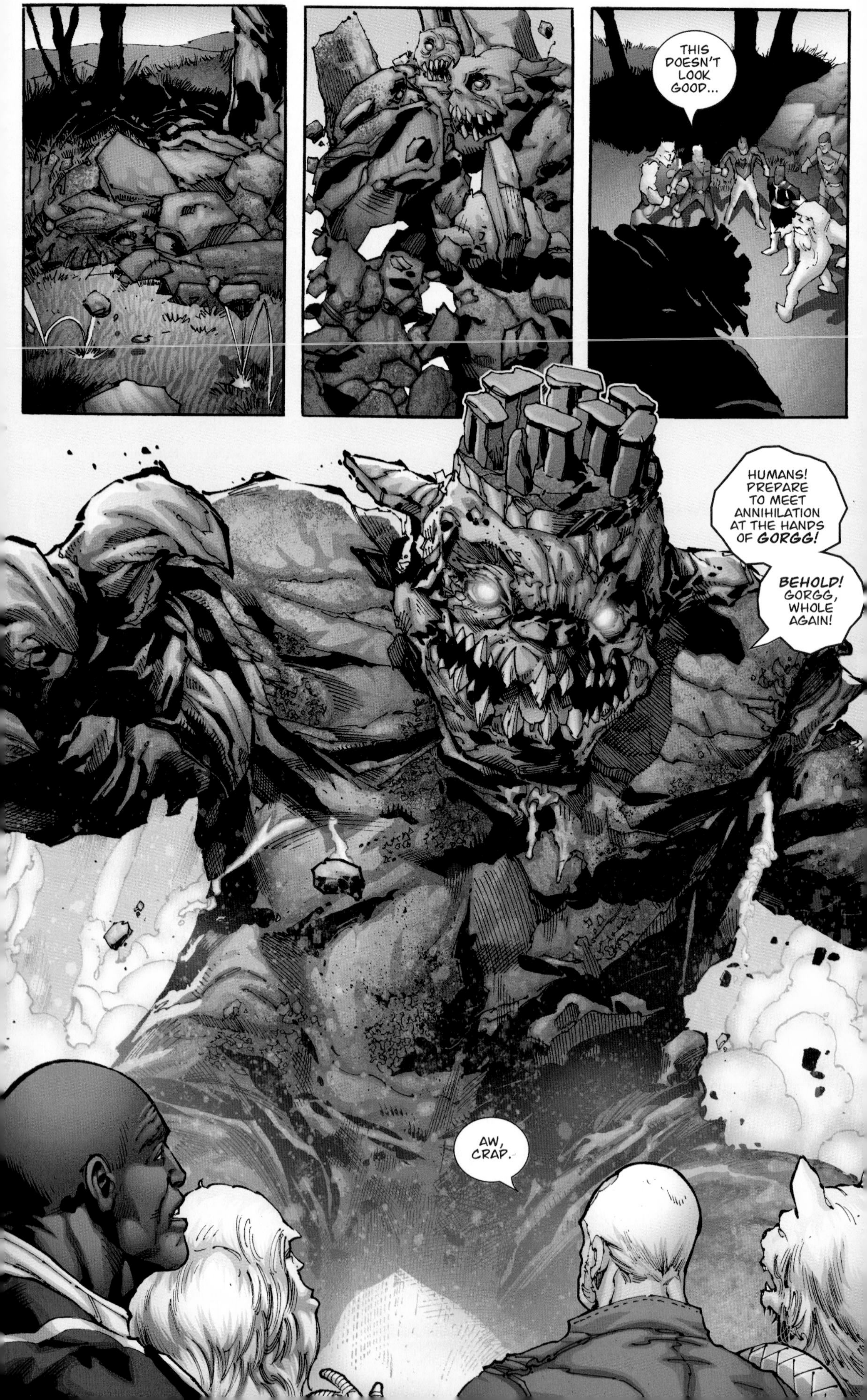
THIS DOESN'T LOOK GOOD...
HUMANS! PREPARE TO MEET ANNIHILATION AT THE HANDS OF **GORGG!**
BEHOLD! GORGG, WHOLE AGAIN!
AW, CRAP.

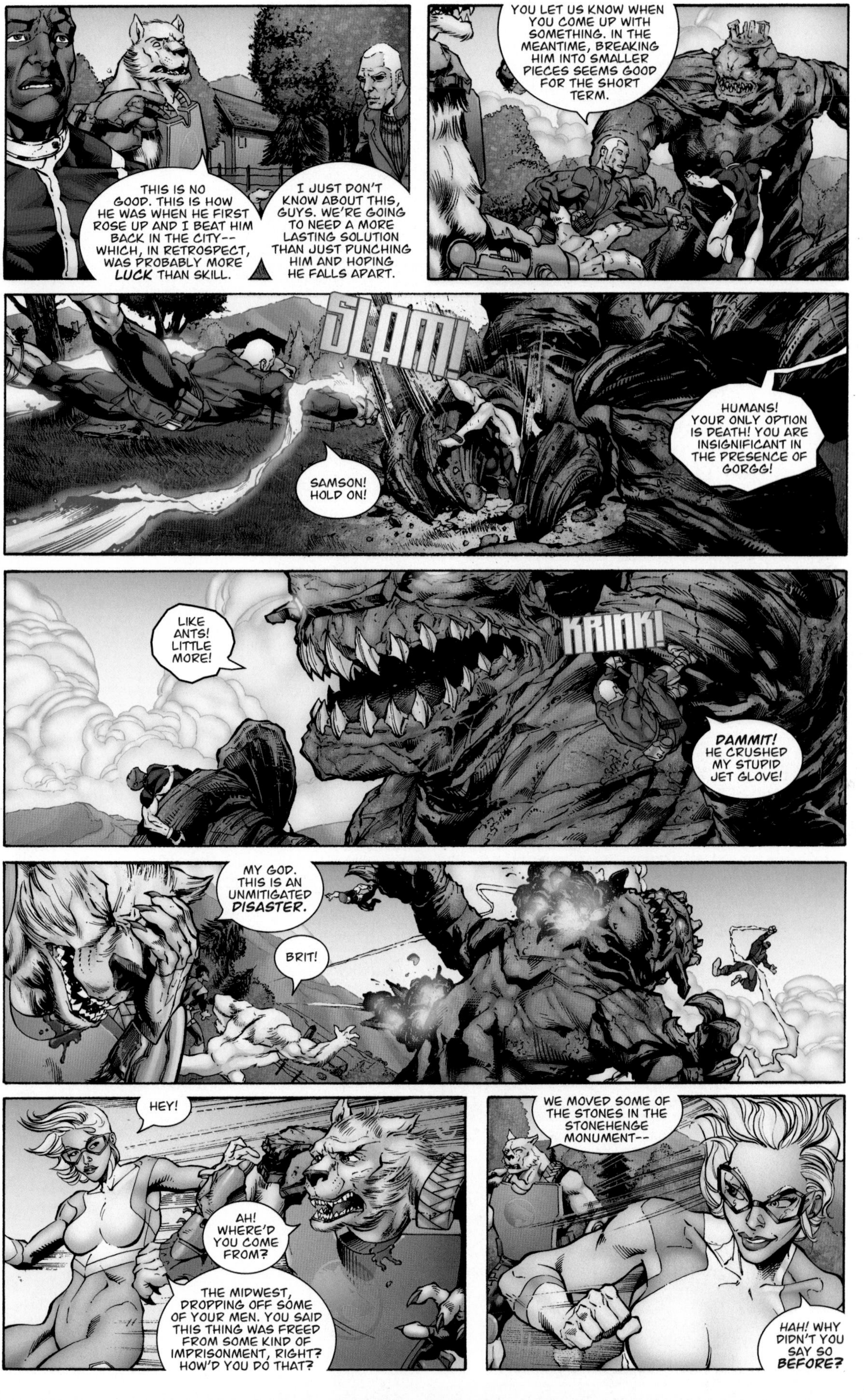
THIS IS NO GOOD. THIS IS HOW HE WAS WHEN HE FIRST ROSE UP AND I BEAT HIM BACK IN THE CITY-- WHICH, IN RETROSPECT, WAS PROBABLY MORE **LUCK** THAN SKILL.
I JUST DON'T KNOW ABOUT THIS, GUYS. WE'RE GOING TO NEED A MORE LASTING SOLUTION THAN JUST PUNCHING HIM AND HOPING HE FALLS APART.
YOU LET US KNOW WHEN YOU COME UP WITH SOMETHING. IN THE MEANTIME, BREAKING HIM INTO SMALLER PIECES SEEMS GOOD FOR THE SHORT TERM.
SLAM!
SAMSON! HOLD ON!
HUMANS! YOUR ONLY OPTION IS DEATH! YOU ARE INSIGNIFICANT IN THE PRESENCE OF GORGG!
LIKE ANTS! LITTLE MORE!
KRINK!
DAMMIT! HE CRUSHED MY STUPID JET GLOVE!
MY GOD. THIS IS AN UNMITIGATED **DISASTER.**
BRIT!
HEY!
AH! WHERE'D YOU COME FROM?
THE MIDWEST, DROPPING OFF SOME OF YOUR MEN. YOU SAID THIS THING WAS FREED FROM SOME KIND OF IMPRISONMENT, RIGHT? HOW'D YOU DO THAT?
WE MOVED SOME OF THE STONES IN THE STONEHENGE MONUMENT--
HAH! WHY DIDN'T YOU SAY SO **BEFORE?**

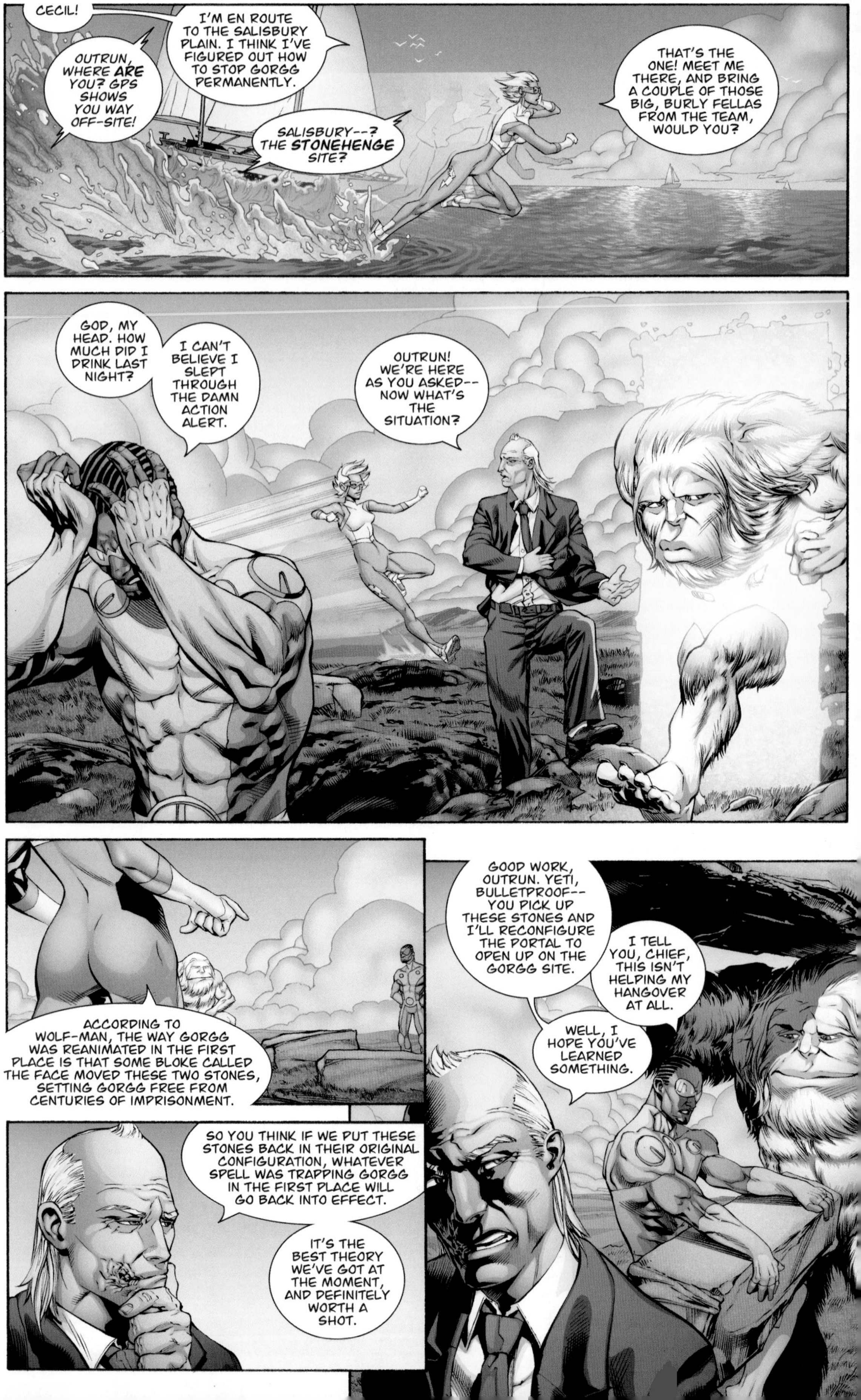
CECIL!
OUTRUN, WHERE ARE YOU? GPS SHOWS YOU WAY OFF-SITE!
I'M EN ROUTE TO THE SALISBURY PLAIN. I THINK I'VE FIGURED OUT HOW TO STOP GORGG PERMANENTLY.
SALISBURY--? THE STONEHENGE SITE?
THAT'S THE ONE! MEET ME THERE, AND BRING A COUPLE OF THOSE BIG, BURLY FELLAS FROM THE TEAM, WOULD YOU?
GOD, MY HEAD. HOW MUCH DID I DRINK LAST NIGHT?
I CAN'T BELIEVE I SLEPT THROUGH THE DAMN ACTION ALERT.
OUTRUN! WE'RE HERE AS YOU ASKED-- NOW WHAT'S THE SITUATION?
ACCORDING TO WOLF-MAN, THE WAY GORGG WAS REANIMATED IN THE FIRST PLACE IS THAT SOME BLOKE CALLED THE FACE MOVED THESE TWO STONES, SETTING GORGG FREE FROM CENTURIES OF IMPRISONMENT.
SO YOU THINK IF WE PUT THESE STONES BACK IN THEIR ORIGINAL CONFIGURATION, WHATEVER SPELL WAS TRAPPING GORGG IN THE FIRST PLACE WILL GO BACK INTO EFFECT.
IT'S THE BEST THEORY WE'VE GOT AT THE MOMENT, AND DEFINITELY WORTH A SHOT.
GOOD WORK, OUTRUN. YETI, BULLETPROOF-- YOU PICK UP THESE STONES AND I'LL RECONFIGURE THE PORTAL TO OPEN UP ON THE GORGG SITE.
I TELL YOU, CHIEF, THIS ISN'T HELPING MY HANGOVER AT ALL.
WELL, I HOPE YOU'VE LEARNED SOMETHING.

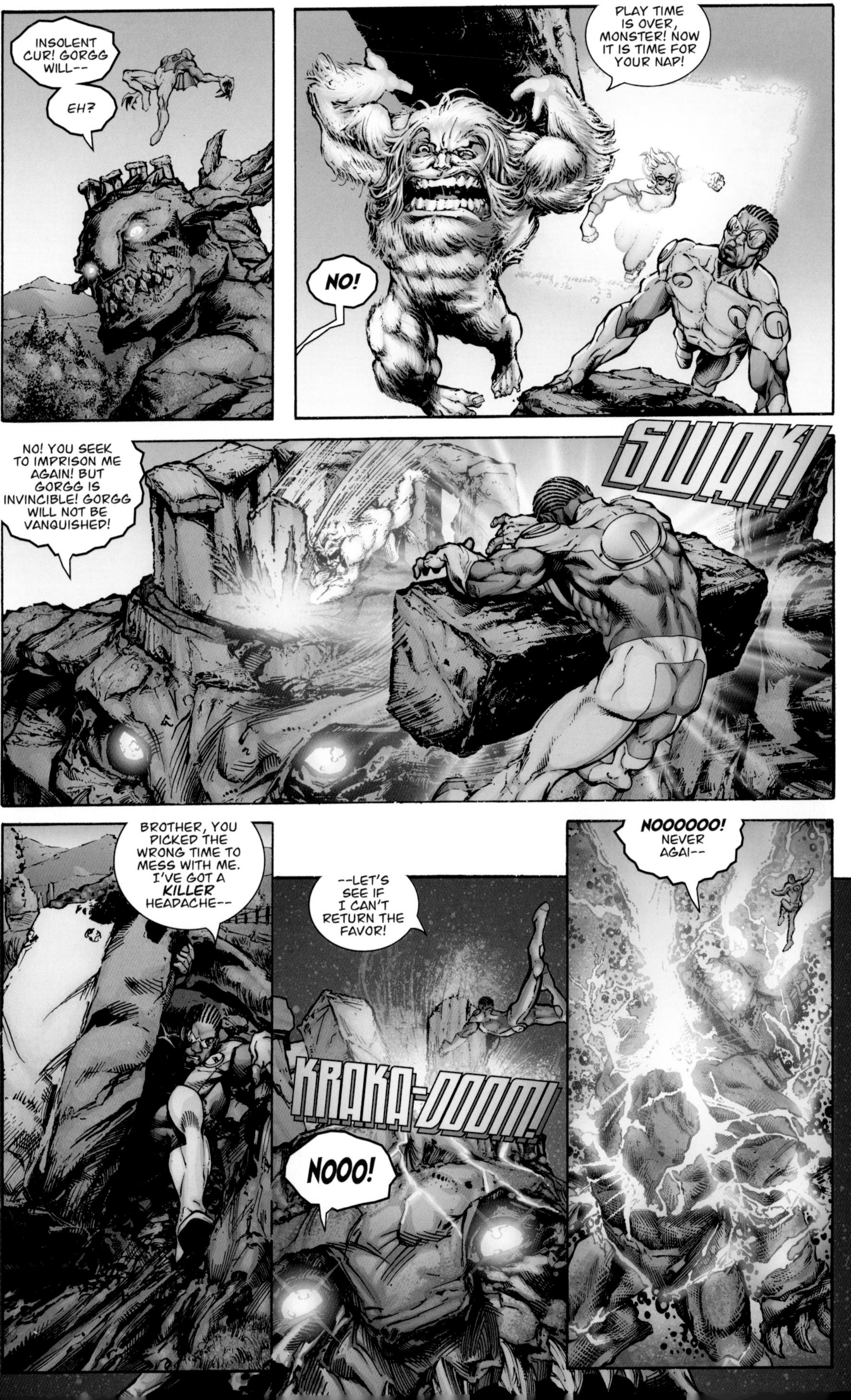

INSOLENT CUR! GORGG WILL--
EH?
PLAY TIME IS OVER, MONSTER! NOW IT IS TIME FOR YOUR NAP!
NO!
NO! YOU SEEK TO IMPRISON ME AGAIN! BUT GORGG IS INVINCIBLE! GORGG WILL NOT BE VANQUISHED!
SWAK!
BROTHER, YOU PICKED THE WRONG TIME TO MESS WITH ME. I'VE GOT A KILLER HEADACHE--
--LET'S SEE IF I CAN'T RETURN THE FAVOR!
KRAKA-DOOM!
NOOO!
NOOOOOO! NEVER AGAI--

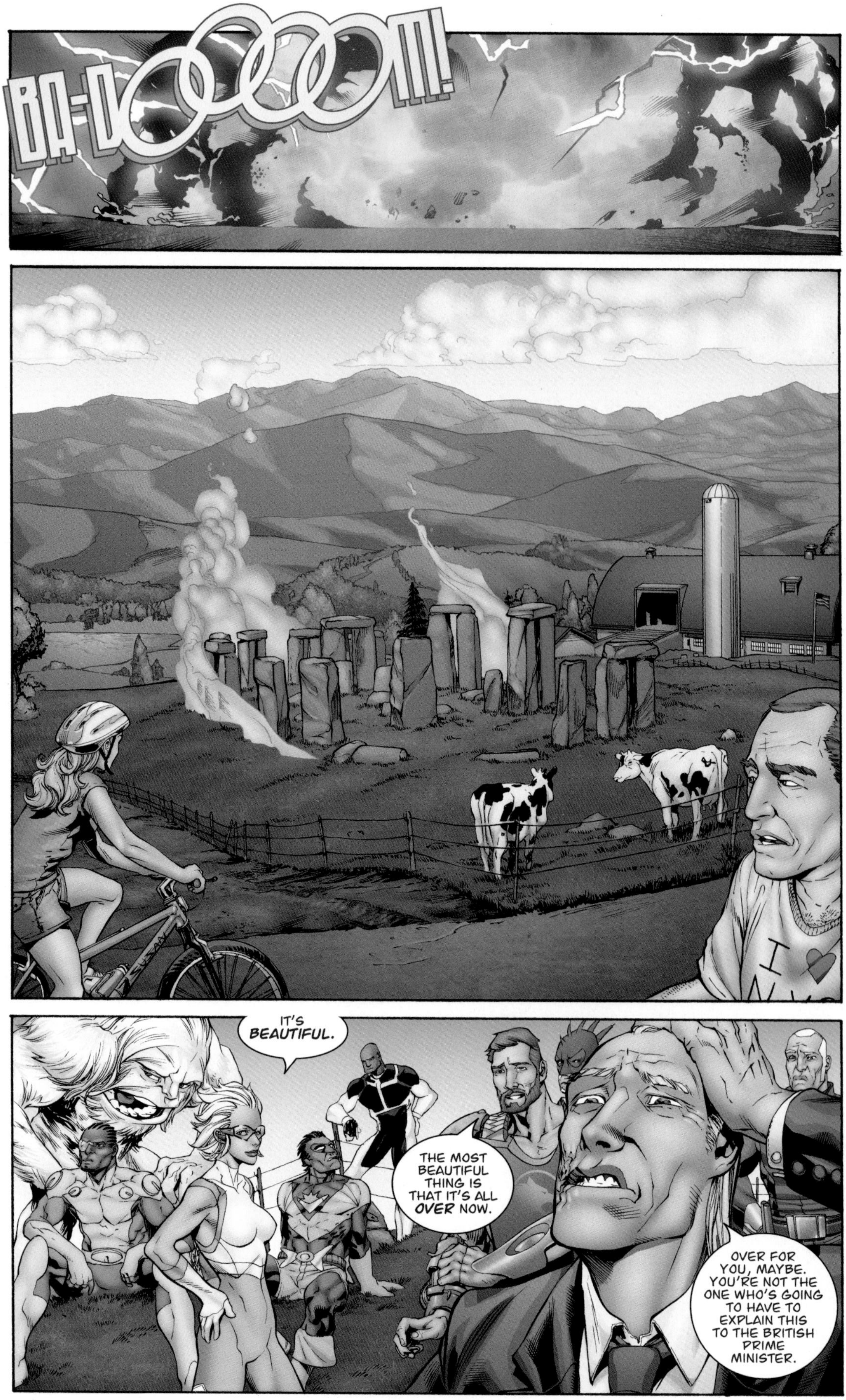
BA-DOOOOM!
IT'S BEAUTIFUL.
THE MOST BEAUTIFUL THING IS THAT IT'S ALL OVER NOW.
OVER FOR YOU, MAYBE. YOU'RE NOT THE ONE WHO'S GOING TO HAVE TO EXPLAIN THIS TO THE BRITISH PRIME MINISTER.

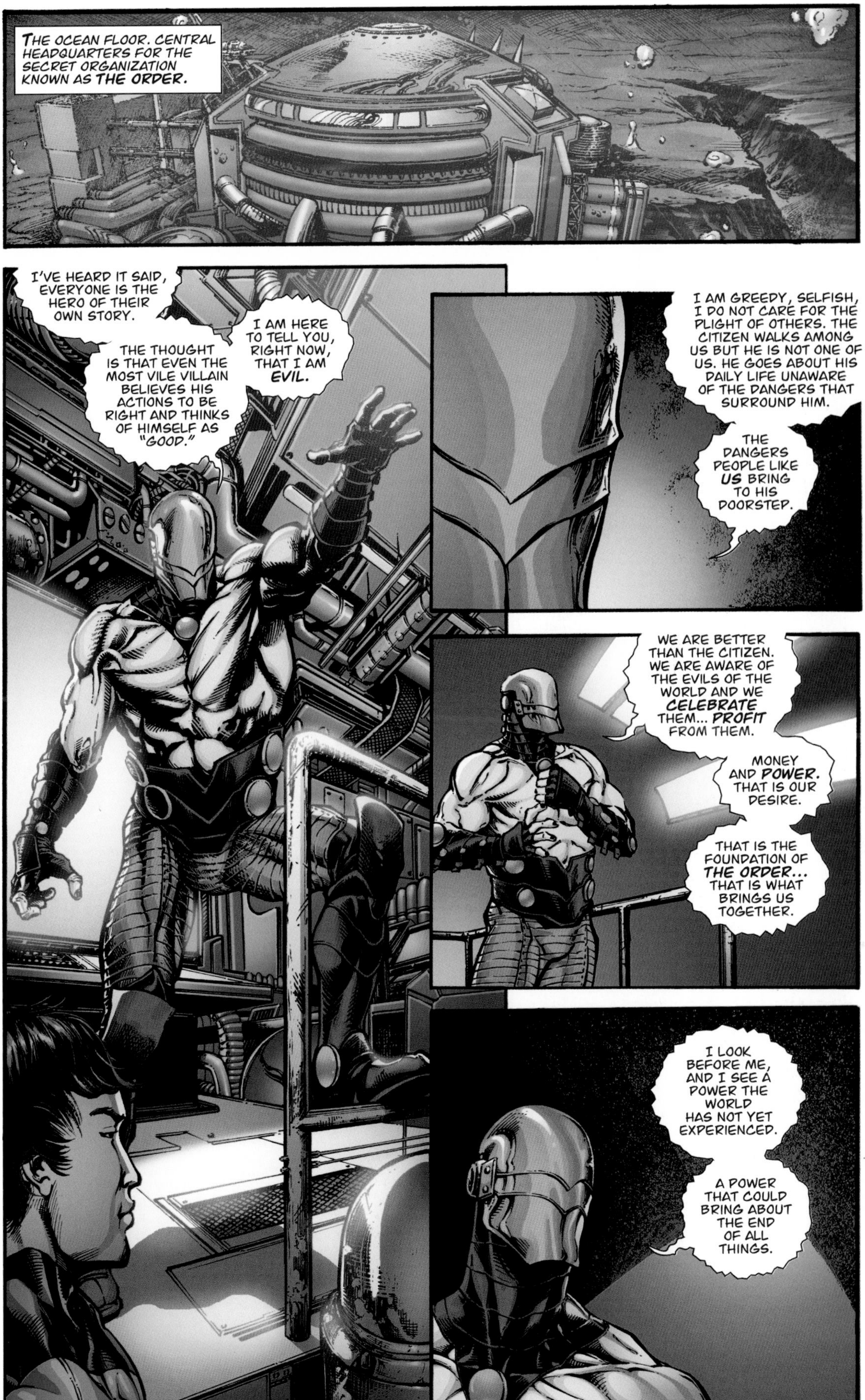

THE OCEAN FLOOR. CENTRAL HEADQUARTERS FOR THE SECRET ORGANIZATION KNOWN AS THE ORDER.
I'VE HEARD IT SAID, EVERYONE IS THE HERO OF THEIR OWN STORY.
THE THOUGHT IS THAT EVEN THE MOST VILE VILLAIN BELIEVES HIS ACTIONS TO BE RIGHT AND THINKS OF HIMSELF AS "GOOD."
I AM HERE TO TELL YOU, RIGHT NOW, THAT I AM EVIL.
I AM GREEDY, SELFISH, I DO NOT CARE FOR THE PLIGHT OF OTHERS. THE CITIZEN WALKS AMONG US BUT HE IS NOT ONE OF US. HE GOES ABOUT HIS DAILY LIFE UNAWARE OF THE DANGERS THAT SURROUND HIM.
THE DANGERS PEOPLE LIKE US BRING TO HIS DOORSTEP.
WE ARE BETTER THAN THE CITIZEN. WE ARE AWARE OF THE EVILS OF THE WORLD AND WE CELEBRATE THEM... PROFIT FROM THEM.
MONEY AND POWER. THAT IS OUR DESIRE.
THAT IS THE FOUNDATION OF THE ORDER... THAT IS WHAT BRINGS US TOGETHER.
I LOOK BEFORE ME, AND I SEE A POWER THE WORLD HAS NOT YET EXPERIENCED.
A POWER THAT COULD BRING ABOUT THE END OF ALL THINGS.

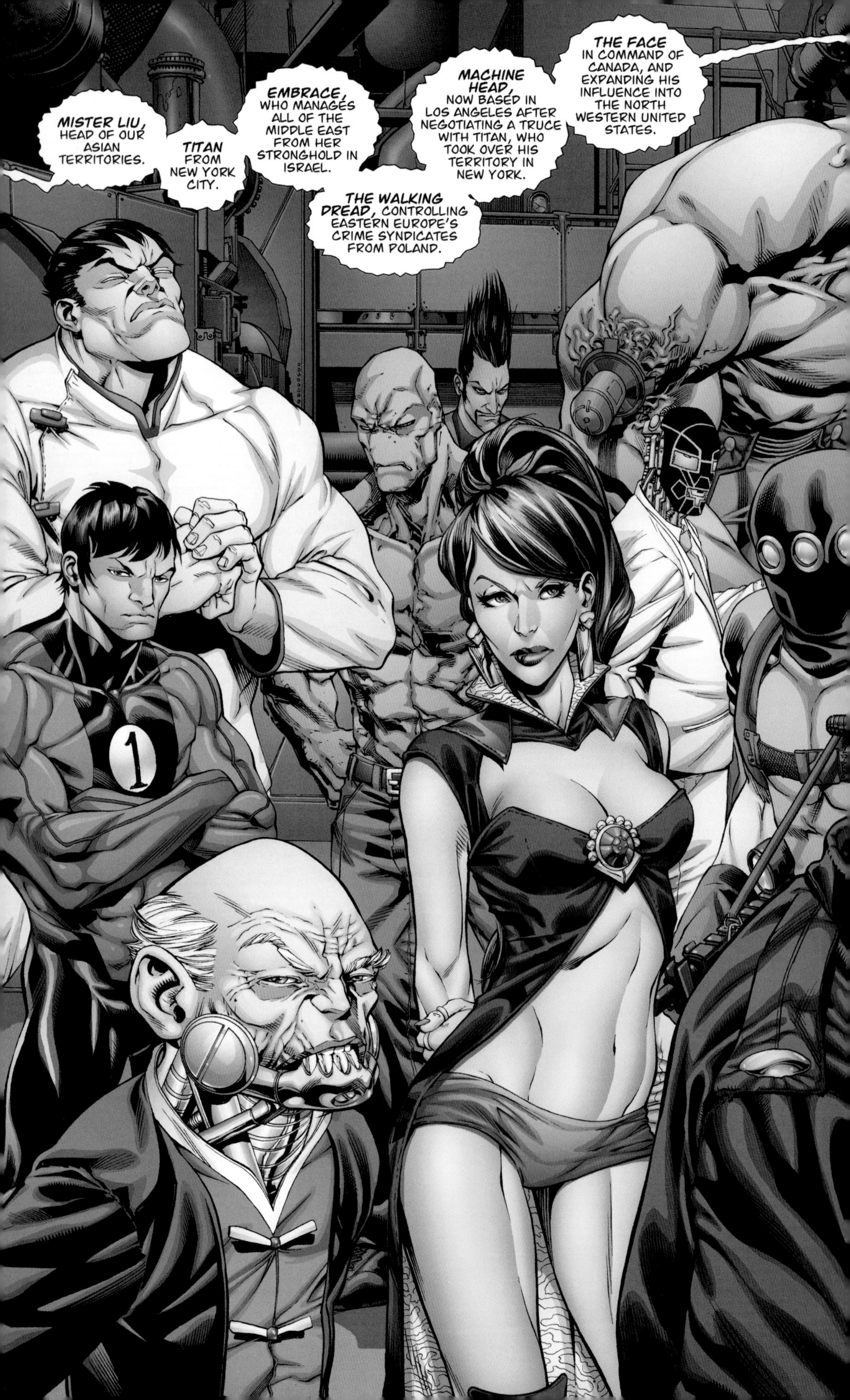
MISTER LIU, HEAD OF OUR ASIAN TERRITORIES.
TITAN FROM NEW YORK CITY.
EMBRACE, WHO MANAGES ALL OF THE MIDDLE EAST FROM HER STRONGHOLD IN ISRAEL.
THE WALKING DREAD, CONTROLLING EASTERN EUROPE'S CRIME SYNDICATES FROM POLAND.
MACHINE HEAD, NOW BASED IN LOS ANGELES AFTER NEGOTIATING A TRUCE WITH TITAN, WHO TOOK OVER HIS TERRITORY IN NEW YORK.
THE FACE IN COMMAND OF CANADA, AND EXPANDING HIS INFLUENCE INTO THE NORTH WESTERN UNITED STATES.
1

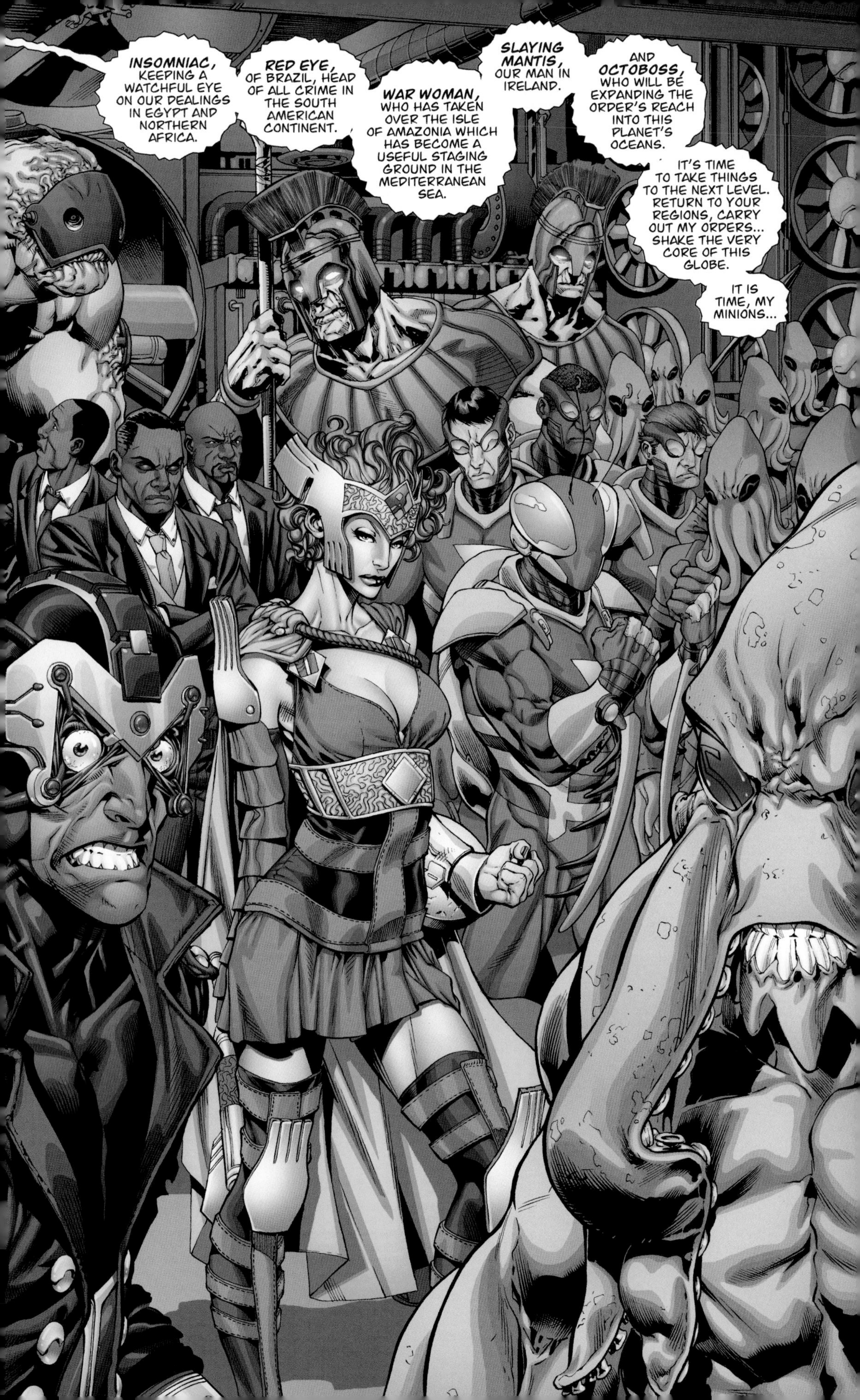
INSOMNIAC, KEEPING A WATCHFUL EYE ON OUR DEALINGS IN EGYPT AND NORTHERN AFRICA.
RED EYE, OF BRAZIL, HEAD OF ALL CRIME IN THE SOUTH AMERICAN CONTINENT.
WAR WOMAN, WHO HAS TAKEN OVER THE ISLE OF AMAZONIA WHICH HAS BECOME A USEFUL STAGING GROUND IN THE MEDITERRANEAN SEA.
SLAYING MANTIS, OUR MAN IN IRELAND.
AND OCTOBOSS, WHO WILL BE EXPANDING THE ORDER'S REACH INTO THIS PLANET'S OCEANS.
IT'S TIME TO TAKE THINGS TO THE NEXT LEVEL. RETURN TO YOUR REGIONS, CARRY OUT MY ORDERS... SHAKE THE VERY CORE OF THIS GLOBE.
IT IS TIME, MY MINIONS...

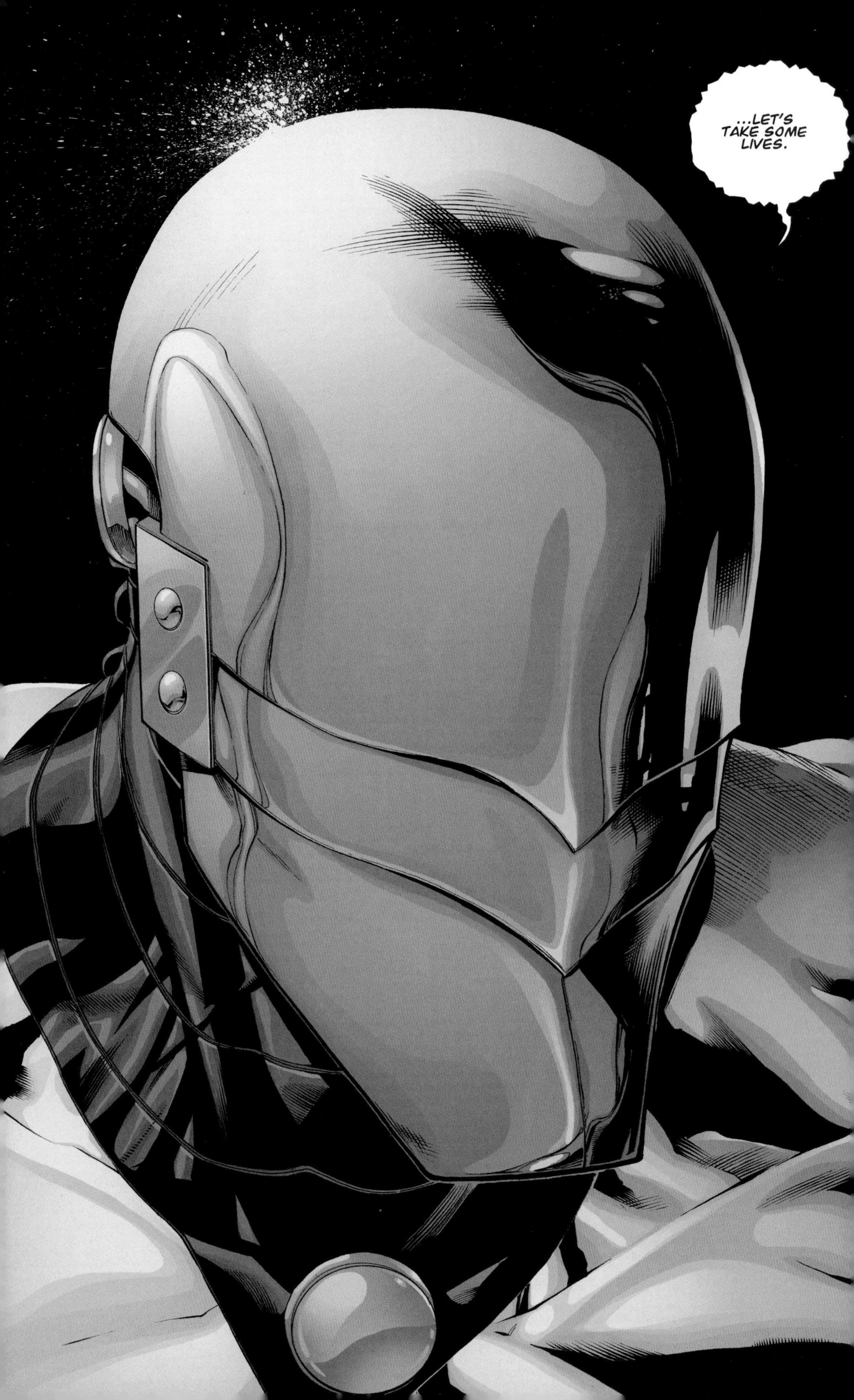
...LET'S TAKE SOME LIVES.

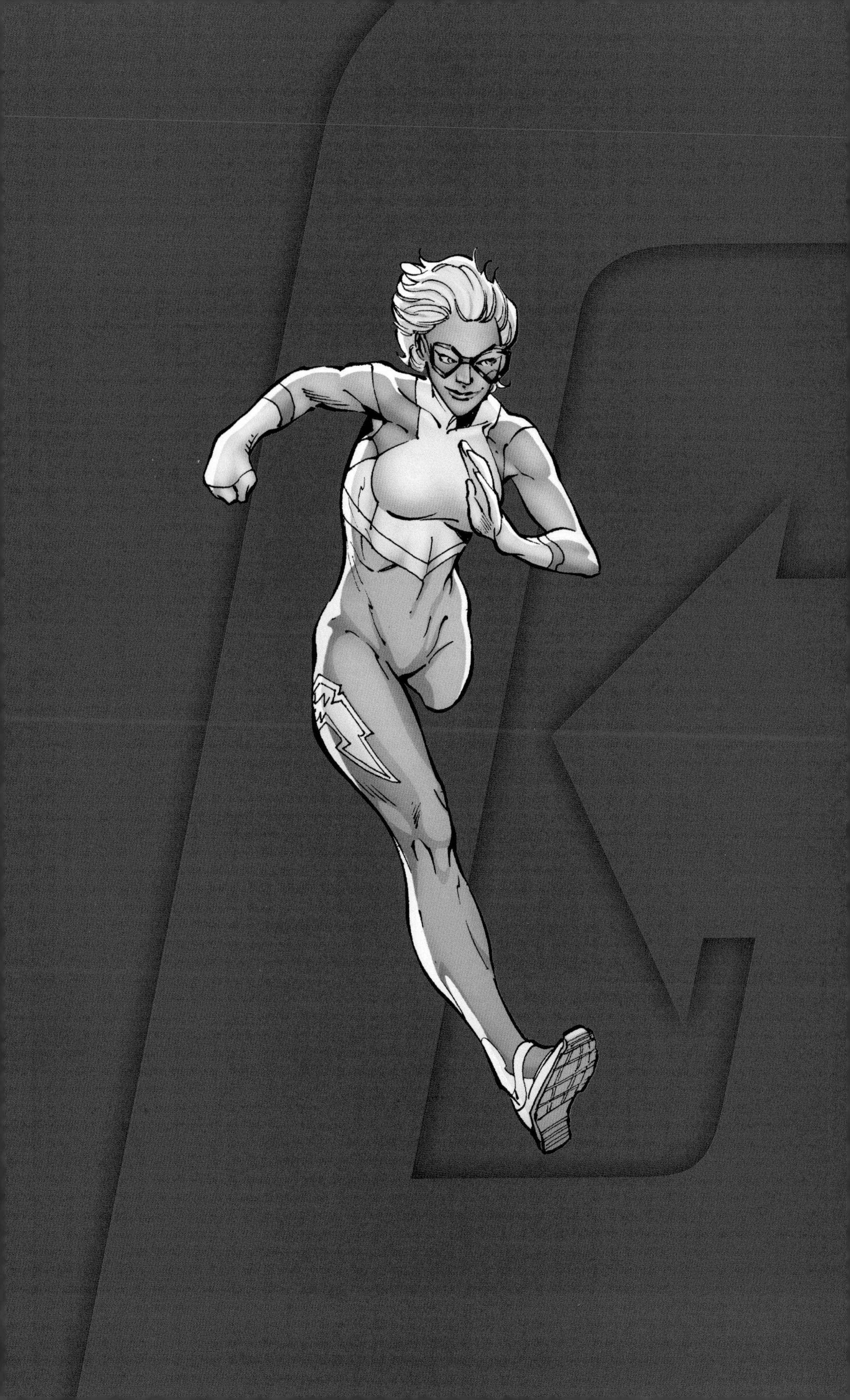

CHAPTER FOUR

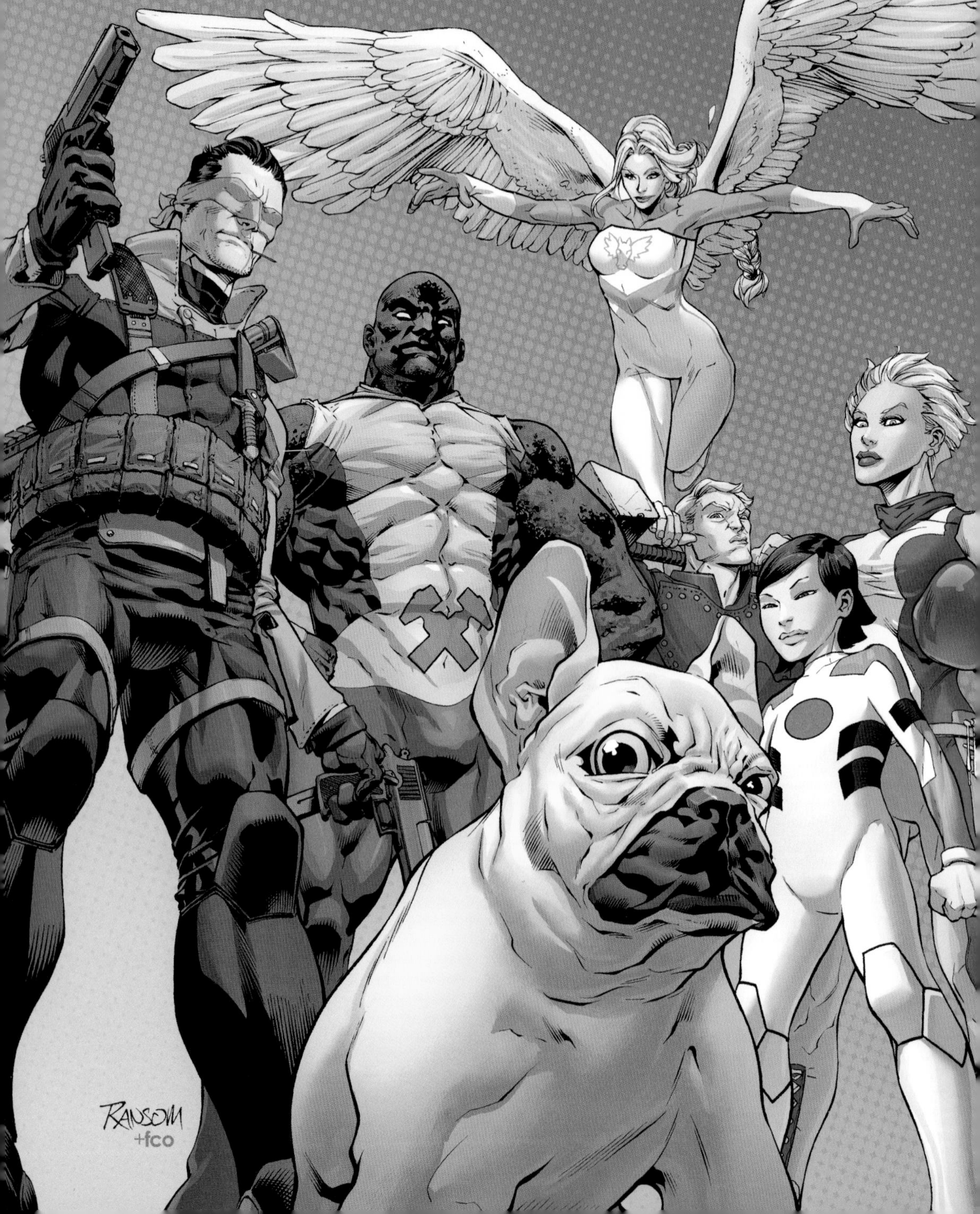
RANSOM
+fco

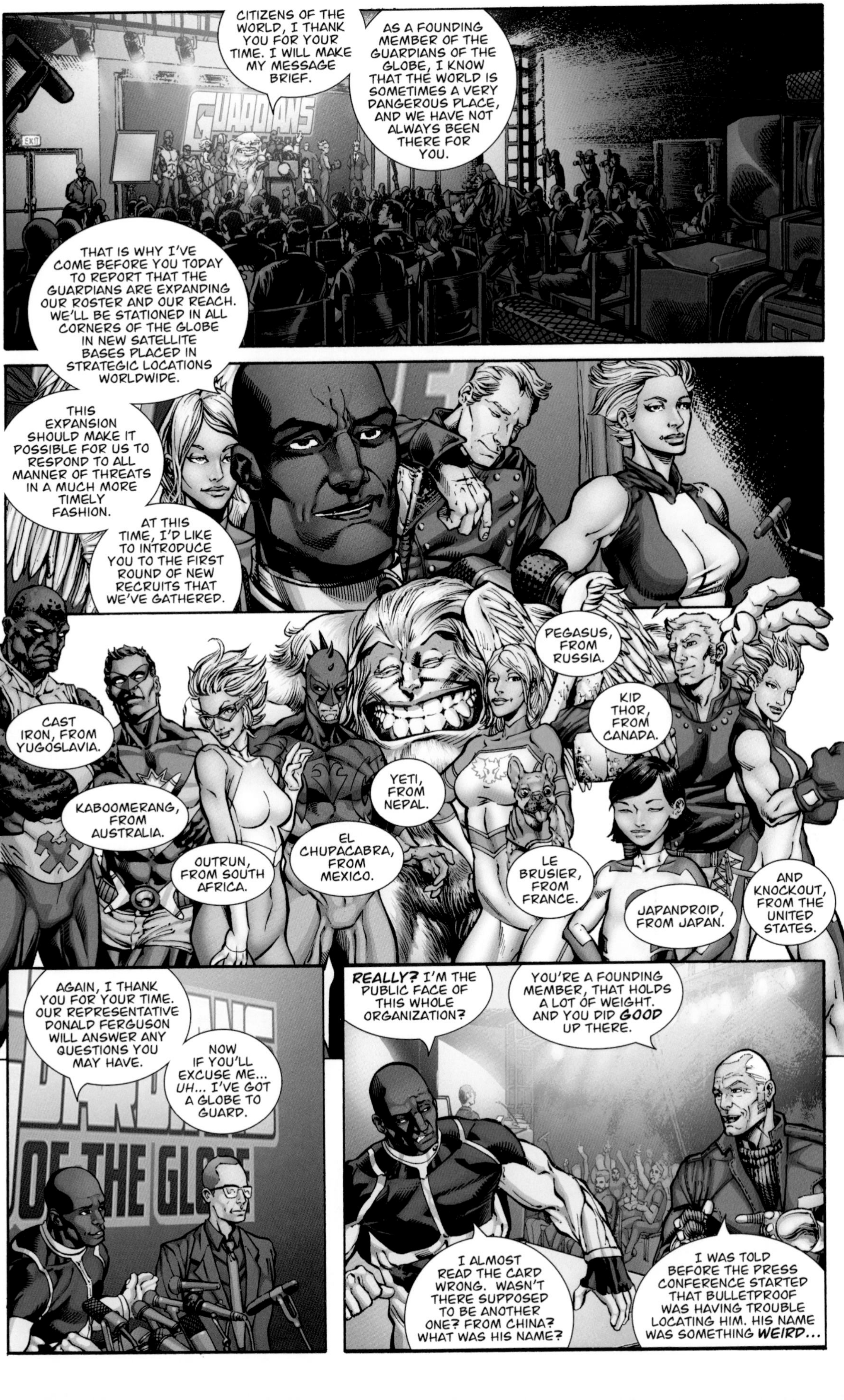
CITIZENS OF THE WORLD, I THANK YOU FOR YOUR TIME. I WILL MAKE MY MESSAGE BRIEF.
AS A FOUNDING MEMBER OF THE GUARDIANS OF THE GLOBE, I KNOW THAT THE WORLD IS SOMETIMES A VERY DANGEROUS PLACE, AND WE HAVE NOT ALWAYS BEEN THERE FOR YOU.
GUARDIANS
EXIT
THAT IS WHY I'VE COME BEFORE YOU TODAY TO REPORT THAT THE GUARDIANS ARE EXPANDING OUR ROSTER AND OUR REACH. WE'LL BE STATIONED IN ALL CORNERS OF THE GLOBE IN NEW SATELLITE BASES PLACED IN STRATEGIC LOCATIONS WORLDWIDE.
THIS EXPANSION SHOULD MAKE IT POSSIBLE FOR US TO RESPOND TO ALL MANNER OF THREATS IN A MUCH MORE TIMELY FASHION.
AT THIS TIME, I'D LIKE TO INTRODUCE YOU TO THE FIRST ROUND OF NEW RECRUITS THAT WE'VE GATHERED.
CAST IRON, FROM YUGOSLAVIA.
KABOOMERANG, FROM AUSTRALIA.
OUTRUN, FROM SOUTH AFRICA.
EL CHUPACABRA, FROM MEXICO.
YETI, FROM NEPAL.
PEGASUS, FROM RUSSIA.
LE BRUSIER, FROM FRANCE.
KID THOR, FROM CANADA.
JAPANDROID, FROM JAPAN.
AND KNOCKOUT, FROM THE UNITED STATES.
AGAIN, I THANK YOU FOR YOUR TIME. OUR REPRESENTATIVE DONALD FERGUSON WILL ANSWER ANY QUESTIONS YOU MAY HAVE.
NOW IF YOU'LL EXCUSE ME... UH... I'VE GOT A GLOBE TO GUARD.
OF THE GLOBE
REALLY? I'M THE PUBLIC FACE OF THIS WHOLE ORGANIZATION?
YOU'RE A FOUNDING MEMBER, THAT HOLDS A LOT OF WEIGHT. AND YOU DID **GOOD** UP THERE.
I ALMOST READ THE CARD WRONG. WASN'T THERE SUPPOSED TO BE ANOTHER ONE? FROM CHINA? WHAT WAS HIS NAME?
I WAS TOLD BEFORE THE PRESS CONFERENCE STARTED THAT BULLETPROOF WAS HAVING TROUBLE LOCATING HIM. HIS NAME WAS SOMETHING **WEIRD...**

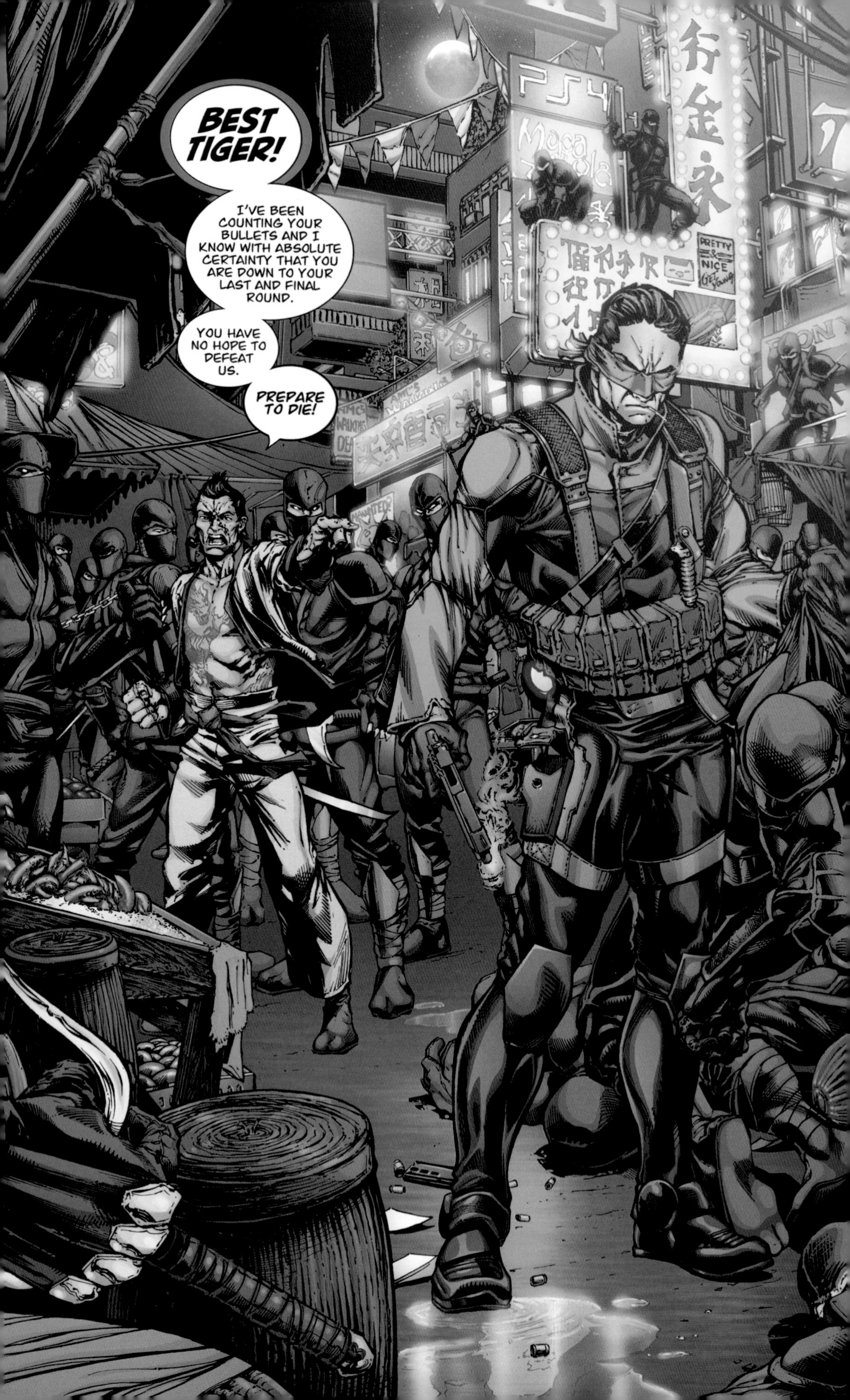
BEST TIGER!
I'VE BEEN COUNTING YOUR BULLETS AND I KNOW WITH ABSOLUTE CERTAINTY THAT YOU ARE DOWN TO YOUR LAST AND FINAL ROUND.
YOU HAVE NO HOPE TO DEFEAT US.
PREPARE TO DIE!

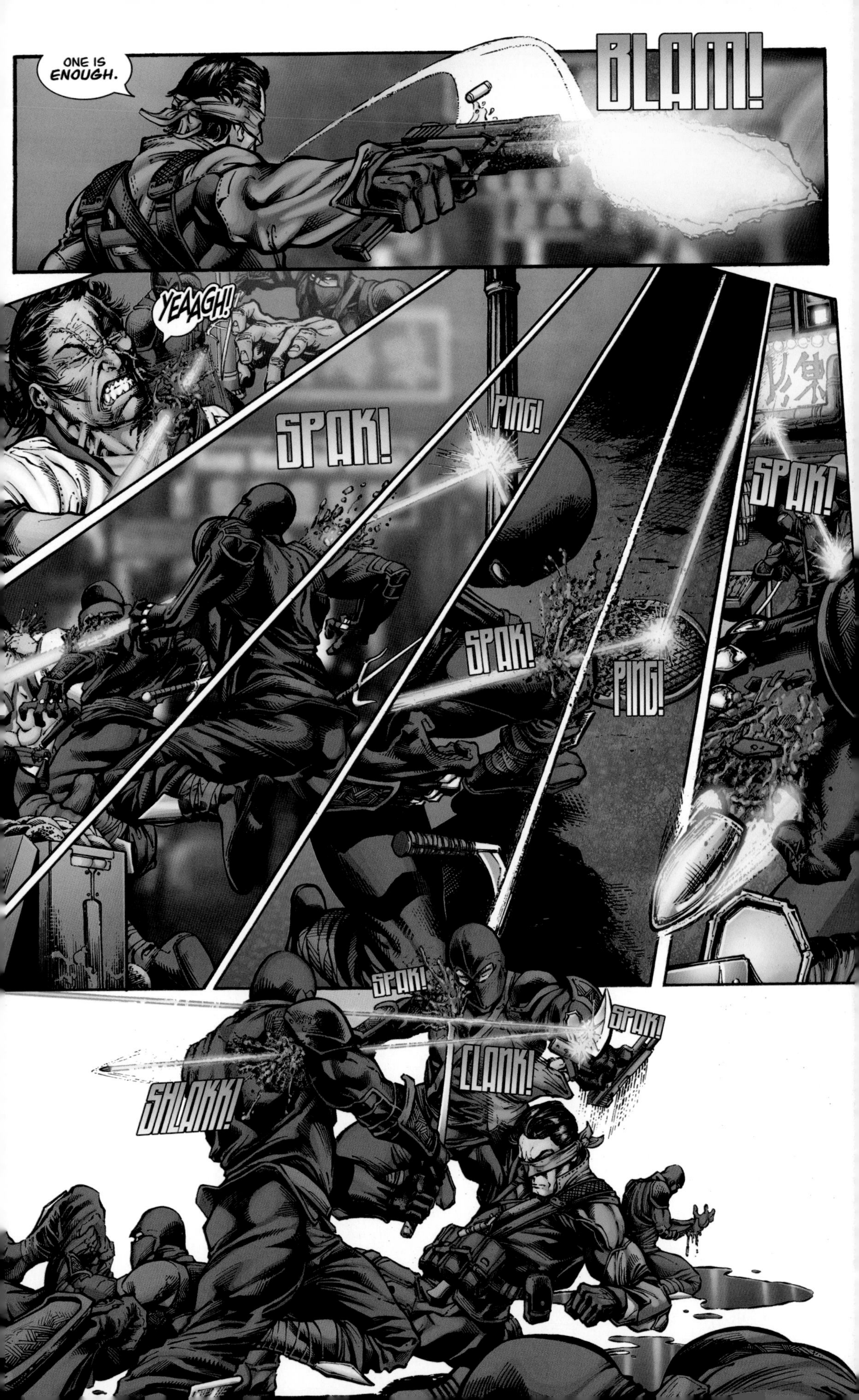
ONE IS ENOUGH.
BLAM!
YEAAGH!
SPAK!
PING!
SPAK!
SPAK!
PING!
SPAK!
SPAK!
CLANK!
SHLAKK!

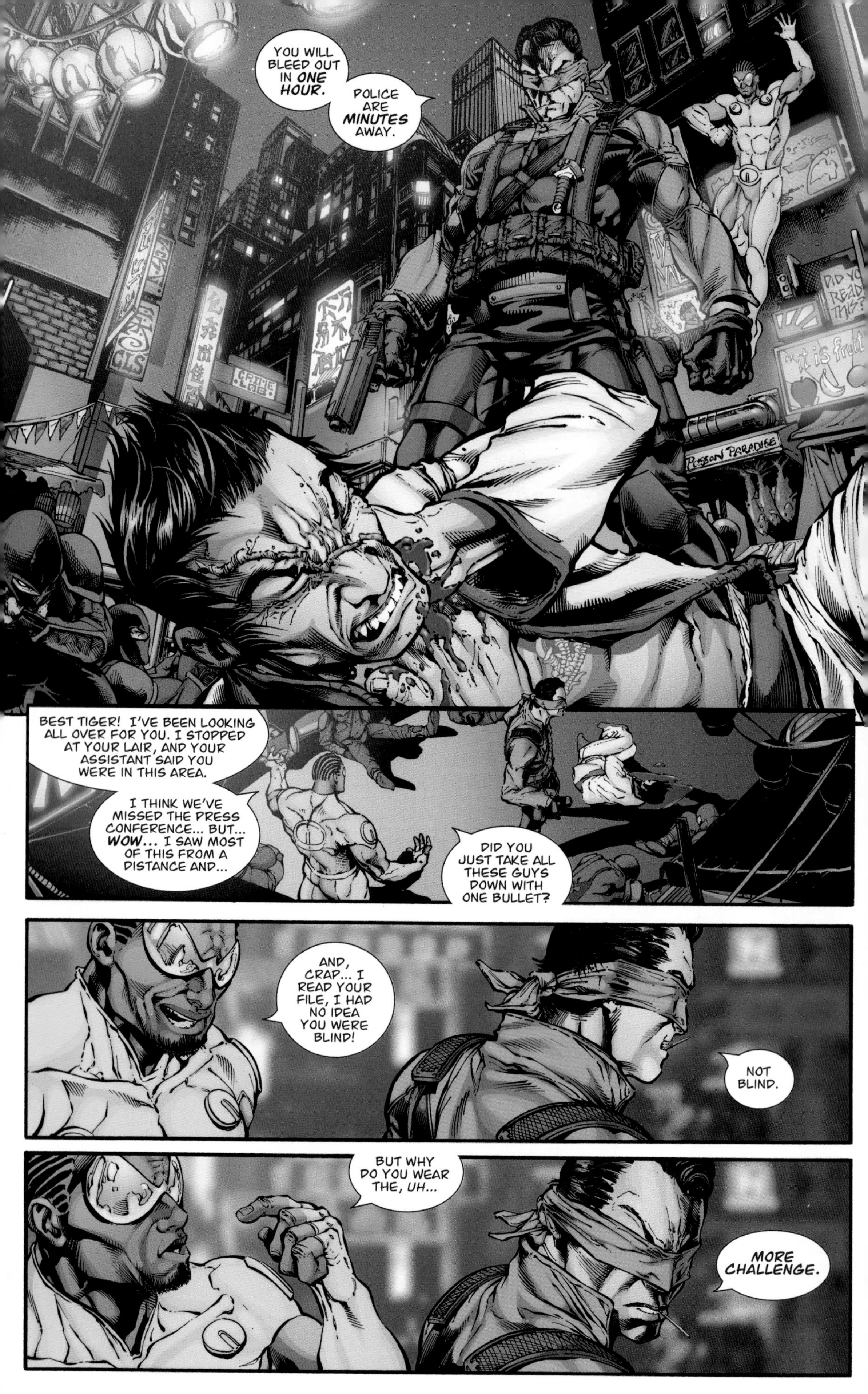
YOU WILL BLEED OUT IN ONE HOUR.
POLICE ARE MINUTES AWAY.
BEST TIGER! I'VE BEEN LOOKING ALL OVER FOR YOU. I STOPPED AT YOUR LAIR, AND YOUR ASSISTANT SAID YOU WERE IN THIS AREA.
I THINK WE'VE MISSED THE PRESS CONFERENCE... BUT... WOW... I SAW MOST OF THIS FROM A DISTANCE AND...
DID YOU JUST TAKE ALL THESE GUYS DOWN WITH ONE BULLET?
AND, CRAP... I READ YOUR FILE, I HAD NO IDEA YOU WERE BLIND!
NOT BLIND.
BUT WHY DO YOU WEAR THE, UH...
MORE CHALLENGE.

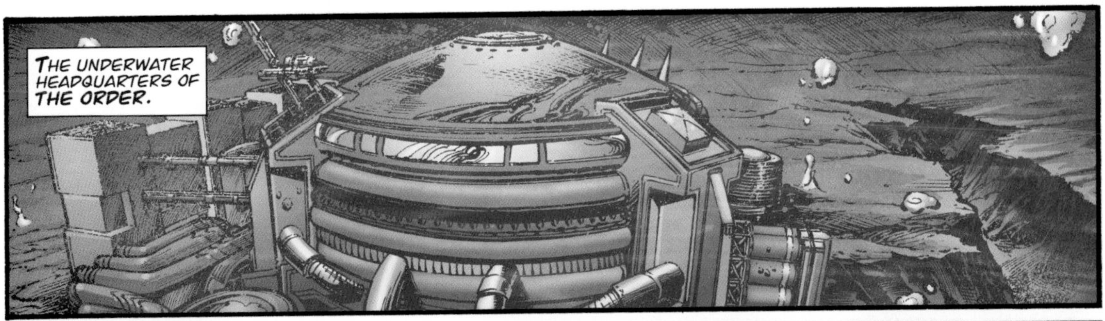
THE UNDERWATER HEADQUARTERS OF THE ORDER.

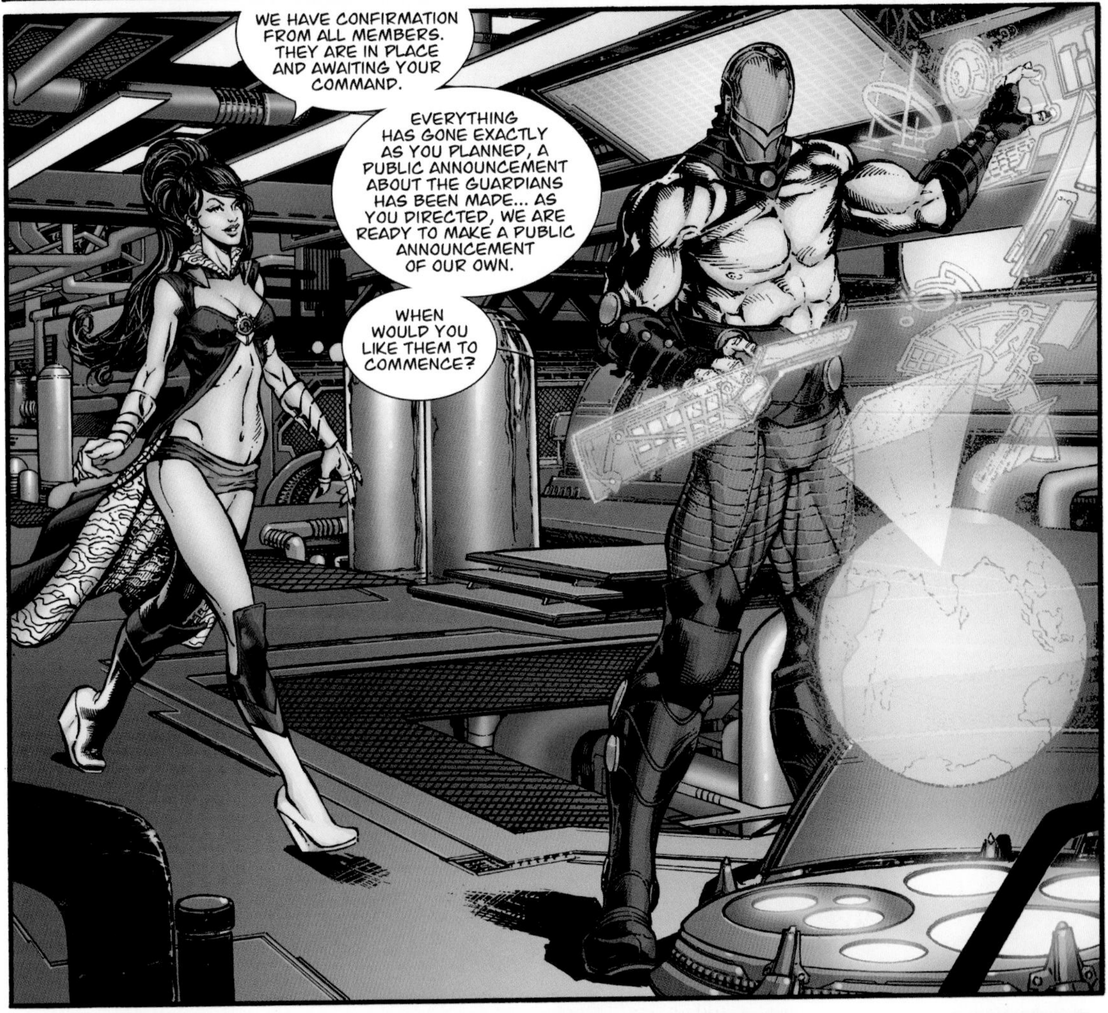
WE HAVE CONFIRMATION FROM ALL MEMBERS. THEY ARE IN PLACE AND AWAITING YOUR COMMAND.
EVERYTHING HAS GONE EXACTLY AS YOU PLANNED, A PUBLIC ANNOUNCEMENT ABOUT THE GUARDIANS HAS BEEN MADE... AS YOU DIRECTED, WE ARE READY TO MAKE A PUBLIC ANNOUNCEMENT OF OUR OWN.
WHEN WOULD YOU LIKE THEM TO COMMENCE?

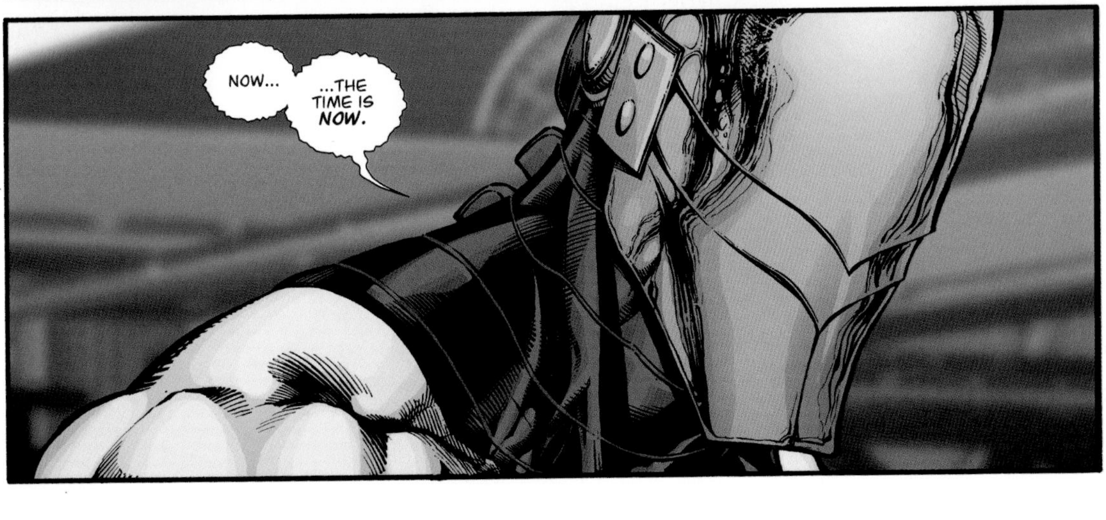
NOW...
...THE TIME IS NOW.

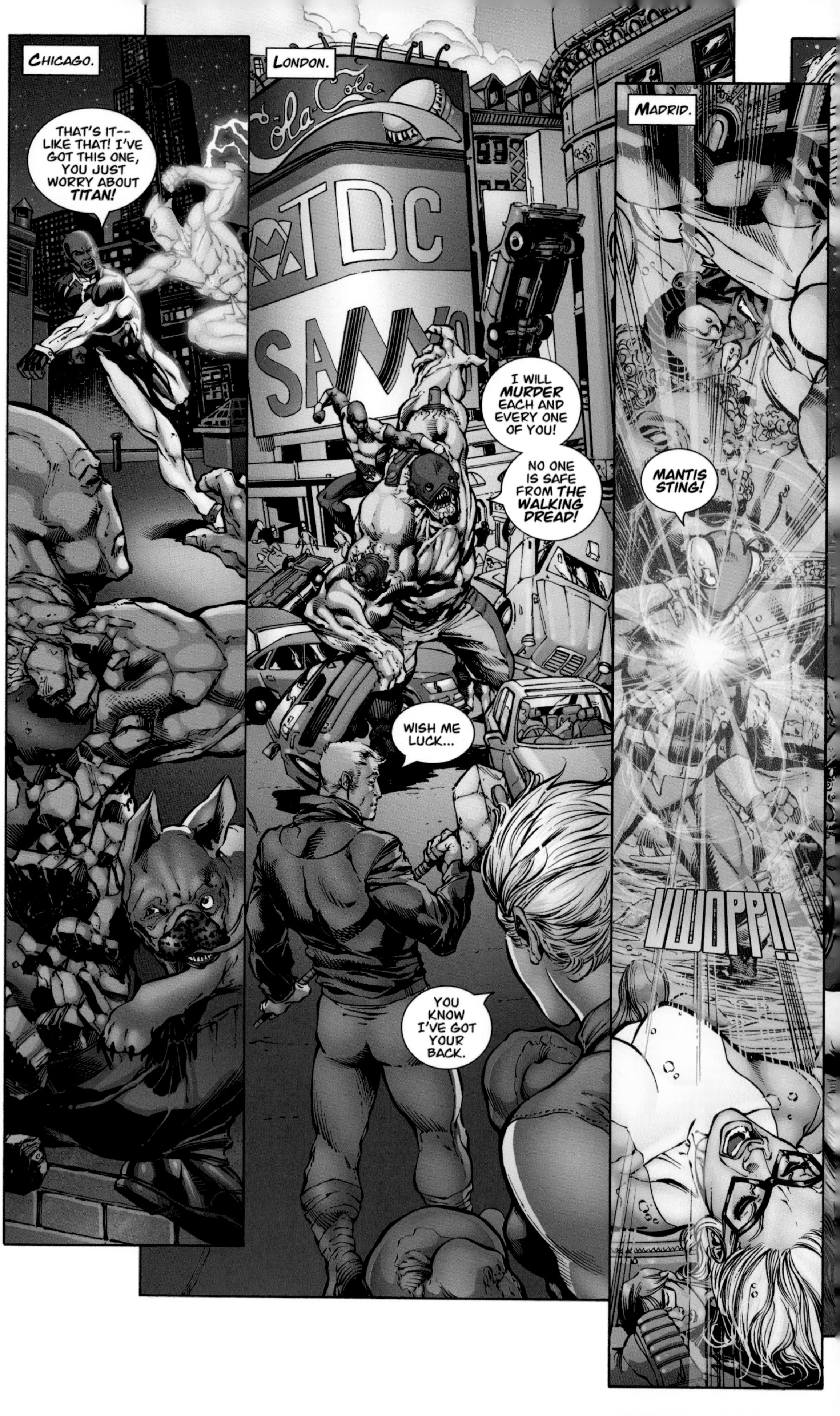
CHICAGO.
THAT'S IT-- LIKE THAT! I'VE GOT THIS ONE, YOU JUST WORRY ABOUT TITAN!
LONDON.
I WILL MURDER EACH AND EVERY ONE OF YOU!
NO ONE IS SAFE FROM THE WALKING DREAD!
WISH ME LUCK...
YOU KNOW I'VE GOT YOUR BACK.
MADRID.
MANTIS STING!
VWOPP!!

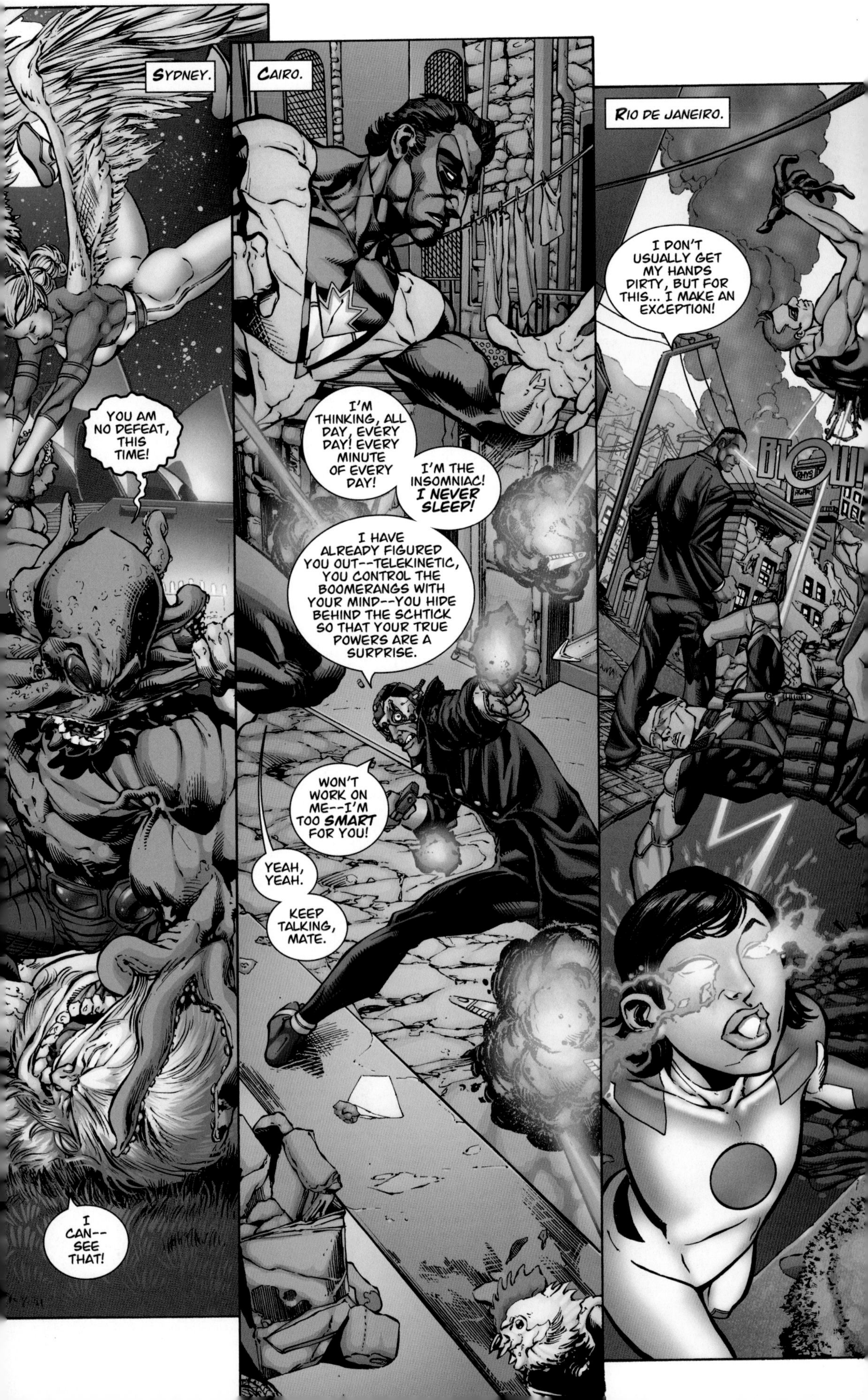
SYDNEY.
YOU AM NO DEFEAT, THIS TIME!
I CAN--SEE THAT!
CAIRO.
I'M THINKING, ALL DAY, EVERY DAY! EVERY MINUTE OF EVERY DAY!
I'M THE INSOMNIAC! I NEVER SLEEP!
I HAVE ALREADY FIGURED YOU OUT--TELEKINETIC, YOU CONTROL THE BOOMERANGS WITH YOUR MIND--YOU HIDE BEHIND THE SCHTICK SO THAT YOUR TRUE POWERS ARE A SURPRISE.
WON'T WORK ON ME--I'M TOO SMART FOR YOU!
YEAH, YEAH.
KEEP TALKING, MATE.
RIO DE JANEIRO.
I DON'T USUALLY GET MY HANDS DIRTY, BUT FOR THIS... I MAKE AN EXCEPTION!
BTOW!

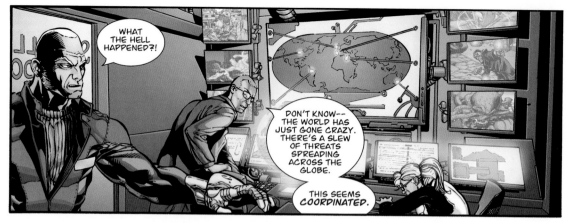

WHAT THE HELL HAPPENED?!

DON'T KNOW-- THE WORLD HAS JUST GONE CRAZY. THERE'S A SLEW OF THREATS SPREADING ACROSS THE GLOBE.

THIS SEEMS *COORDINATED.*

OKAY, THAT SOUNDS REALLY BAD.

HOW'S THIS ONE?

MS. POPPER? SHE'S *FINE,* JUST TIRED.

CECIL'S GOT HER USING HER POWERS TO HELP OUT WITH ALL OUR TELEPORTATION. WE HAD TO GET FIFTEEN PEOPLE TO SIX DIFFERENT LOCATIONS. SHE'LL BE BACK AT ONE-HUNDRED PERCENT IN AN HOUR, TOPS.

WAIT A MINUTE--WHY IS KABOOMERANG OUT THERE ON HIS OWN?

WE'RE NOT SPREAD SO THIN WE'VE GOT PEOPLE GOING ON SOLO MISSIONS...

HE'S NOT SOLO. EL CHUPACABRA IS...

...*NOT THERE.* THAT CAN'T BE RIGHT. I SENT THEM IN. THEY WERE BOTH AT THE EGYPT GUARDIAN STATION TOGETHER.

POPPER, CAN YOU GET ME THERE?

YEAH, I THINK SO. JUST NEEDED A MINUTE.

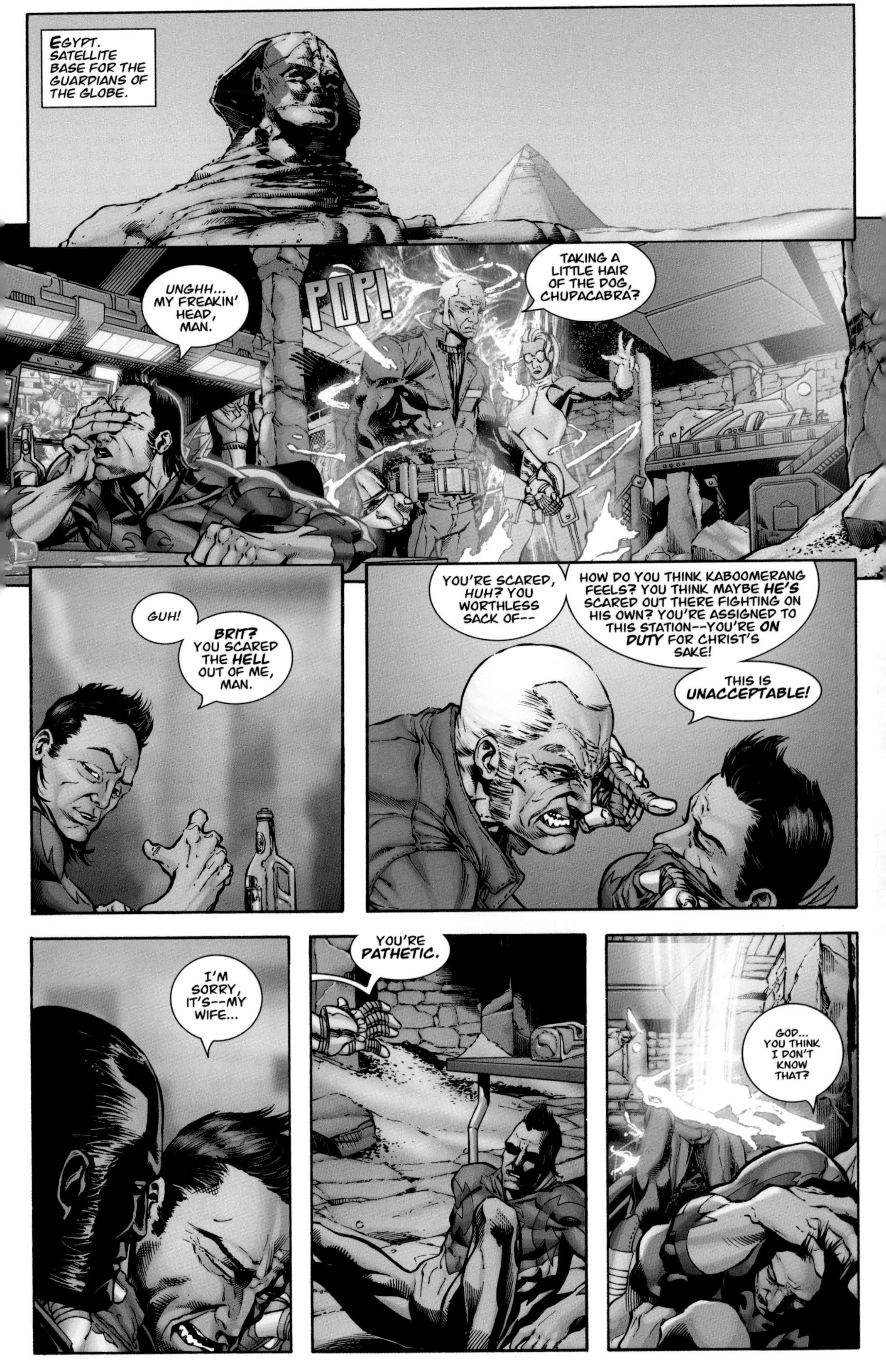
EGYPT. SATELLITE BASE FOR THE GUARDIANS OF THE GLOBE.
UNGHH... MY FREAKIN' HEAD, MAN.
POP!
TAKING A LITTLE HAIR OF THE DOG, CHUPACABRA?
GUH!
BRIT? YOU SCARED THE HELL OUT OF ME, MAN.
YOU'RE SCARED, HUH? YOU WORTHLESS SACK OF--
HOW DO YOU THINK KABOOMERANG FEELS? YOU THINK MAYBE HE'S SCARED OUT THERE FIGHTING ON HIS OWN? YOU'RE ASSIGNED TO THIS STATION--YOU'RE ON DUTY FOR CHRIST'S SAKE!
THIS IS UNACCEPTABLE!
I'M SORRY, IT'S--MY WIFE...
YOU'RE PATHETIC.
GOD... YOU THINK I DON'T KNOW THAT?

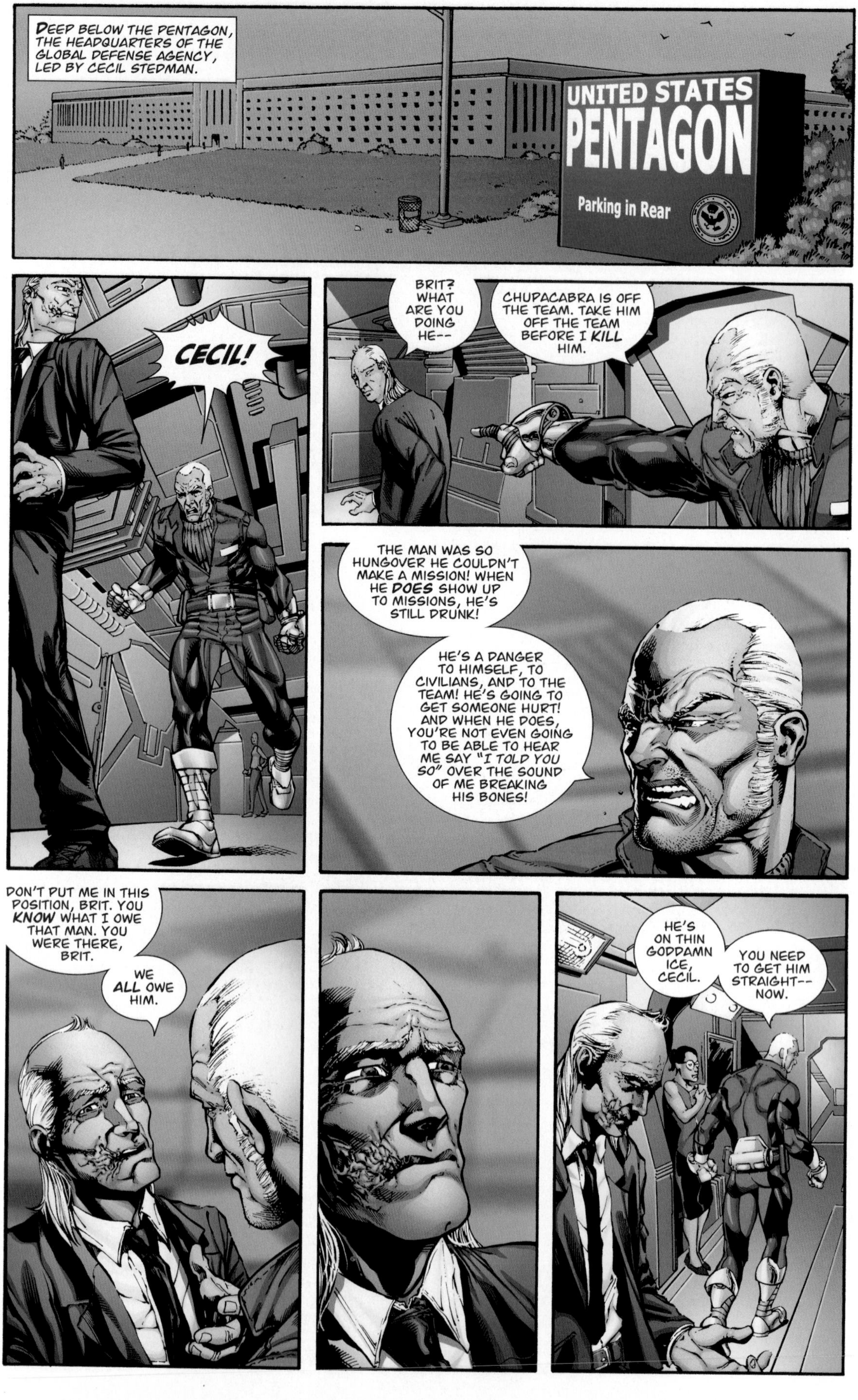
DEEP BELOW THE PENTAGON, THE HEADQUARTERS OF THE GLOBAL DEFENSE AGENCY, LED BY CECIL STEDMAN.
UNITED STATES PENTAGON
Parking in Rear
CECIL!
BRIT? WHAT ARE YOU DOING HE--
CHUPACABRA IS OFF THE TEAM. TAKE HIM OFF THE TEAM BEFORE I KILL HIM.
THE MAN WAS SO HUNGOVER HE COULDN'T MAKE A MISSION! WHEN HE DOES SHOW UP TO MISSIONS, HE'S STILL DRUNK!
HE'S A DANGER TO HIMSELF, TO CIVILIANS, AND TO THE TEAM! HE'S GOING TO GET SOMEONE HURT! AND WHEN HE DOES, YOU'RE NOT EVEN GOING TO BE ABLE TO HEAR ME SAY "I TOLD YOU SO" OVER THE SOUND OF ME BREAKING HIS BONES!
DON'T PUT ME IN THIS POSITION, BRIT. YOU KNOW WHAT I OWE THAT MAN. YOU WERE THERE, BRIT.
WE ALL OWE HIM.
HE'S ON THIN GODDAMN ICE, CECIL.
YOU NEED TO GET HIM STRAIGHT-- NOW.

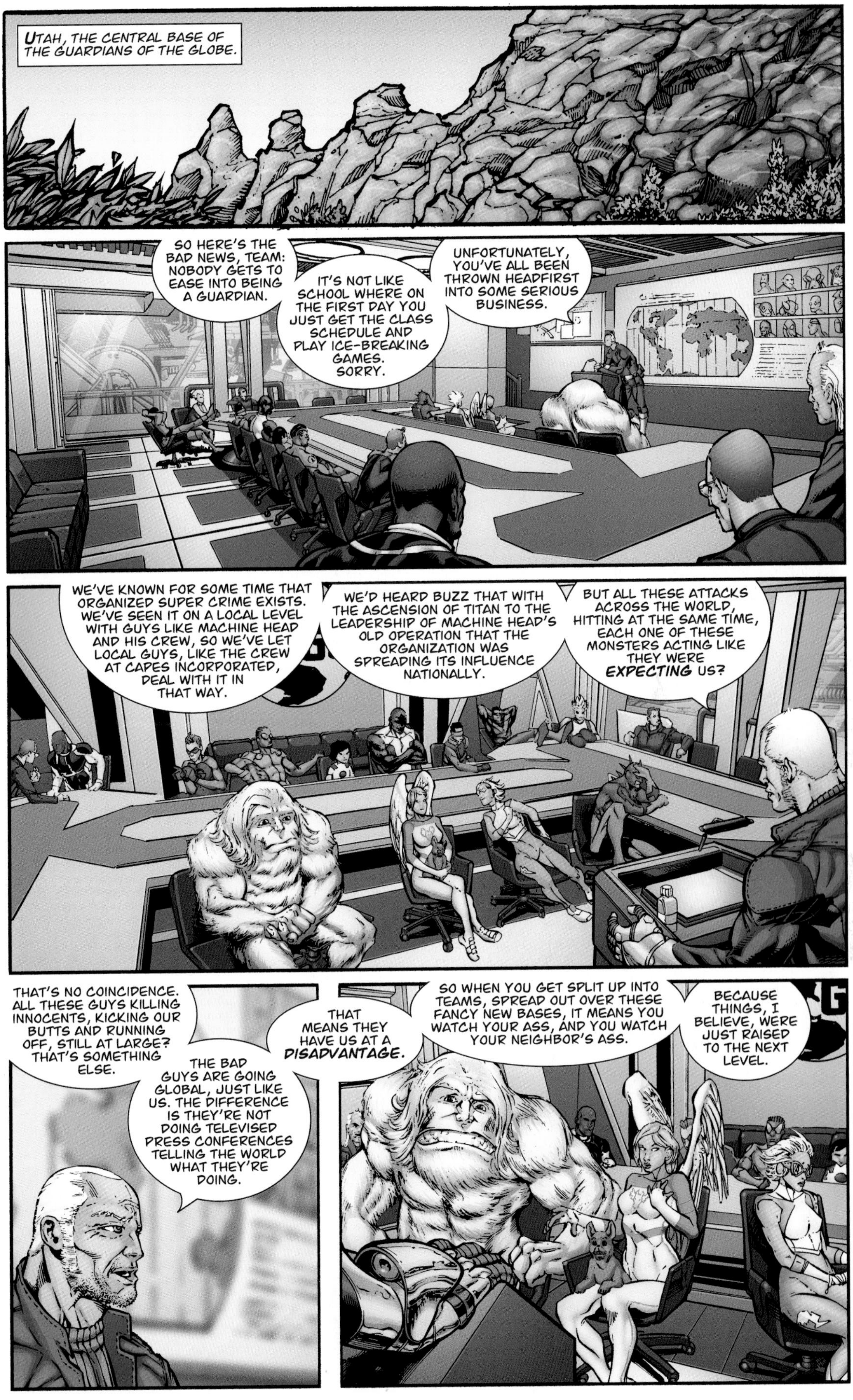
UTAH, THE CENTRAL BASE OF THE GUARDIANS OF THE GLOBE.
SO HERE'S THE BAD NEWS, TEAM: NOBODY GETS TO EASE INTO BEING A GUARDIAN.
IT'S NOT LIKE SCHOOL WHERE ON THE FIRST DAY YOU JUST GET THE CLASS SCHEDULE AND PLAY ICE-BREAKING GAMES. SORRY.
UNFORTUNATELY, YOU'VE ALL BEEN THROWN HEADFIRST INTO SOME SERIOUS BUSINESS.
WE'VE KNOWN FOR SOME TIME THAT ORGANIZED SUPER CRIME EXISTS. WE'VE SEEN IT ON A LOCAL LEVEL WITH GUYS LIKE MACHINE HEAD AND HIS CREW, SO WE'VE LET LOCAL GUYS, LIKE THE CREW AT CAPES INCORPORATED, DEAL WITH IT IN THAT WAY.
WE'D HEARD BUZZ THAT WITH THE ASCENSION OF TITAN TO THE LEADERSHIP OF MACHINE HEAD'S OLD OPERATION THAT THE ORGANIZATION WAS SPREADING ITS INFLUENCE NATIONALLY.
BUT ALL THESE ATTACKS ACROSS THE WORLD, HITTING AT THE SAME TIME, EACH ONE OF THESE MONSTERS ACTING LIKE THEY WERE EXPECTING US?
THAT'S NO COINCIDENCE. ALL THESE GUYS KILLING INNOCENTS, KICKING OUR BUTTS AND RUNNING OFF, STILL AT LARGE? THAT'S SOMETHING ELSE.
THE BAD GUYS ARE GOING GLOBAL, JUST LIKE US. THE DIFFERENCE IS THEY'RE NOT DOING TELEVISED PRESS CONFERENCES TELLING THE WORLD WHAT THEY'RE DOING.
THAT MEANS THEY HAVE US AT A DISADVANTAGE.
SO WHEN YOU GET SPLIT UP INTO TEAMS, SPREAD OUT OVER THESE FANCY NEW BASES, IT MEANS YOU WATCH YOUR ASS, AND YOU WATCH YOUR NEIGHBOR'S ASS.
BECAUSE THINGS, I BELIEVE, WERE JUST RAISED TO THE NEXT LEVEL.

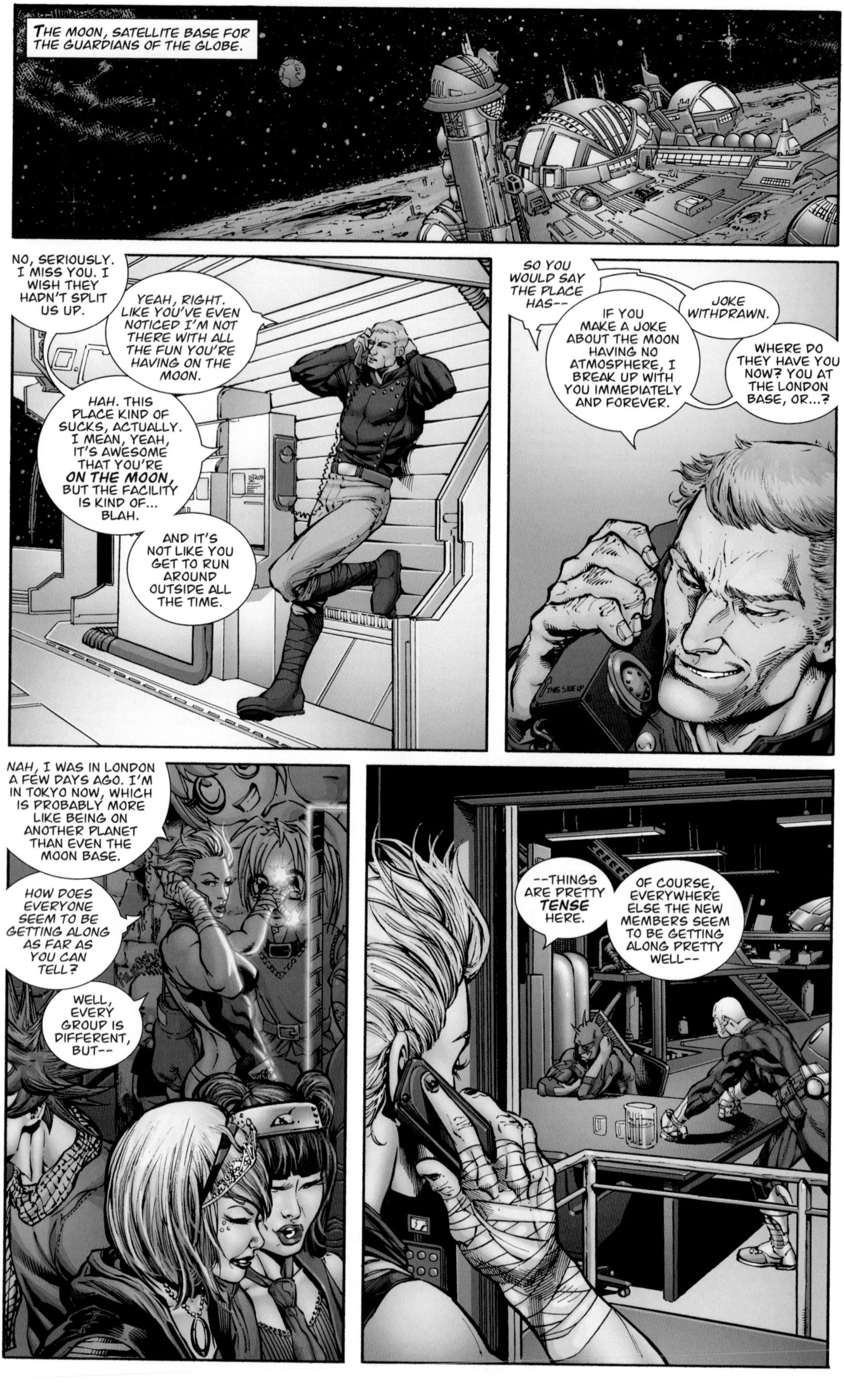
THE MOON, SATELLITE BASE FOR THE GUARDIANS OF THE GLOBE.
NO, SERIOUSLY. I MISS YOU. I WISH THEY HADN'T SPLIT US UP.
YEAH, RIGHT. LIKE YOU'VE EVEN NOTICED I'M NOT THERE WITH ALL THE FUN YOU'RE HAVING ON THE MOON.
HAH. THIS PLACE KIND OF SUCKS, ACTUALLY. I MEAN, YEAH, IT'S AWESOME THAT YOU'RE ON THE MOON, BUT THE FACILITY IS KIND OF... BLAH.
AND IT'S NOT LIKE YOU GET TO RUN AROUND OUTSIDE ALL THE TIME.
SO YOU WOULD SAY THE PLACE HAS--
IF YOU MAKE A JOKE ABOUT THE MOON HAVING NO ATMOSPHERE, I BREAK UP WITH YOU IMMEDIATELY AND FOREVER.
JOKE WITHDRAWN.
WHERE DO THEY HAVE YOU NOW? YOU AT THE LONDON BASE, OR...?
THIS SIDE UP
NAH, I WAS IN LONDON A FEW DAYS AGO. I'M IN TOKYO NOW, WHICH IS PROBABLY MORE LIKE BEING ON ANOTHER PLANET THAN EVEN THE MOON BASE.
HOW DOES EVERYONE SEEM TO BE GETTING ALONG AS FAR AS YOU CAN TELL?
WELL, EVERY GROUP IS DIFFERENT, BUT--
--THINGS ARE PRETTY TENSE HERE.
OF COURSE, EVERYWHERE ELSE THE NEW MEMBERS SEEM TO BE GETTING ALONG PRETTY WELL--

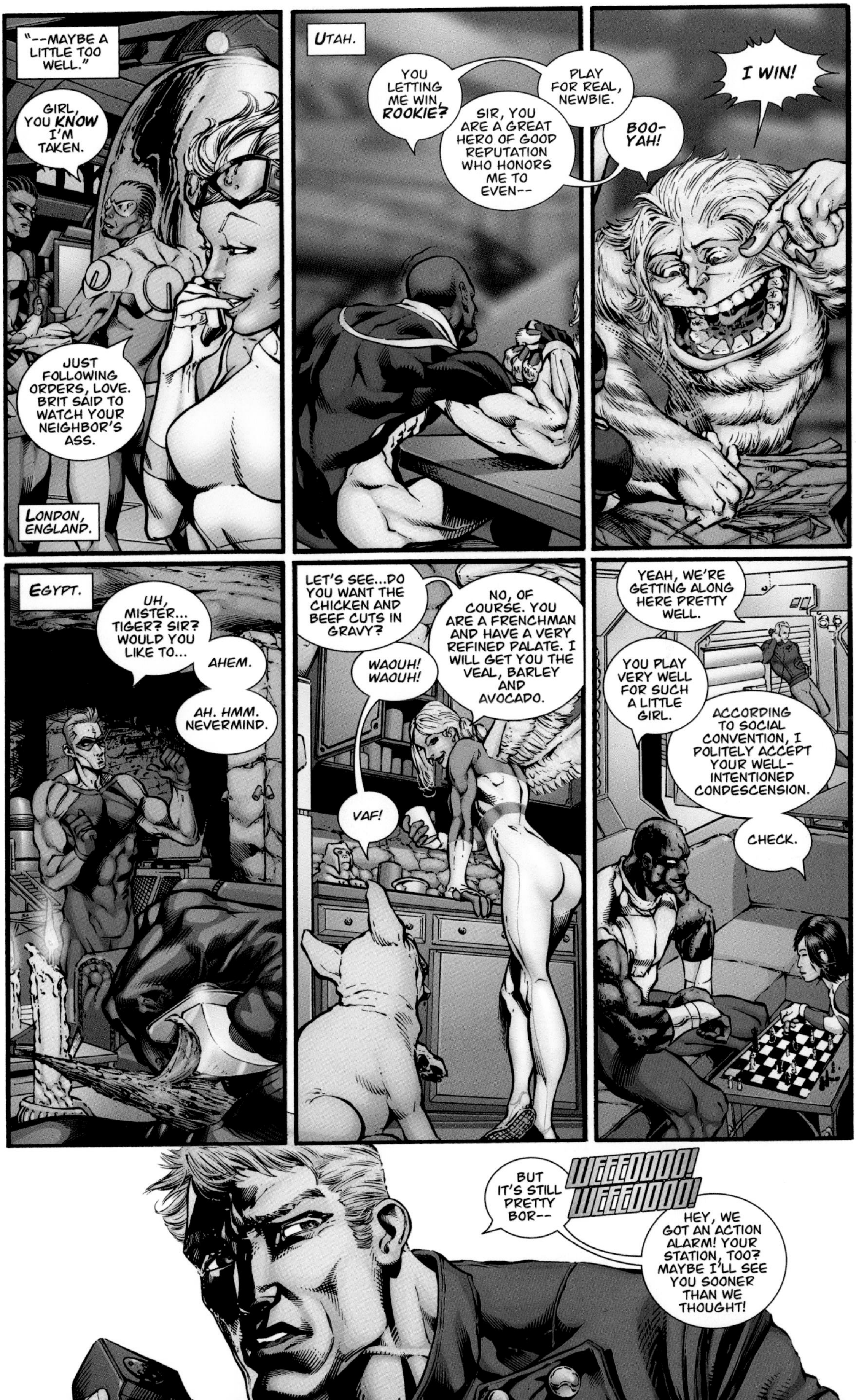

"--MAYBE A LITTLE TOO WELL."
GIRL, YOU KNOW I'M TAKEN.
JUST FOLLOWING ORDERS, LOVE. BRIT SAID TO WATCH YOUR NEIGHBOR'S ASS.
LONDON, ENGLAND.
UTAH.
YOU LETTING ME WIN, ROOKIE?
SIR, YOU ARE A GREAT HERO OF GOOD REPUTATION WHO HONORS ME TO EVEN--
PLAY FOR REAL, NEWBIE.
BOO-YAH!
I WIN!
EGYPT.
UH, MISTER... TIGER? SIR? WOULD YOU LIKE TO...
AHEM.
AH. HMM. NEVERMIND.
LET'S SEE...DO YOU WANT THE CHICKEN AND BEEF CUTS IN GRAVY?
WAOUH! WAOUH!
NO, OF COURSE. YOU ARE A FRENCHMAN AND HAVE A VERY REFINED PALATE. I WILL GET YOU THE VEAL, BARLEY AND AVOCADO.
VAF!
YEAH, WE'RE GETTING ALONG HERE PRETTY WELL.
YOU PLAY VERY WELL FOR SUCH A LITTLE GIRL.
ACCORDING TO SOCIAL CONVENTION, I POLITELY ACCEPT YOUR WELL-INTENTIONED CONDESCENSION.
CHECK.
BUT IT'S STILL PRETTY BOR--
WEEEOOOO! WEEEOOOO!
HEY, WE GOT AN ACTION ALARM! YOUR STATION, TOO? MAYBE I'LL SEE YOU SOONER THAN WE THOUGHT!

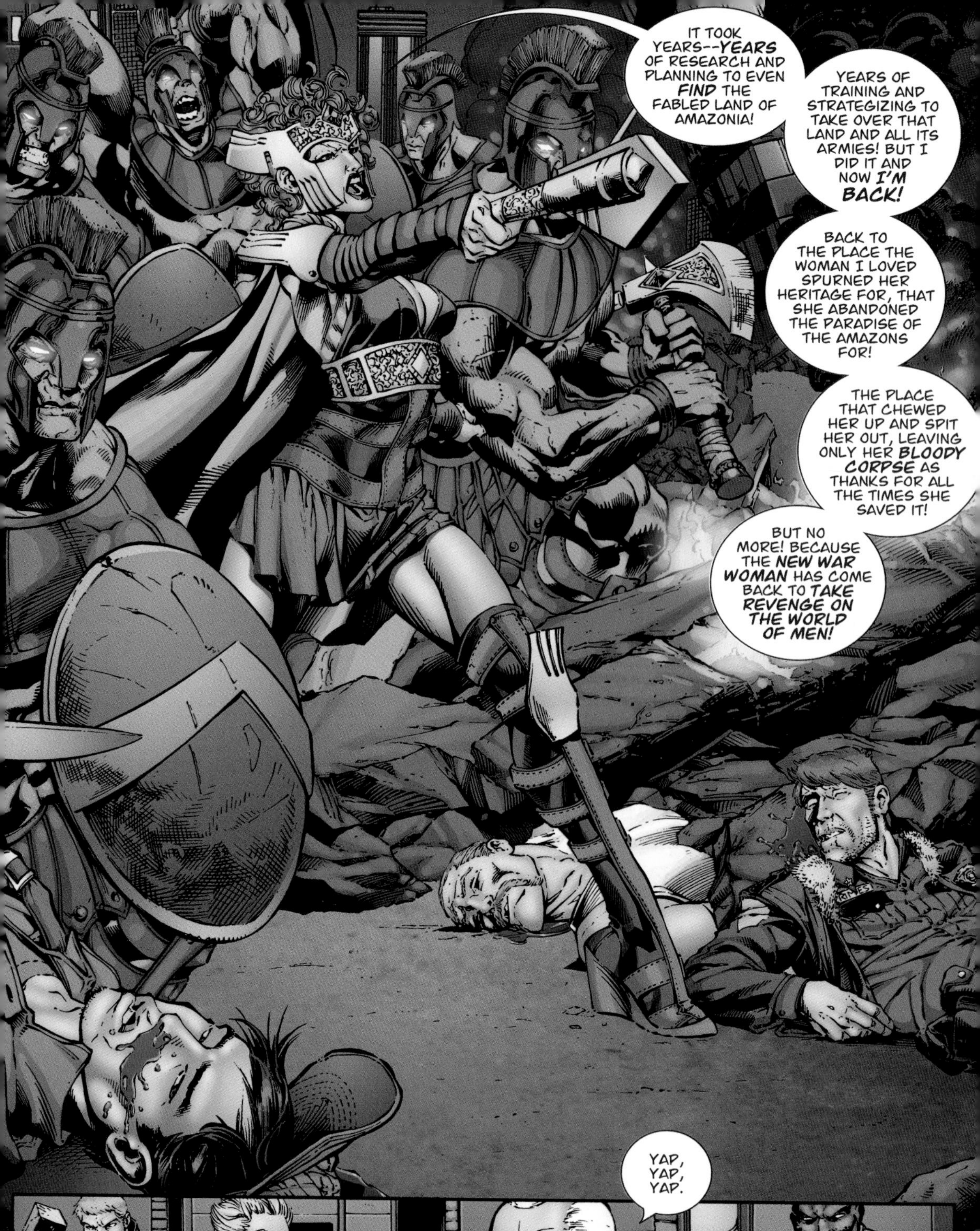
IT TOOK YEARS--YEARS OF RESEARCH AND PLANNING TO EVEN FIND THE FABLED LAND OF AMAZONIA!
YEARS OF TRAINING AND STRATEGIZING TO TAKE OVER THAT LAND AND ALL ITS ARMIES! BUT I DID IT AND NOW I'M BACK!
BACK TO THE PLACE THE WOMAN I LOVED SPURNED HER HERITAGE FOR, THAT SHE ABANDONED THE PARADISE OF THE AMAZONS FOR!
THE PLACE THAT CHEWED HER UP AND SPIT HER OUT, LEAVING ONLY HER BLOODY CORPSE AS THANKS FOR ALL THE TIMES SHE SAVED IT!
BUT NO MORE! BECAUSE THE NEW WAR WOMAN HAS COME BACK TO TAKE REVENGE ON THE WORLD OF MEN!
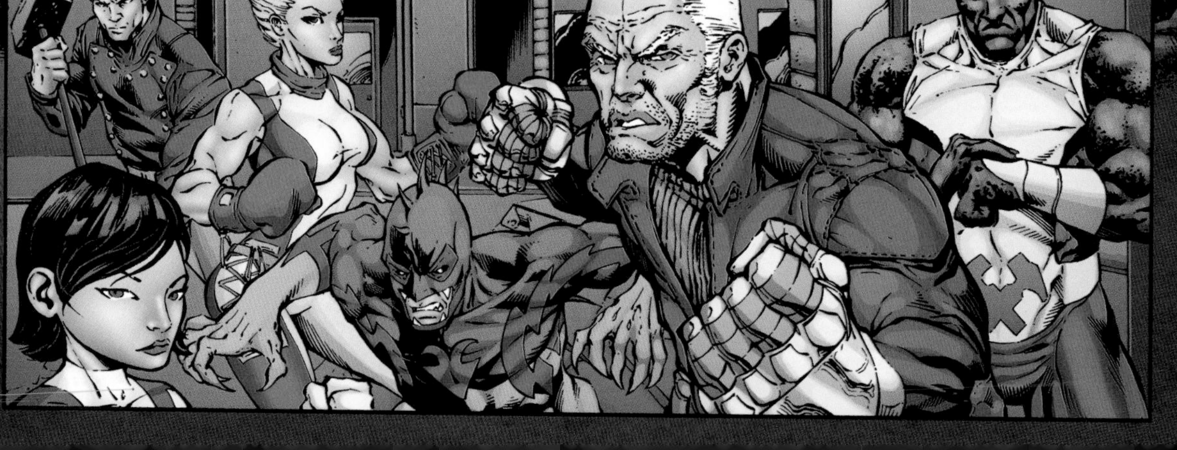
YAP, YAP, YAP.

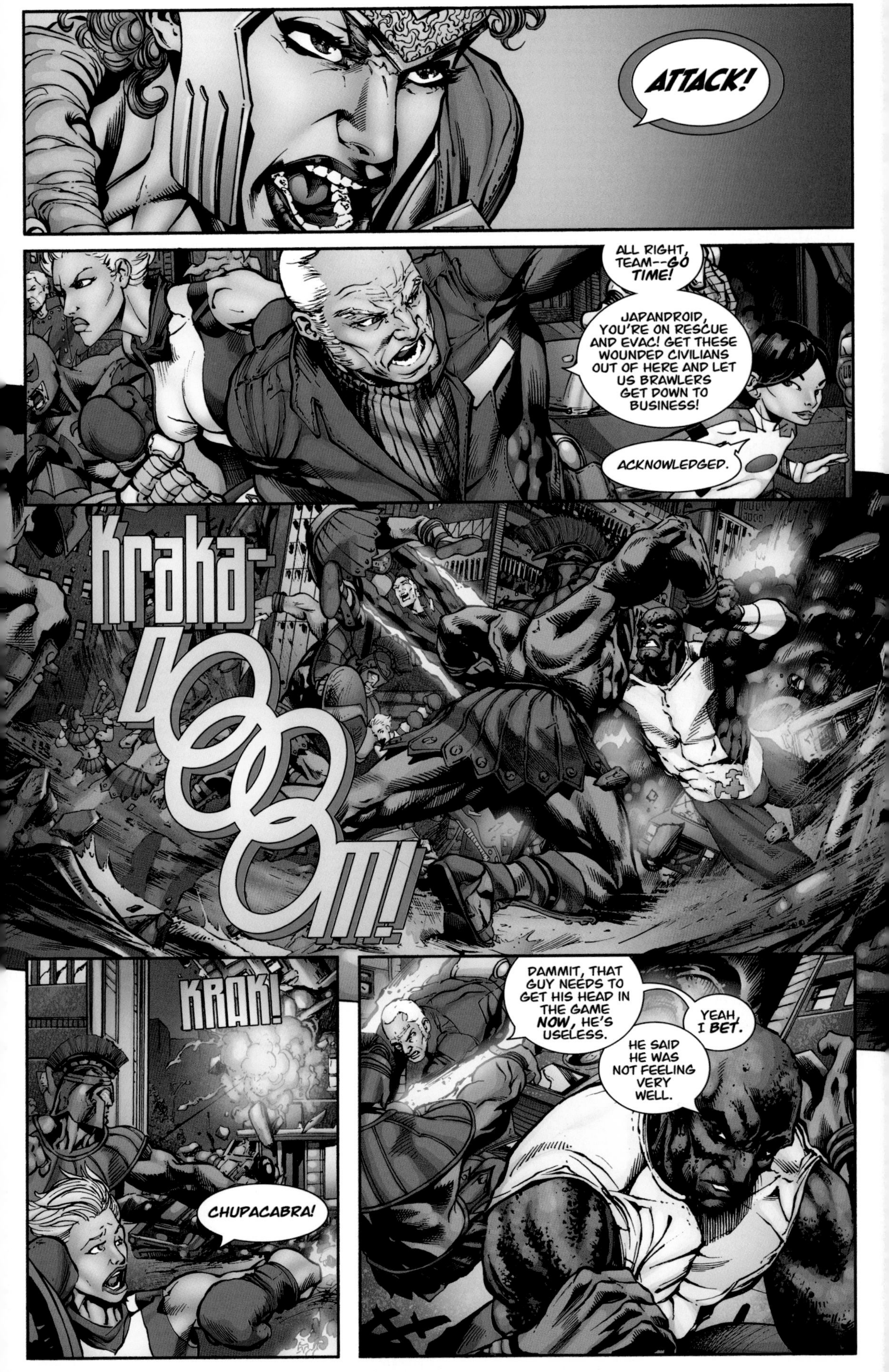
ATTACK!
ALL RIGHT, TEAM--GO TIME!
JAPANDROID, YOU'RE ON RESCUE AND EVAC! GET THESE WOUNDED CIVILIANS OUT OF HERE AND LET US BRAWLERS GET DOWN TO BUSINESS!
ACKNOWLEDGED.
Kraka-Doooom!
KRAK!
CHUPACABRA!
DAMMIT, THAT GUY NEEDS TO GET HIS HEAD IN THE GAME NOW, HE'S USELESS.
YEAH, I BET.
HE SAID HE WAS NOT FEELING VERY WELL.

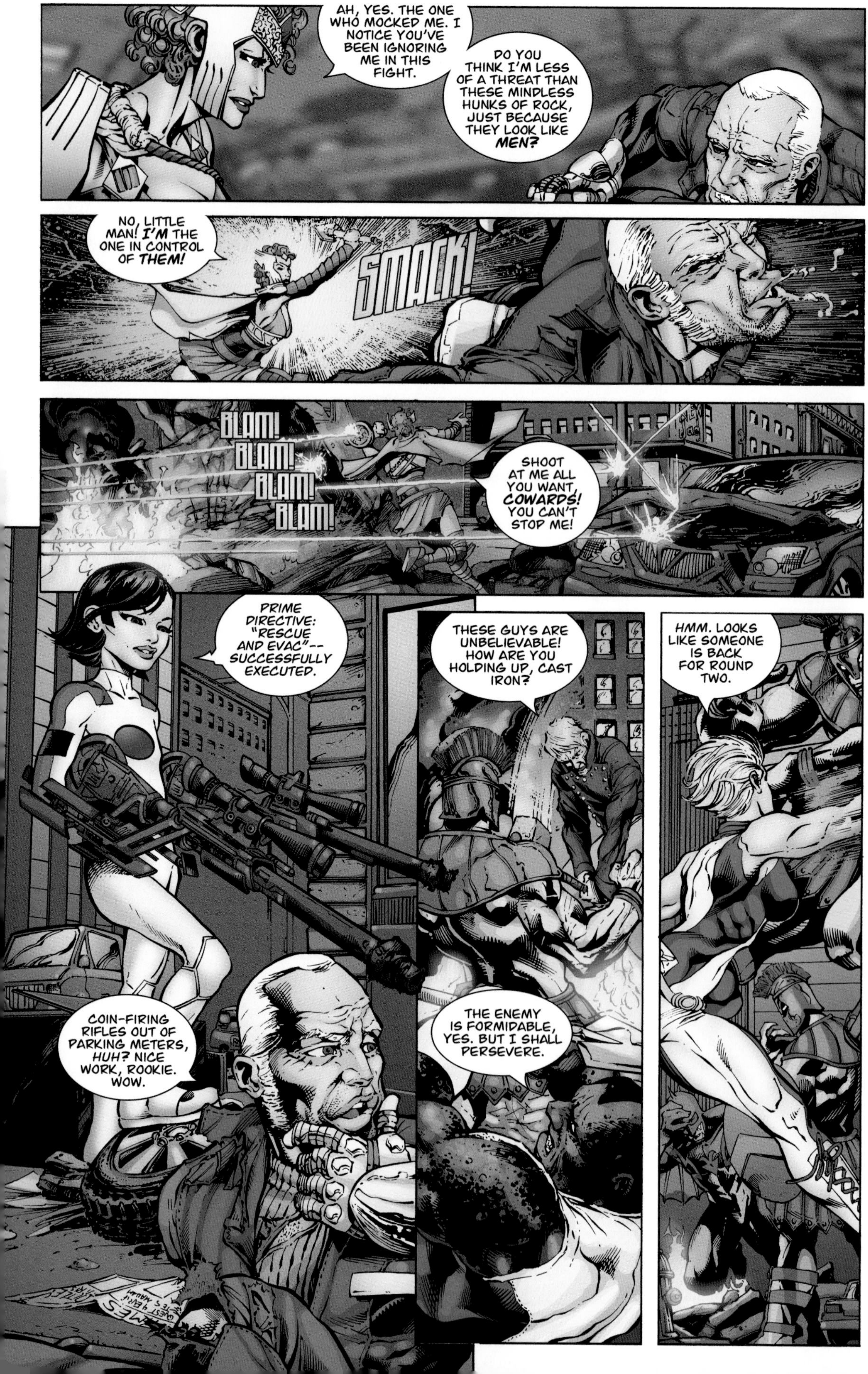

AH, YES. THE ONE WHO MOCKED ME. I NOTICE YOU'VE BEEN IGNORING ME IN THIS FIGHT.
DO YOU THINK I'M LESS OF A THREAT THAN THESE MINDLESS HUNKS OF ROCK, JUST BECAUSE THEY LOOK LIKE MEN?
NO, LITTLE MAN! I'M THE ONE IN CONTROL OF THEM!
SMACK!
BLAM! BLAM! BLAM! BLAM!
SHOOT AT ME ALL YOU WANT, COWARDS! YOU CAN'T STOP ME!
PRIME DIRECTIVE: "RESCUE AND EVAC"-- SUCCESSFULLY EXECUTED.
COIN-FIRING RIFLES OUT OF PARKING METERS, HUH? NICE WORK, ROOKIE. WOW.
THESE GUYS ARE UNBELIEVABLE! HOW ARE YOU HOLDING UP, CAST IRON?
THE ENEMY IS FORMIDABLE, YES. BUT I SHALL PERSEVERE.
HMM. LOOKS LIKE SOMEONE IS BACK FOR ROUND TWO.

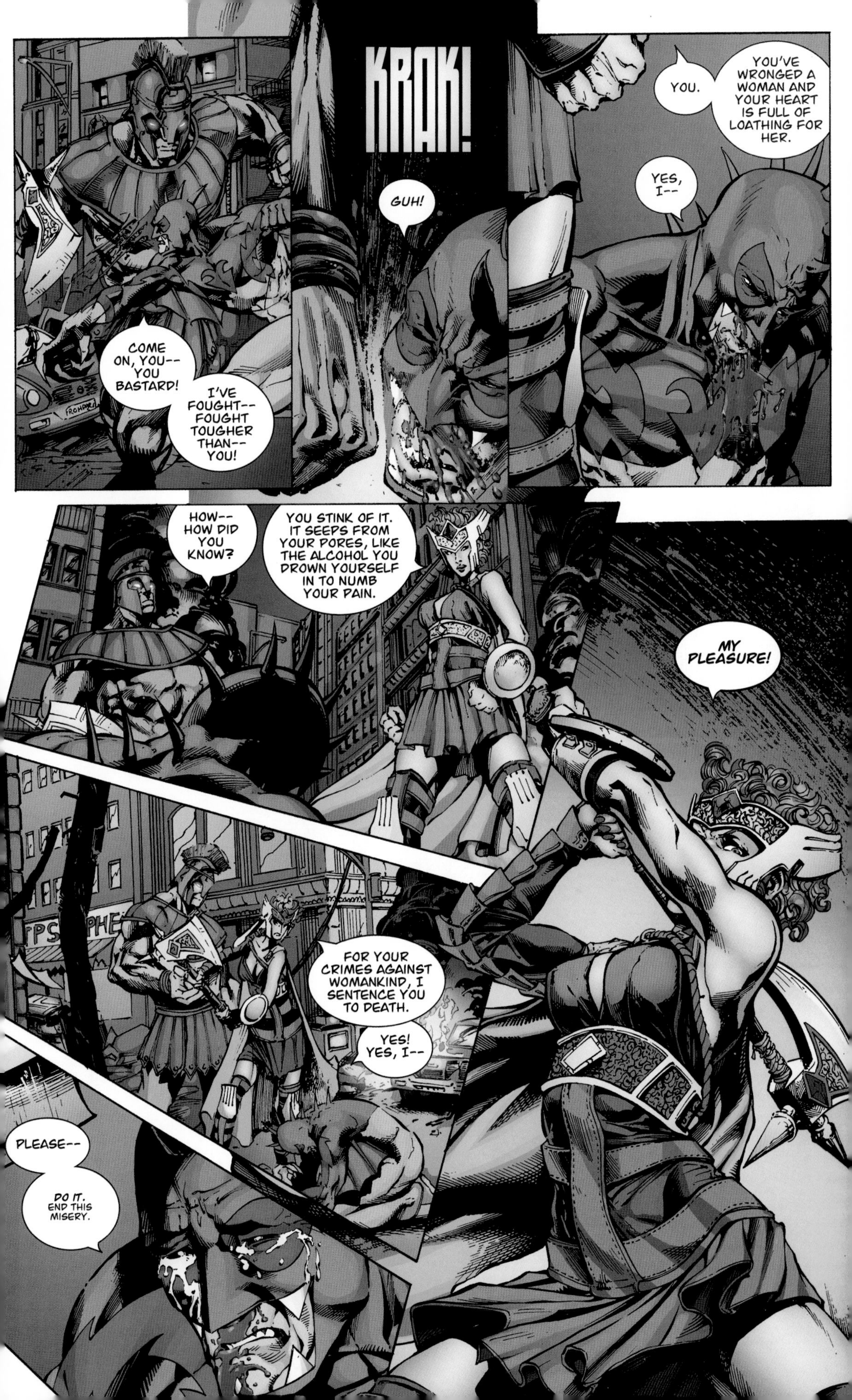
COME ON, YOU-- YOU BASTARD!
I'VE FOUGHT-- FOUGHT TOUGHER THAN-- YOU!
KRAK!
GUH!
YOU.
YOU'VE WRONGED A WOMAN AND YOUR HEART IS FULL OF LOATHING FOR HER.
YES, I--
HOW-- HOW DID YOU KNOW?
YOU STINK OF IT. IT SEEPS FROM YOUR PORES, LIKE THE ALCOHOL YOU DROWN YOURSELF IN TO NUMB YOUR PAIN.
FOR YOUR CRIMES AGAINST WOMANKIND, I SENTENCE YOU TO DEATH.
YES! YES, I--
PLEASE--
DO IT. END THIS MISERY.
MY PLEASURE!

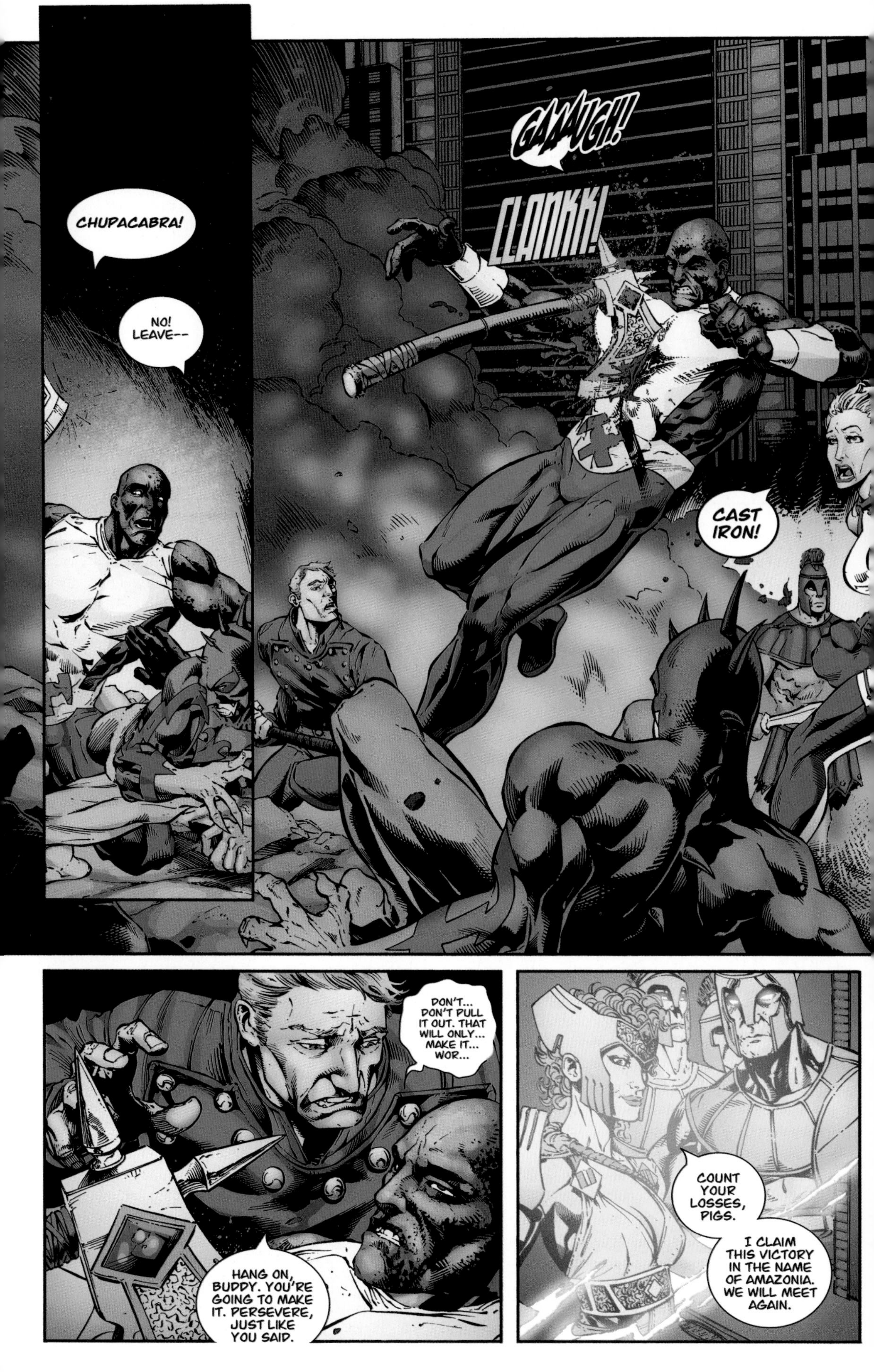
CHUPACABRA!
NO! LEAVE--
GAAAUGH!
CLANKK!
CAST IRON!
DON'T... DON'T PULL IT OUT. THAT WILL ONLY... MAKE IT... WOR...
HANG ON, BUDDY. YOU'RE GOING TO MAKE IT. PERSEVERE, JUST LIKE YOU SAID.
COUNT YOUR LOSSES, PIGS.
I CLAIM THIS VICTORY IN THE NAME OF AMAZONIA. WE WILL MEET AGAIN.

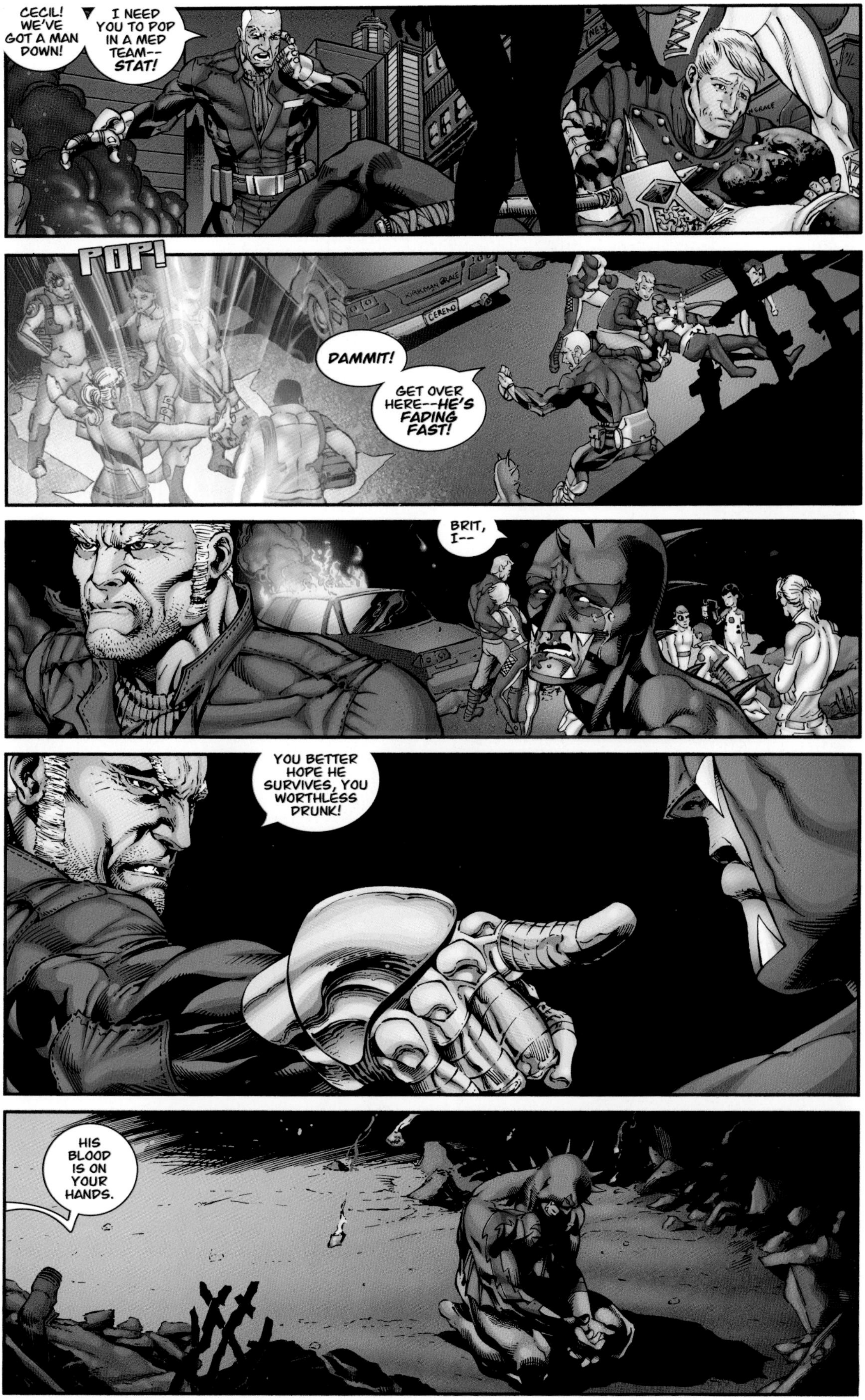
CECIL! WE'VE GOT A MAN DOWN!
I NEED YOU TO POP IN A MED TEAM-- STAT!
POP!
DAMMIT!
GET OVER HERE--HE'S FADING FAST!
BRIT, I--
YOU BETTER HOPE HE SURVIVES, YOU WORTHLESS DRUNK!
HIS BLOOD IS ON YOUR HANDS.

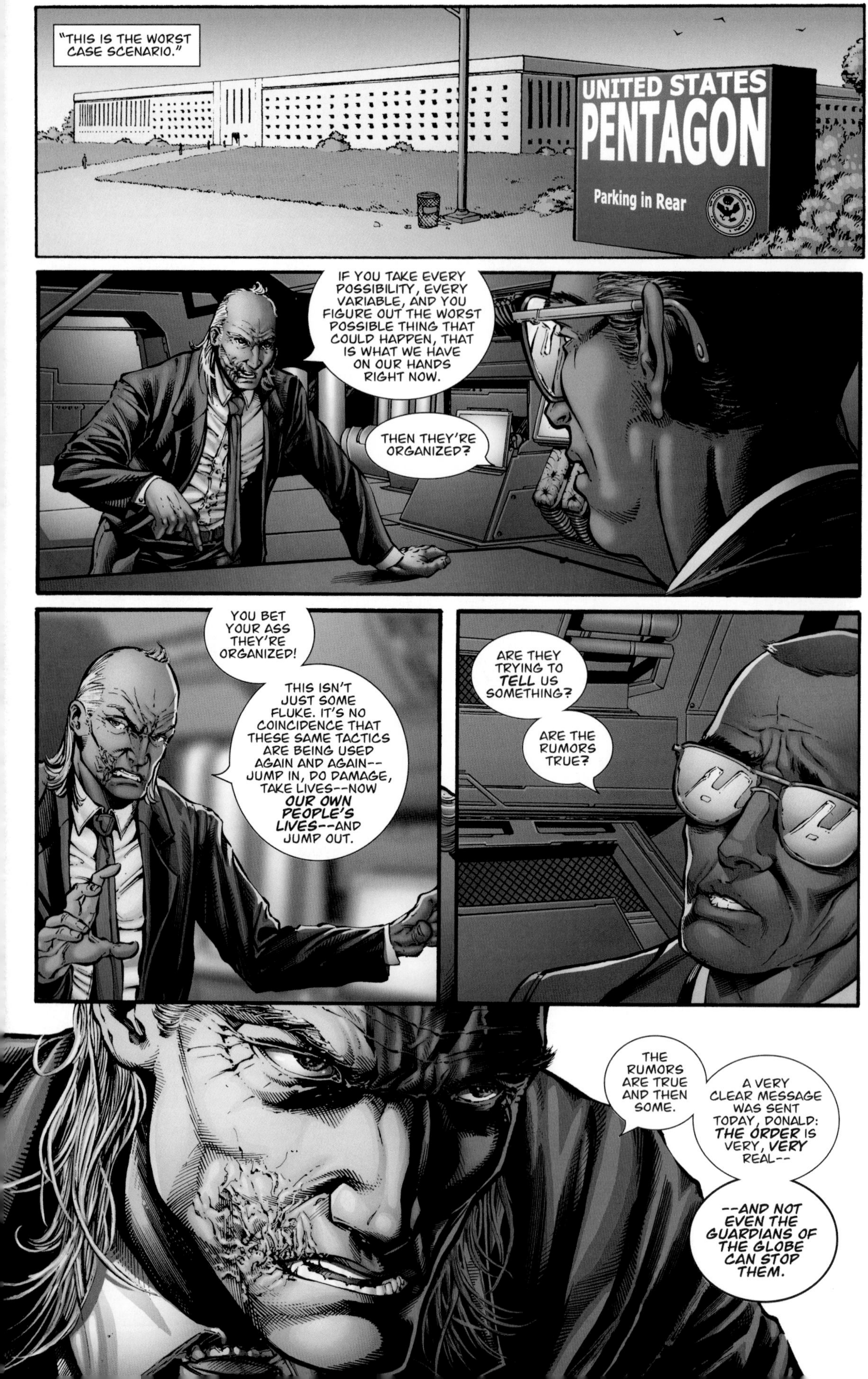
"THIS IS THE WORST CASE SCENARIO."
UNITED STATES PENTAGON
Parking in Rear
IF YOU TAKE EVERY POSSIBILITY, EVERY VARIABLE, AND YOU FIGURE OUT THE WORST POSSIBLE THING THAT COULD HAPPEN, THAT IS WHAT WE HAVE ON OUR HANDS RIGHT NOW.
THEN THEY'RE ORGANIZED?
YOU BET YOUR ASS THEY'RE ORGANIZED!
THIS ISN'T JUST SOME FLUKE. IT'S NO COINCIDENCE THAT THESE SAME TACTICS ARE BEING USED AGAIN AND AGAIN--JUMP IN, DO DAMAGE, TAKE LIVES--NOW ***OUR OWN PEOPLE'S LIVES***--AND JUMP OUT.
ARE THEY TRYING TO ***TELL*** US SOMETHING?
ARE THE RUMORS TRUE?
THE RUMORS ARE TRUE AND THEN SOME.
A VERY CLEAR MESSAGE WAS SENT TODAY, DONALD: ***THE ORDER*** IS VERY, ***VERY*** REAL--
--AND NOT EVEN THE GUARDIANS OF THE GLOBE CAN STOP THEM.

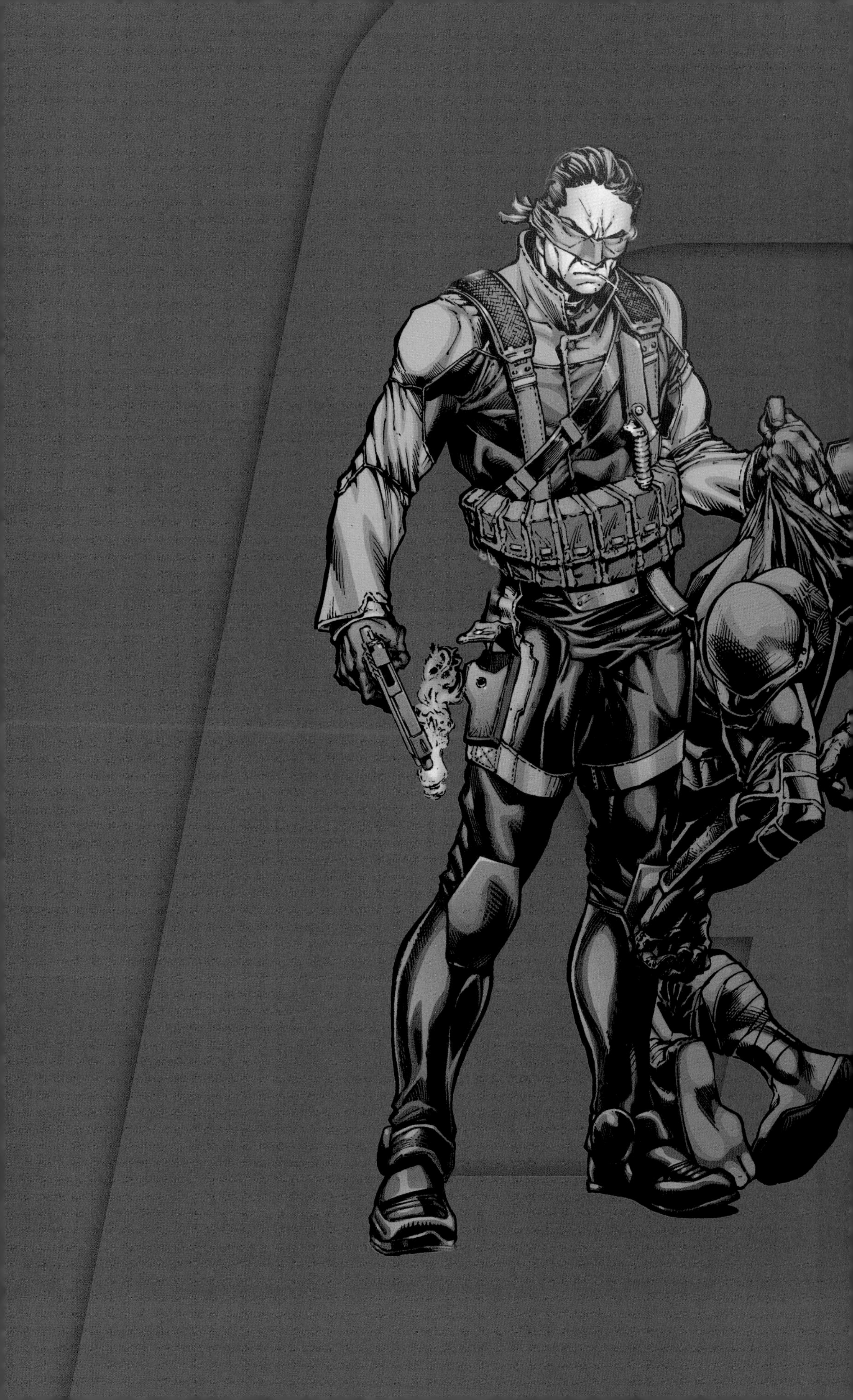

CHAPTER FIVE

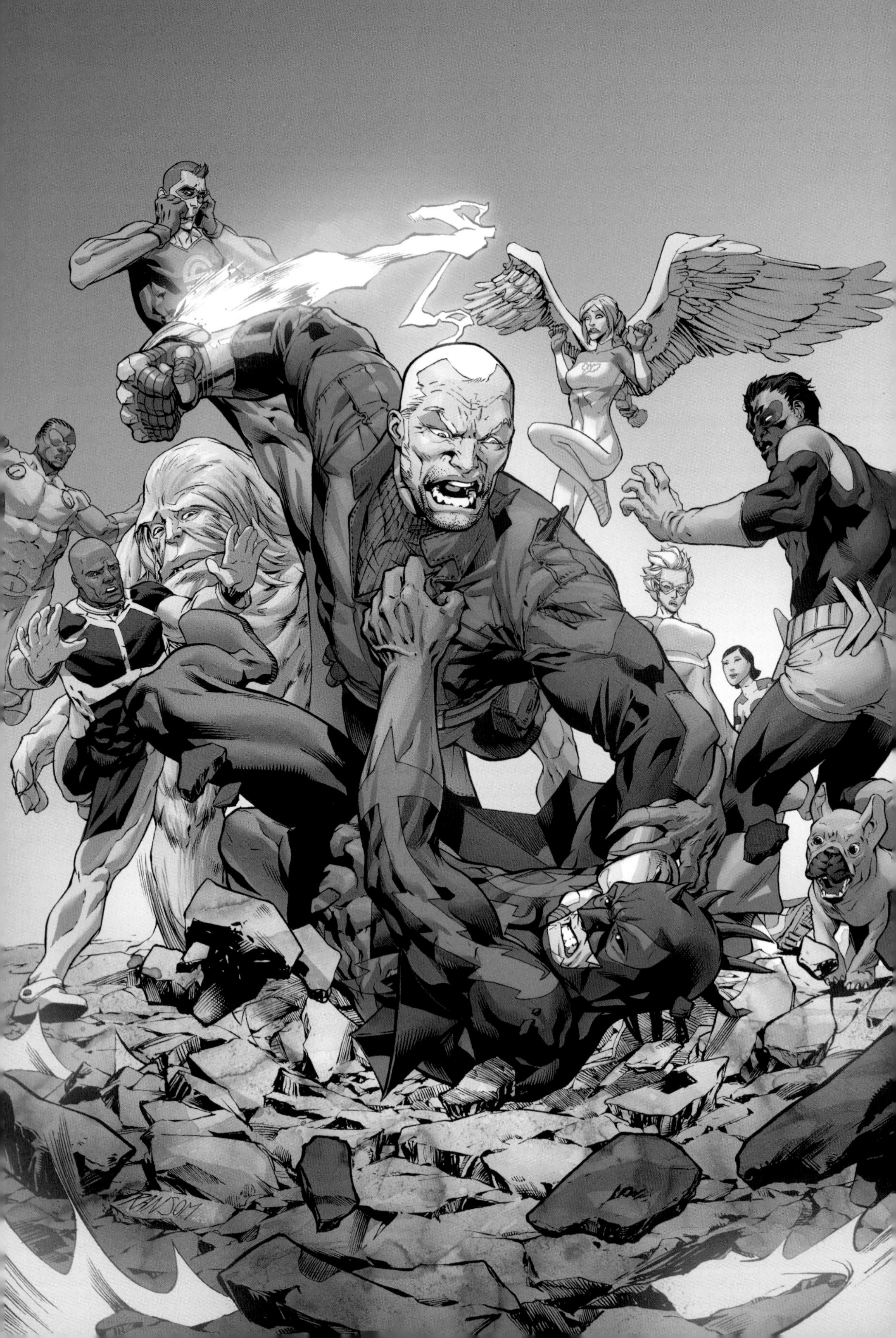

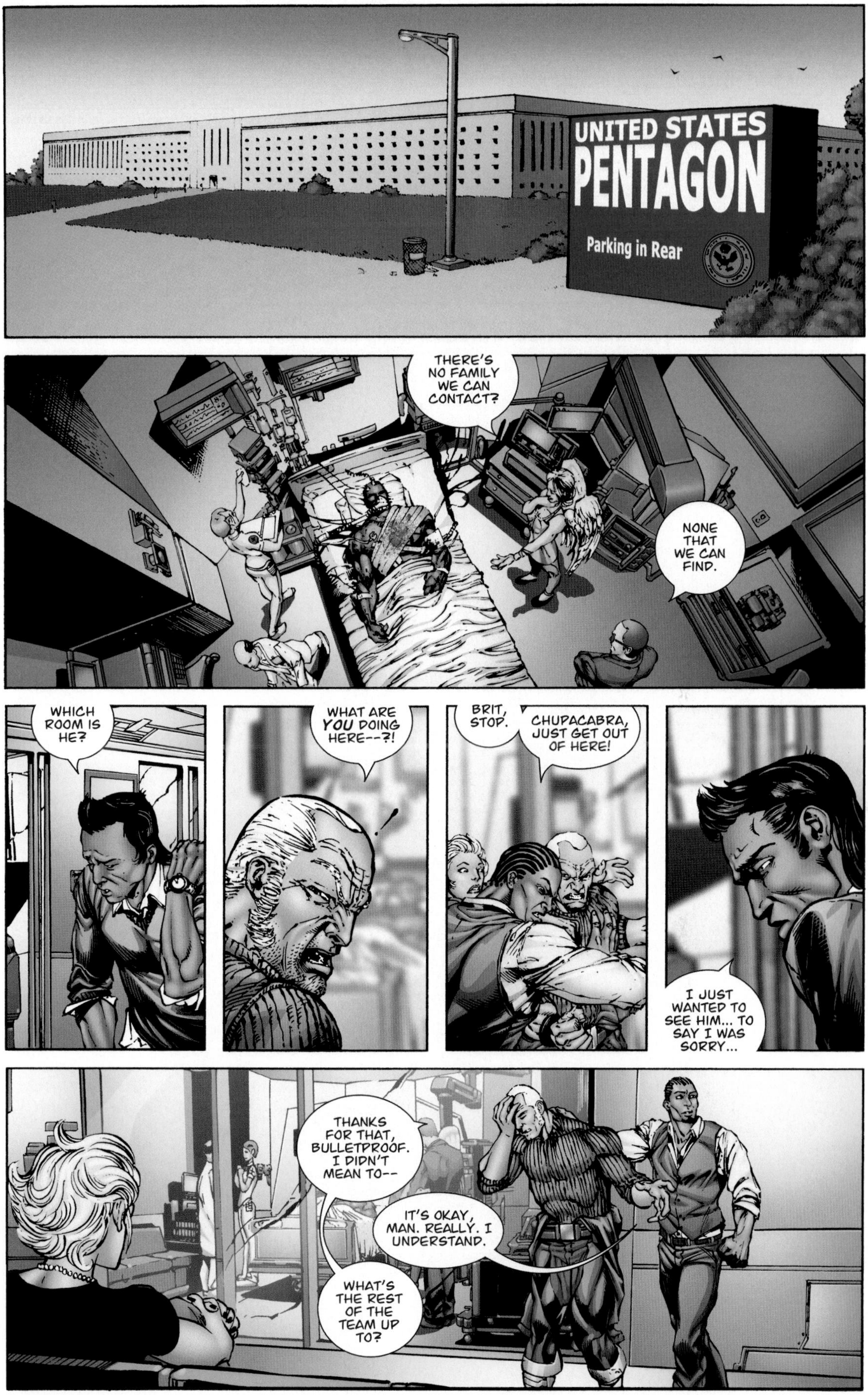
UNITED STATES
PENTAGON
Parking in Rear
THERE'S NO FAMILY WE CAN CONTACT?
NONE THAT WE CAN FIND.
WHICH ROOM IS HE?
WHAT ARE YOU DOING HERE--?!
BRIT, STOP.
CHUPACABRA, JUST GET OUT OF HERE!
I JUST WANTED TO SEE HIM... TO SAY I WAS SORRY...
THANKS FOR THAT, BULLETPROOF. I DIDN'T MEAN TO--
IT'S OKAY, MAN. REALLY. I UNDERSTAND.
WHAT'S THE REST OF THE TEAM UP TO?

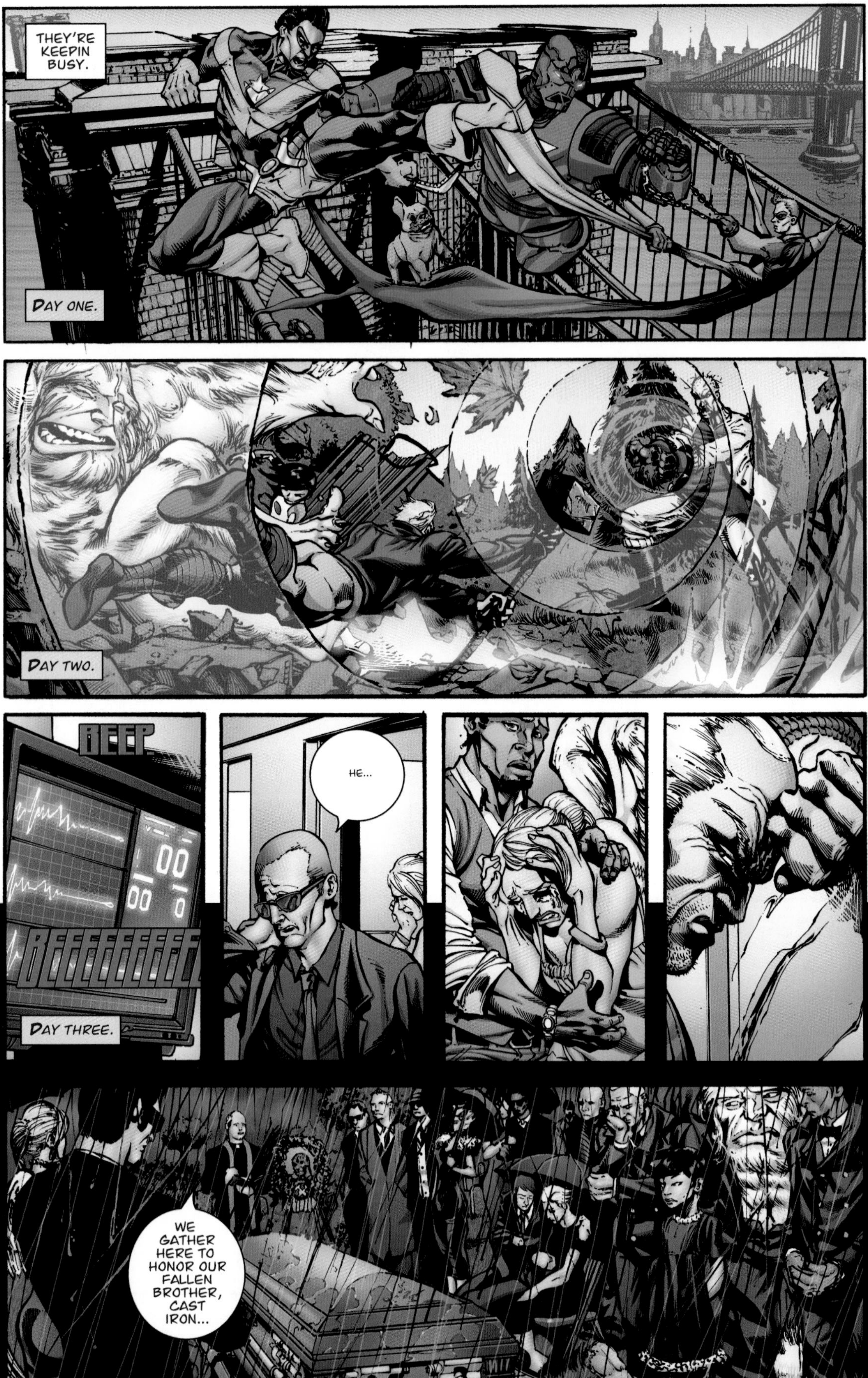
THEY'RE KEEPIN BUSY.
DAY ONE.
DAY TWO.
BEEP.
BEEEEEEEEE
DAY THREE.
HE...
WE GATHER HERE TO HONOR OUR FALLEN BROTHER, CAST IRON...

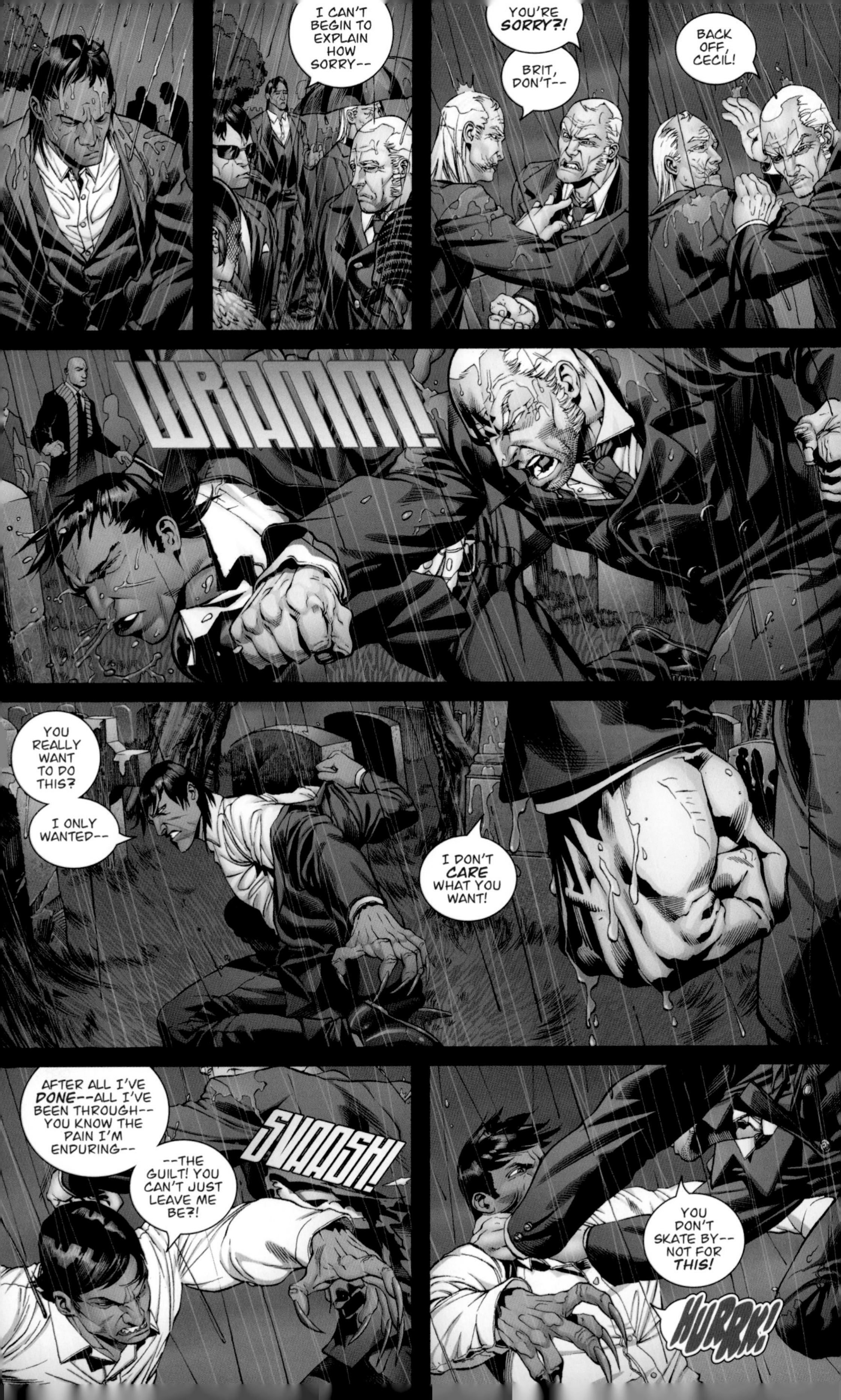
I CAN'T BEGIN TO EXPLAIN HOW SORRY--
YOU'RE SORRY?!
BRIT, DON'T--
BACK OFF, CECIL!
WRAMM!
YOU REALLY WANT TO DO THIS?
I ONLY WANTED--
I DON'T CARE WHAT YOU WANT!
AFTER ALL I'VE DONE--ALL I'VE BEEN THROUGH--YOU KNOW THE PAIN I'M ENDURING--
SWOOSH!
--THE GUILT! YOU CAN'T JUST LEAVE ME BE?!
YOU DON'T SKATE BY--NOT FOR THIS!
HURRK!

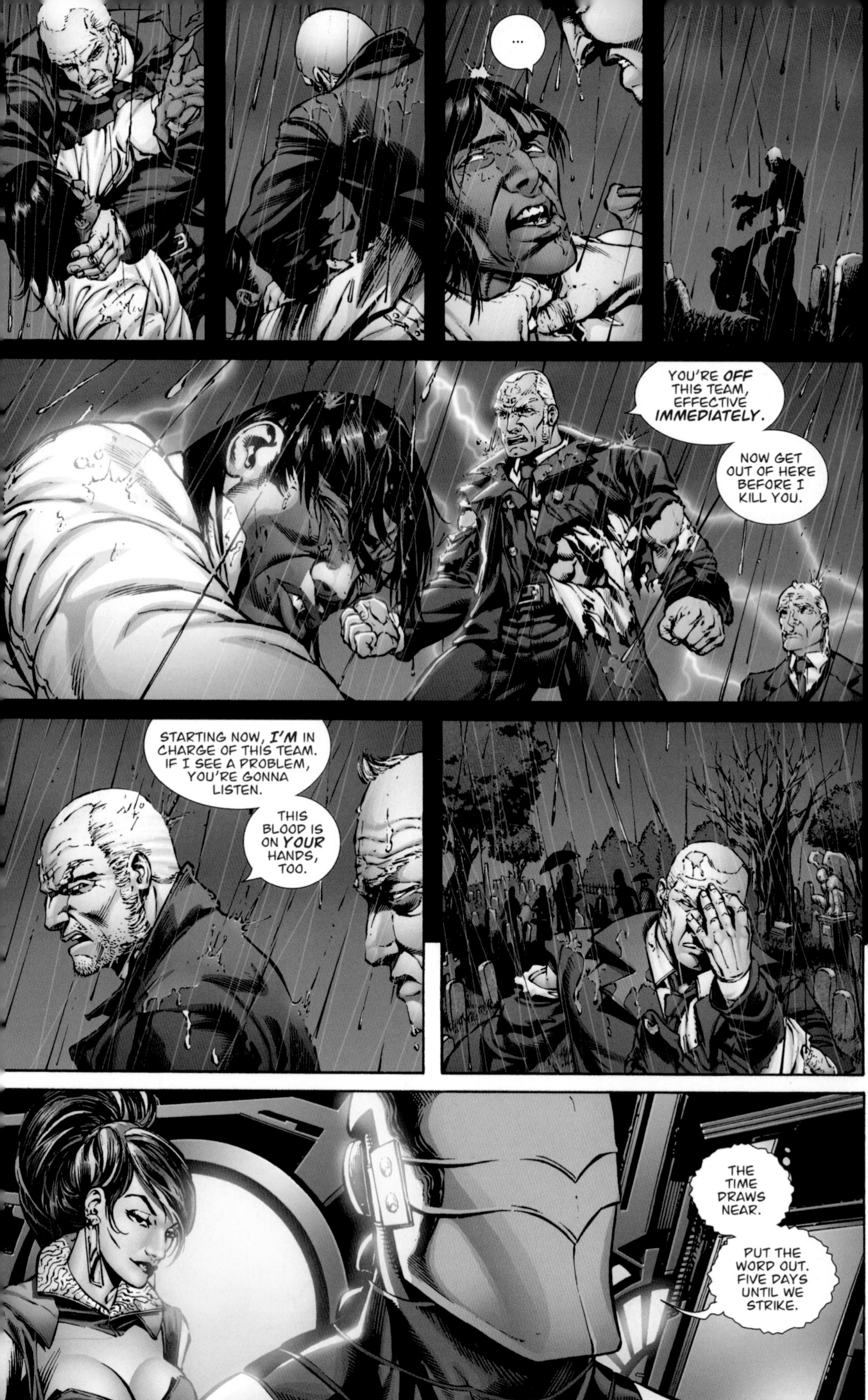
...
YOU'RE OFF THIS TEAM, EFFECTIVE IMMEDIATELY.
NOW GET OUT OF HERE BEFORE I KILL YOU.
STARTING NOW, I'M IN CHARGE OF THIS TEAM. IF I SEE A PROBLEM, YOU'RE GONNA LISTEN.
THIS BLOOD IS ON YOUR HANDS, TOO.
THE TIME DRAWS NEAR.
PUT THE WORD OUT. FIVE DAYS UNTIL WE STRIKE.

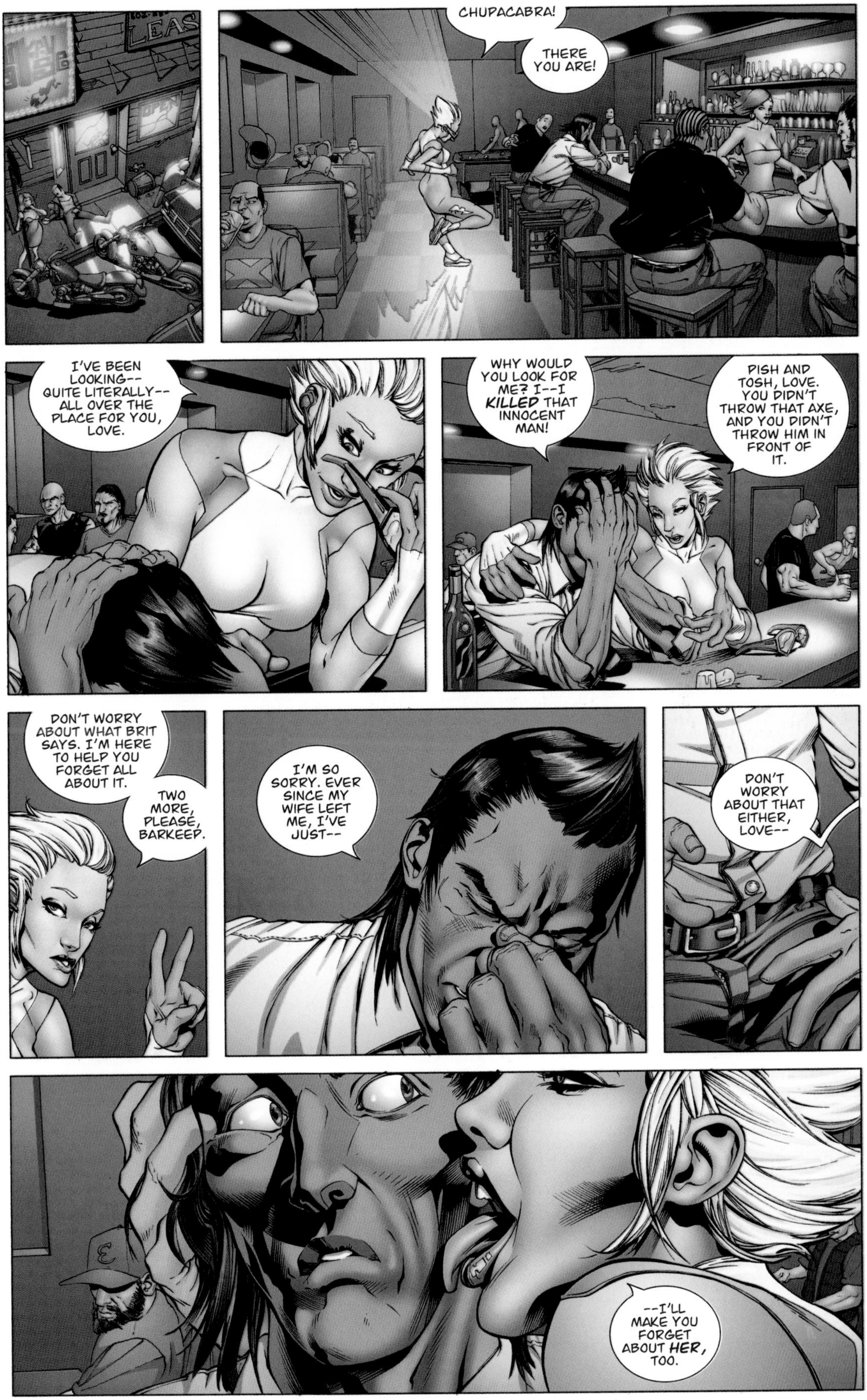

CHUPACABRA!
THERE YOU ARE!
I'VE BEEN LOOKING--QUITE LITERALLY--ALL OVER THE PLACE FOR YOU, LOVE.
WHY WOULD YOU LOOK FOR ME? I--I KILLED THAT INNOCENT MAN!
PISH AND TOSH, LOVE. YOU DIDN'T THROW THAT AXE, AND YOU DIDN'T THROW HIM IN FRONT OF IT.
DON'T WORRY ABOUT WHAT BRIT SAYS. I'M HERE TO HELP YOU FORGET ALL ABOUT IT.
TWO MORE, PLEASE, BARKEEP.
I'M SO SORRY. EVER SINCE MY WIFE LEFT ME, I'VE JUST--
DON'T WORRY ABOUT THAT EITHER, LOVE--
--I'LL MAKE YOU FORGET ABOUT HER, TOO.

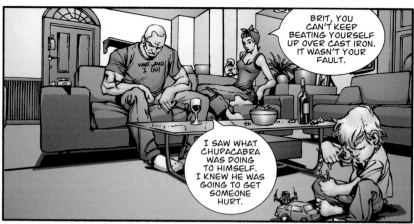

BRIT, YOU CAN'T KEEP BEATING YOURSELF UP OVER CAST IRON. IT WASN'T YOUR FAULT.

I SAW WHAT CHUPACABRA WAS DOING TO HIMSELF. I KNEW HE WAS GOING TO GET SOMEONE HURT.

IT WAS ON ME TO STOP HIM, AND I DIDN'T DO ENOUGH.

THAT BOY'S DEATH HAPPENED ON *MY* WATCH.

WELL, CAST IRON KNEW THE RISKS WHEN HE SIGNED UP WITH THE GUARDIANS, THAT'S ALL.

MORE WINE?

NO, I...

I THINK I'VE HAD ENOUGH.

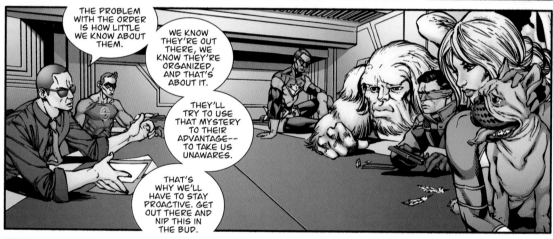

THE PROBLEM WITH THE ORDER IS HOW LITTLE WE KNOW ABOUT THEM.

WE KNOW THEY'RE OUT THERE, WE KNOW THEY'RE ORGANIZED, AND THAT'S ABOUT IT.

THEY'LL TRY TO USE THAT MYSTERY TO THEIR ADVANTAGE-- TO TAKE US UNAWARES.

THAT'S WHY WE'LL HAVE TO STAY PROACTIVE. GET OUT THERE AND NIP THIS IN THE BUD.

FIND ALL THE SUPER-CRIMINAL ACTIVITY YOU CAN, AND LOOK FOR SIGNS THAT IT'S RELATED TO THE ORDER.

GETTING INSIDE INFORMATION ON THIS ORGANIZATION IS THE ONLY WAY WE'RE GOING TO BE ABLE TO STOP THEM BEFORE THEY DO SOMETHING TRULY DEVASTATING.

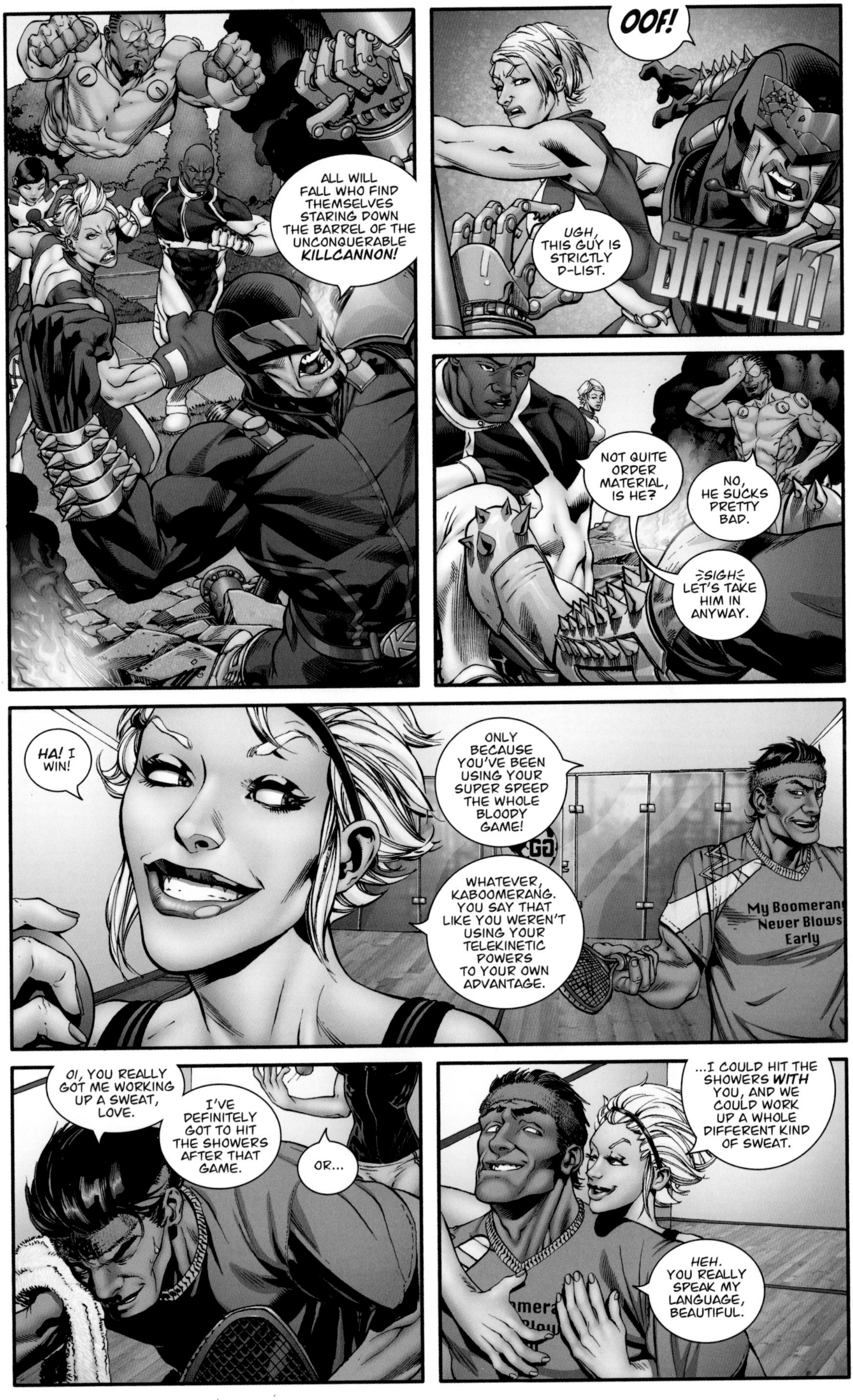
ALL WILL FALL WHO FIND THEMSELVES STARING DOWN THE BARREL OF THE UNCONQUERABLE KILLCANNON!
OOF!
UGH, THIS GUY IS STRICTLY D-LIST.
SMACK!
NOT QUITE ORDER MATERIAL, IS HE?
NO, HE SUCKS PRETTY BAD.
SIGH LET'S TAKE HIM IN ANYWAY.
HA! I WIN!
ONLY BECAUSE YOU'VE BEEN USING YOUR SUPER SPEED THE WHOLE BLOODY GAME!
WHATEVER, KABOOMERANG. YOU SAY THAT LIKE YOU WEREN'T USING YOUR TELEKINETIC POWERS TO YOUR OWN ADVANTAGE.
My Boomerang Never Blows Early
OI, YOU REALLY GOT ME WORKING UP A SWEAT, LOVE.
I'VE DEFINITELY GOT TO HIT THE SHOWERS AFTER THAT GAME.
OR...
...I COULD HIT THE SHOWERS WITH YOU, AND WE COULD WORK UP A WHOLE DIFFERENT KIND OF SWEAT.
HEH. YOU REALLY SPEAK MY LANGUAGE, BEAUTIFUL.

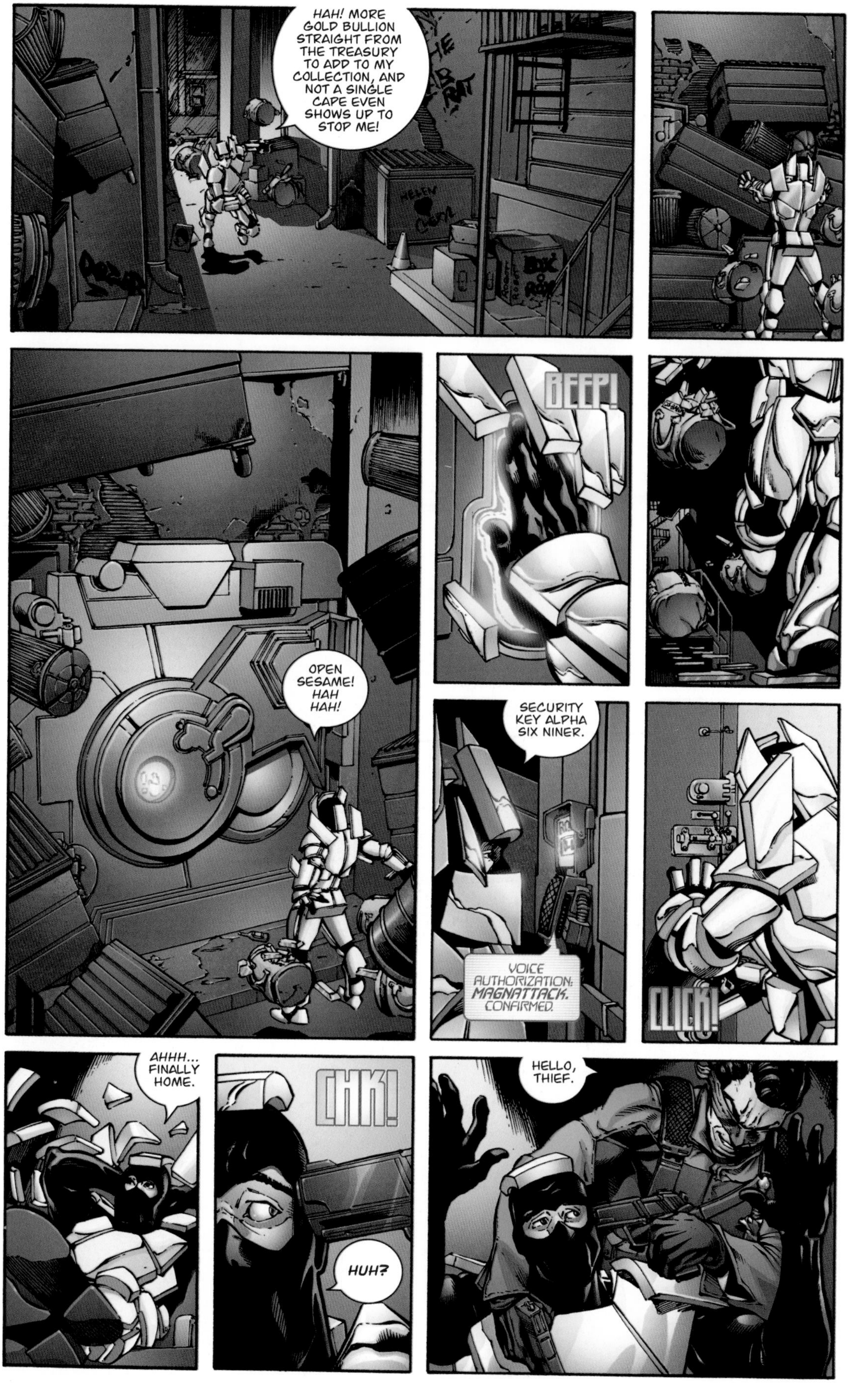
HAH! MORE GOLD BULLION STRAIGHT FROM THE TREASURY TO ADD TO MY COLLECTION, AND NOT A SINGLE CAPE EVEN SHOWS UP TO STOP ME!
OPEN SESAME! HAH HAH!
BEEP!
SECURITY KEY ALPHA SIX NINER.
VOICE AUTHORIZATION: MAGNATTACK. CONFIRMED.
CLICK!
AHHH... FINALLY HOME.
CHK!
HUH?
HELLO, THIEF.

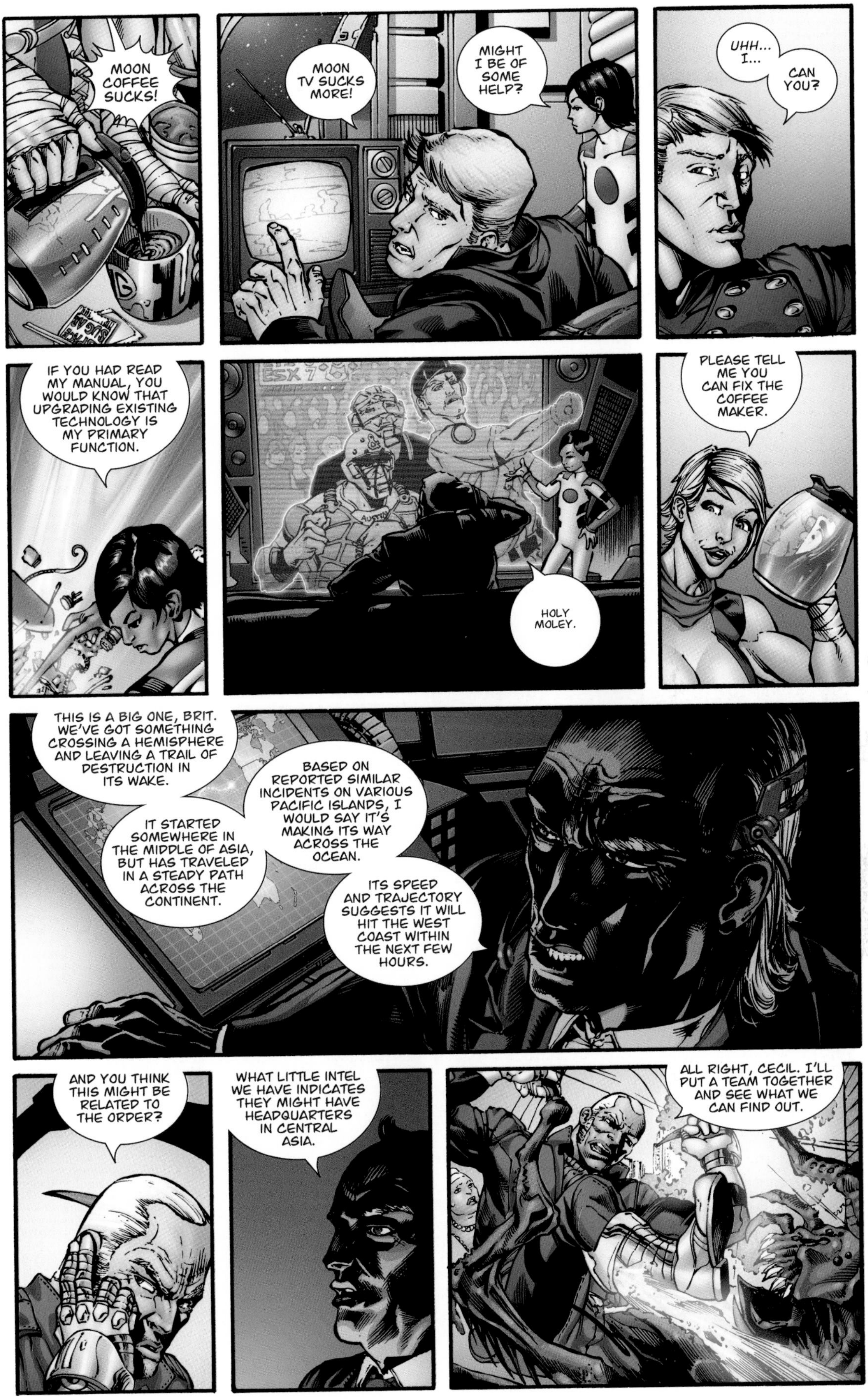
MOON COFFEE SUCKS!
MOON TV SUCKS MORE!
MIGHT I BE OF SOME HELP?
UHH... I...
CAN YOU?
IF YOU HAD READ MY MANUAL, YOU WOULD KNOW THAT UPGRADING EXISTING TECHNOLOGY IS MY PRIMARY FUNCTION.
HOLY MOLEY.
PLEASE TELL ME YOU CAN FIX THE COFFEE MAKER.
THIS IS A BIG ONE, BRIT. WE'VE GOT SOMETHING CROSSING A HEMISPHERE AND LEAVING A TRAIL OF DESTRUCTION IN ITS WAKE.
IT STARTED SOMEWHERE IN THE MIDDLE OF ASIA, BUT HAS TRAVELED IN A STEADY PATH ACROSS THE CONTINENT.
BASED ON REPORTED SIMILAR INCIDENTS ON VARIOUS PACIFIC ISLANDS, I WOULD SAY IT'S MAKING ITS WAY ACROSS THE OCEAN.
ITS SPEED AND TRAJECTORY SUGGESTS IT WILL HIT THE WEST COAST WITHIN THE NEXT FEW HOURS.
AND YOU THINK THIS MIGHT BE RELATED TO THE ORDER?
WHAT LITTLE INTEL WE HAVE INDICATES THEY MIGHT HAVE HEADQUARTERS IN CENTRAL ASIA.
ALL RIGHT, CECIL. I'LL PUT A TEAM TOGETHER AND SEE WHAT WE CAN FIND OUT.

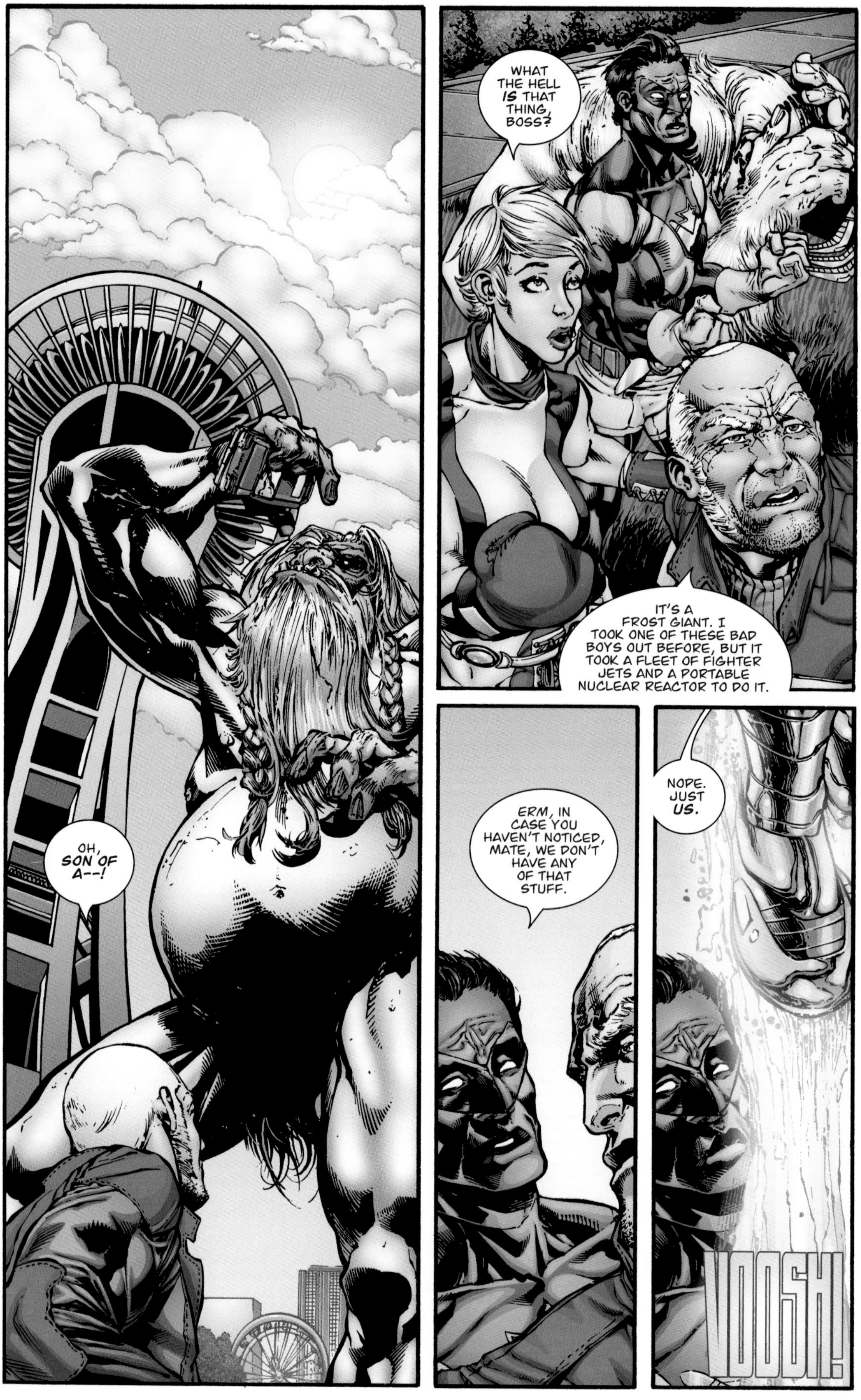
OH, SON OF A--!
WHAT THE HELL IS THAT THING, BOSS?
IT'S A FROST GIANT. I TOOK ONE OF THESE BAD BOYS OUT BEFORE, BUT IT TOOK A FLEET OF FIGHTER JETS AND A PORTABLE NUCLEAR REACTOR TO DO IT.
ERM, IN CASE YOU HAVEN'T NOTICED, MATE, WE DON'T HAVE ANY OF THAT STUFF.
NOPE. JUST US.
VOOSH!

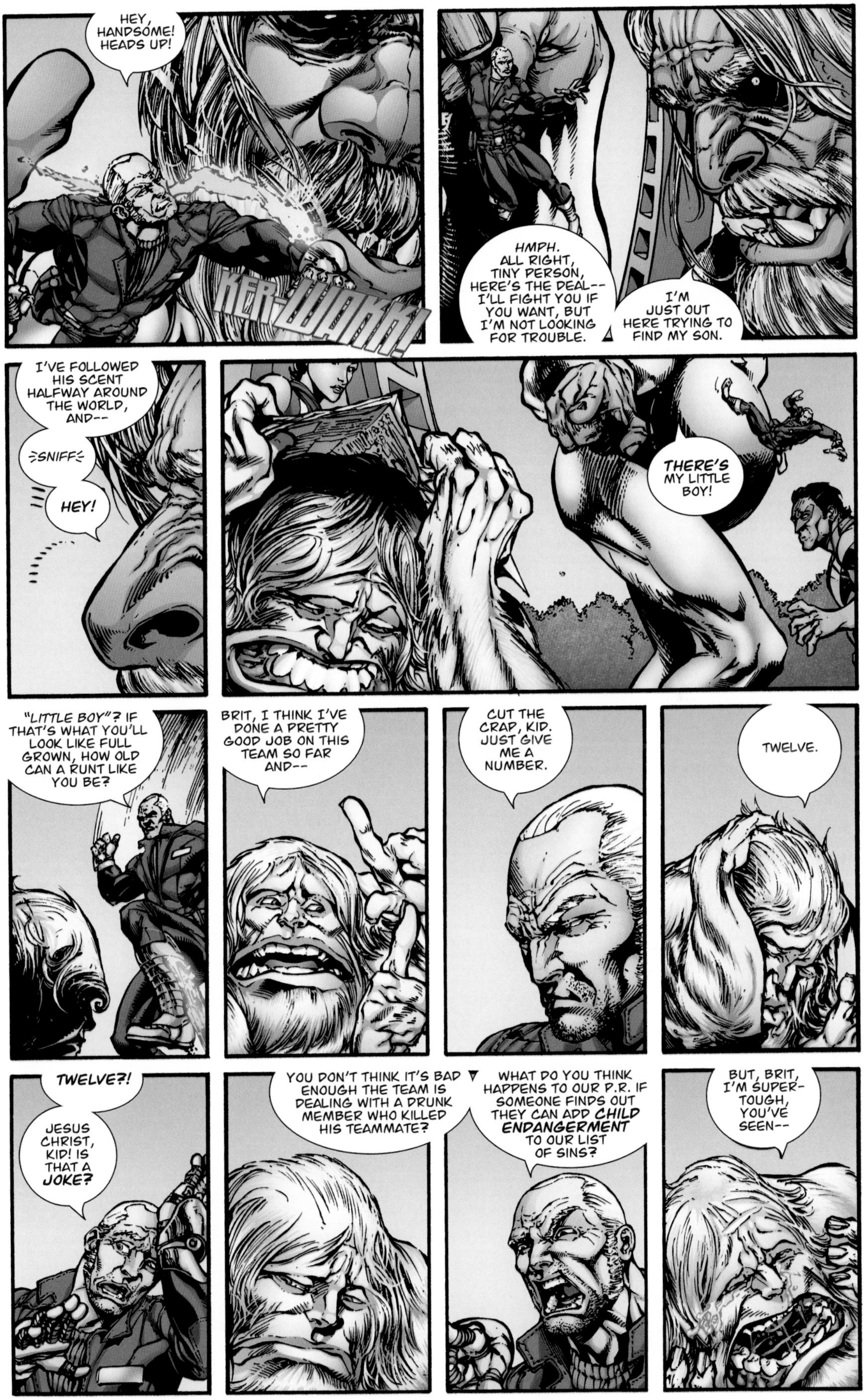
HEY, HANDSOME! HEADS UP!
KER-WOKK!
HMPH. ALL RIGHT, TINY PERSON, HERE'S THE DEAL-- I'LL FIGHT YOU IF YOU WANT, BUT I'M NOT LOOKING FOR TROUBLE.
I'M JUST OUT HERE TRYING TO FIND MY SON.
I'VE FOLLOWED HIS SCENT HALFWAY AROUND THE WORLD, AND--
SNIFF
HEY!
THERE'S MY LITTLE BOY!
"LITTLE BOY"? IF THAT'S WHAT YOU'LL LOOK LIKE FULL GROWN, HOW OLD CAN A RUNT LIKE YOU BE?
BRIT, I THINK I'VE DONE A PRETTY GOOD JOB ON THIS TEAM SO FAR AND--
CUT THE CRAP, KID. JUST GIVE ME A NUMBER.
TWELVE.
TWELVE?!
JESUS CHRIST, KID! IS THAT A JOKE?
YOU DON'T THINK IT'S BAD ENOUGH THE TEAM IS DEALING WITH A DRUNK MEMBER WHO KILLED HIS TEAMMATE?
WHAT DO YOU THINK HAPPENS TO OUR P.R. IF SOMEONE FINDS OUT THEY CAN ADD CHILD ENDANGERMENT TO OUR LIST OF SINS?
BUT, BRIT, I'M SUPER-TOUGH, YOU'VE SEEN--

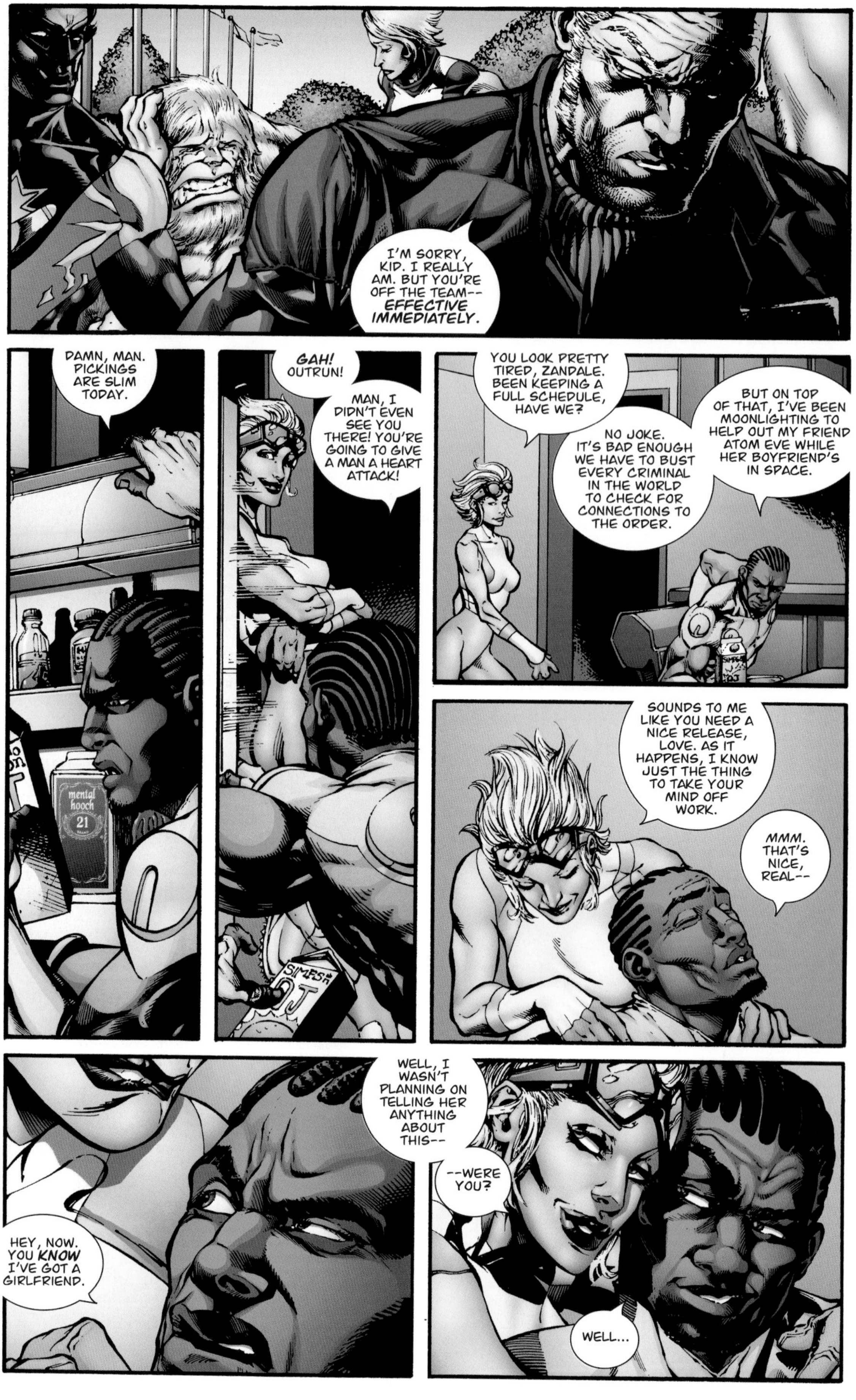
I'M SORRY, KID. I REALLY AM. BUT YOU'RE OFF THE TEAM-- *EFFECTIVE IMMEDIATELY*.
DAMN, MAN. PICKINGS ARE SLIM TODAY.
GAH! OUTRUN!
MAN, I DIDN'T EVEN SEE YOU THERE! YOU'RE GOING TO GIVE A MAN A HEART ATTACK!
YOU LOOK PRETTY TIRED, ZANDALE. BEEN KEEPING A FULL SCHEDULE, HAVE WE?
NO JOKE. IT'S BAD ENOUGH WE HAVE TO BUST EVERY CRIMINAL IN THE WORLD TO CHECK FOR CONNECTIONS TO THE ORDER.
BUT ON TOP OF THAT, I'VE BEEN MOONLIGHTING TO HELP OUT MY FRIEND ATOM EVE WHILE HER BOYFRIEND'S IN SPACE.
SOUNDS TO ME LIKE YOU NEED A NICE RELEASE, LOVE. AS IT HAPPENS, I KNOW JUST THE THING TO TAKE YOUR MIND OFF WORK.
MMM. THAT'S NICE, REAL--
HEY, NOW. YOU *KNOW* I'VE GOT A GIRLFRIEND.
WELL, I WASN'T PLANNING ON TELLING HER ANYTHING ABOUT THIS--
--WERE YOU?
WELL...

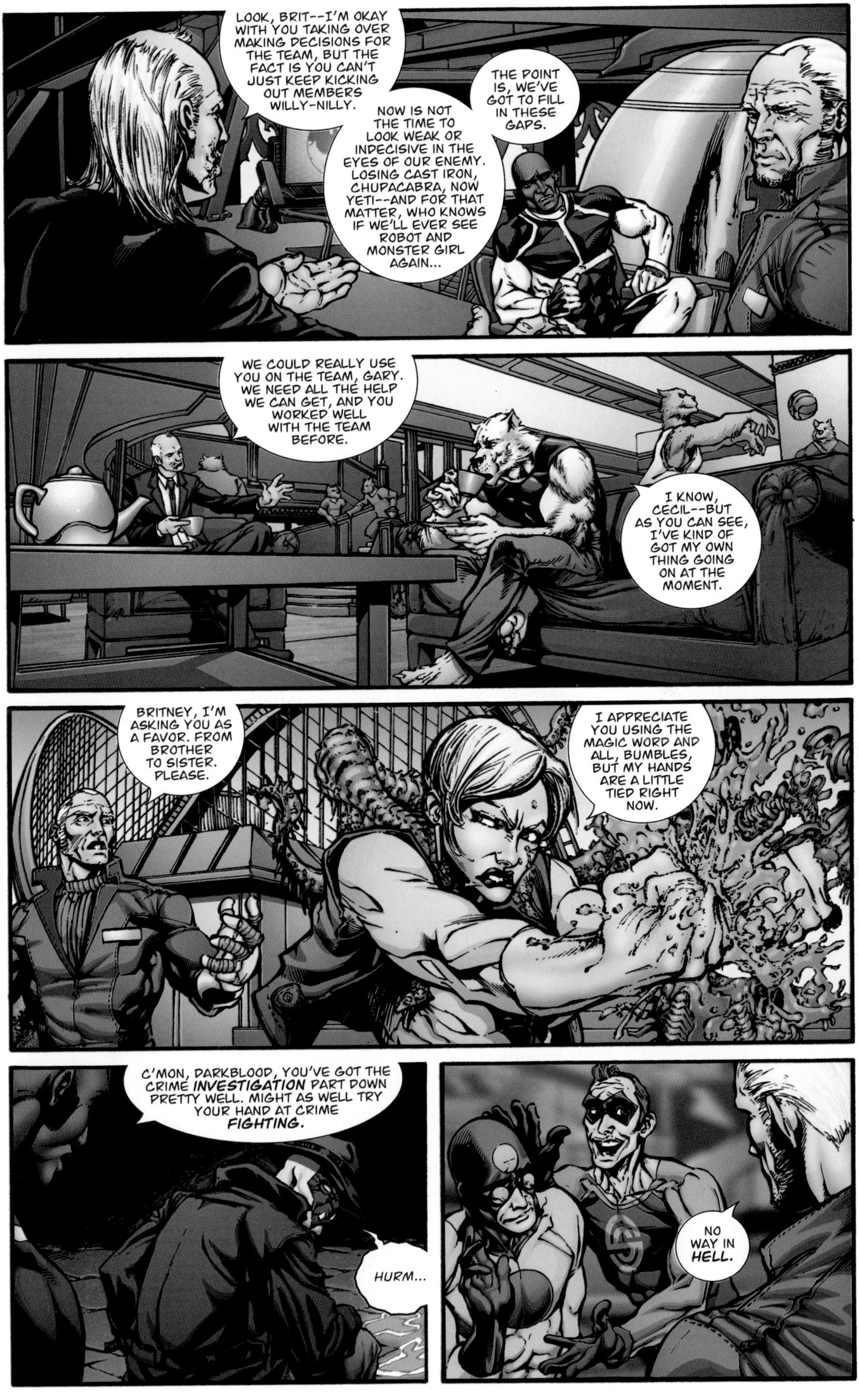
LOOK, BRIT--I'M OKAY WITH YOU TAKING OVER MAKING DECISIONS FOR THE TEAM, BUT THE FACT IS YOU CAN'T JUST KEEP KICKING OUT MEMBERS WILLY-NILLY.
NOW IS NOT THE TIME TO LOOK WEAK OR INDECISIVE IN THE EYES OF OUR ENEMY. LOSING CAST IRON, CHUPACABRA, NOW YETI--AND FOR THAT MATTER, WHO KNOWS IF WE'LL EVER SEE ROBOT AND MONSTER GIRL AGAIN...
THE POINT IS, WE'VE GOT TO FILL IN THESE GAPS.
WE COULD REALLY USE YOU ON THE TEAM, GARY. WE NEED ALL THE HELP WE CAN GET, AND YOU WORKED WELL WITH THE TEAM BEFORE.
I KNOW, CECIL--BUT AS YOU CAN SEE, I'VE KIND OF GOT MY OWN THING GOING ON AT THE MOMENT.
BRITNEY, I'M ASKING YOU AS A FAVOR. FROM BROTHER TO SISTER. PLEASE.
I APPRECIATE YOU USING THE MAGIC WORD AND ALL, BUMBLES, BUT MY HANDS ARE A LITTLE TIED RIGHT NOW.
C'MON, DARKBLOOD, YOU'VE GOT THE CRIME INVESTIGATION PART DOWN PRETTY WELL. MIGHT AS WELL TRY YOUR HAND AT CRIME FIGHTING.
HURM...
NO WAY IN HELL.

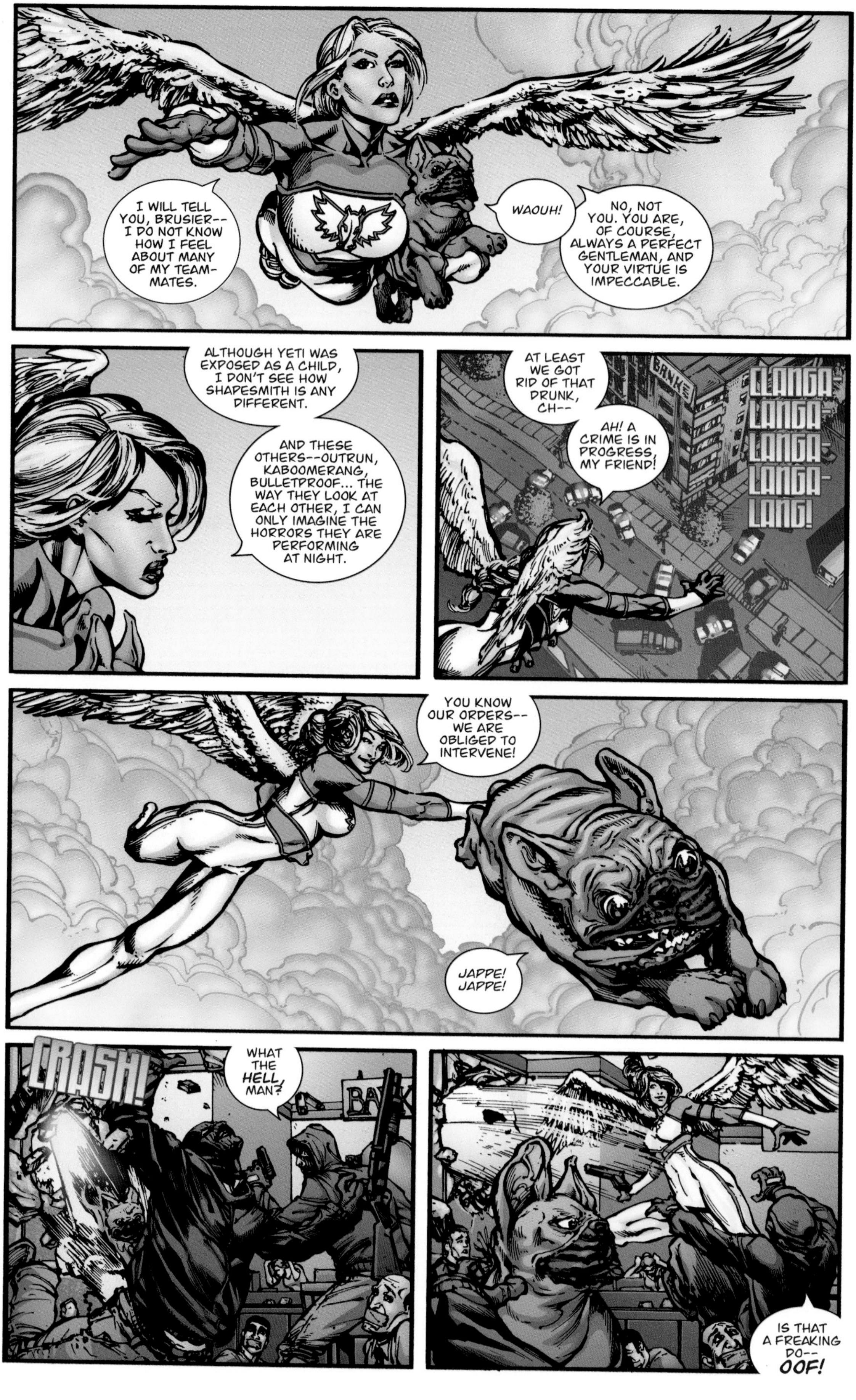

I WILL TELL YOU, BRUSIER-- I DO NOT KNOW HOW I FEEL ABOUT MANY OF MY TEAM-MATES.
WAOUH!
NO, NOT YOU. YOU ARE, OF COURSE, ALWAYS A PERFECT GENTLEMAN, AND YOUR VIRTUE IS IMPECCABLE.
ALTHOUGH YETI WAS EXPOSED AS A CHILD, I DON'T SEE HOW SHAPESMITH IS ANY DIFFERENT.
AND THESE OTHERS--OUTRUN, KABOOMERANG, BULLETPROOF... THE WAY THEY LOOK AT EACH OTHER, I CAN ONLY IMAGINE THE HORRORS THEY ARE PERFORMING AT NIGHT.
AT LEAST WE GOT RID OF THAT DRUNK, CH--
BANK
CLANGA-LANGA-LANGA-LANGA-LANG!
AH! A CRIME IS IN PROGRESS, MY FRIEND!
YOU KNOW OUR ORDERS-- WE ARE OBLIGED TO INTERVENE!
JAPPE! JAPPE!
CRASH!
WHAT THE HELL, MAN?
BANK
IS THAT A FREAKING DO-- OOF!

NOW, TELL ME, GENTLEMEN-- DO EITHER OF YOU WORK FOR THE ORDER?

LADY, I GOT NO IDEA WHAT THAT EVEN MEANS.

THEY ARE ALL YOURS, OFFICER. TAKE THEM AWAY.

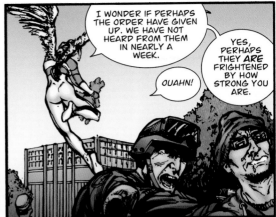

I WONDER IF PERHAPS THE ORDER HAVE GIVEN UP. WE HAVE NOT HEARD FROM THEM IN NEARLY A WEEK.

OUAHN!

YES, PERHAPS THEY ARE FRIGHTENED BY HOW STRONG YOU ARE.

HELLO, SHAPESMITH. ARE WE THE ONLY ONES STILL IN THE BASE?

I DUNNO. I GUESS SO.

SO, WHAT ARE YOU DOING THERE? SOMETHING IMPORTANT?

YEAH. PLAYING SOME VIDEO GAMES.

WHAT ARE YOUR PLANS FOR AFTER THE GAME?

I WAS THINKING ABOUT EATING CANDY UNTIL A CRIME HAPPENS.

I HEARD A RUMOR YOU LIKE LOOKING AT HUMAN FEMALE BODY PARTS. WOULD YOU LIKE TO SEE SOME?

I MEAN, I GUESS I COULD PAUSE MY GAME FOR A FEW MINUTES...

IS IT TRUE THAT YOU CAN TURN YOUR BODY INTO ANY SHAPE, LOVE?

YEAH, PRETTY MUCH.

UH... WHAT DOES THAT HAVE TO DO WITH ANYTHING?

SOMETHING'S HAPPENING IN PARIS!

BRING IT UP ON SCREEN!

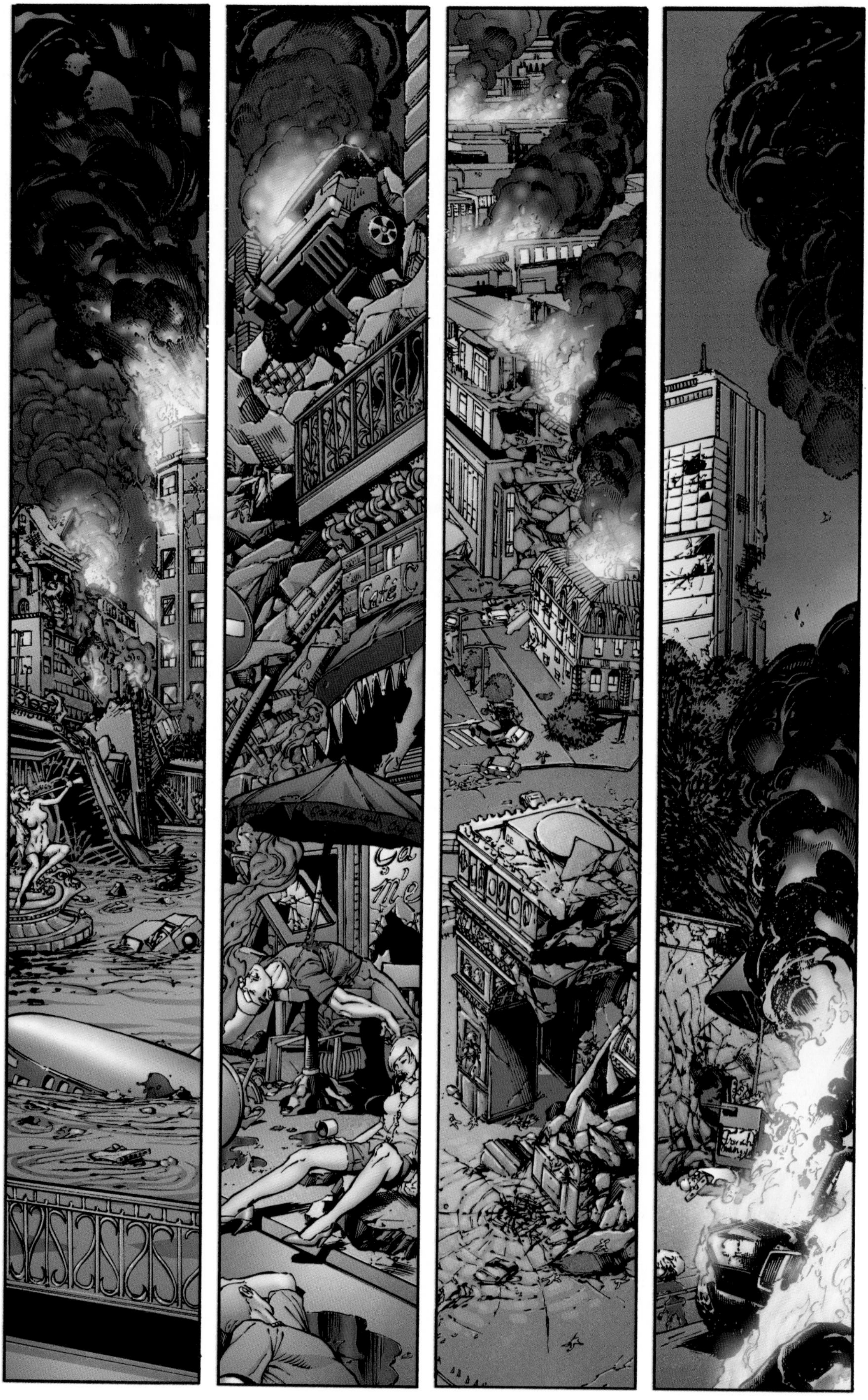
Café C

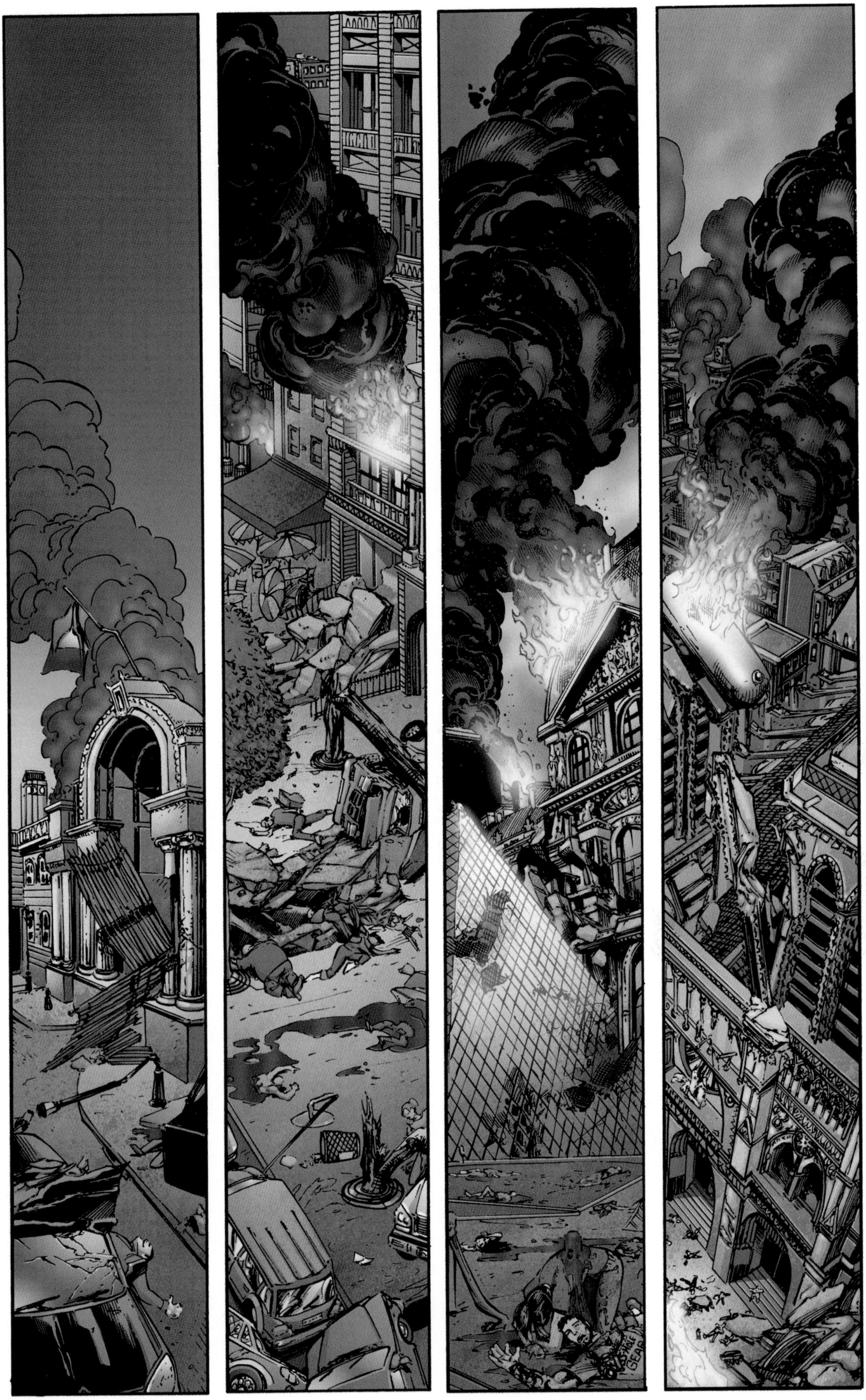

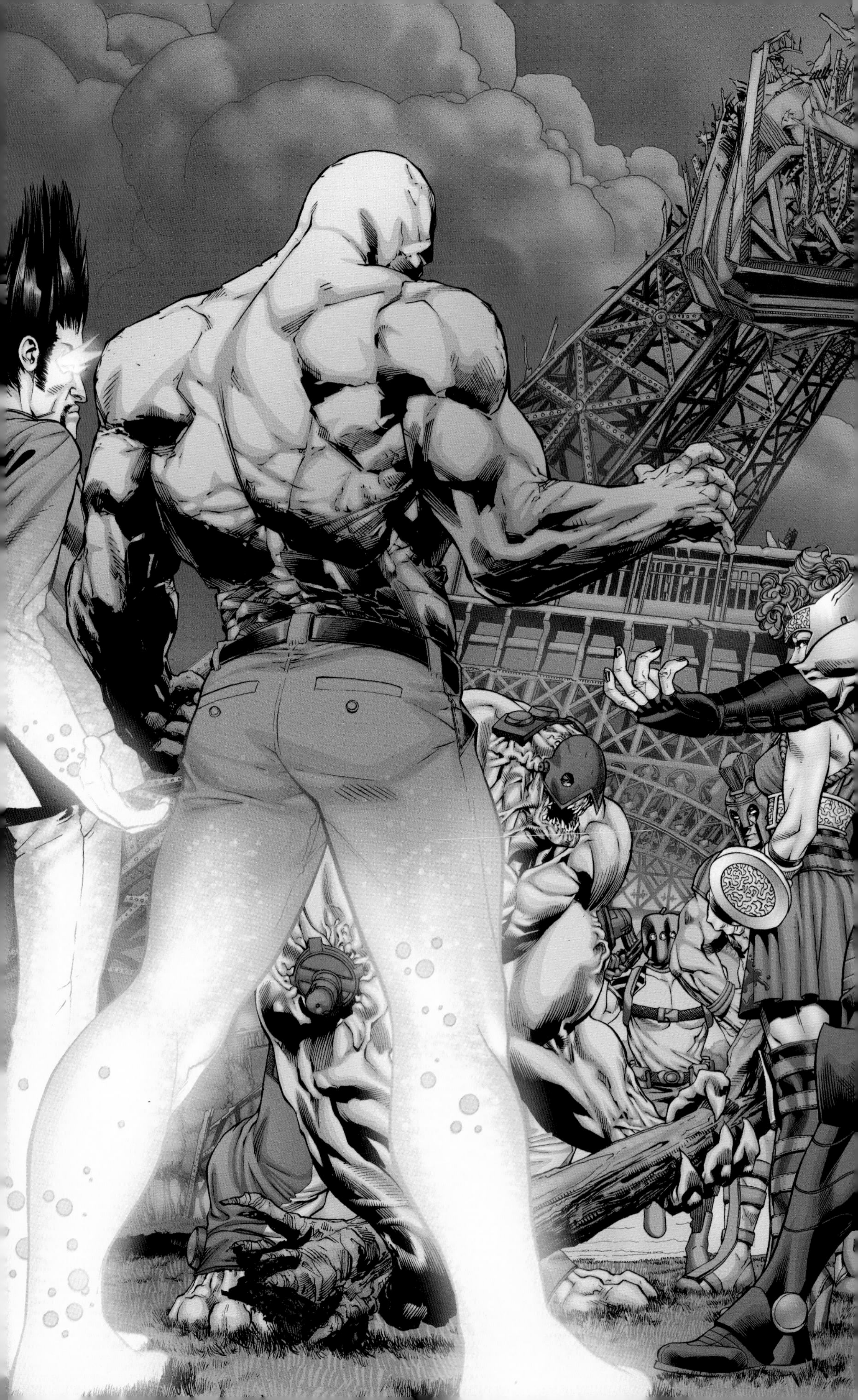

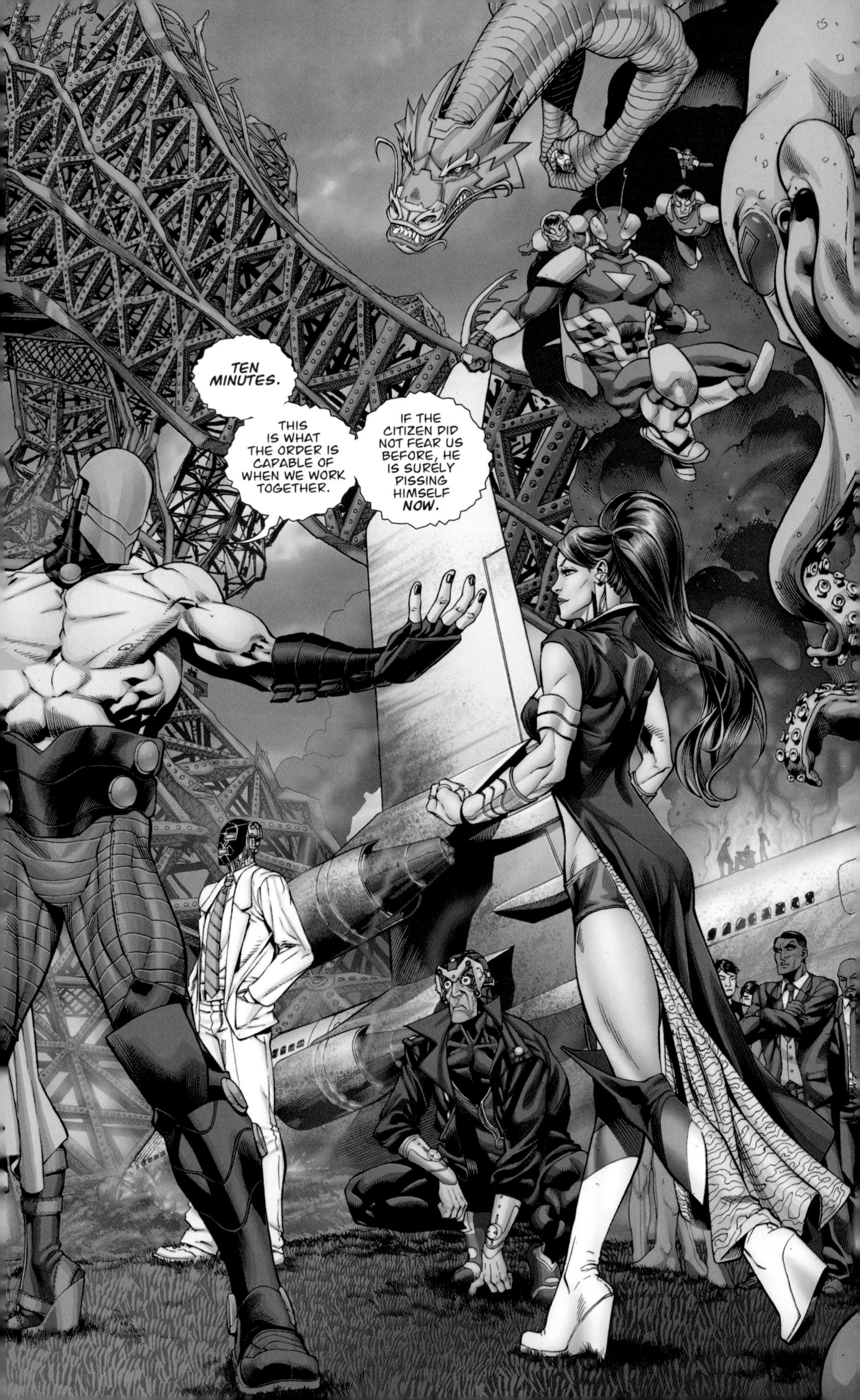
TEN MINUTES.
THIS IS WHAT THE ORDER IS CAPABLE OF WHEN WE WORK TOGETHER.
IF THE CITIZEN DID NOT FEAR US BEFORE, HE IS SURELY PISSING HIMSELF NOW.

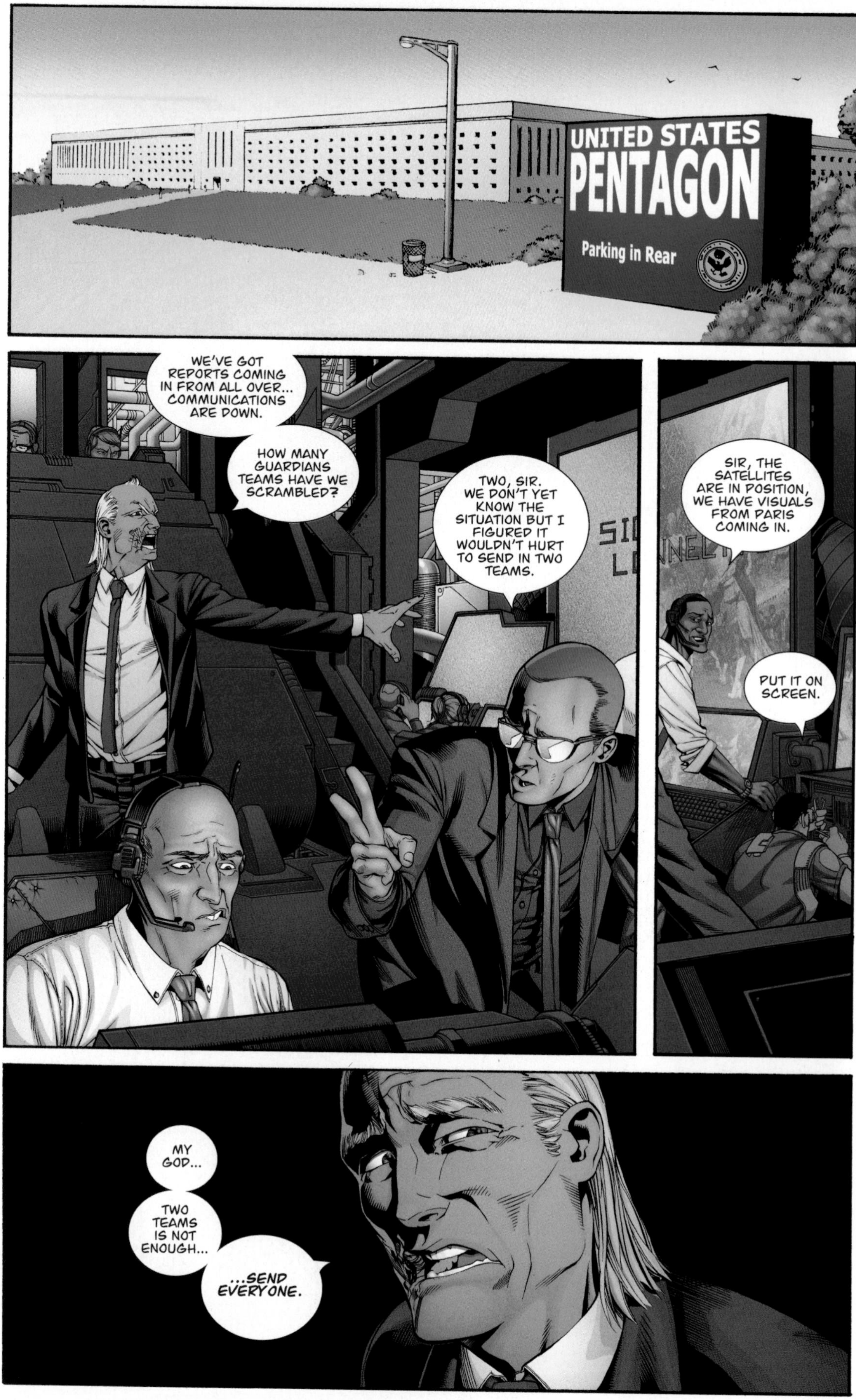
UNITED STATES
PENTAGON
Parking in Rear
WE'VE GOT REPORTS COMING IN FROM ALL OVER... COMMUNICATIONS ARE DOWN.
HOW MANY GUARDIANS TEAMS HAVE WE SCRAMBLED?
TWO, SIR. WE DON'T YET KNOW THE SITUATION BUT I FIGURED IT WOULDN'T HURT TO SEND IN TWO TEAMS.
SIR, THE SATELLITES ARE IN POSITION, WE HAVE VISUALS FROM PARIS COMING IN.
PUT IT ON SCREEN.
MY GOD...
TWO TEAMS IS NOT ENOUGH...
...SEND EVERYONE.

CHAPTER SIX

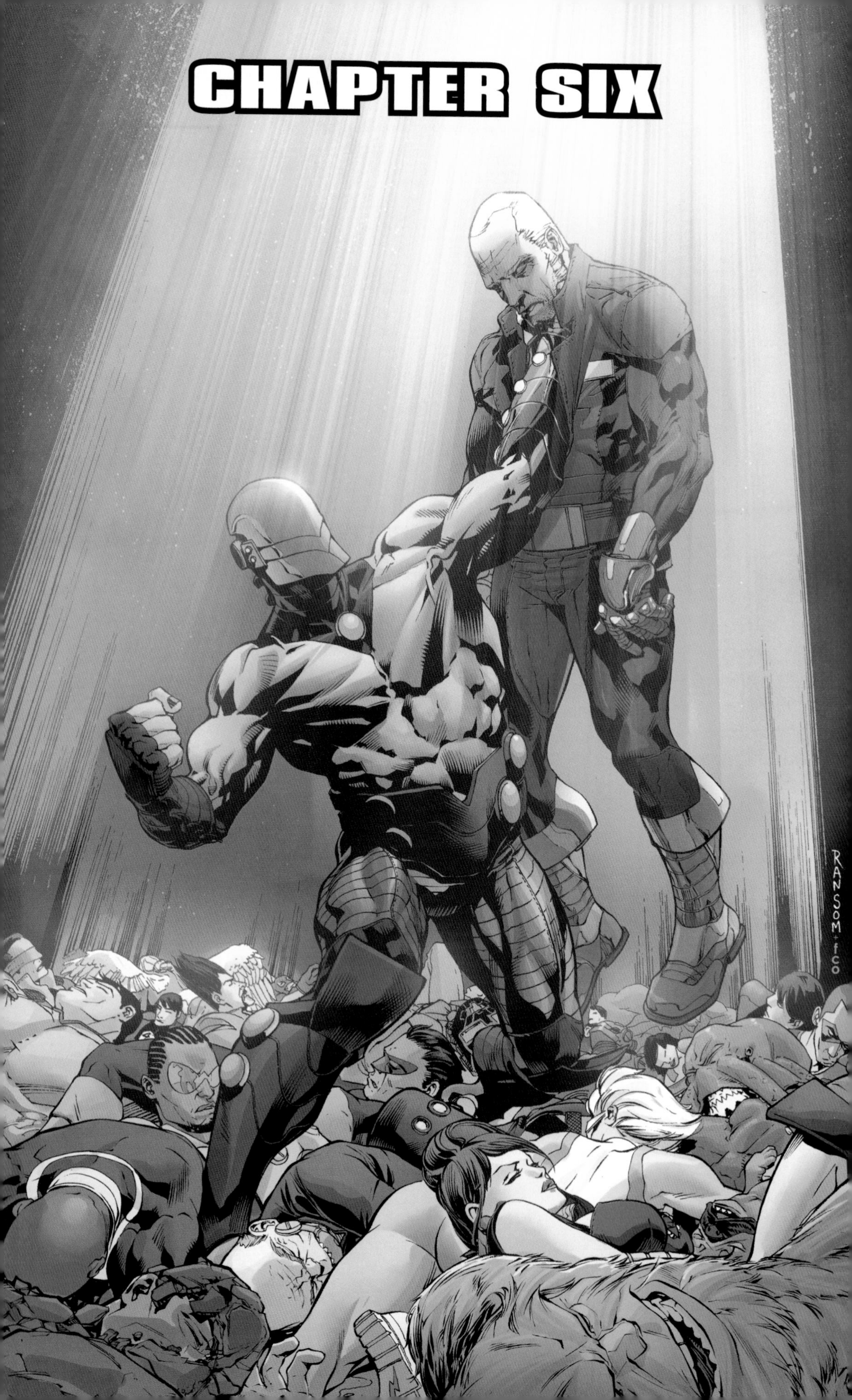
RANSOM+ICO

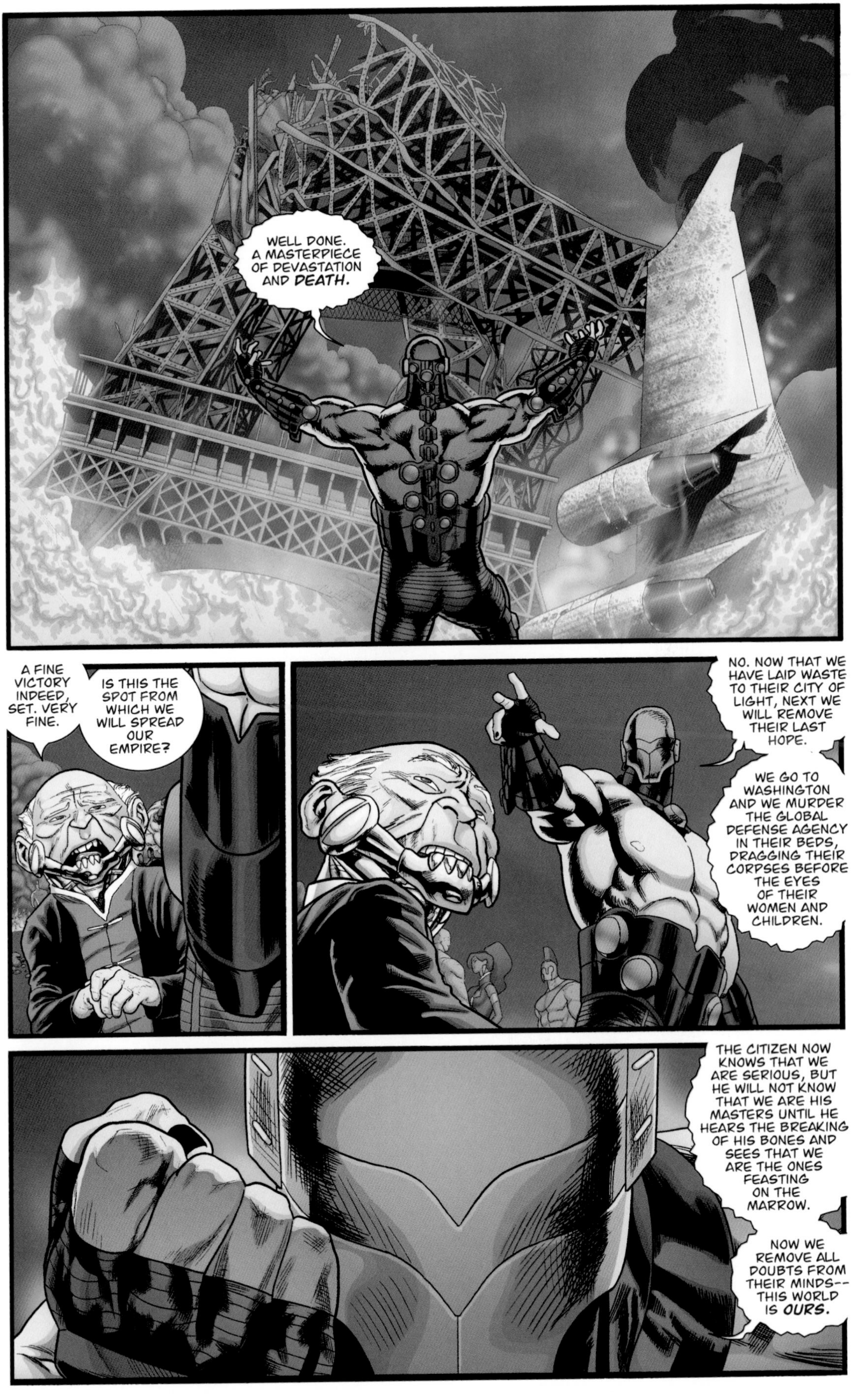
WELL DONE. A MASTERPIECE OF DEVASTATION AND DEATH.
A FINE VICTORY INDEED, SET. VERY FINE.
IS THIS THE SPOT FROM WHICH WE WILL SPREAD OUR EMPIRE?
NO. NOW THAT WE HAVE LAID WASTE TO THEIR CITY OF LIGHT, NEXT WE WILL REMOVE THEIR LAST HOPE.
WE GO TO WASHINGTON AND WE MURDER THE GLOBAL DEFENSE AGENCY IN THEIR BEDS, DRAGGING THEIR CORPSES BEFORE THE EYES OF THEIR WOMEN AND CHILDREN.
THE CITIZEN NOW KNOWS THAT WE ARE SERIOUS, BUT HE WILL NOT KNOW THAT WE ARE HIS MASTERS UNTIL HE HEARS THE BREAKING OF HIS BONES AND SEES THAT WE ARE THE ONES FEASTING ON THE MARROW.
NOW WE REMOVE ALL DOUBTS FROM THEIR MINDS-- THIS WORLD IS OURS.

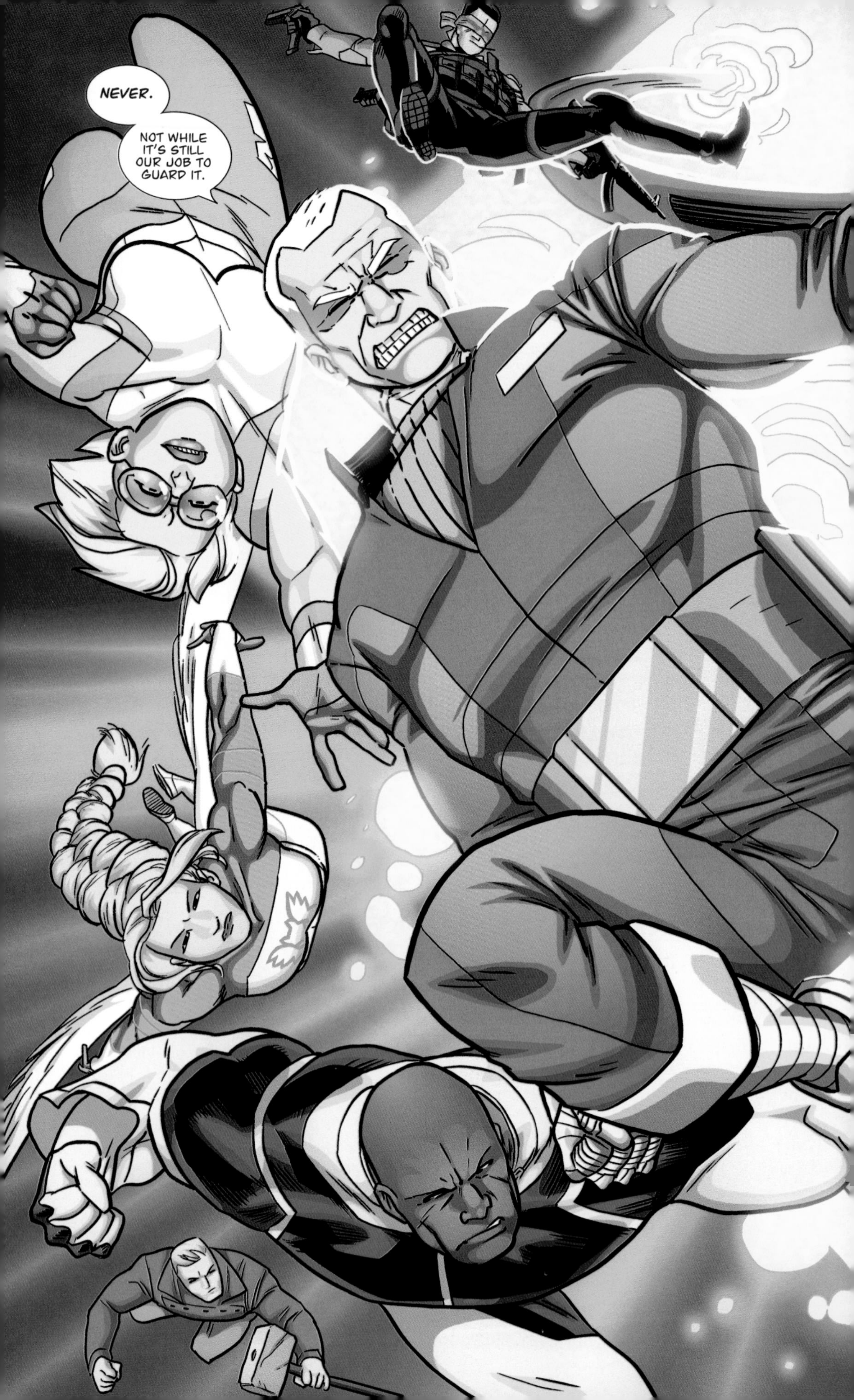
NEVER.
NOT WHILE IT'S STILL OUR JOB TO GUARD IT.

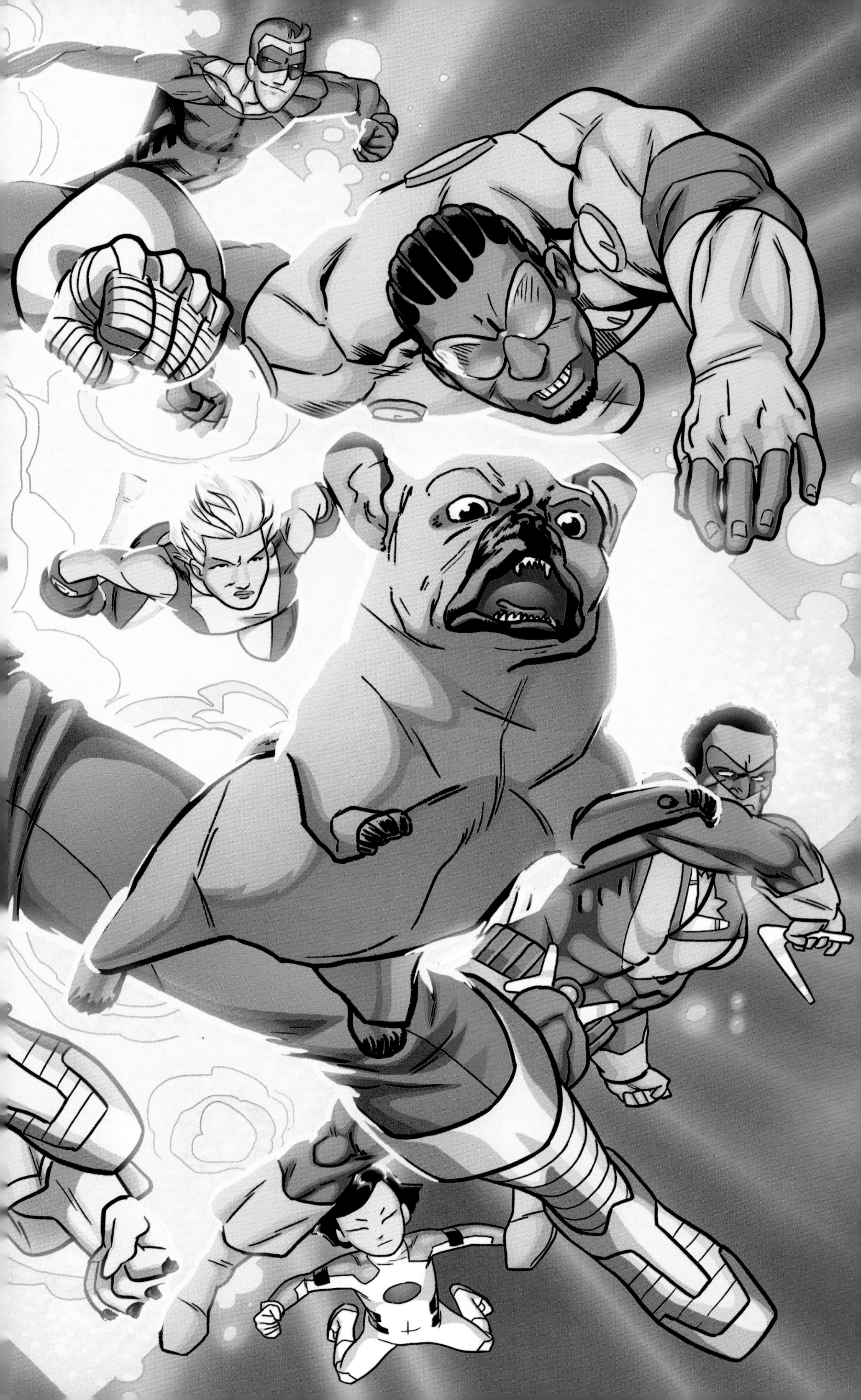

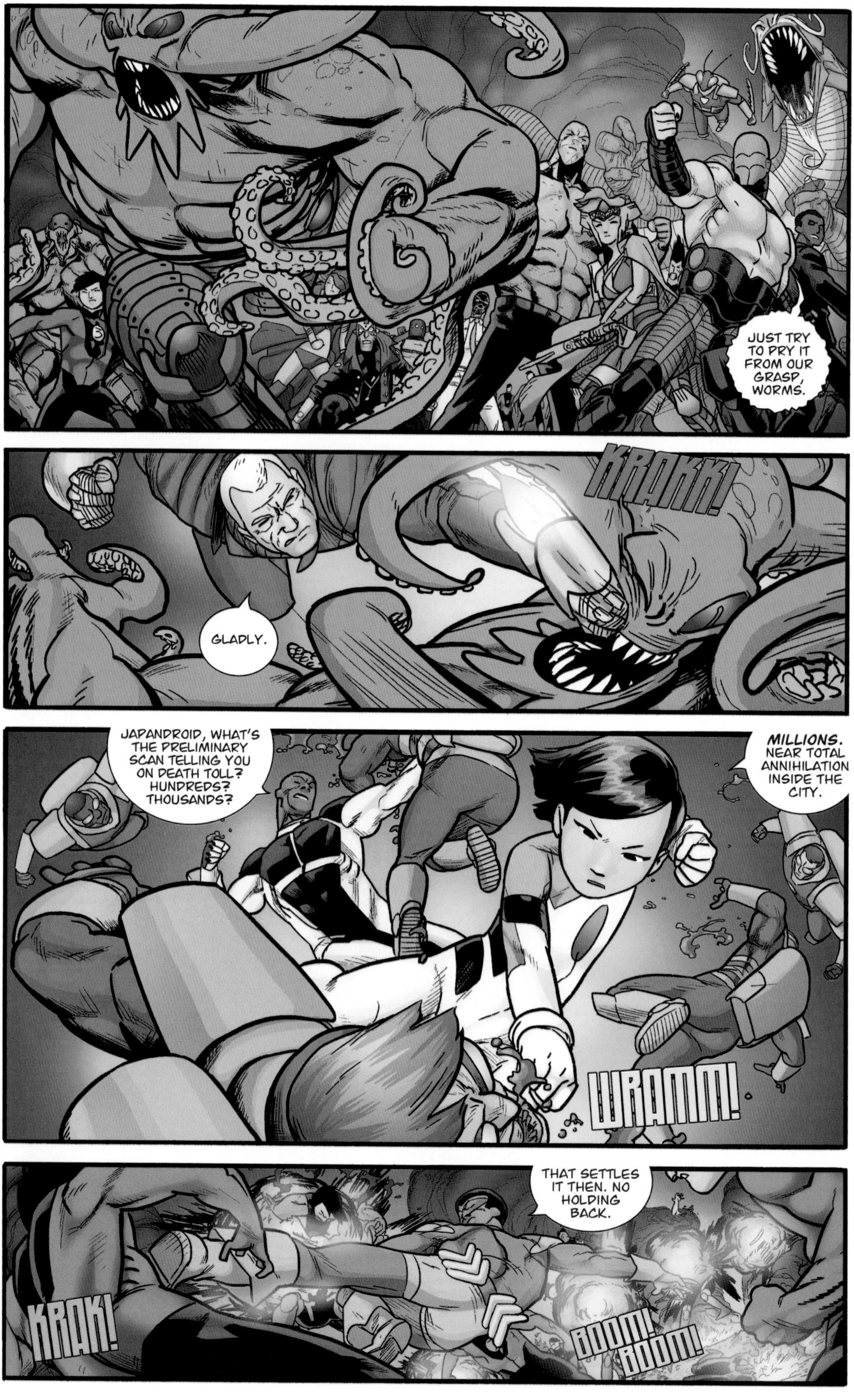
JUST TRY TO PRY IT FROM OUR GRASP, WORMS.
KRAKK!
GLADLY.
JAPANDROID, WHAT'S THE PRELIMINARY SCAN TELLING YOU ON DEATH TOLL? HUNDREDS? THOUSANDS?
MILLIONS. NEAR TOTAL ANNIHILATION INSIDE THE CITY.
WRAMM!
THAT SETTLES IT THEN. NO HOLDING BACK.
KRAK!
BOOM! BOOM!

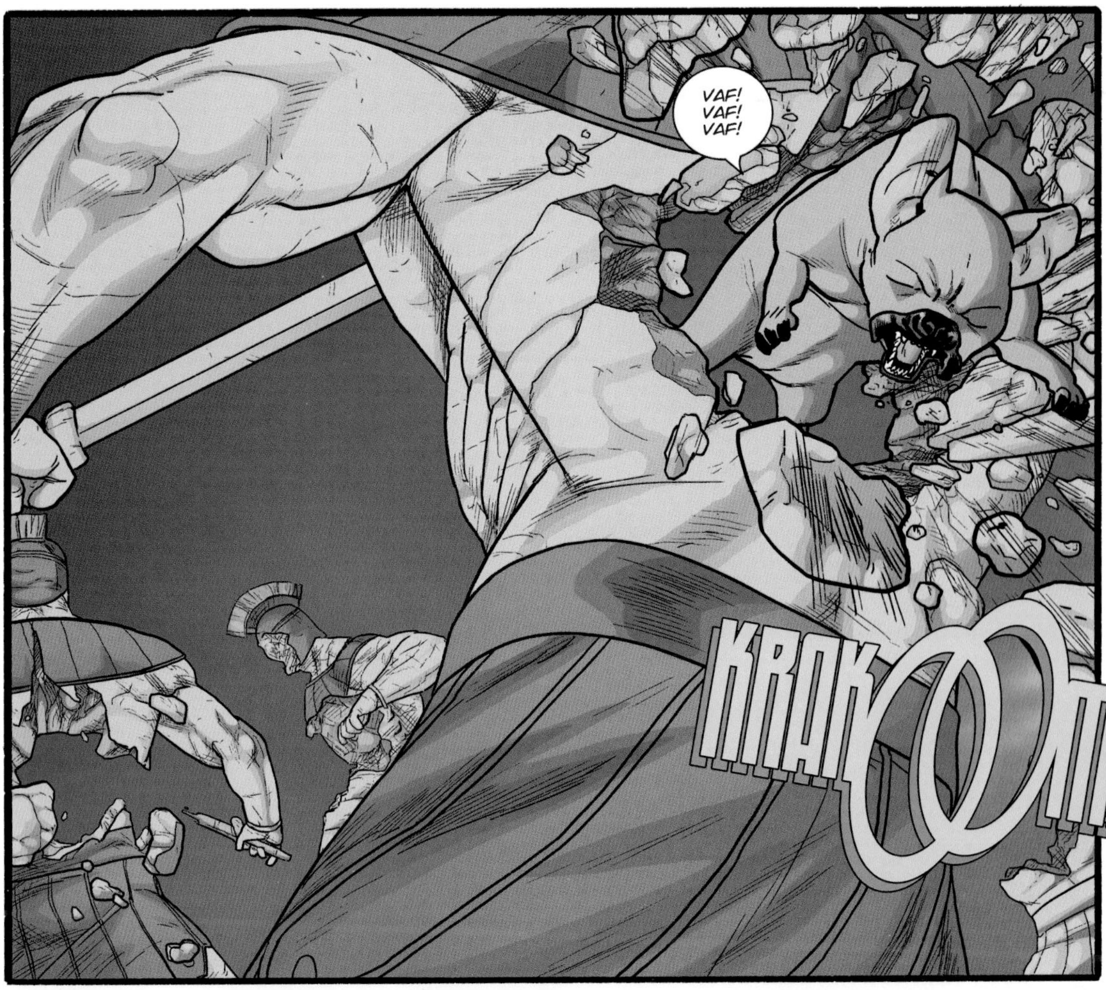
VAF! VAF! VAF!
KRAKOOM!

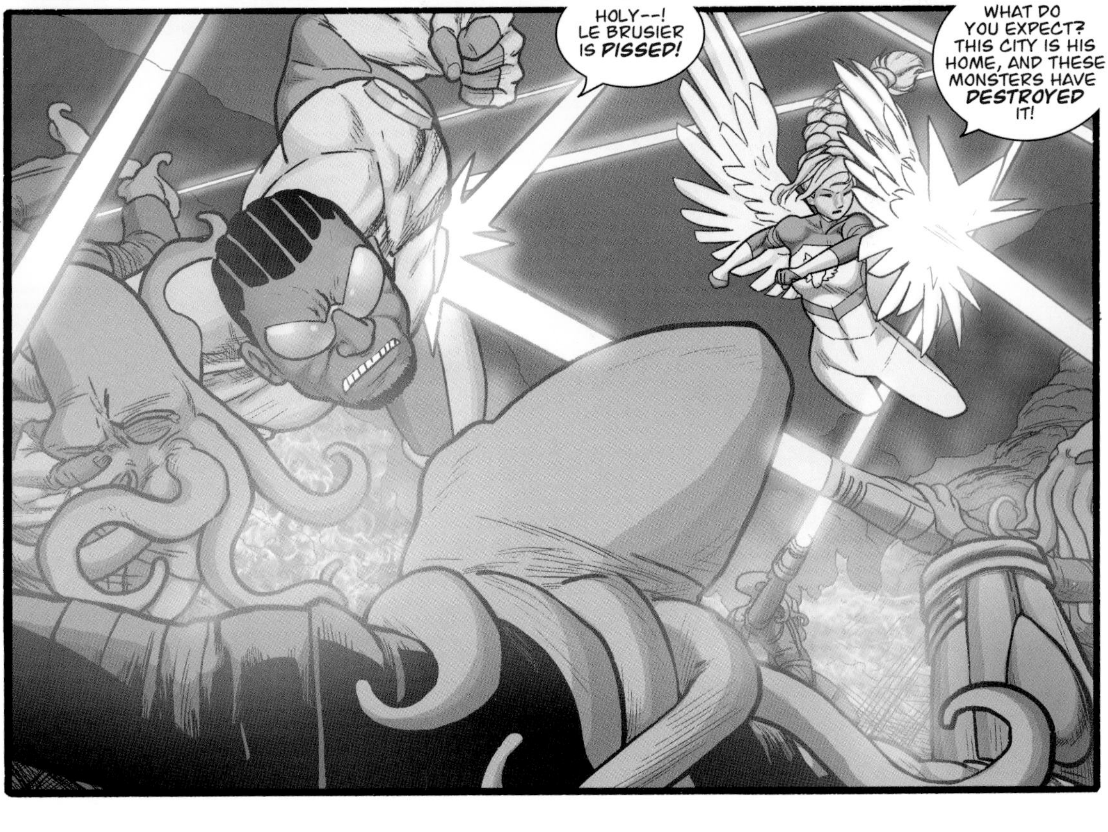
HOLY--! LE BRUSIER IS PISSED!
WHAT DO YOU EXPECT? THIS CITY IS HIS HOME, AND THESE MONSTERS HAVE DESTROYED IT!

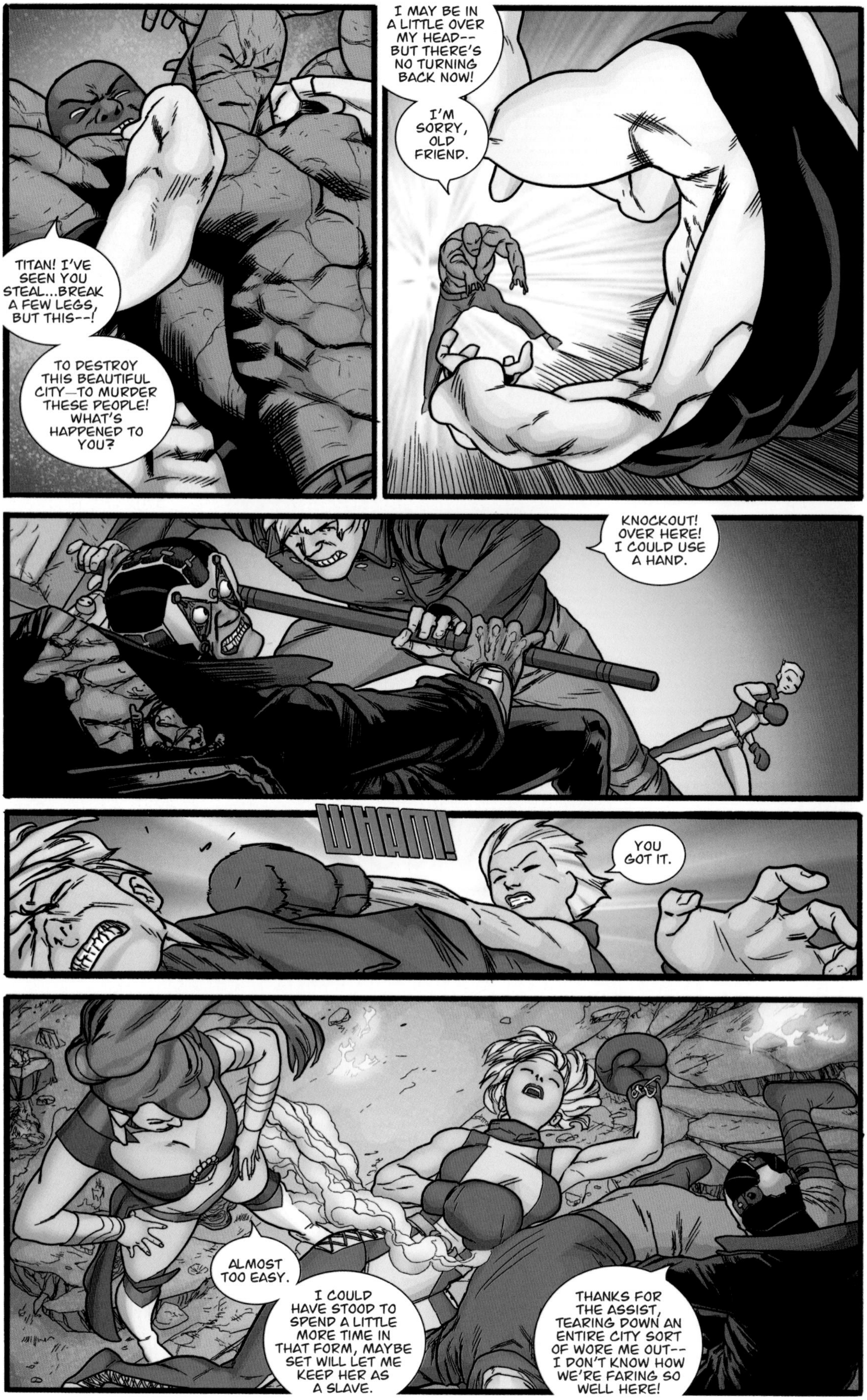
TITAN! I'VE SEEN YOU STEAL...BREAK A FEW LEGS, BUT THIS--!
TO DESTROY THIS BEAUTIFUL CITY—TO MURDER THESE PEOPLE! WHAT'S HAPPENED TO YOU?
I MAY BE IN A LITTLE OVER MY HEAD-- BUT THERE'S NO TURNING BACK NOW!
I'M SORRY, OLD FRIEND.
KNOCKOUT! OVER HERE! I COULD USE A HAND.
WHAM!
YOU GOT IT.
ALMOST TOO EASY.
I COULD HAVE STOOD TO SPEND A LITTLE MORE TIME IN THAT FORM, MAYBE SET WILL LET ME KEEP HER AS A SLAVE.
THANKS FOR THE ASSIST, TEARING DOWN AN ENTIRE CITY SORT OF WORE ME OUT-- I DON'T KNOW HOW WE'RE FARING SO WELL HERE!

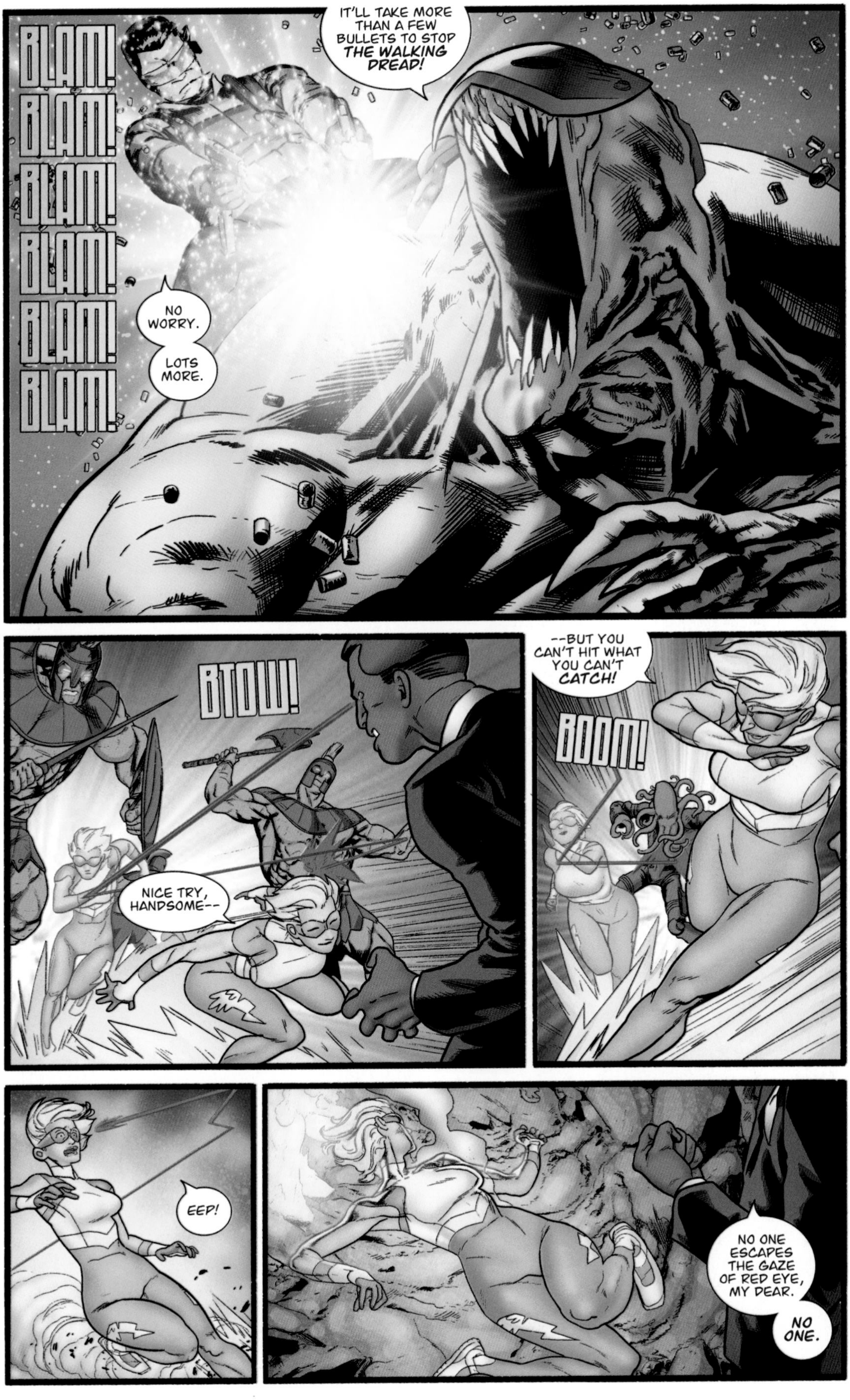
BLAM! BLAM! BLAM! BLAM! BLAM! BLAM!
IT'LL TAKE MORE THAN A FEW BULLETS TO STOP THE WALKING DREAD!
NO WORRY.
LOTS MORE.
BTOW!
NICE TRY, HANDSOME--
--BUT YOU CAN'T HIT WHAT YOU CAN'T CATCH!
BOOM!
EEP!
NO ONE ESCAPES THE GAZE OF RED EYE, MY DEAR.
NO ONE.

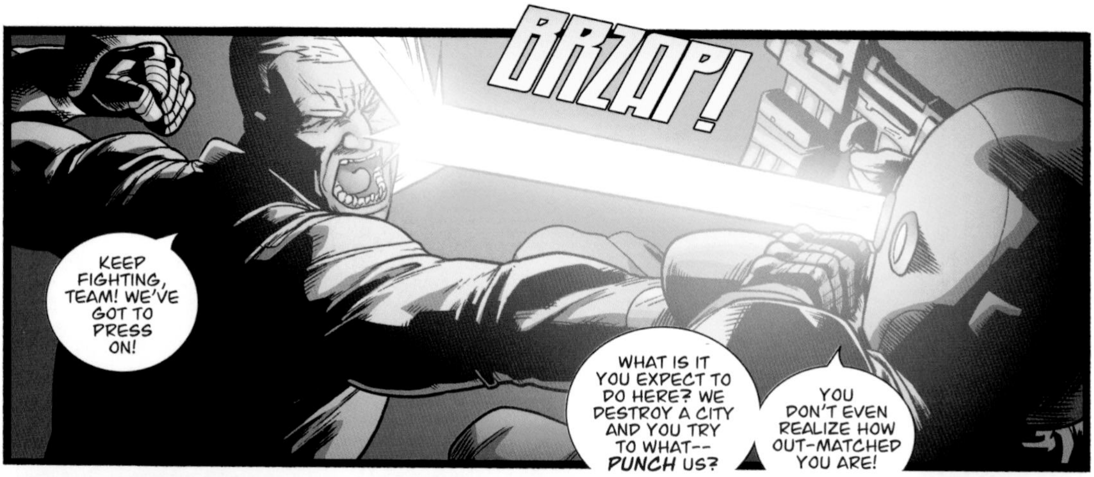
BRZAP!
KEEP FIGHTING, TEAM! WE'VE GOT TO PRESS ON!
WHAT IS IT YOU EXPECT TO DO HERE? WE DESTROY A CITY AND YOU TRY TO WHAT-- PUNCH US?
YOU DON'T EVEN REALIZE HOW OUT-MATCHED YOU ARE!

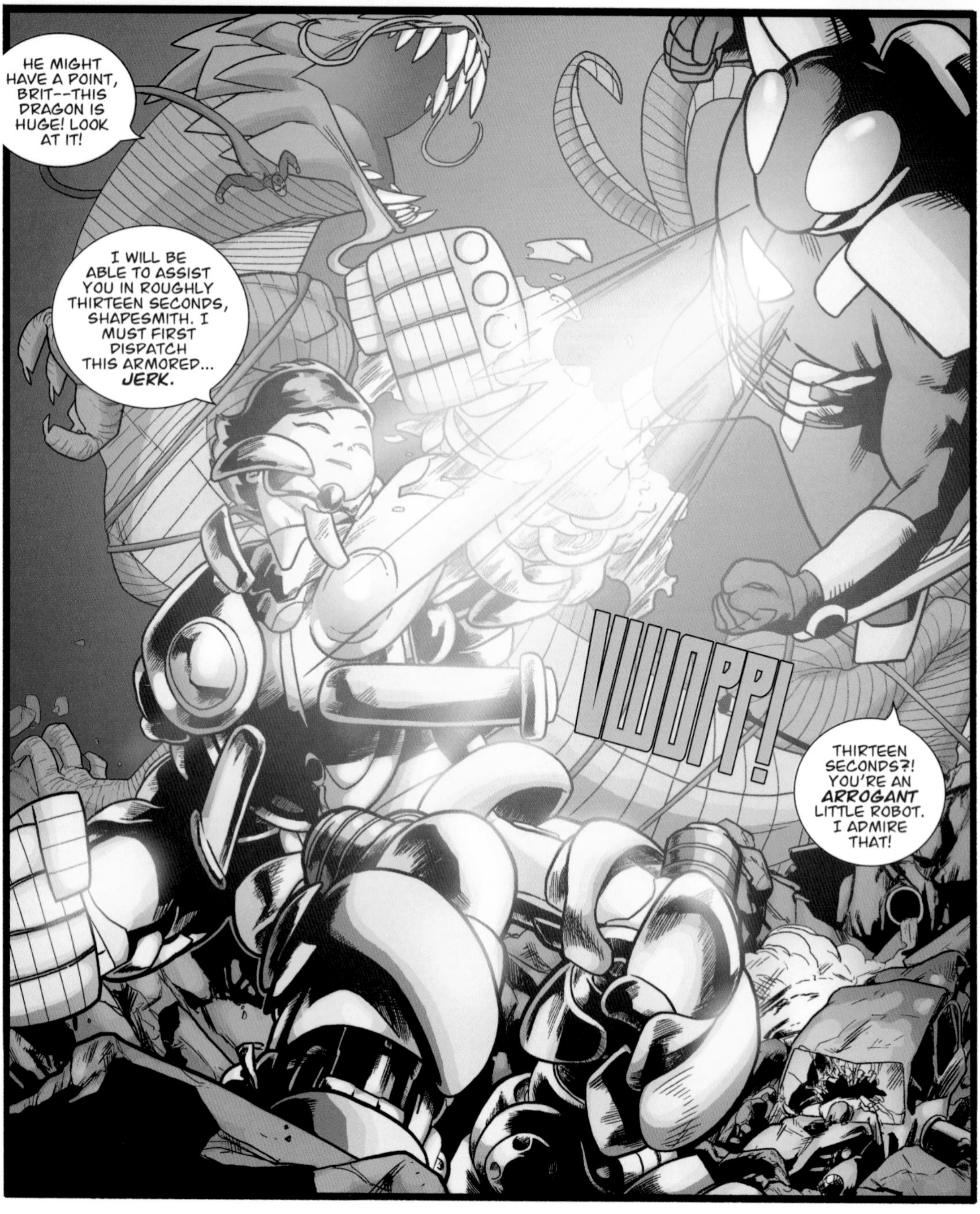
HE MIGHT HAVE A POINT, BRIT--THIS DRAGON IS HUGE! LOOK AT IT!
I WILL BE ABLE TO ASSIST YOU IN ROUGHLY THIRTEEN SECONDS, SHAPESMITH. I MUST FIRST DISPATCH THIS ARMORED... JERK.
VWOPP!
THIRTEEN SECONDS?! YOU'RE AN ARROGANT LITTLE ROBOT. I ADMIRE THAT!

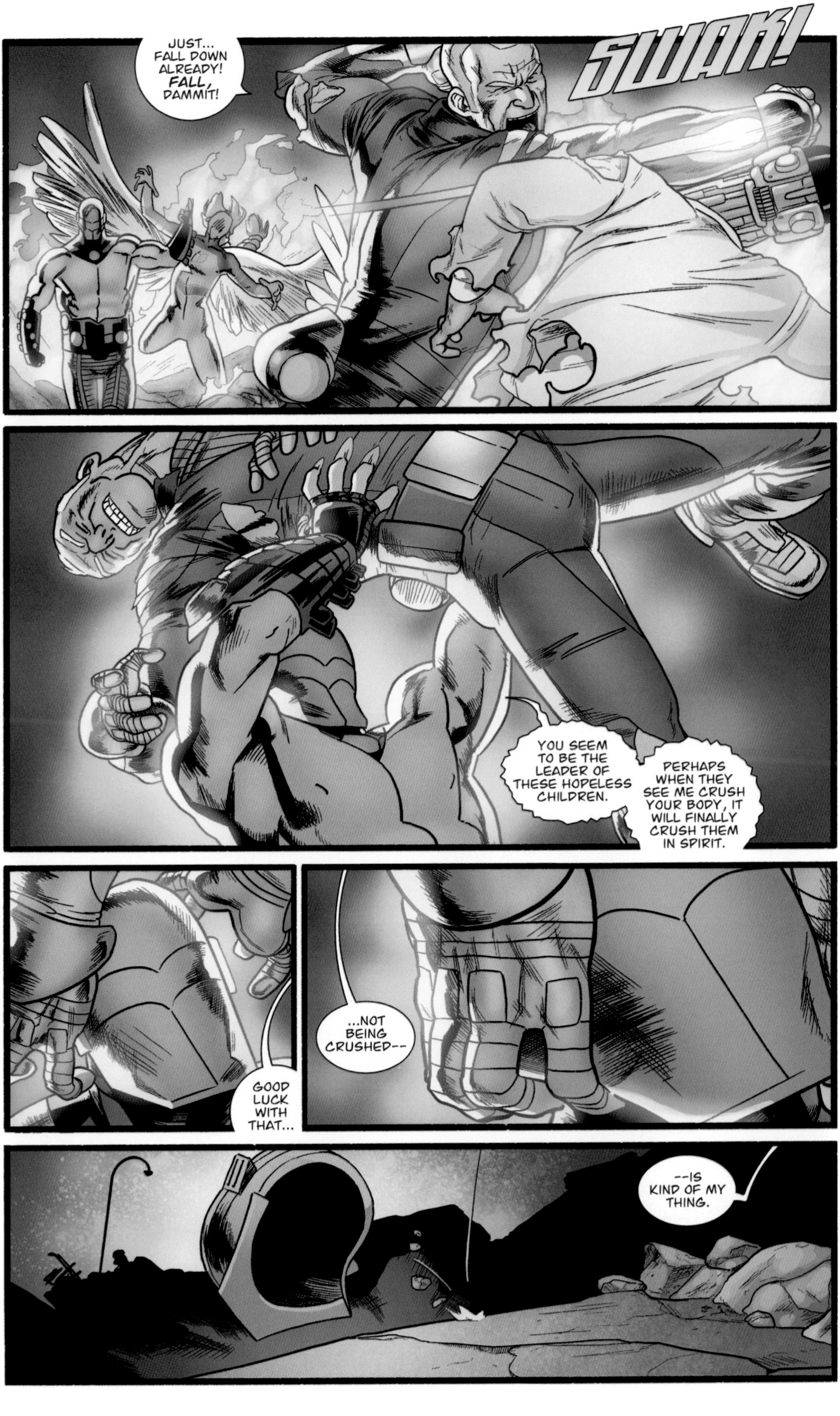
SWAK!
JUST... FALL DOWN ALREADY! FALL, DAMMIT!
YOU SEEM TO BE THE LEADER OF THESE HOPELESS CHILDREN.
PERHAPS WHEN THEY SEE ME CRUSH YOUR BODY, IT WILL FINALLY CRUSH THEM IN SPIRIT.
GOOD LUCK WITH THAT...
...NOT BEING CRUSHED--
--IS KIND OF MY THING.

NO!

MY HELMET!

WHAT HAVE YOU DONE?!

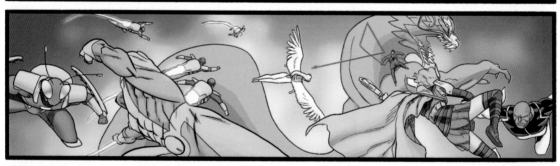

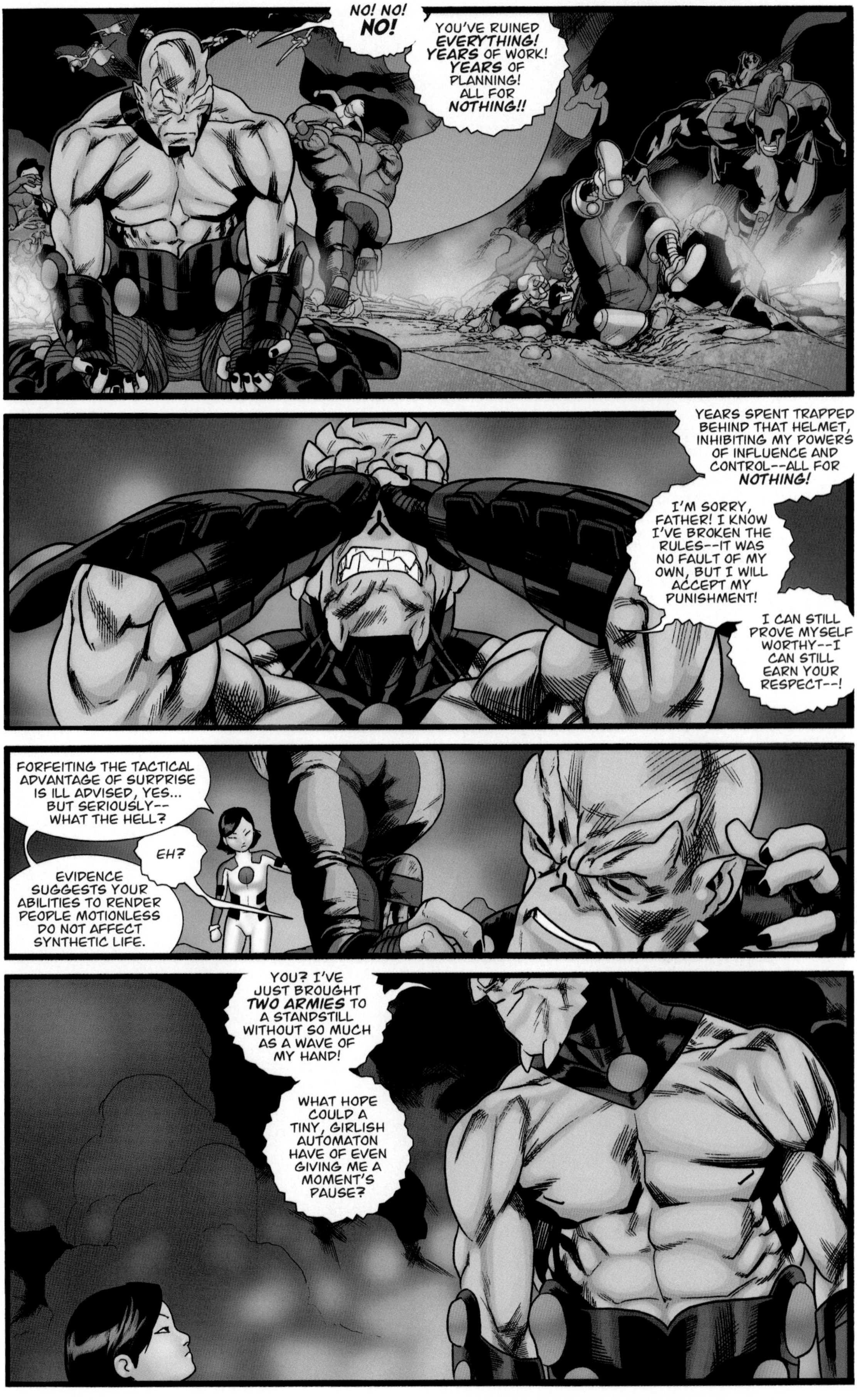
NO! NO! NO!
YOU'VE RUINED EVERYTHING! YEARS OF WORK! YEARS OF PLANNING! ALL FOR NOTHING!!
YEARS SPENT TRAPPED BEHIND THAT HELMET, INHIBITING MY POWERS OF INFLUENCE AND CONTROL--ALL FOR NOTHING!
I'M SORRY, FATHER! I KNOW I'VE BROKEN THE RULES--IT WAS NO FAULT OF MY OWN, BUT I WILL ACCEPT MY PUNISHMENT!
I CAN STILL PROVE MYSELF WORTHY--I CAN STILL EARN YOUR RESPECT--!
FORFEITING THE TACTICAL ADVANTAGE OF SURPRISE IS ILL ADVISED, YES... BUT SERIOUSLY-- WHAT THE HELL?
EH?
EVIDENCE SUGGESTS YOUR ABILITIES TO RENDER PEOPLE MOTIONLESS DO NOT AFFECT SYNTHETIC LIFE.
YOU? I'VE JUST BROUGHT TWO ARMIES TO A STANDSTILL WITHOUT SO MUCH AS A WAVE OF MY HAND!
WHAT HOPE COULD A TINY, GIRLISH AUTOMATON HAVE OF EVEN GIVING ME A MOMENT'S PAUSE?

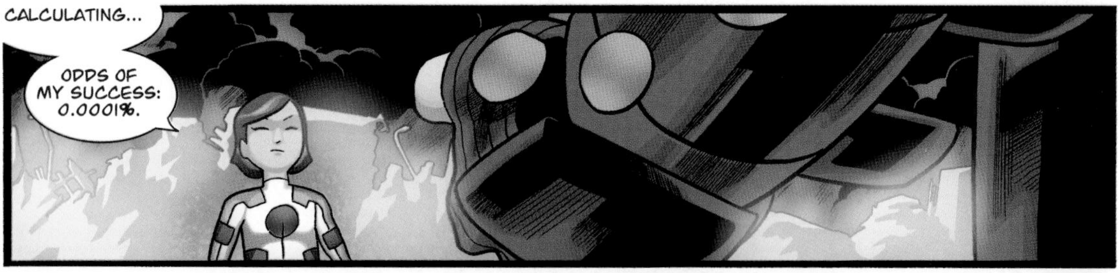
CALCULATING...
ODDS OF MY SUCCESS: 0.0001%.

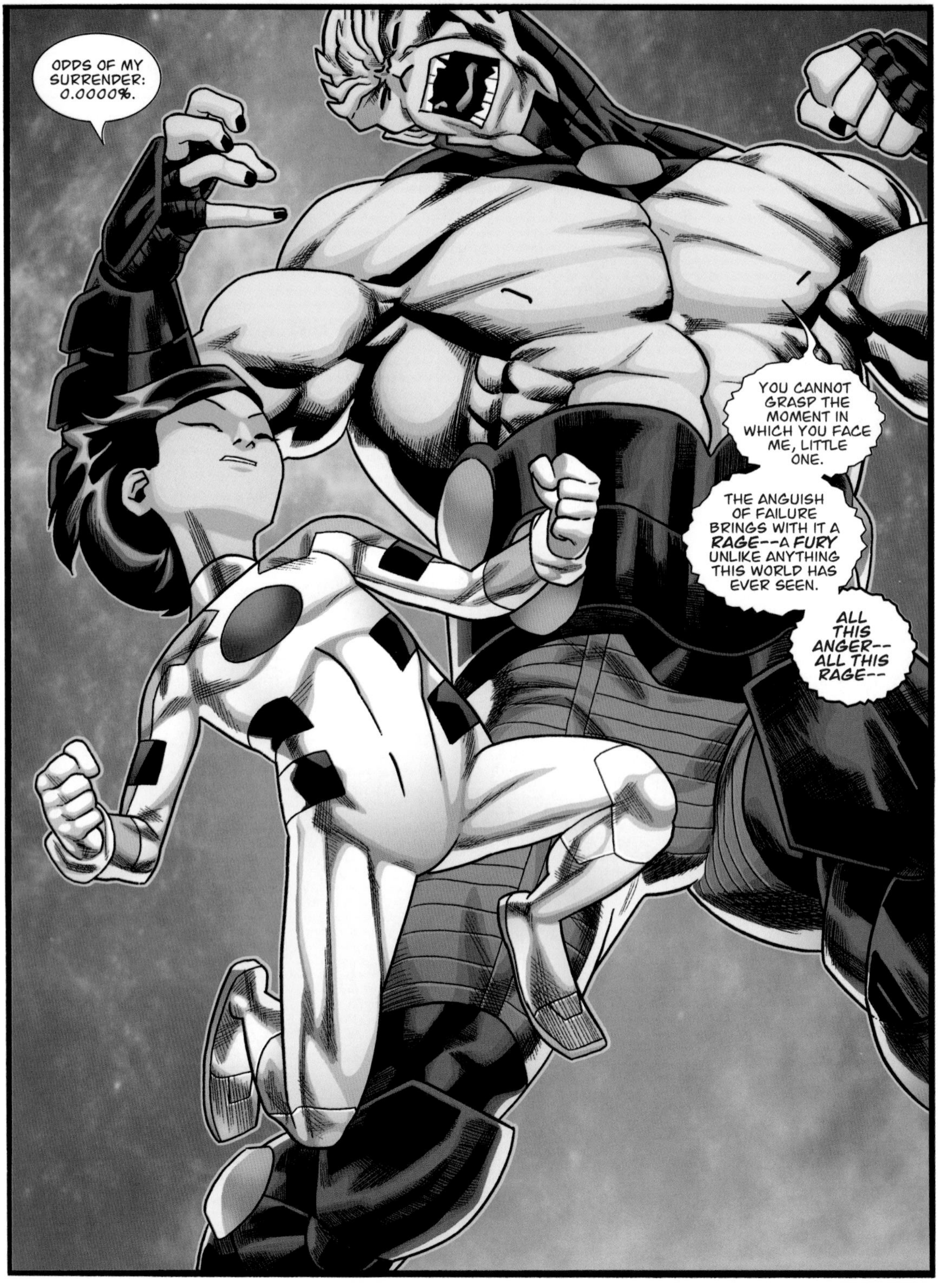
ODDS OF MY SURRENDER: 0.0000%.
YOU CANNOT GRASP THE MOMENT IN WHICH YOU FACE ME, LITTLE ONE.
THE ANGUISH OF FAILURE BRINGS WITH IT A RAGE--A FURY UNLIKE ANYTHING THIS WORLD HAS EVER SEEN.
ALL THIS ANGER-- ALL THIS RAGE--

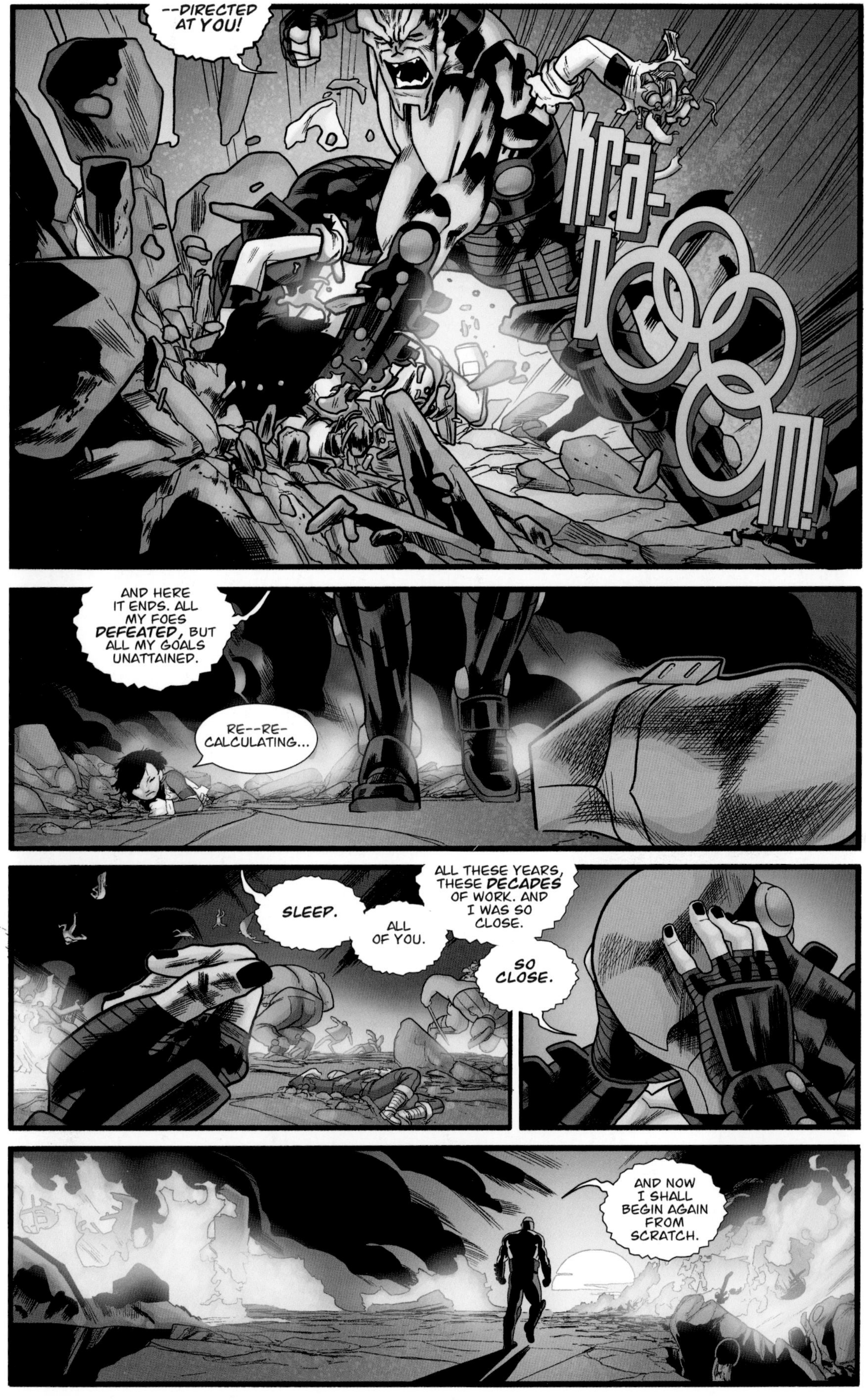
--DIRECTED AT YOU!
KRA-BOOOOM!!
AND HERE IT ENDS. ALL MY FOES DEFEATED, BUT ALL MY GOALS UNATTAINED.
RE--RE-CALCULATING...
SLEEP.
ALL OF YOU.
ALL THESE YEARS, THESE DECADES OF WORK. AND I WAS SO CLOSE.
SO CLOSE.
AND NOW I SHALL BEGIN AGAIN FROM SCRATCH.

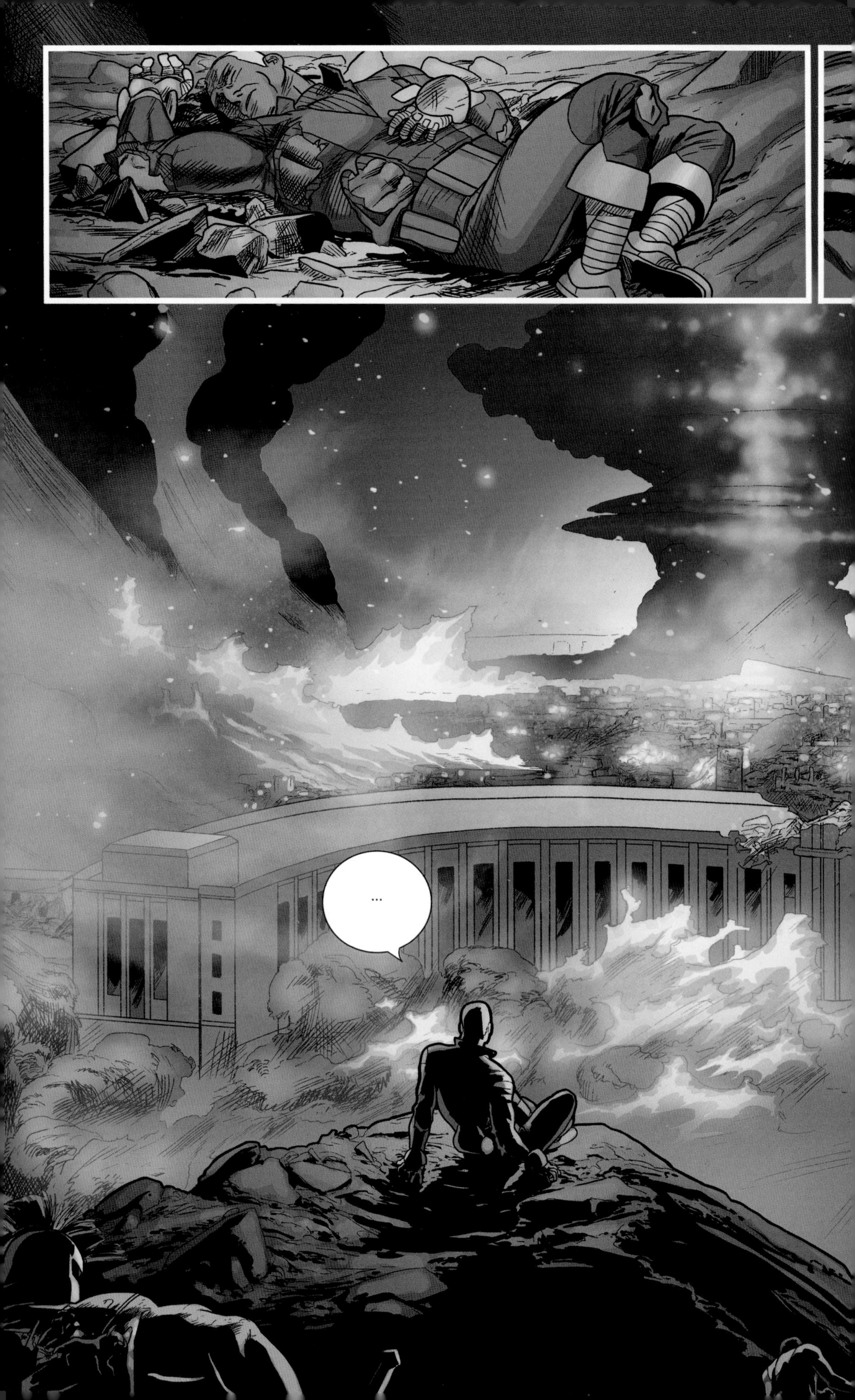
...

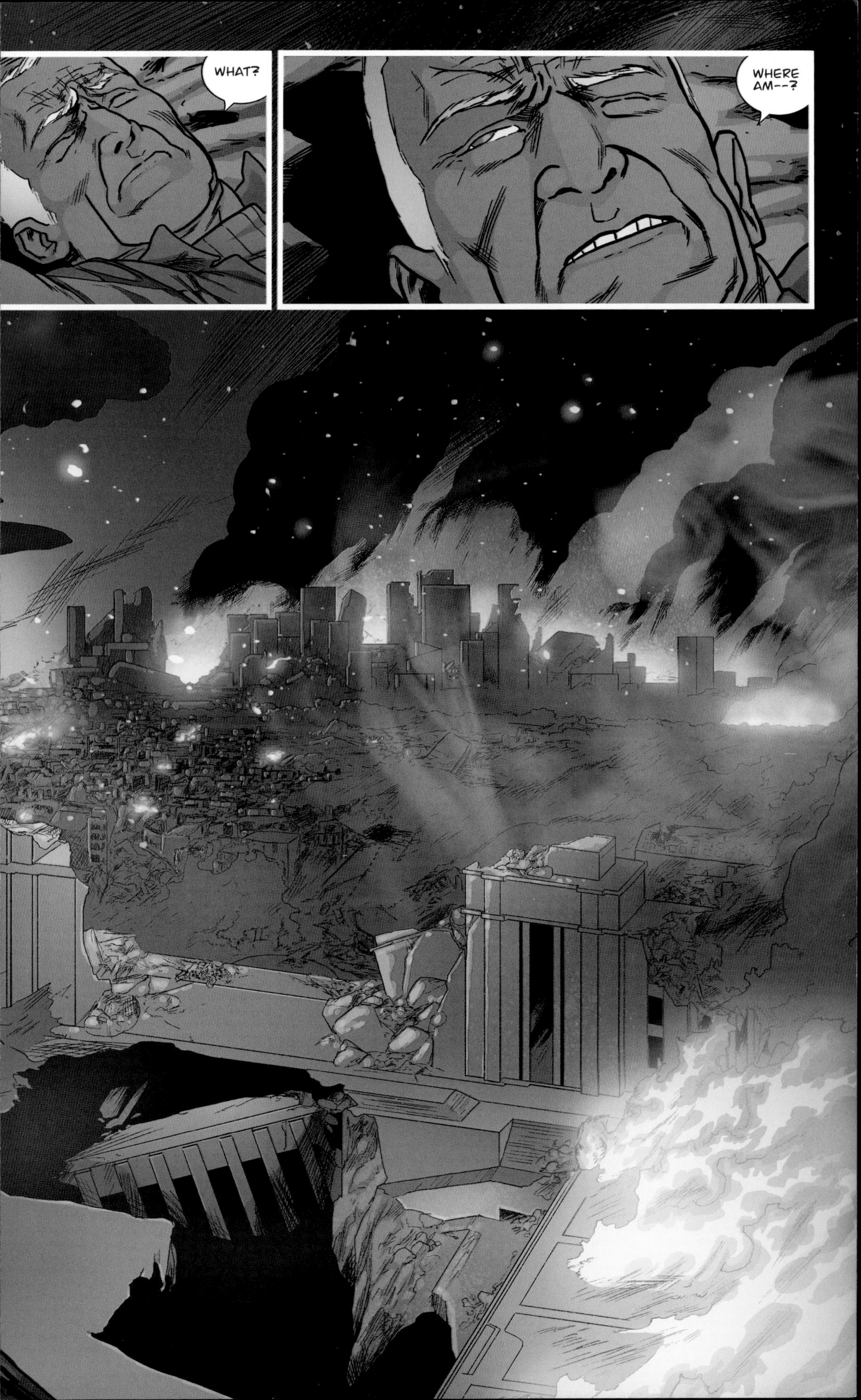
WHAT?
WHERE AM--?

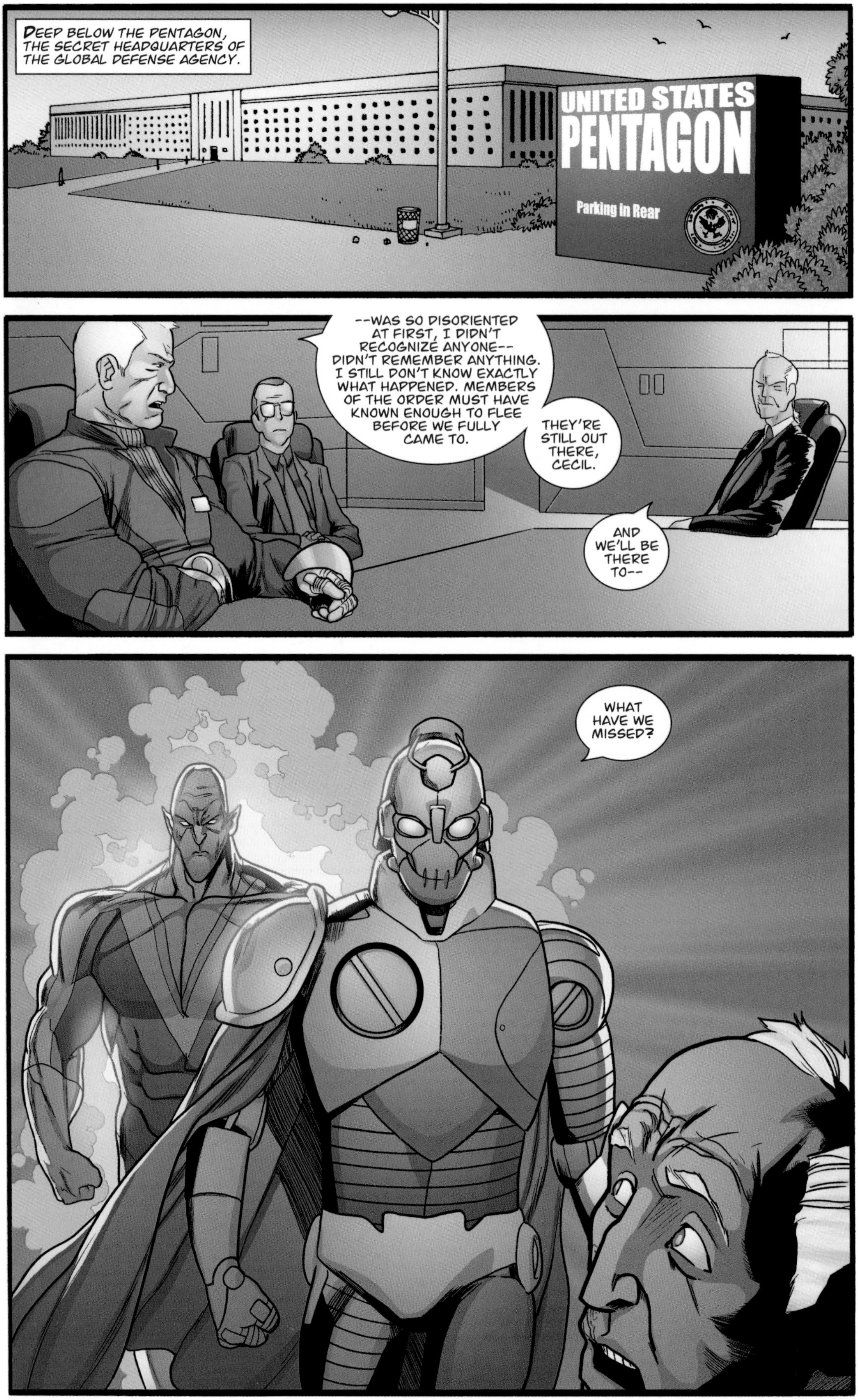
DEEP BELOW THE PENTAGON, THE SECRET HEADQUARTERS OF THE GLOBAL DEFENSE AGENCY.
UNITED STATES PENTAGON
Parking in Rear
--WAS SO DISORIENTED AT FIRST, I DIDN'T RECOGNIZE ANYONE-- DIDN'T REMEMBER ANYTHING. I STILL DON'T KNOW EXACTLY WHAT HAPPENED. MEMBERS OF THE ORDER MUST HAVE KNOWN ENOUGH TO FLEE BEFORE WE FULLY CAME TO.
THEY'RE STILL OUT THERE, CECIL.
AND WE'LL BE THERE TO--
WHAT HAVE WE MISSED?

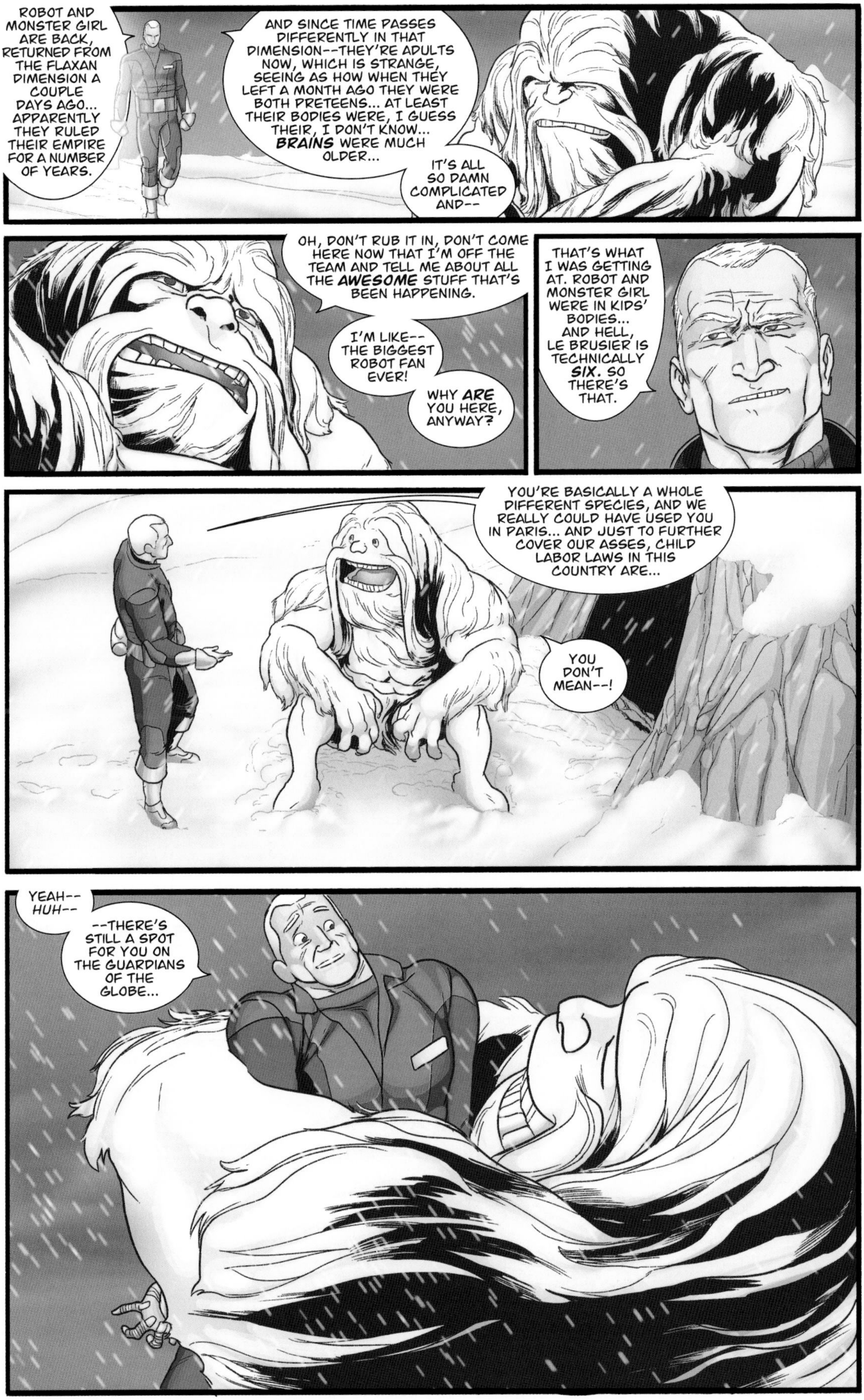

ROBOT AND MONSTER GIRL ARE BACK, RETURNED FROM THE FLAXAN DIMENSION A COUPLE DAYS AGO... APPARENTLY THEY RULED THEIR EMPIRE FOR A NUMBER OF YEARS.
AND SINCE TIME PASSES DIFFERENTLY IN THAT DIMENSION--THEY'RE ADULTS NOW, WHICH IS STRANGE, SEEING AS HOW WHEN THEY LEFT A MONTH AGO THEY WERE BOTH PRETEENS... AT LEAST THEIR BODIES WERE, I GUESS THEIR, I DON'T KNOW... **BRAINS** WERE MUCH OLDER...
IT'S ALL SO DAMN COMPLICATED AND--
OH, DON'T RUB IT IN, DON'T COME HERE NOW THAT I'M OFF THE TEAM AND TELL ME ABOUT ALL THE **AWESOME** STUFF THAT'S BEEN HAPPENING.
I'M LIKE-- THE BIGGEST ROBOT FAN EVER!
WHY **ARE** YOU HERE, ANYWAY?
THAT'S WHAT I WAS GETTING AT. ROBOT AND MONSTER GIRL WERE IN KIDS' BODIES... AND HELL, LE BRUSIER IS TECHNICALLY **SIX.** SO THERE'S THAT.
YOU'RE BASICALLY A WHOLE DIFFERENT SPECIES, AND WE REALLY COULD HAVE USED YOU IN PARIS... AND JUST TO FURTHER COVER OUR ASSES, CHILD LABOR LAWS IN THIS COUNTRY ARE...
YOU DON'T MEAN--!
YEAH-- HUH--
--THERE'S STILL A SPOT FOR YOU ON THE GUARDIANS OF THE GLOBE...

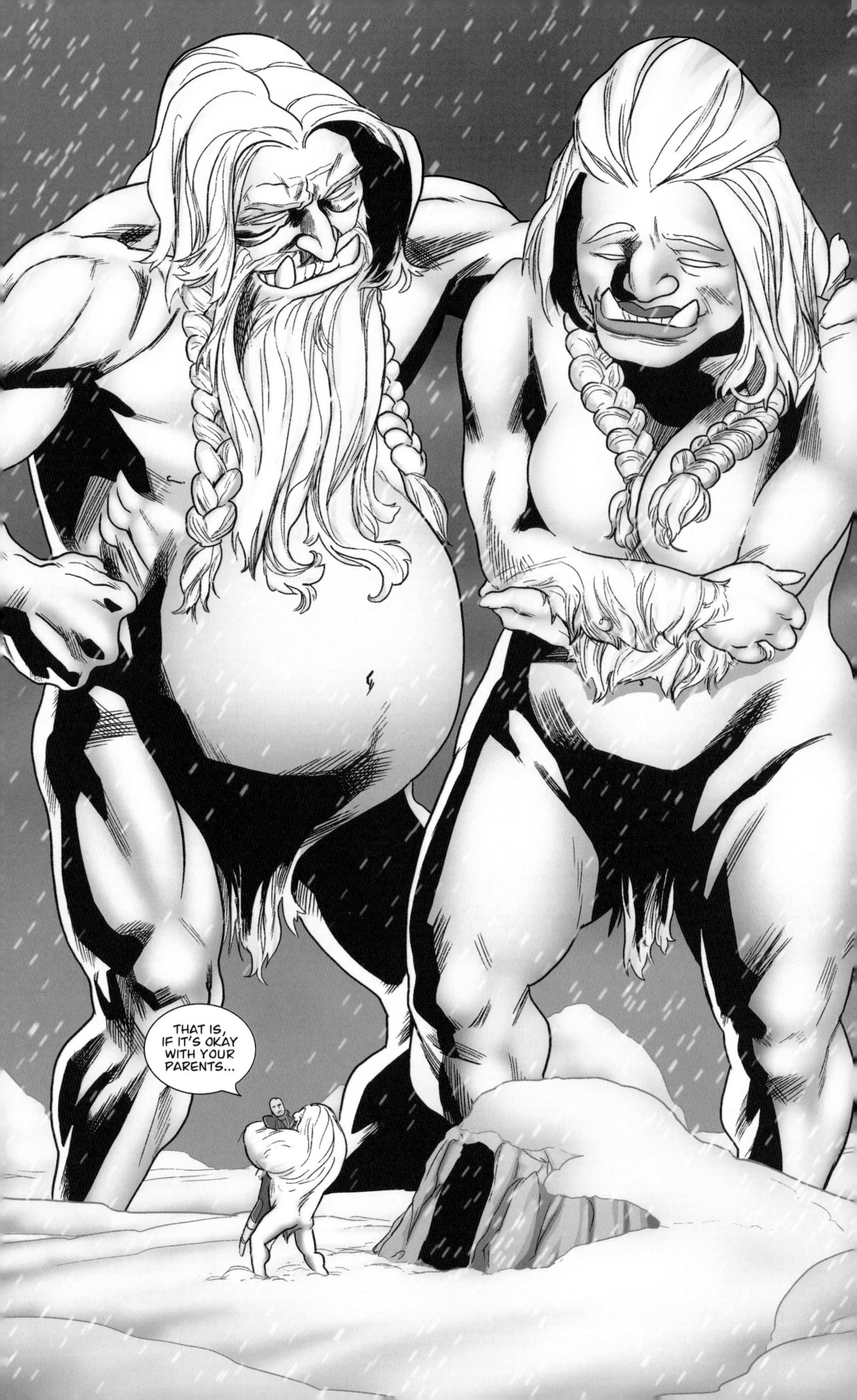
THAT IS, IF IT'S OKAY WITH YOUR PARENTS...

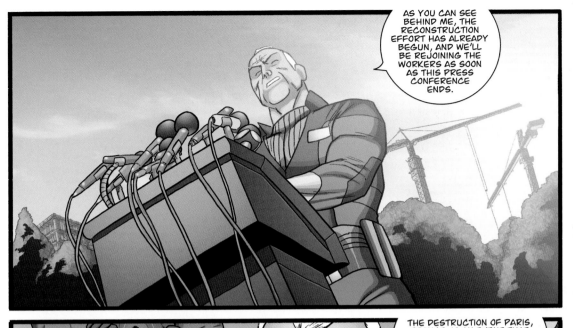

AS YOU CAN SEE BEHIND ME, THE RECONSTRUCTION EFFORT HAS ALREADY BEGUN, AND WE'LL BE REJOINING THE WORKERS AS SOON AS THIS PRESS CONFERENCE ENDS.

THE DESTRUCTION OF PARIS, FRANCE, IS AN EVENT THAT HAS SENT SHOCK WAVES THROUGH THE INTERNATIONAL COMMUNITY. IT IS NOT A LOSS CONTAINED WITHIN THIS COUNTRY'S BORDERS.

NEVER HAS IT BEEN MORE CLEAR, THAT WE ARE ONE WORLD, ONE COMMUNITY-- WE ALL SURVIVE IN THIS WORLD, BY COMING *TOGETHER*.

MY TEAM COMES FROM EVERY CORNER OF THIS GLOBE, AND TOGETHER, WE WILL BE EXPANDING OUR EFFORTS TO GUARD IT AND ITS CITIZENS.

WE COULDN'T STOP THIS TRAGEDY FROM OCCURRING, BUT IN THE FUTURE WE WILL BE PREPARED FOR ATTACKS ON SUCH A SCALE.

THAT IS OUR MESSAGE TODAY, THAT WE ARE *HERE*.

WE STAND BEFORE YOU, ASSEMBLED, AS A SHOW OF OUR STRENGTH, TO TELL THE WORLD, WE ARE HERE FOR YOU, WE WILL ALWAYS BE HERE FOR YOU...

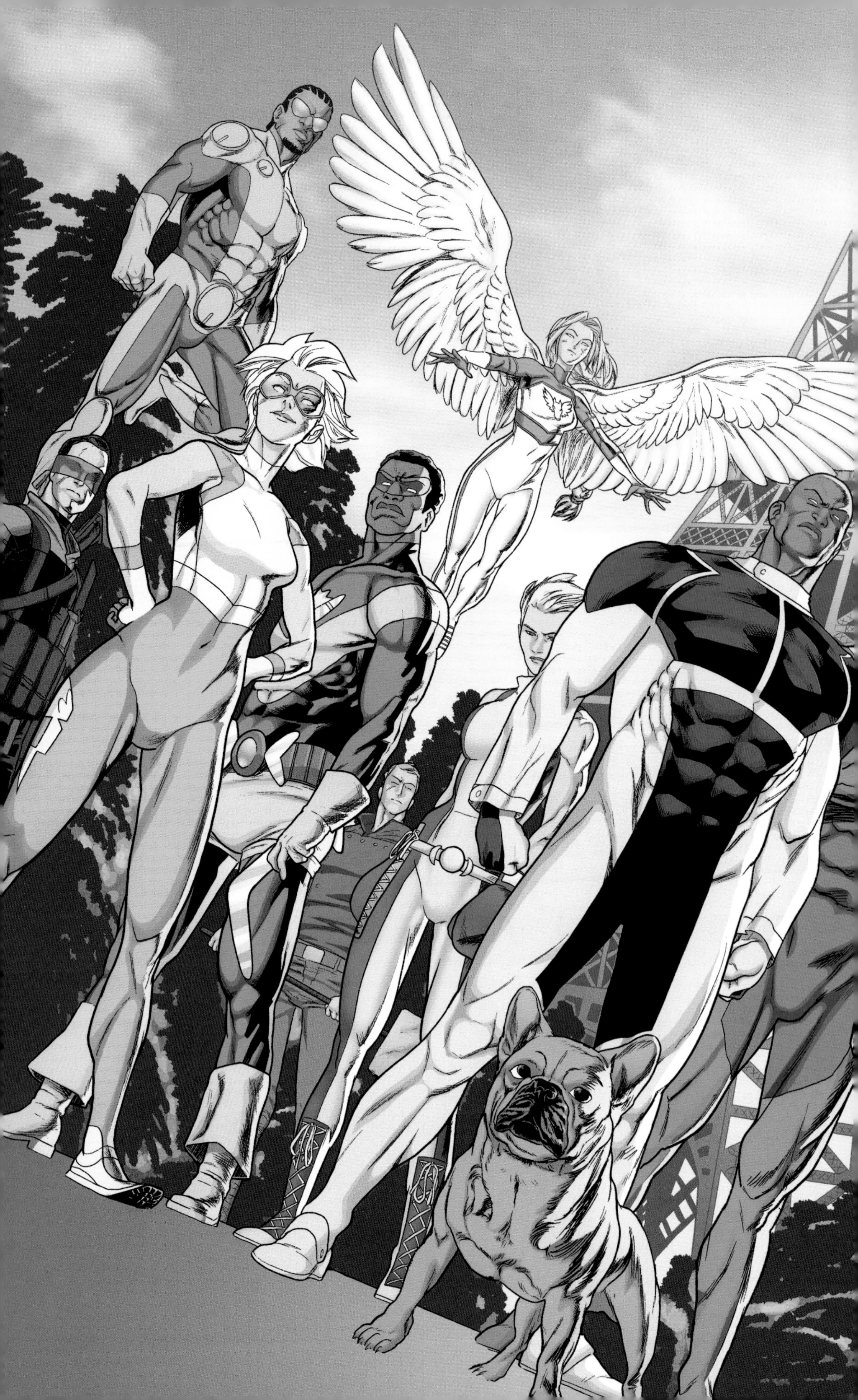

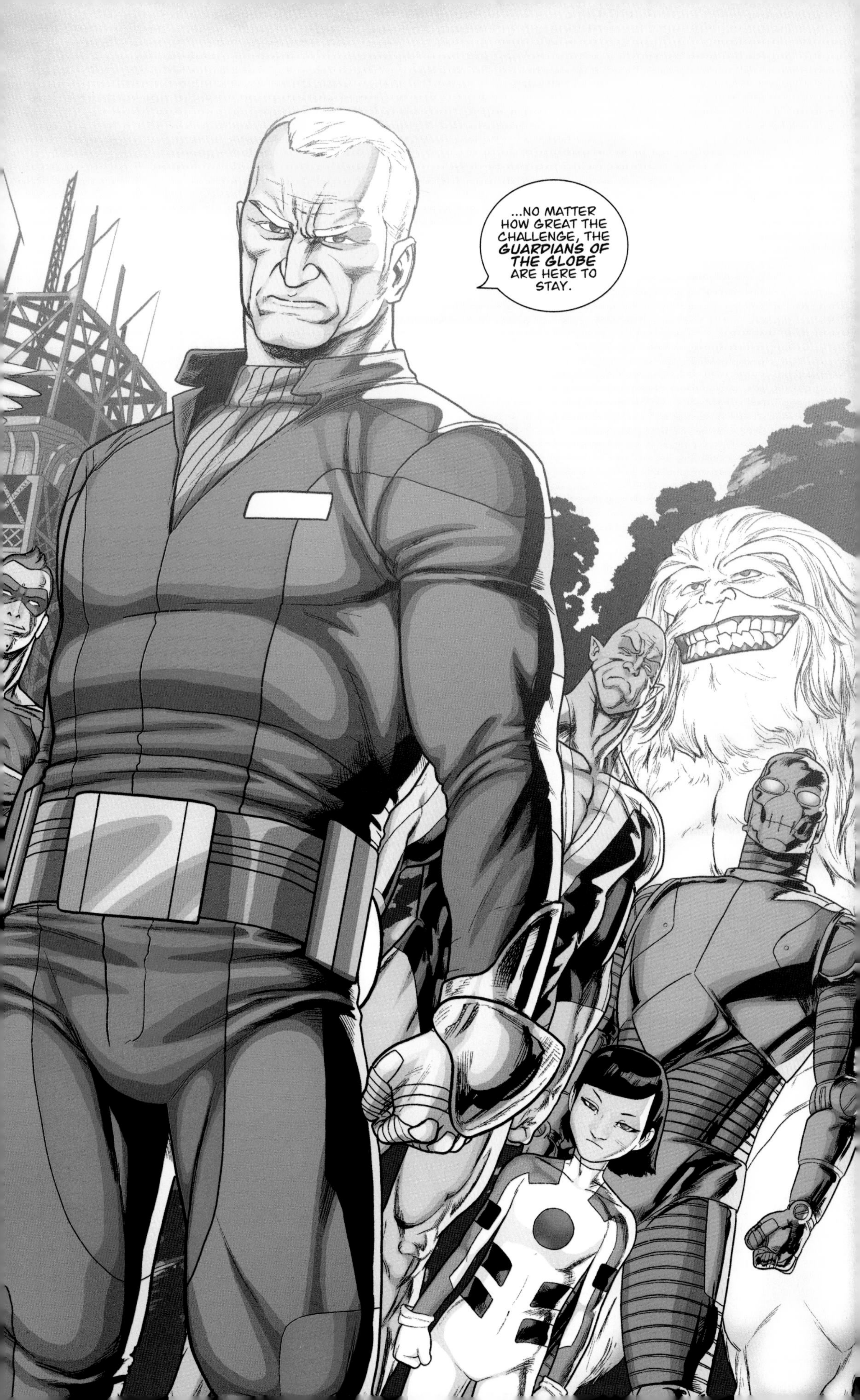
...NO MATTER HOW GREAT THE CHALLENGE, THE GUARDIANS OF THE GLOBE ARE HERE TO STAY.

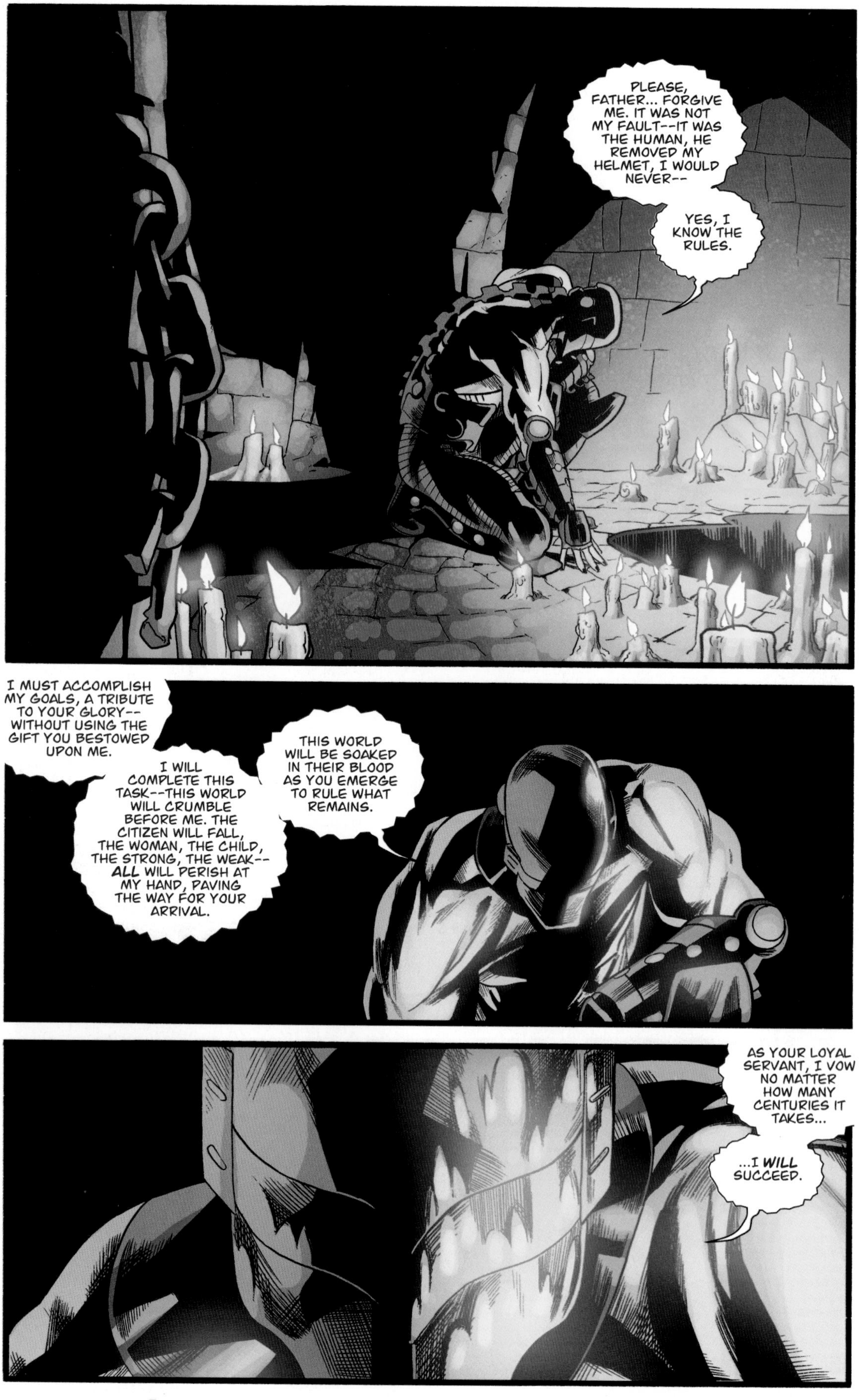
PLEASE, FATHER... FORGIVE ME. IT WAS NOT MY FAULT--IT WAS THE HUMAN, HE REMOVED MY HELMET, I WOULD NEVER--
YES, I KNOW THE RULES.
I MUST ACCOMPLISH MY GOALS, A TRIBUTE TO YOUR GLORY--WITHOUT USING THE GIFT YOU BESTOWED UPON ME.
I WILL COMPLETE THIS TASK--THIS WORLD WILL CRUMBLE BEFORE ME. THE CITIZEN WILL FALL, THE WOMAN, THE CHILD, THE STRONG, THE WEAK--ALL WILL PERISH AT MY HAND, PAVING THE WAY FOR YOUR ARRIVAL.
THIS WORLD WILL BE SOAKED IN THEIR BLOOD AS YOU EMERGE TO RULE WHAT REMAINS.
AS YOUR LOYAL SERVANT, I VOW NO MATTER HOW MANY CENTURIES IT TAKES...
...I WILL SUCCEED.

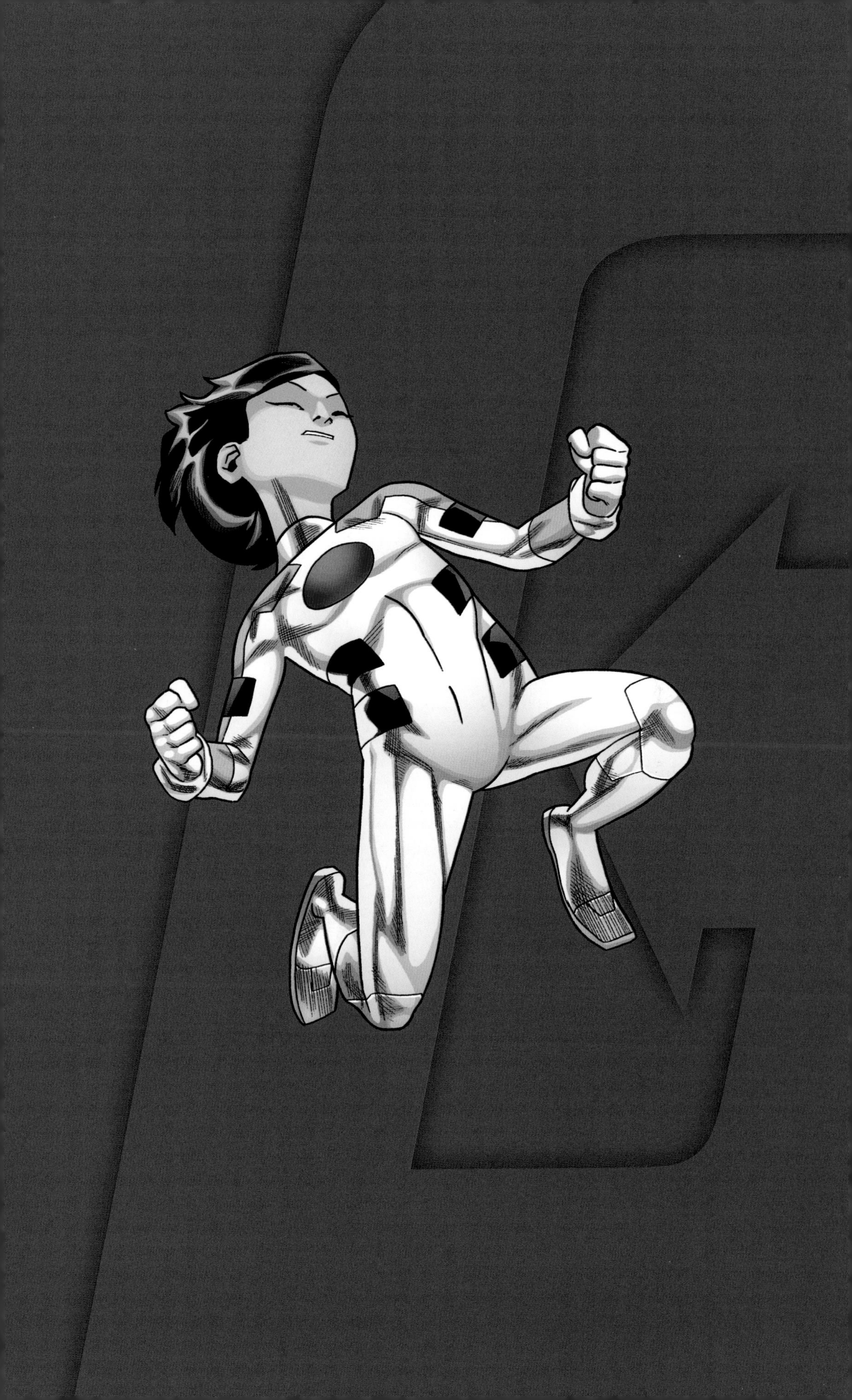

SKETCHBOOK

ROBERT KIRKMAN: As this is an Invincible Universe title, we had to go with the standard, put a bunch of cool stuff behind a figure of our hero motif for the trade cover... the only problem, this is a team book! EEK! What an ill-advised plan. Luckily, Todd Nauck was able to make it look spectacular.

TODD NAUCK: I love choreographing large numbers of superheroes. Things I try to consider are the powers, personalities, and costume colors of each character and where to place them. It's a challenge but I love it! After discussing the first volume's cover with Robert and Sina, we decided to focus on the main Guardians and put the newest recruits in a side panel. We didn't want to crowd out the main image with the whole team. I figured a globe of some sort would make a nice background element in the team's theme. I left space for colorist, John Rauch, to place in the globe and he totally nailed what I was hoping for.

For the other two panels, I felt I should put Mark in there since this series spins out of his book and is an anchor for the fans. Plus, he did appear in the first issue.

Then of course, the other panel would feature the main villain, Set, from the mini-series. I'd have loved to have worked in all the other villains, but that would've been way too many characters for this cover.

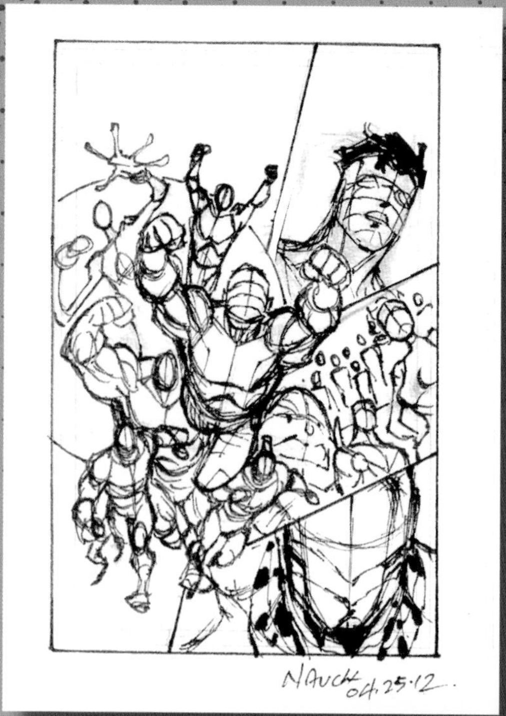
NAUCK 04.25.12.

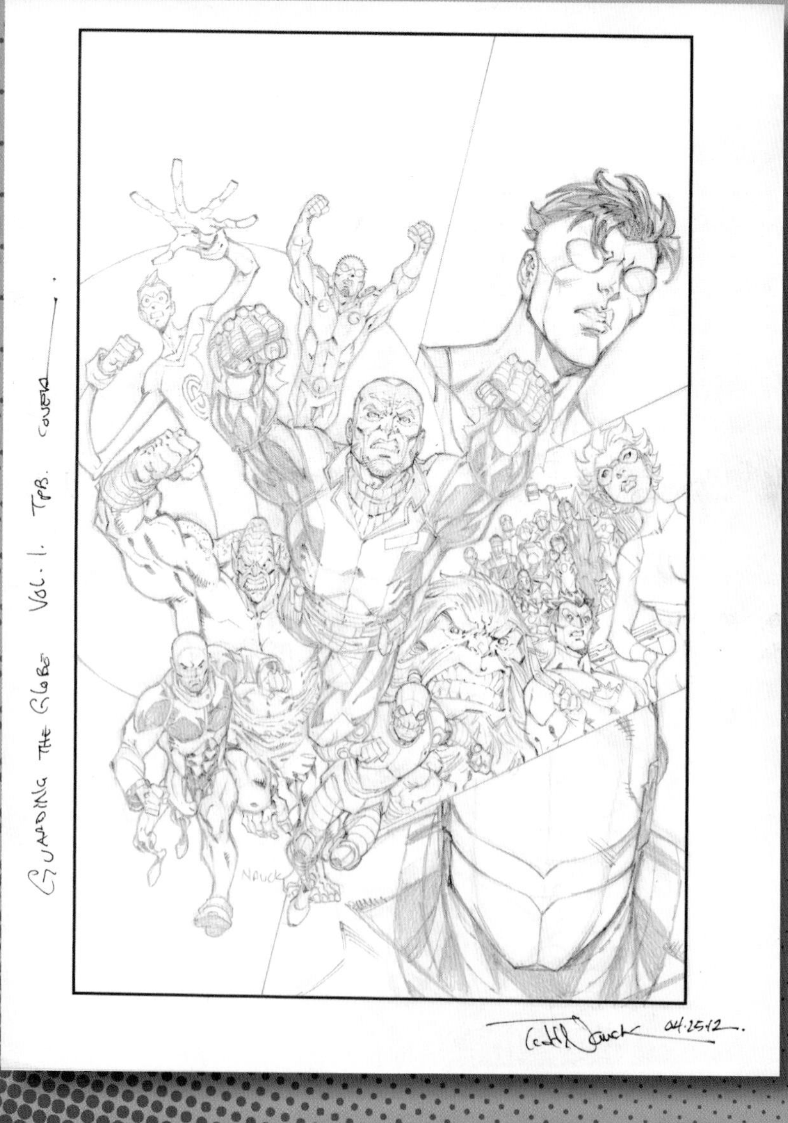
GUARDING THE GLOBE VOL. 1. TPB. COVER
NAUCK
Todd Nauck 04.25.12.

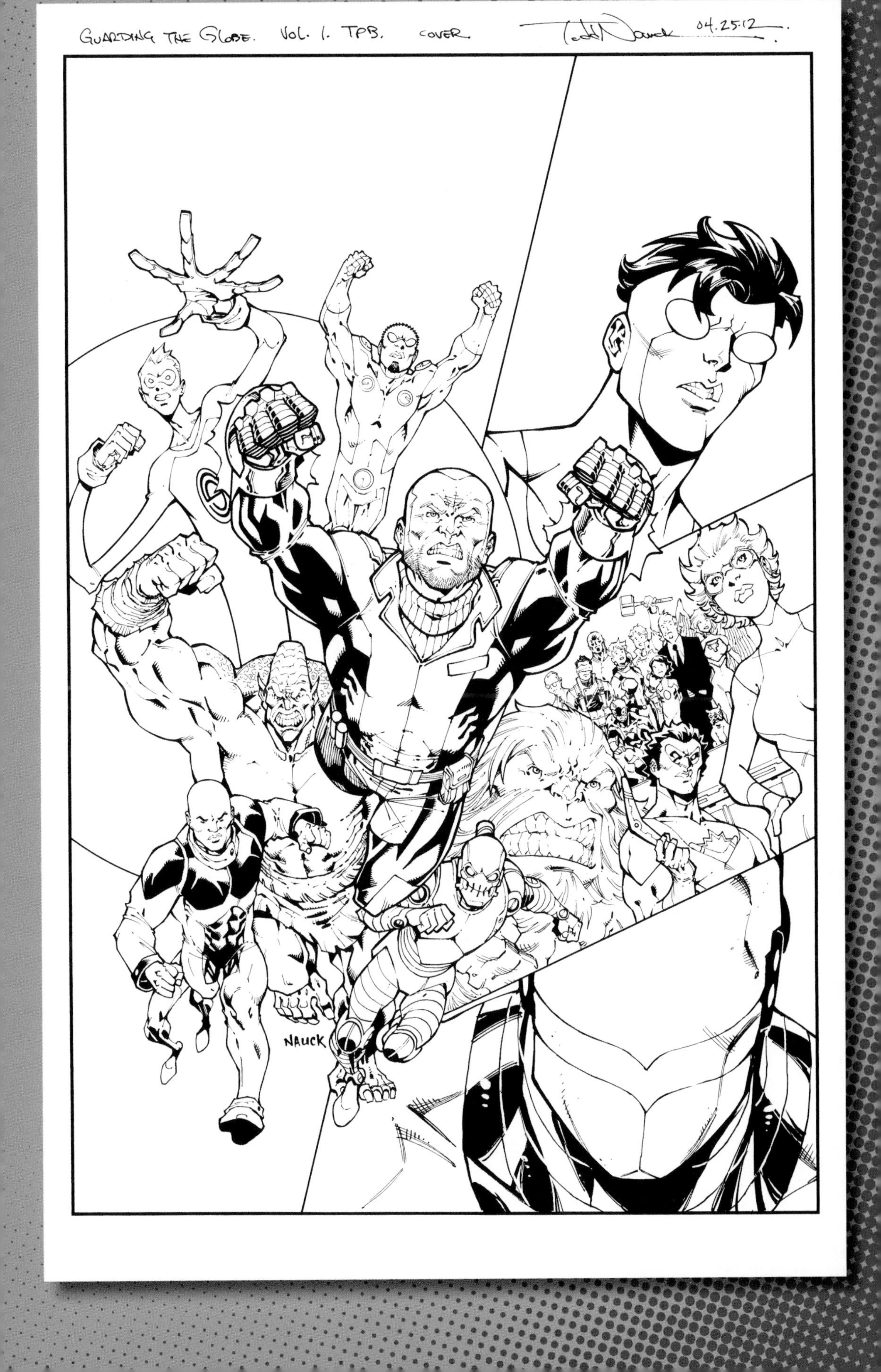
GUARDING THE GLOBE. VOL. 1. TPB. COVER.
04.25.12
NAUCK

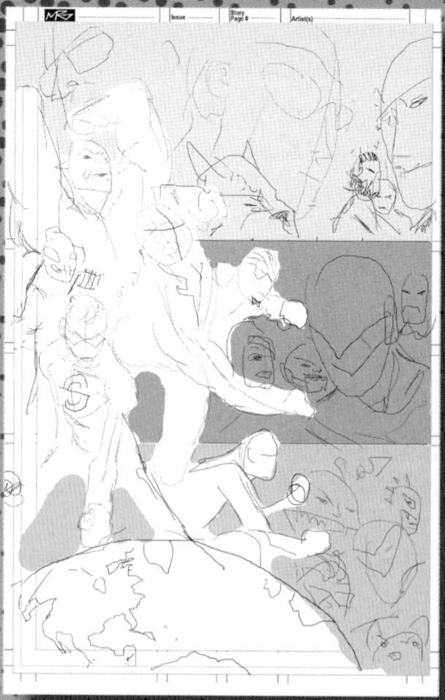

KIRKMAN: **The artist for (most of) this mini-series Ransom Getty actually did a cover for this book. The only reason we didn't end up using it is that Todd Nauck was chosen to draw the regular series and therefore will be doing the covers of other volumes, and I figured having them match would be better.**

RANSOM GETTY: Being a huge fan of the other Invincible Universe covers, I had a blast trying to do my own version. I was so relieved when I was able to fit all 1,483 characters on the cover.

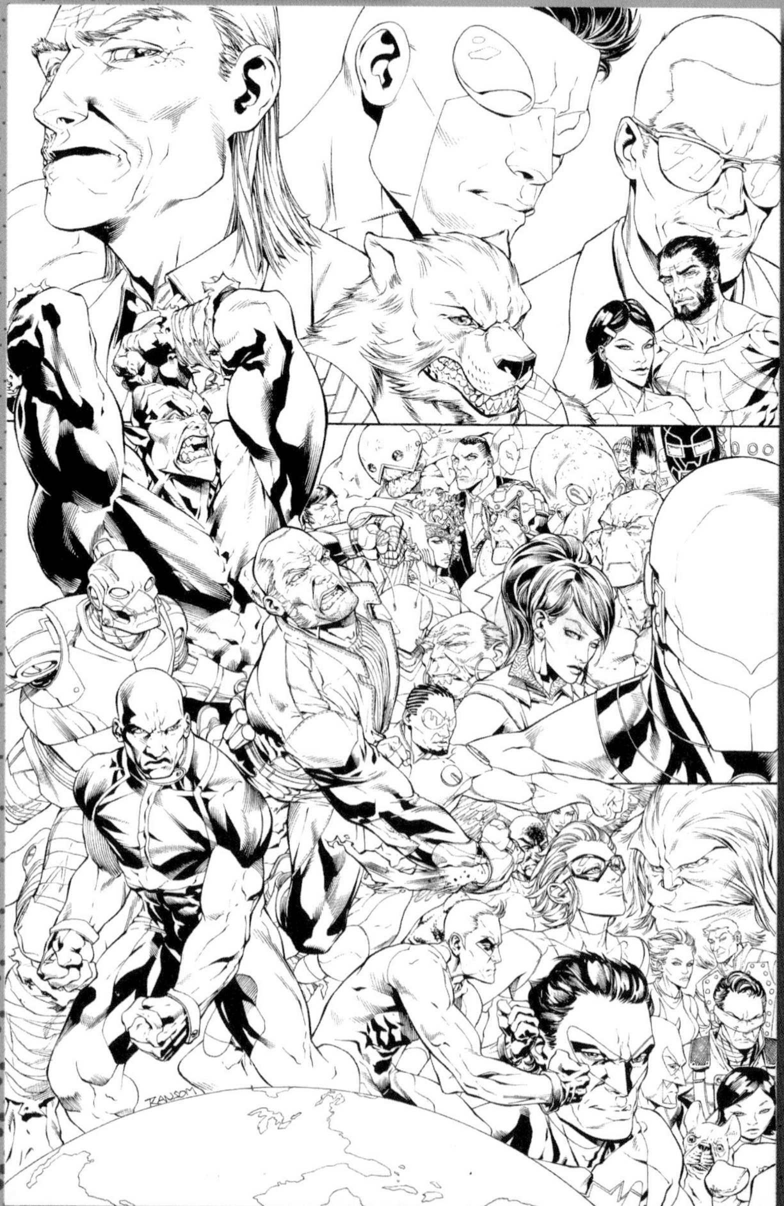

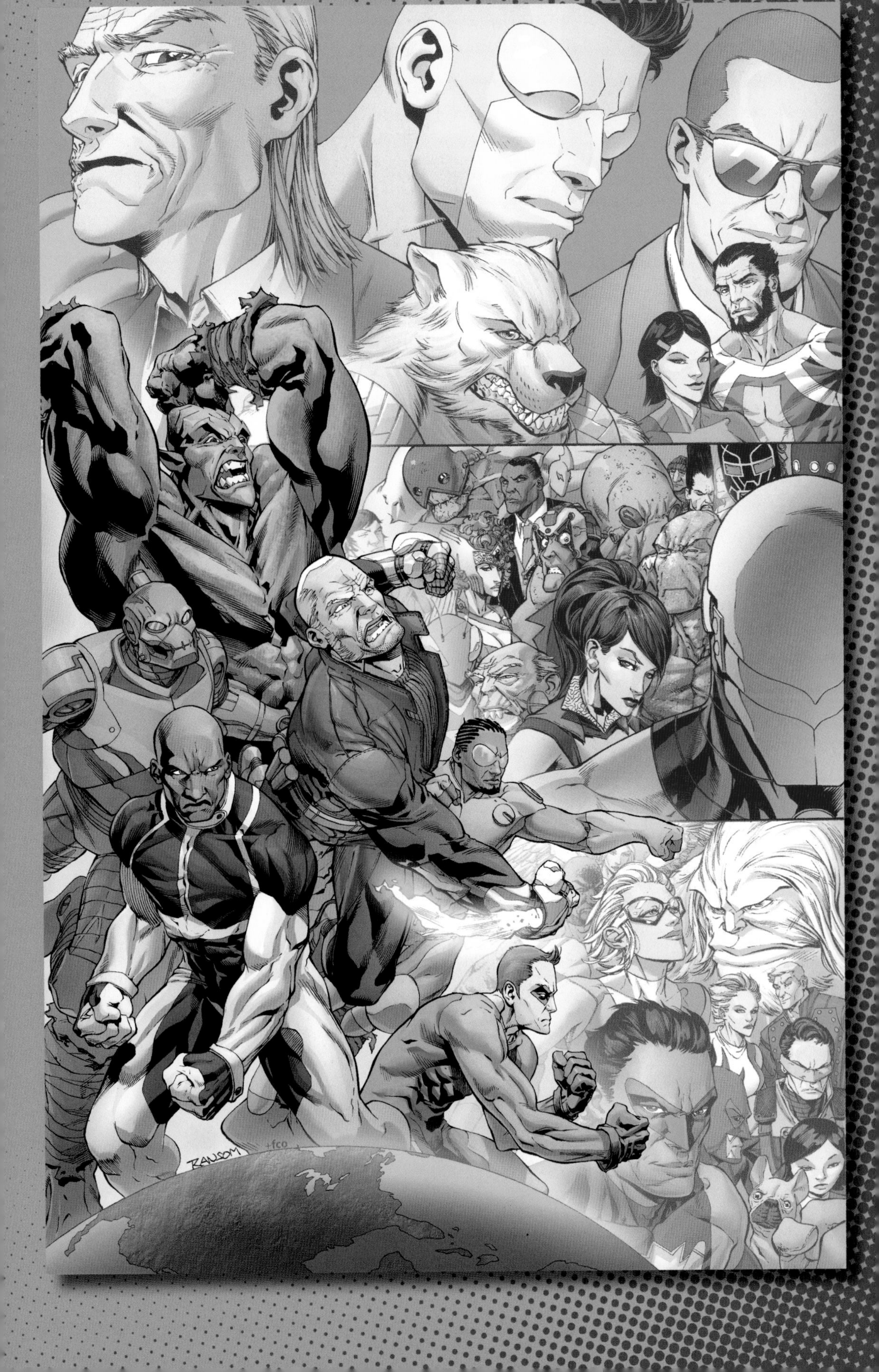
RANSOM
+fco

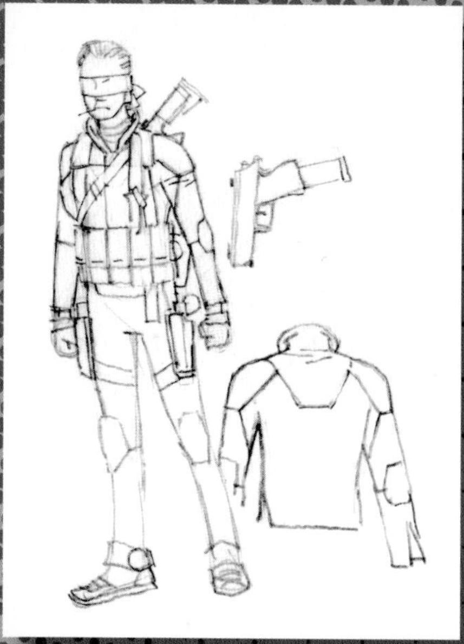
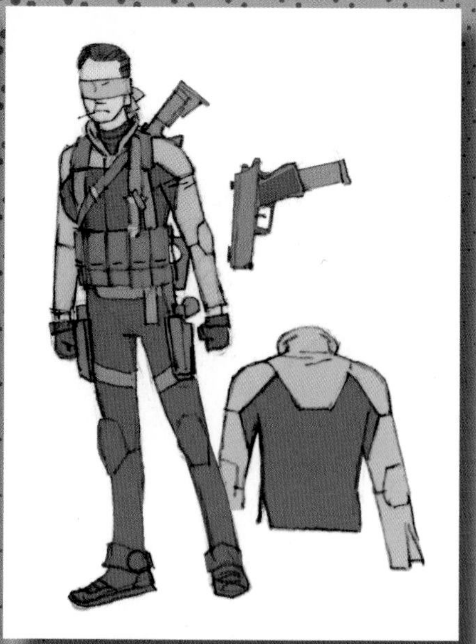
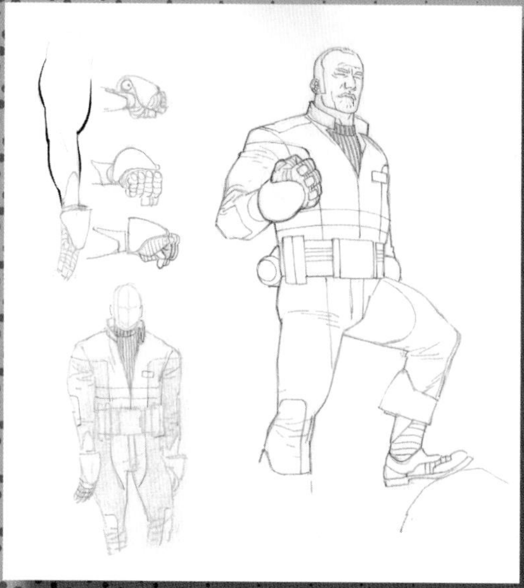
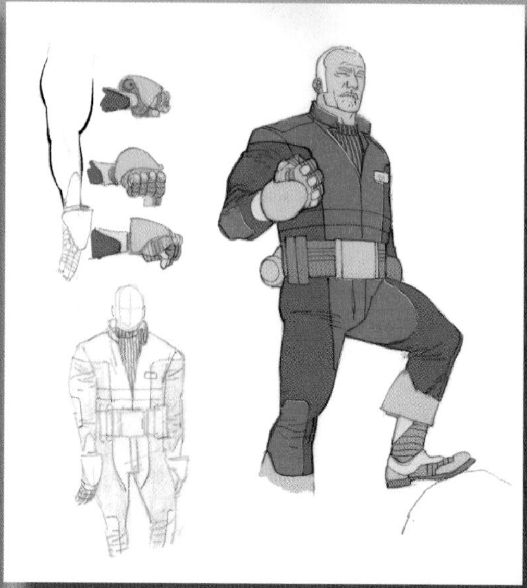
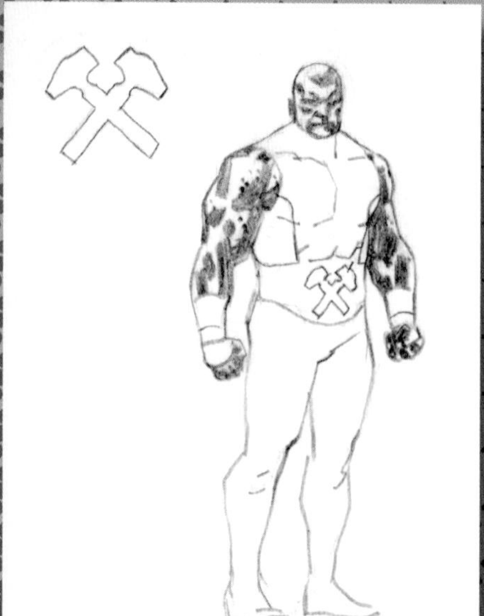
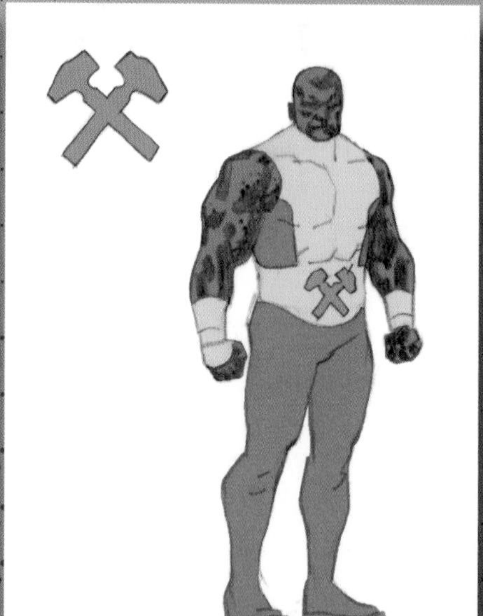

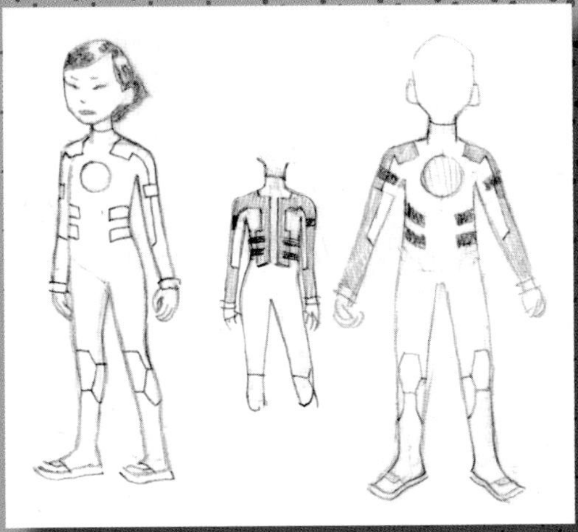

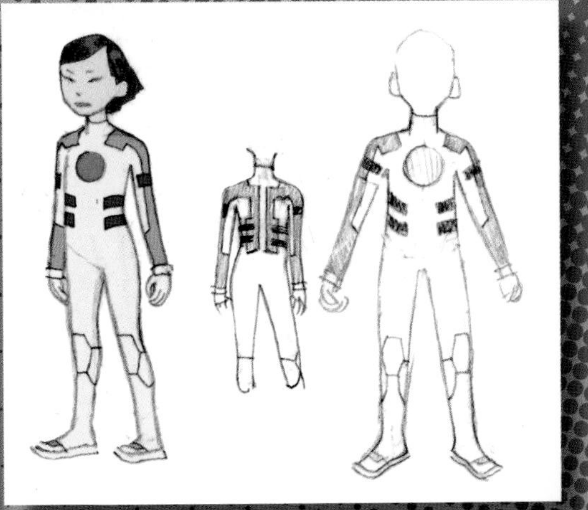

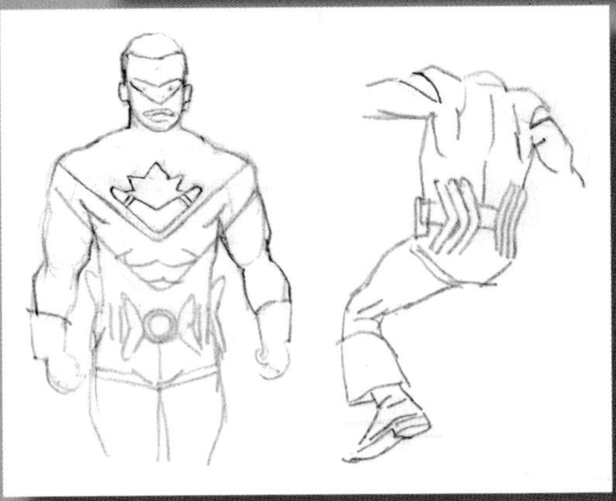

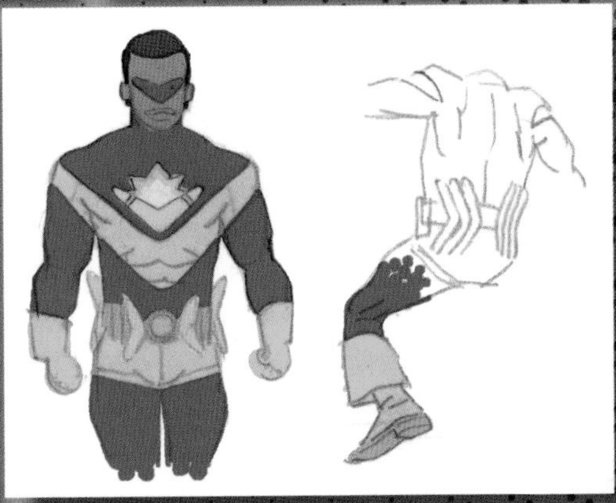

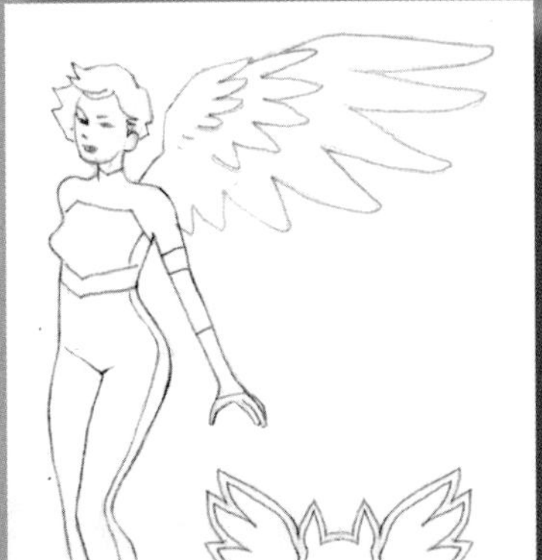

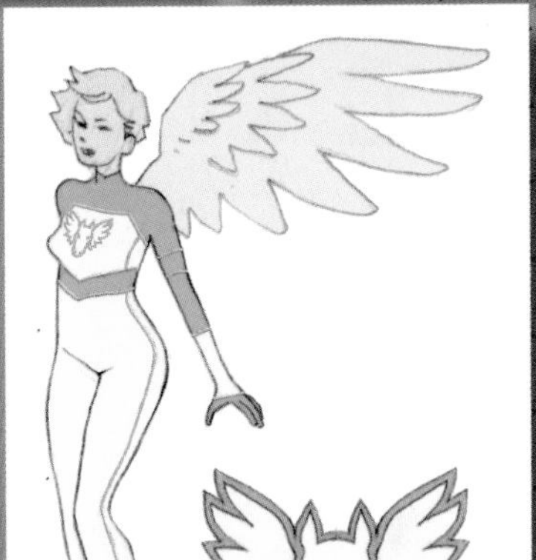

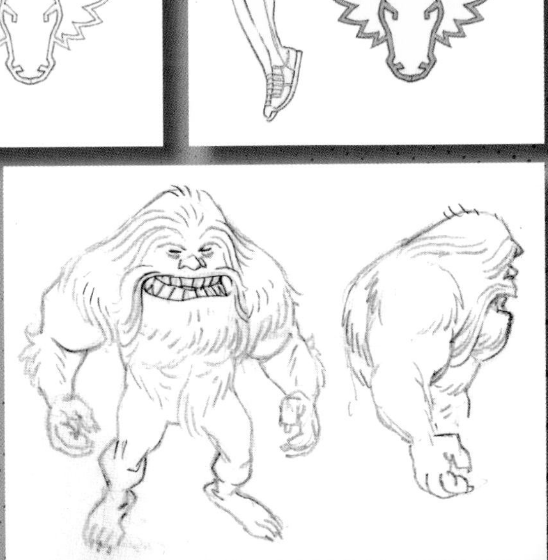

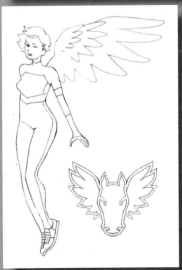

ROBERT KIRKMAN: One of the most fun things about this series, for me, was getting to sit down with Invincible co-creator Cory Walker and create a bunch of new characters. It may not be clear but the idea for this series was to show superheroes from other countries. So Cory and I just sat down and picked a bunch of countries and tried to come up with what kind of super hero would be from there.

On these pages you'll find Cory's designs for Best Tiger, Cast Iron, Japandroid, Kaboomerang, Pegasus, Yeti, and also a new costume for existing super-hero Brit. I had the idea to give him jet boots and hands to empower his indestructible (but otherwise powerless body). Now he can use jets to slam his indestructible fists into you.

Also, Best Tiger is the greatest character I've ever had a hand in creating. I want to do a Best Tiger series some day. He's literally my favorite.

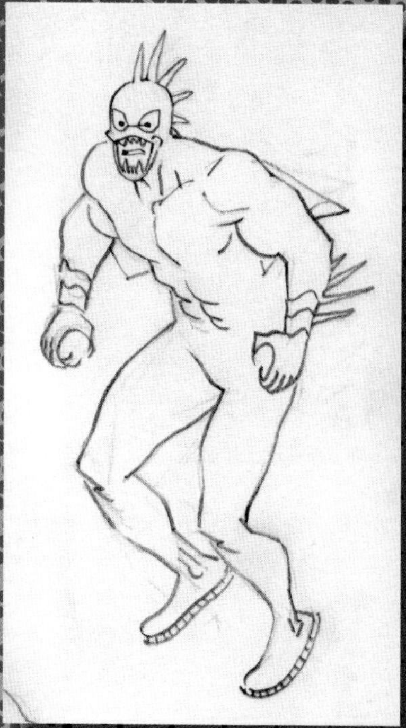

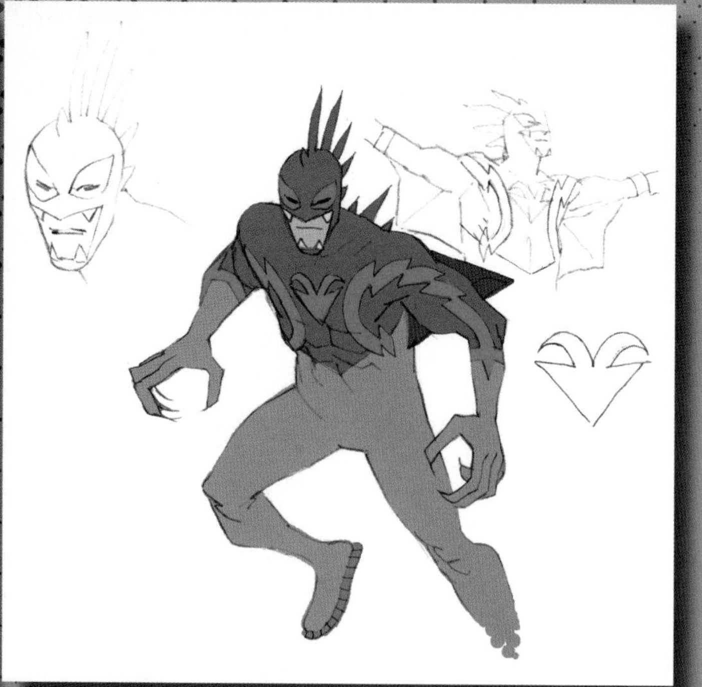

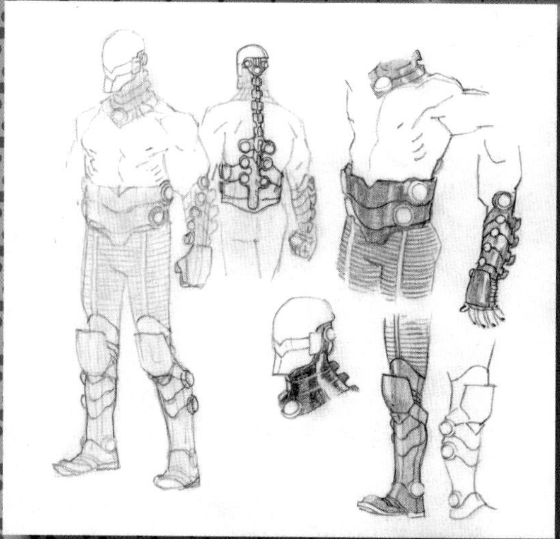

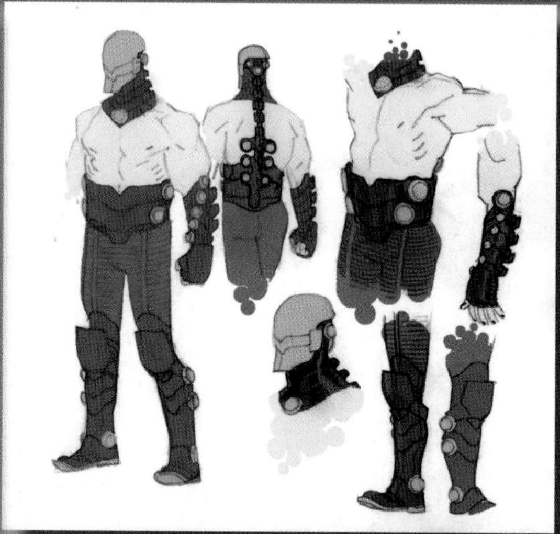

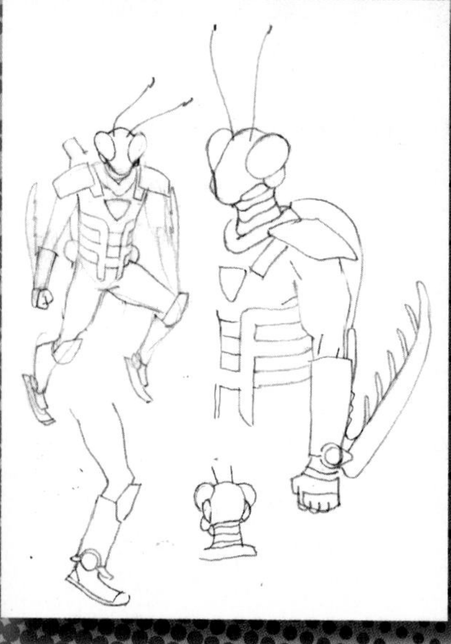

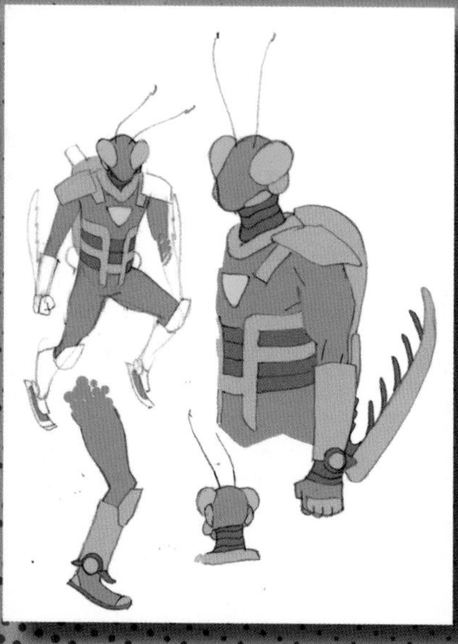

ROBERT KIRKMAN: El Chupacabra, Set and Slaying Mantis. El Chupacabra is from Mexico--get it? I have to give a shout out to Cory here. These designs are spectacular. El Chupacabra is so so so great. And Set just looks cool.

Slaying Mantis is pretty awesome as well... these are all great. Cory is great--even if he refuses to write commentary for sketchbook sections sometimes.

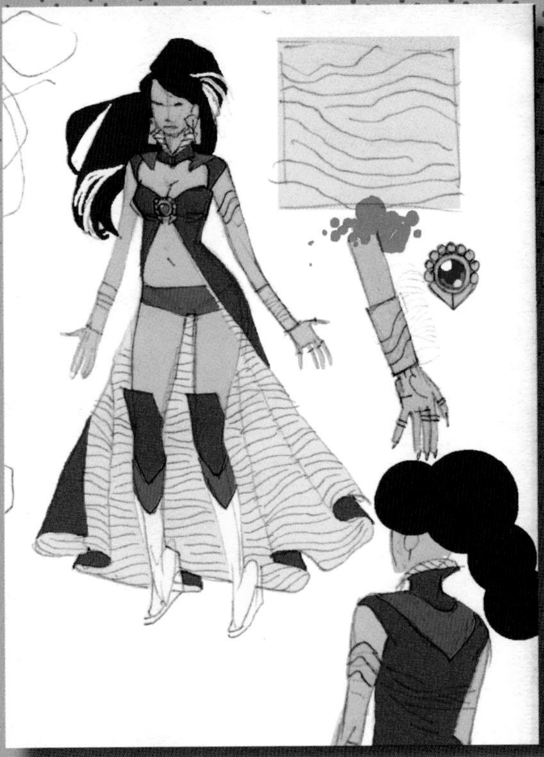

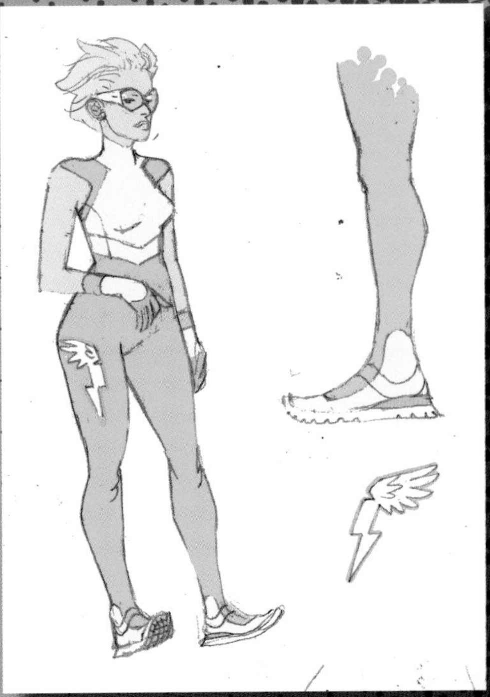

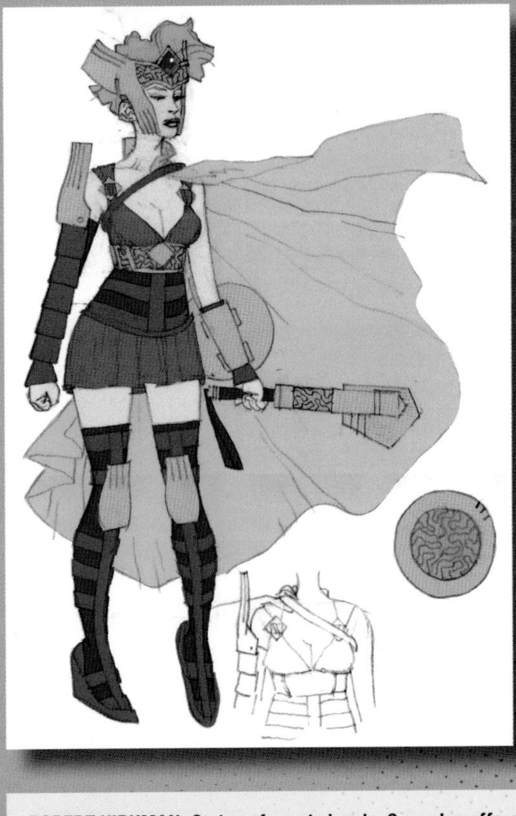

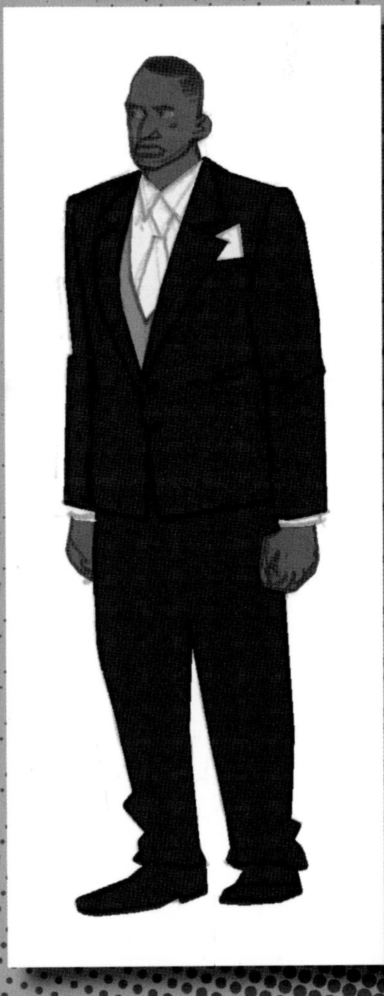

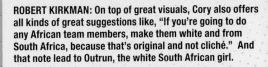

ROBERT KIRKMAN: On top of great visuals, Cory also offers all kinds of great suggestions like, "If you're going to do any African team members, make them white and from South Africa, because that's original and not cliché." And that note lead to Outrun, the white South African girl.

Also on this page, Red Eye, Embrace and the new villainous War Woman, a character who actually made her debut waaaaay back in issue 7 for anyone who was actually paying attention.

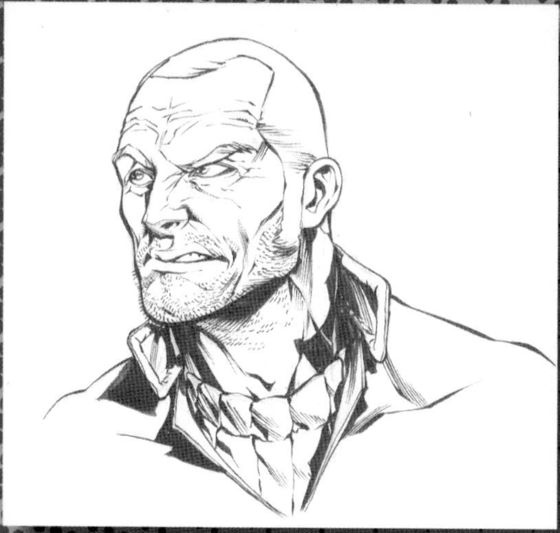

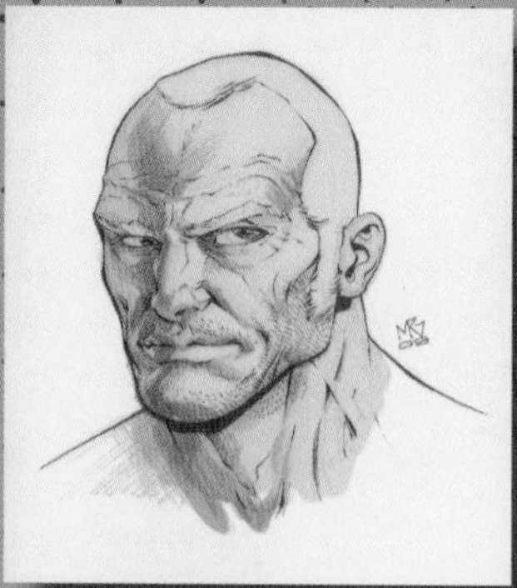

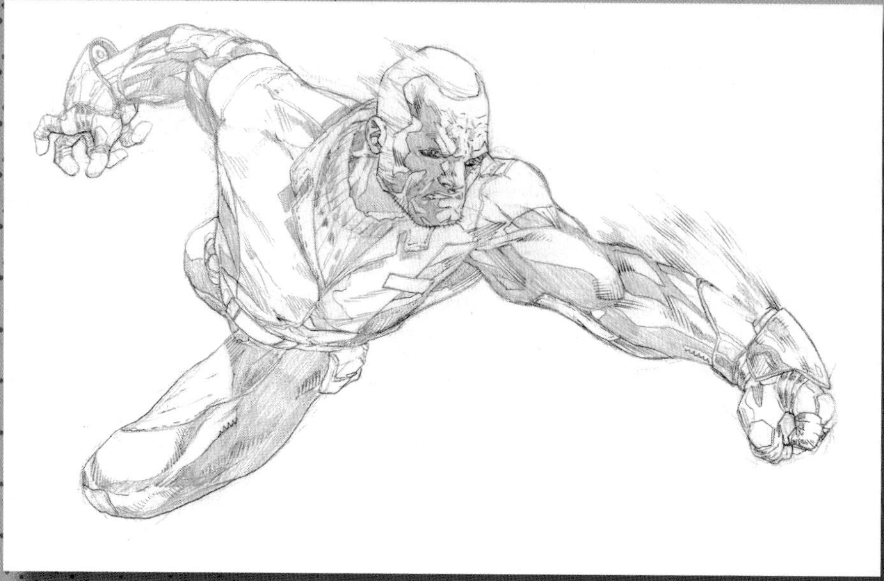

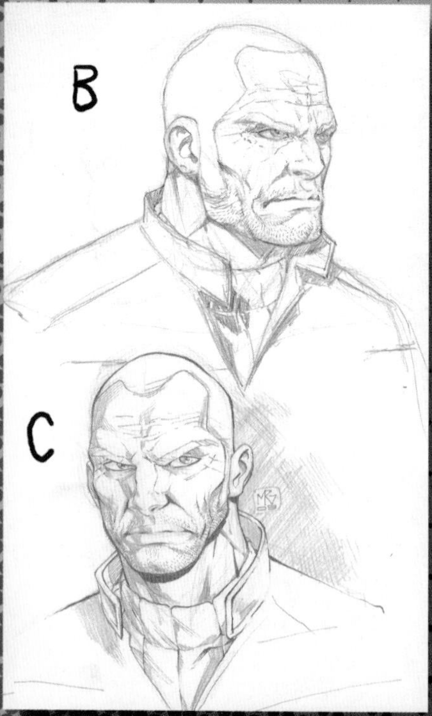
B
C

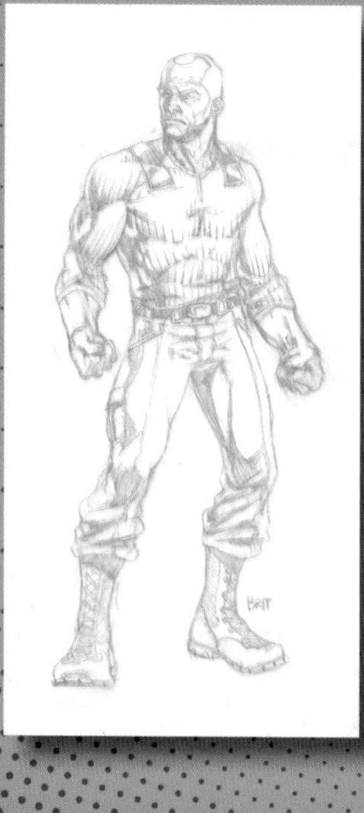
BRIT

GETTY: Here are some sketches that I did leading up to the series and some I did as warm-ups.

KIRKMAN: It was great to see Getty diving in, figuring out Brit. He's a really talented dude.

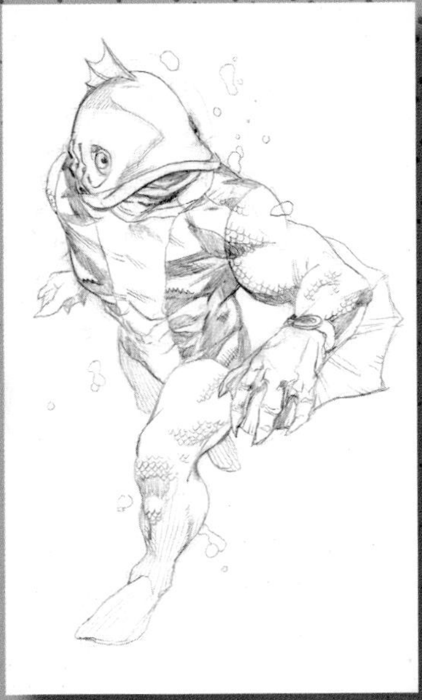

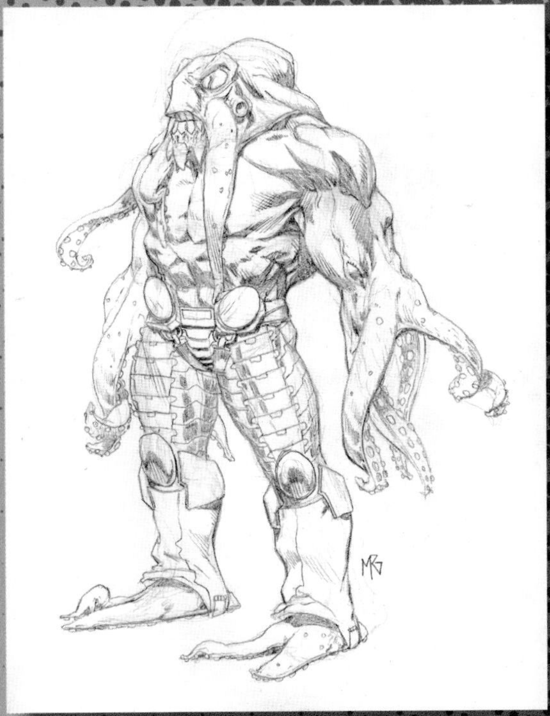

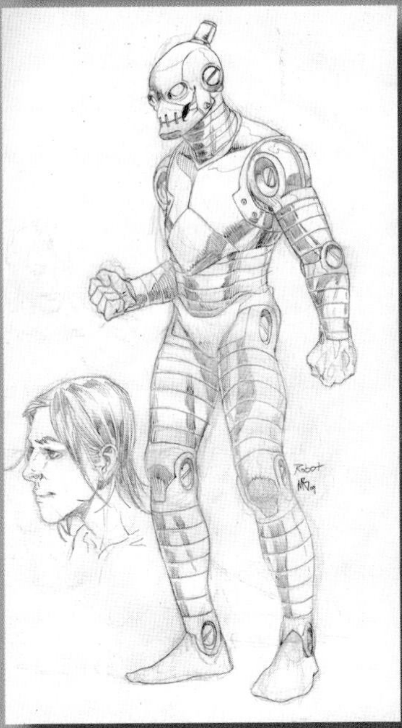
Robot

GETTY: As a fan, I loved getting Cory Walker's sketches in my email. I just tried to not screw them up.

Yeti was almost impossible for me to wrap my head around, and I think Robert got exhausted with my inability to pull off the glory of Cory's design. I'm still waiting for Cory's Le Brusier design sketch...

KIRKMAN: He sent a photo of a French bulldog! That counts!

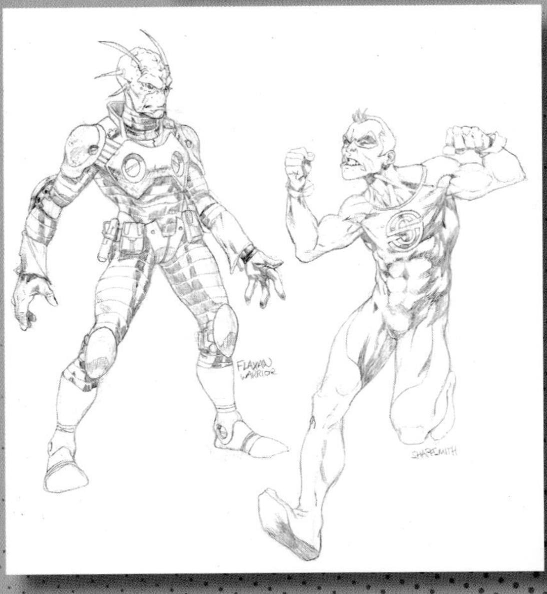
FLAXAN WARRIOR
SHAPESMITH

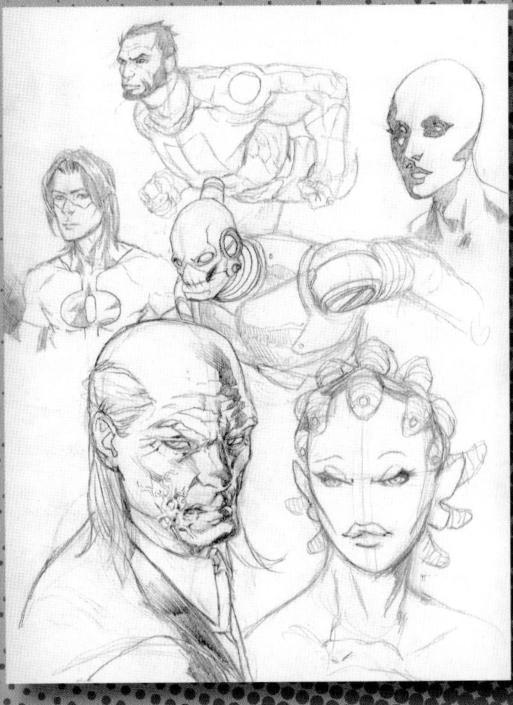

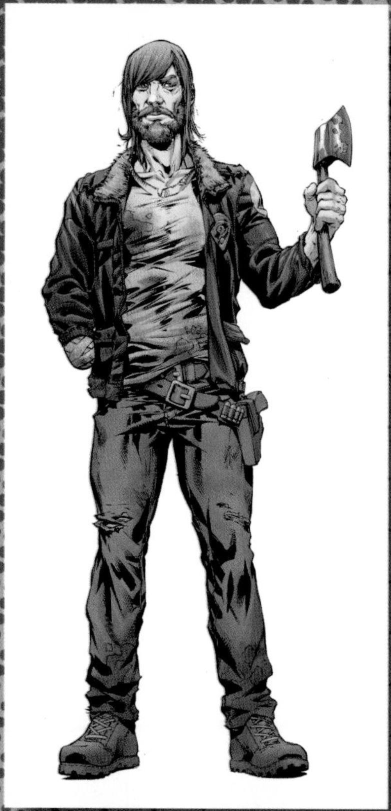

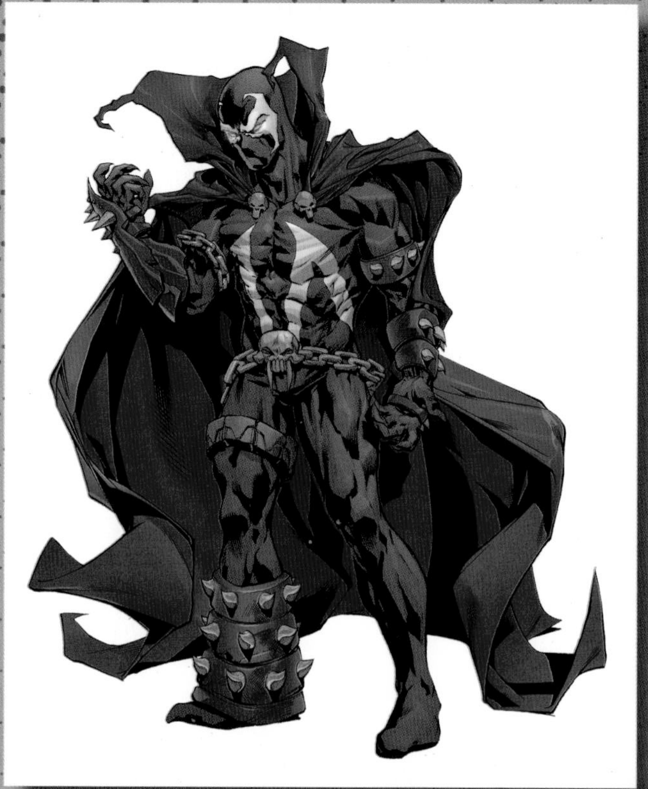

KIRKMAN: To promote this book, I thought it would be pretty funny to make a team up from the most commercially blatant team available to me. Rick Grimes from THE WALKING DEAD, Spawn from SPAWN, Invincible from INVINCIBLE, Barack Obama from Hawaii and, y'know... Perry Hotter. These teasers were a big success online.

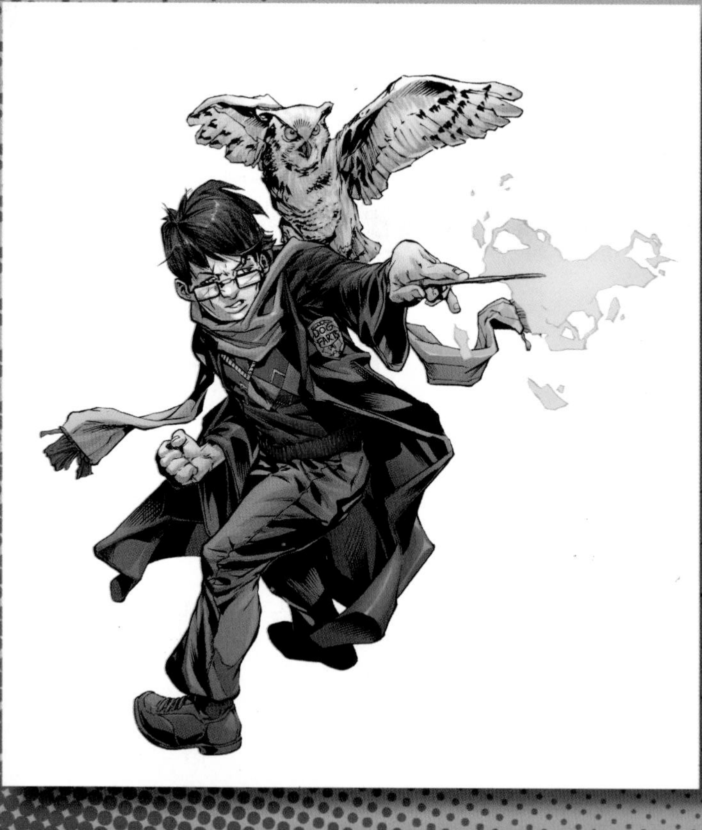

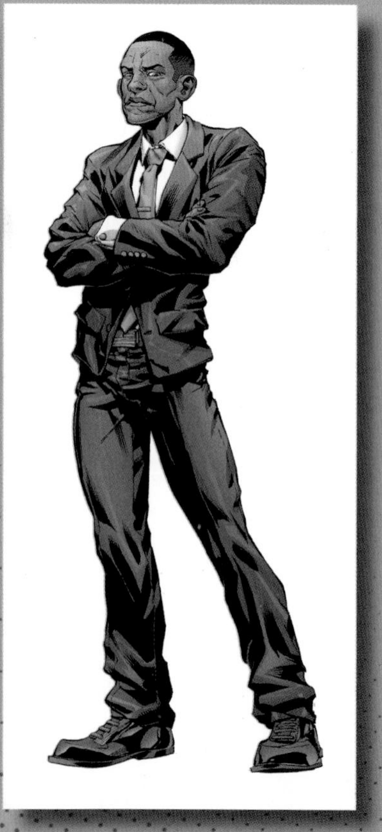

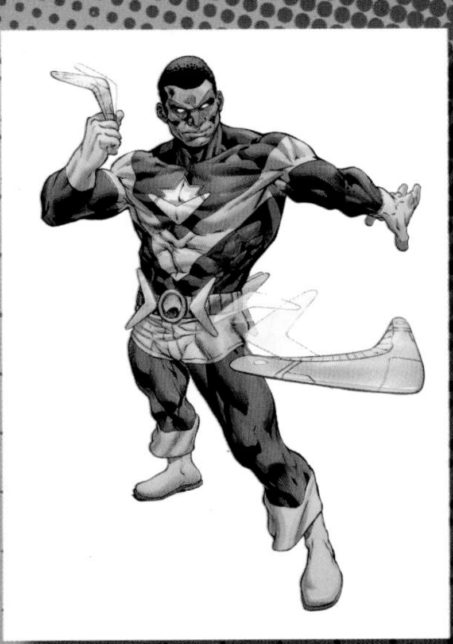

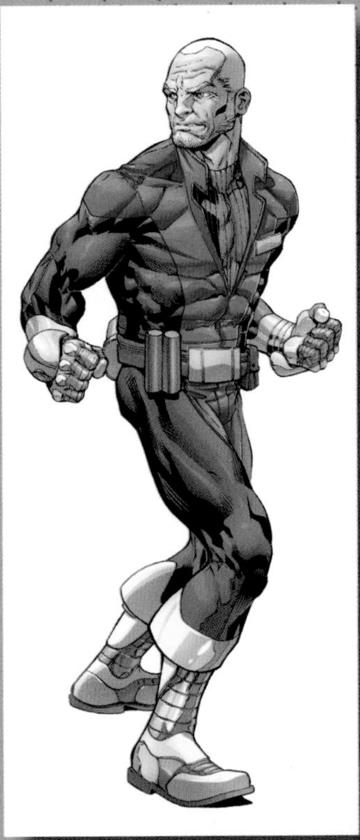

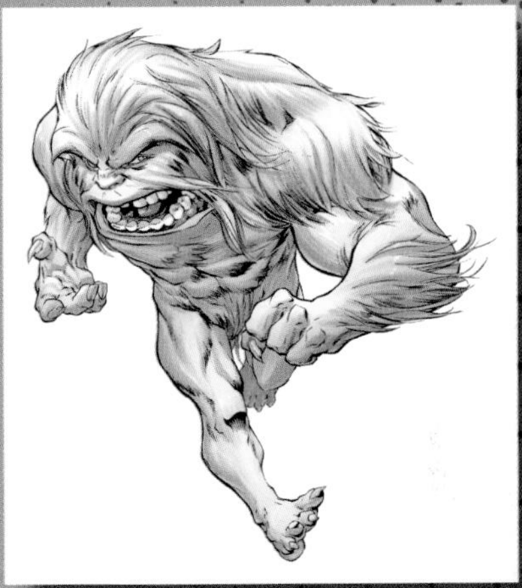

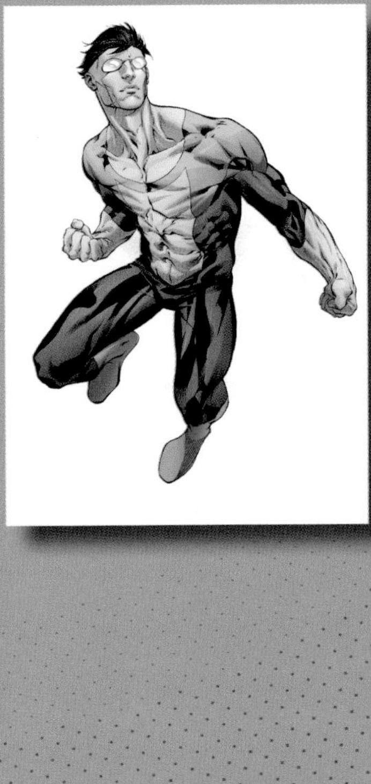

KIRKMAN: Then we did these real teasers showing off some of the new characters for this series... and Bulletproof…why was Bulletproof included? I don't think we'd designed any other new characters yet! Boo ya!

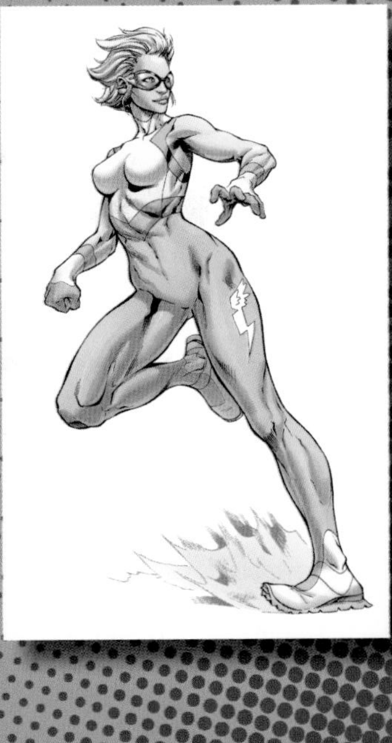

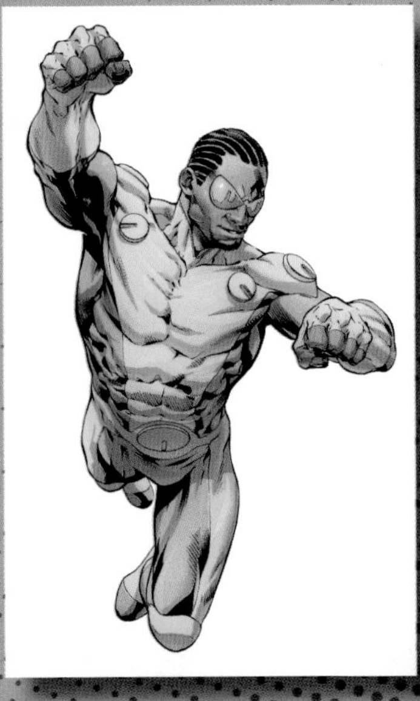

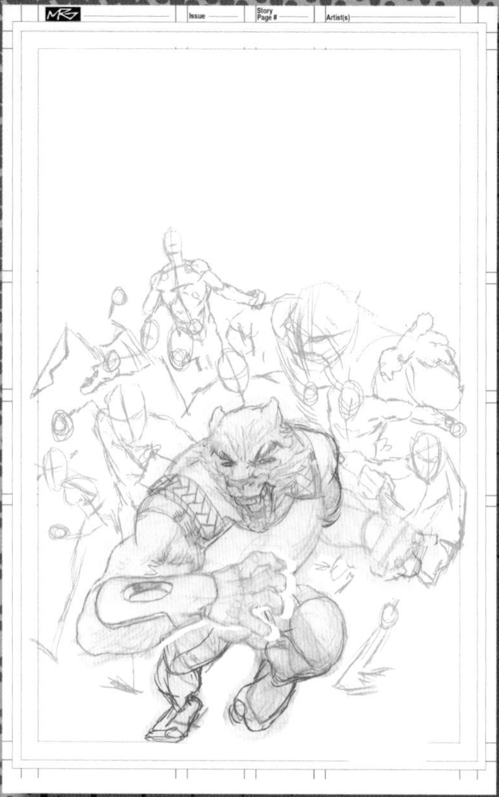
Issue
Story Page #
Artist(s)

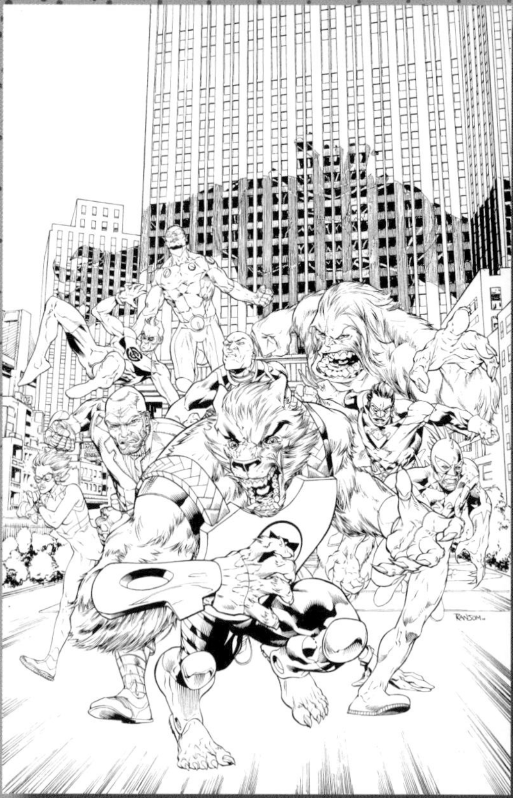
RANSOM

GETTY: Robert gave me a sweet cover composition sketch and I was excited to get to draw everyone's favorite Astounding Wolf-Person. After finishing the inks on this page, Robert made me redo Wolfman, which, while being annoying, it wasn't nearly as annoying as realizing he was totally right and the cover looks way better thanks to the change. Smart man.

KIRKMAN: Sorry. And don't you forget it!

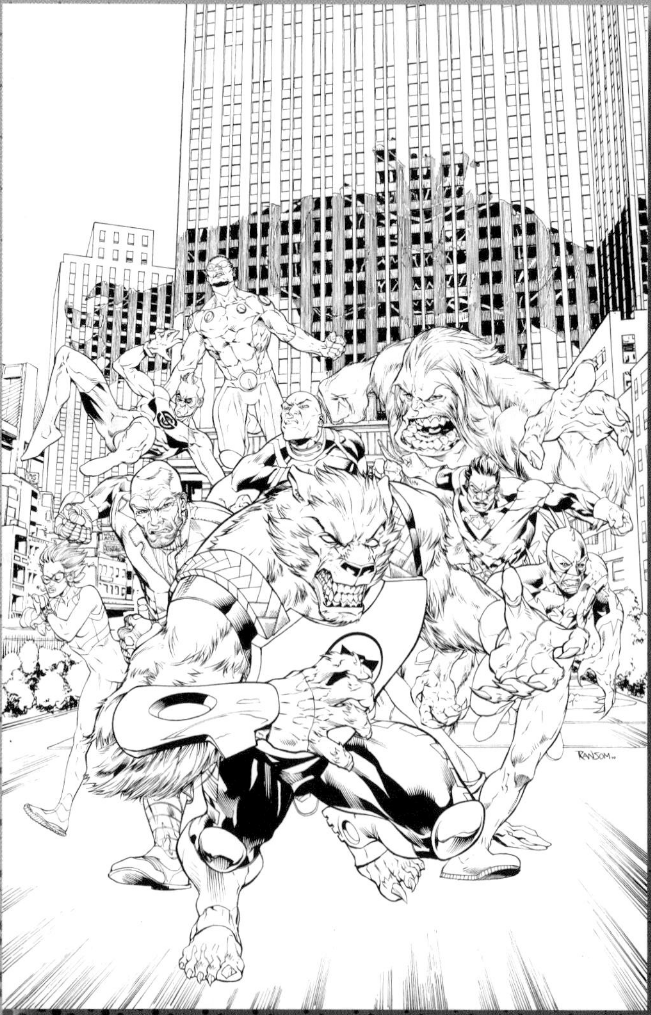
RANSOM

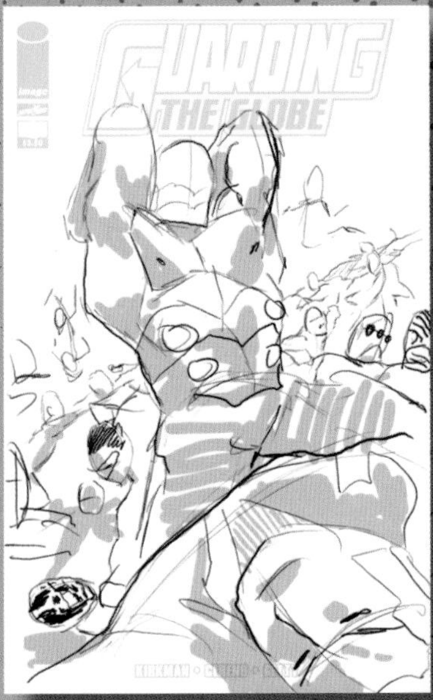

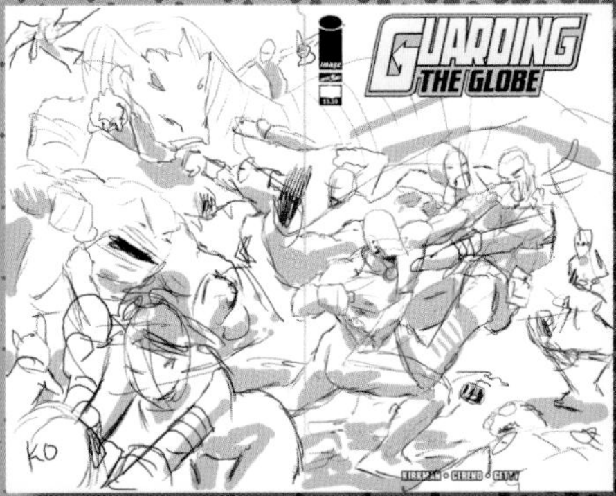
GUARDING THE GLOBE

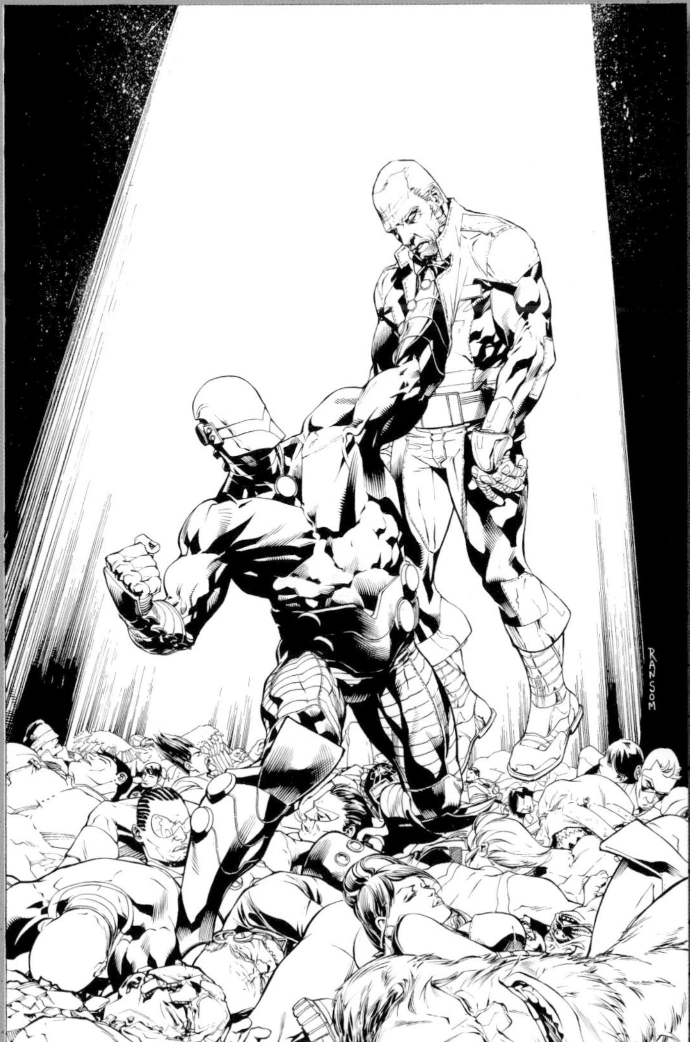
RANSOM

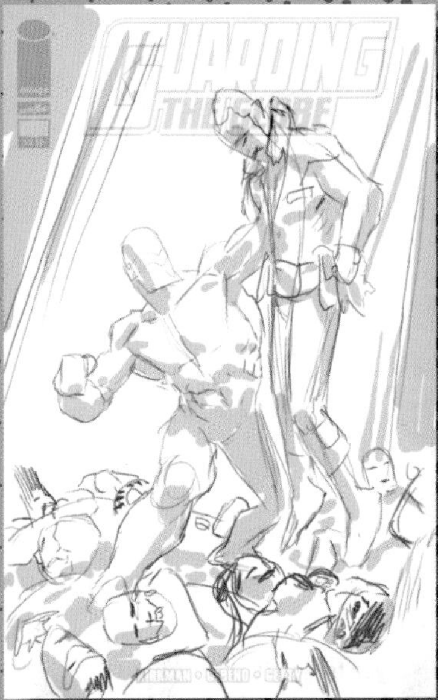

GETTY: I played around with three different compositions for this cover and we eventually picked this one knowing full well that it would be exhausting for FCO to figure out who belonged to what body part, and whose knee needed to be colored what. He ended up doing a dandy job... as we demanded.

KIRKMAN: This is my favorite cover from this mini-series. I love it.

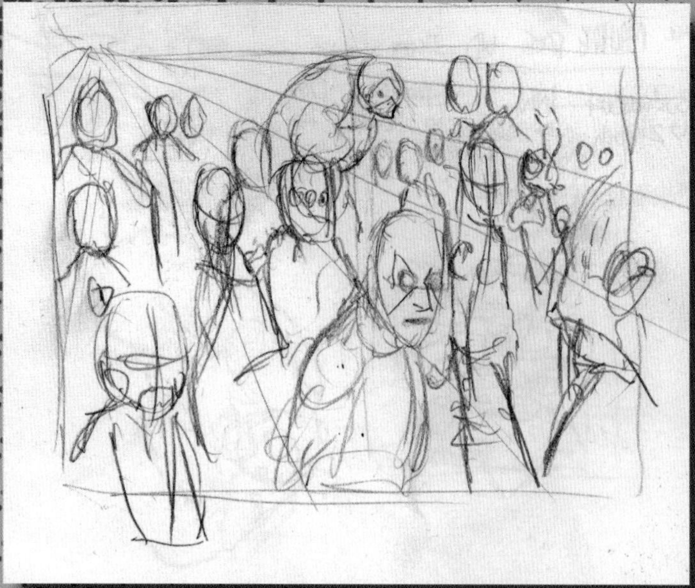

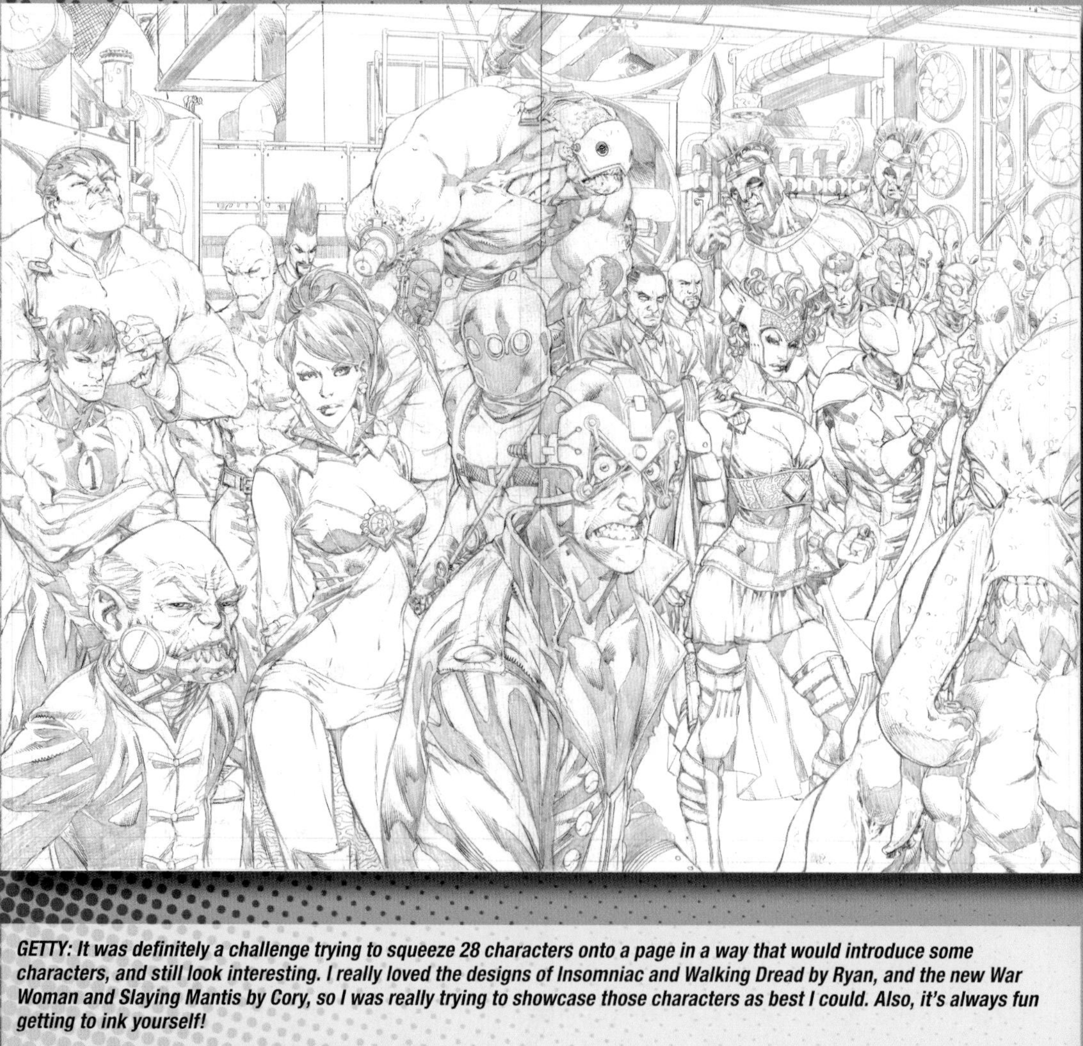

***GETTY:** It was definitely a challenge trying to squeeze 28 characters onto a page in a way that would introduce some characters, and still look interesting. I really loved the designs of Insomniac and Walking Dread by Ryan, and the new War Woman and Slaying Mantis by Cory, so I was really trying to showcase those characters as best I could. Also, it's always fun getting to ink yourself!*

KIRKMAN: Oh, come on--this page wasn't so hard.

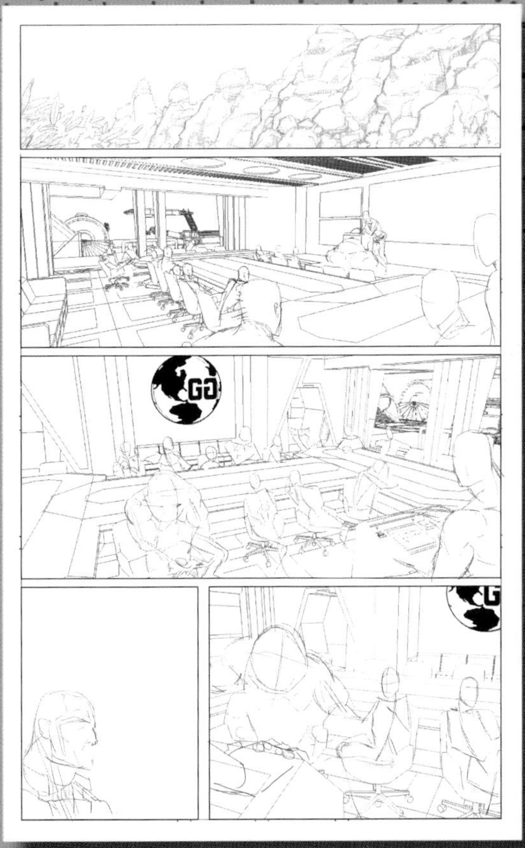

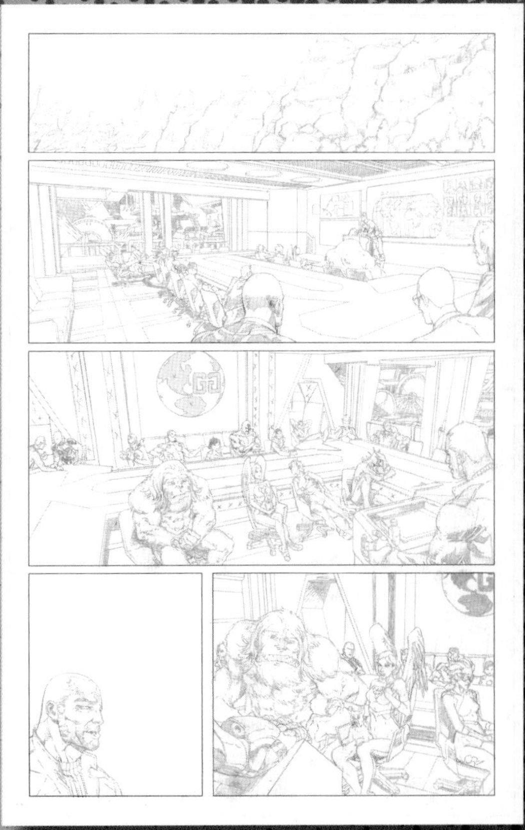

GETTY: I normally start pages digitally, laying down gesture underdrawings on top of 3D modeled backgrounds. Figuring I'd be drawing it a lot, I modeled almost the complete Guardians base to save time. I keep telling myself it saved time.

KIRKMAN: Hey, is that a page from issue 5 drawn by RYAN OTTLEY? But Ryan didn't draw any pages in that issue, did he?! Oh, wait... he did... because we hadn't heard from Getty in weeks and we were waiting on one measly page! And wouldn't you know it, as soon as Ryan batted his out--Getty magically turned his in. We opted to run Getty's to keep the book consistent.

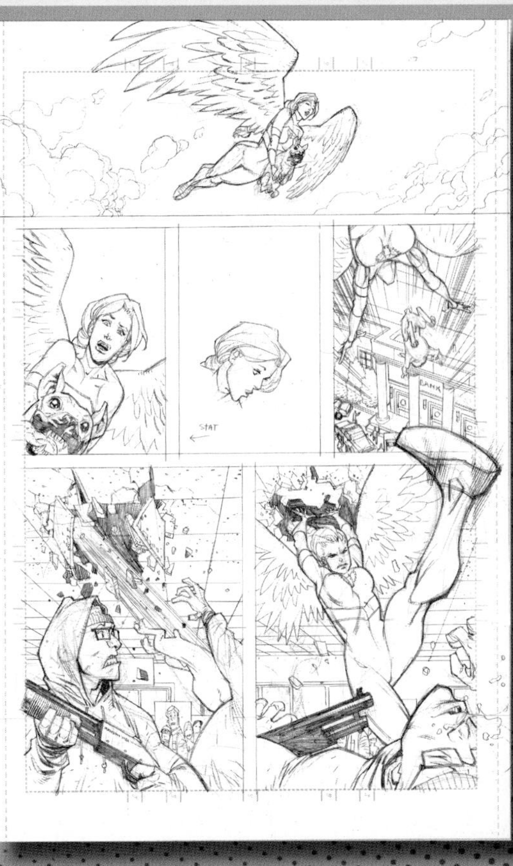

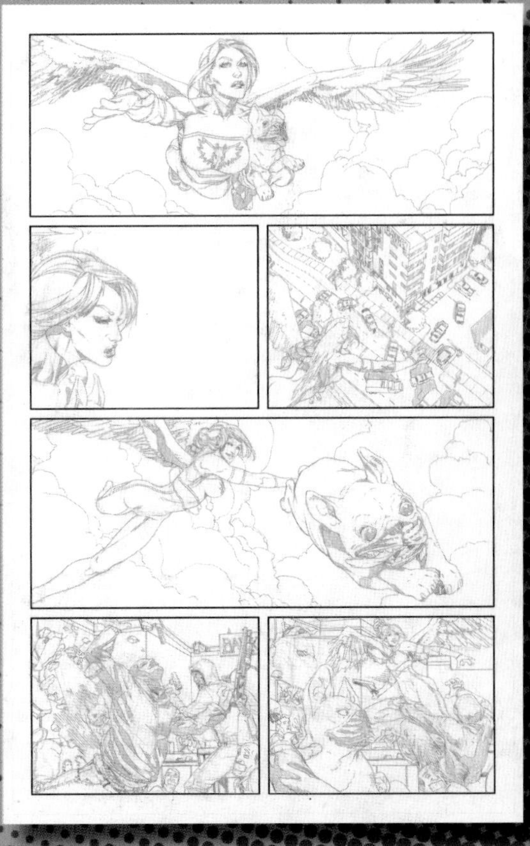

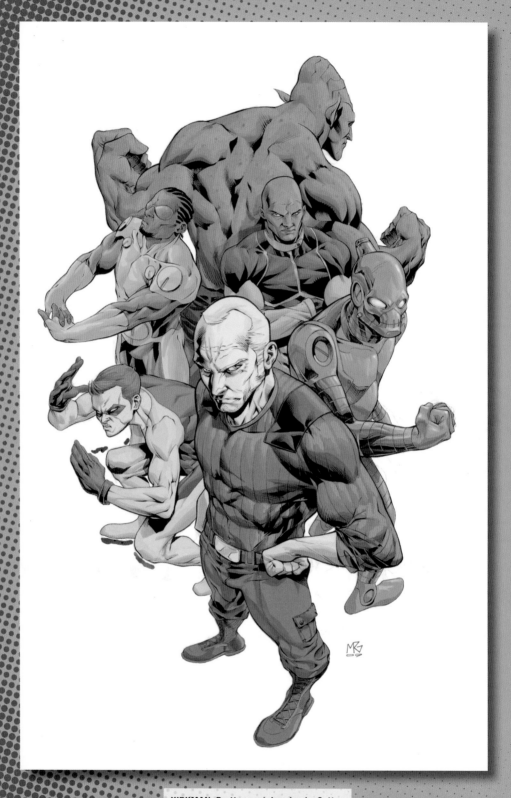

KIRKMAN: Pretty great drawing by Getty,
done early to get a feel for the characters.

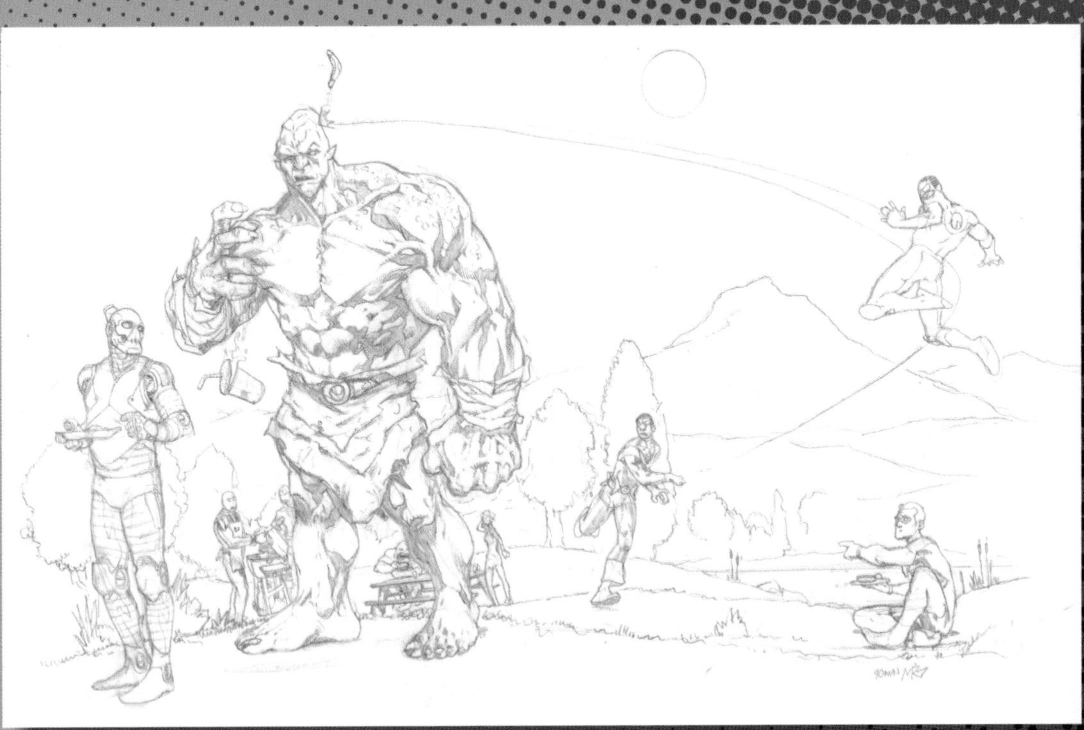

KIRKMAN: More Getty Goodies.

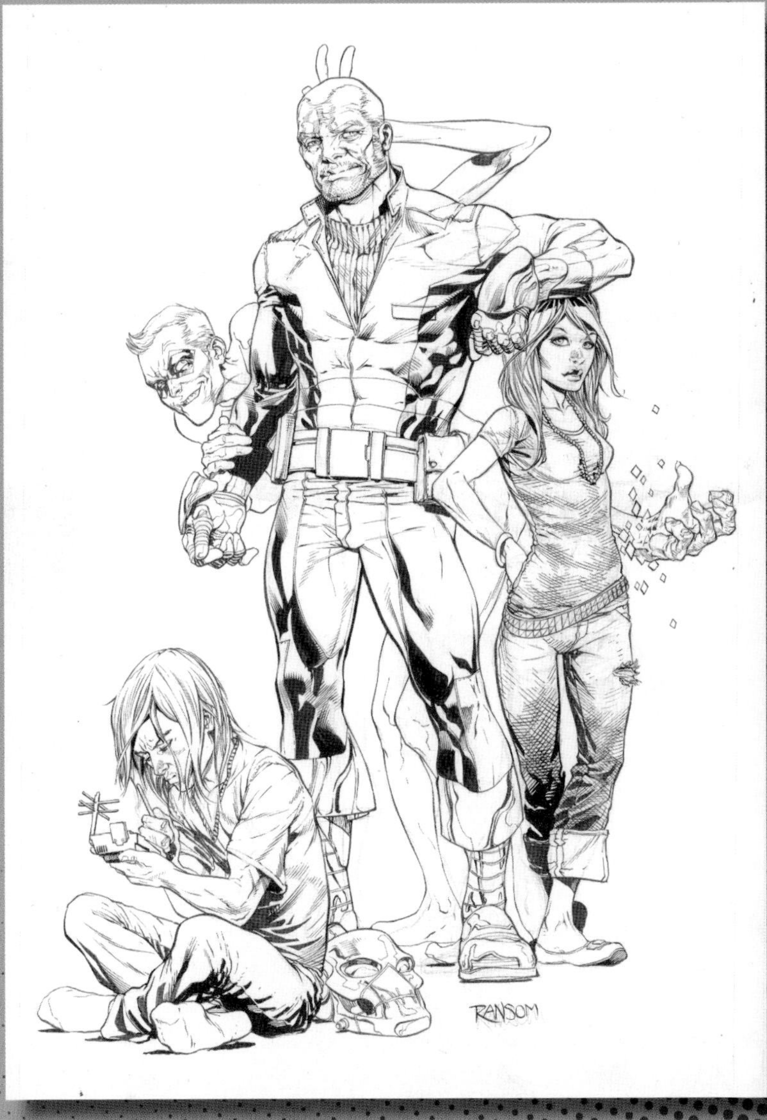
RANSOM

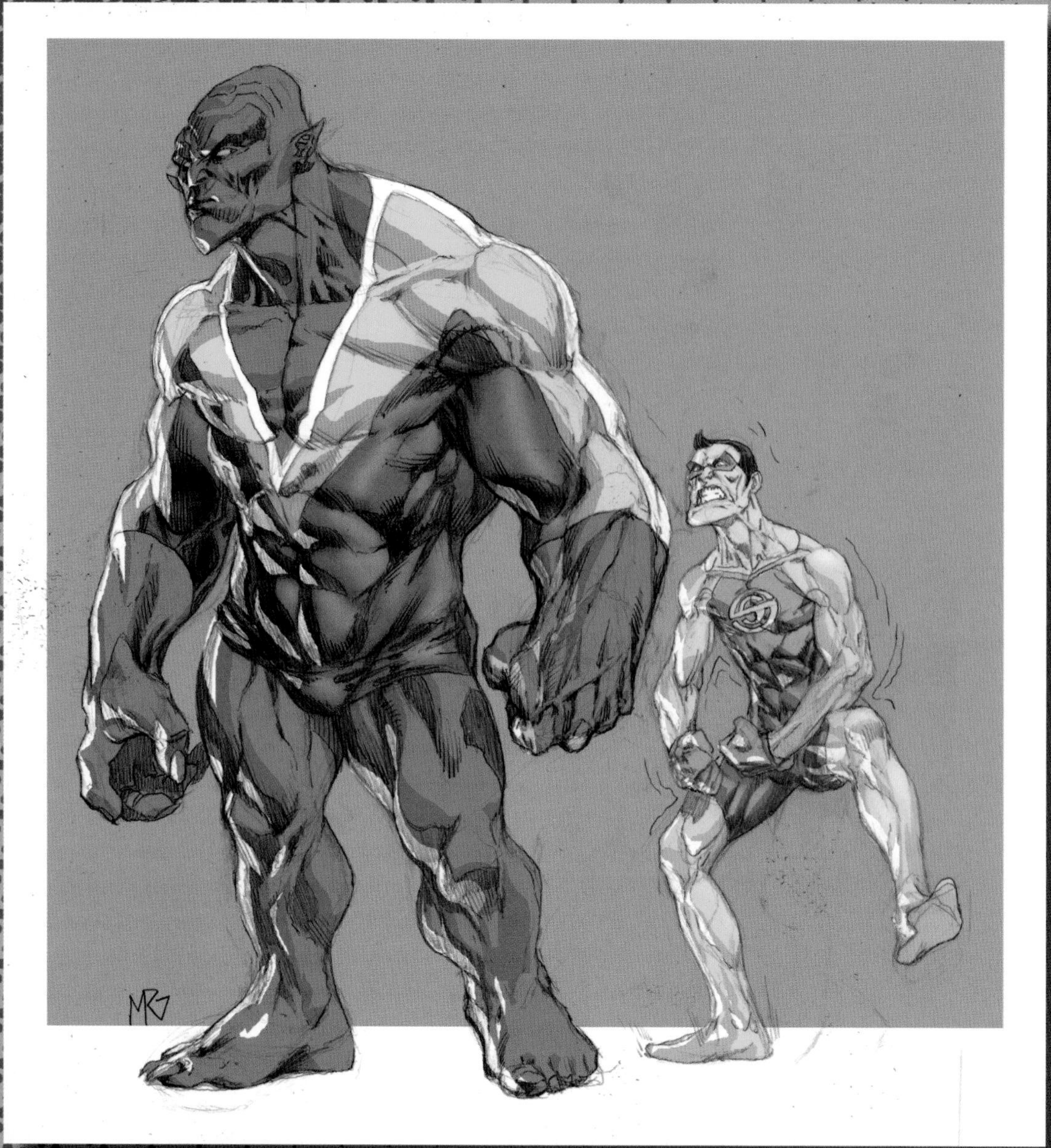

KIRKMAN: Octomom, get it? YEESH. Love Getty's rendition of Shapesmith, great stuff.

And on the following page--you'll see a damn awesome illustration of Kaboomerang. Sweet!

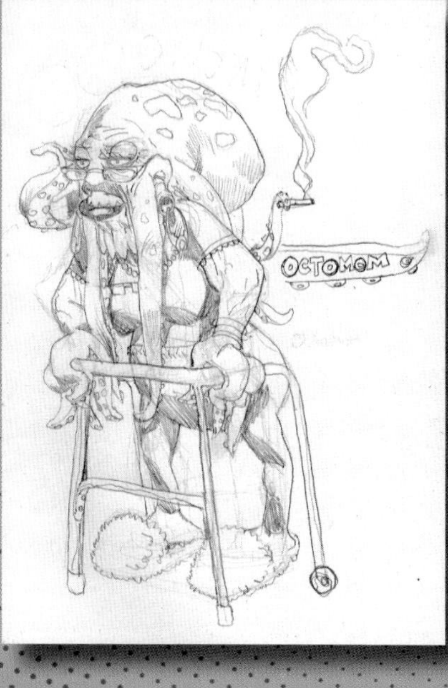
OCTOMOM

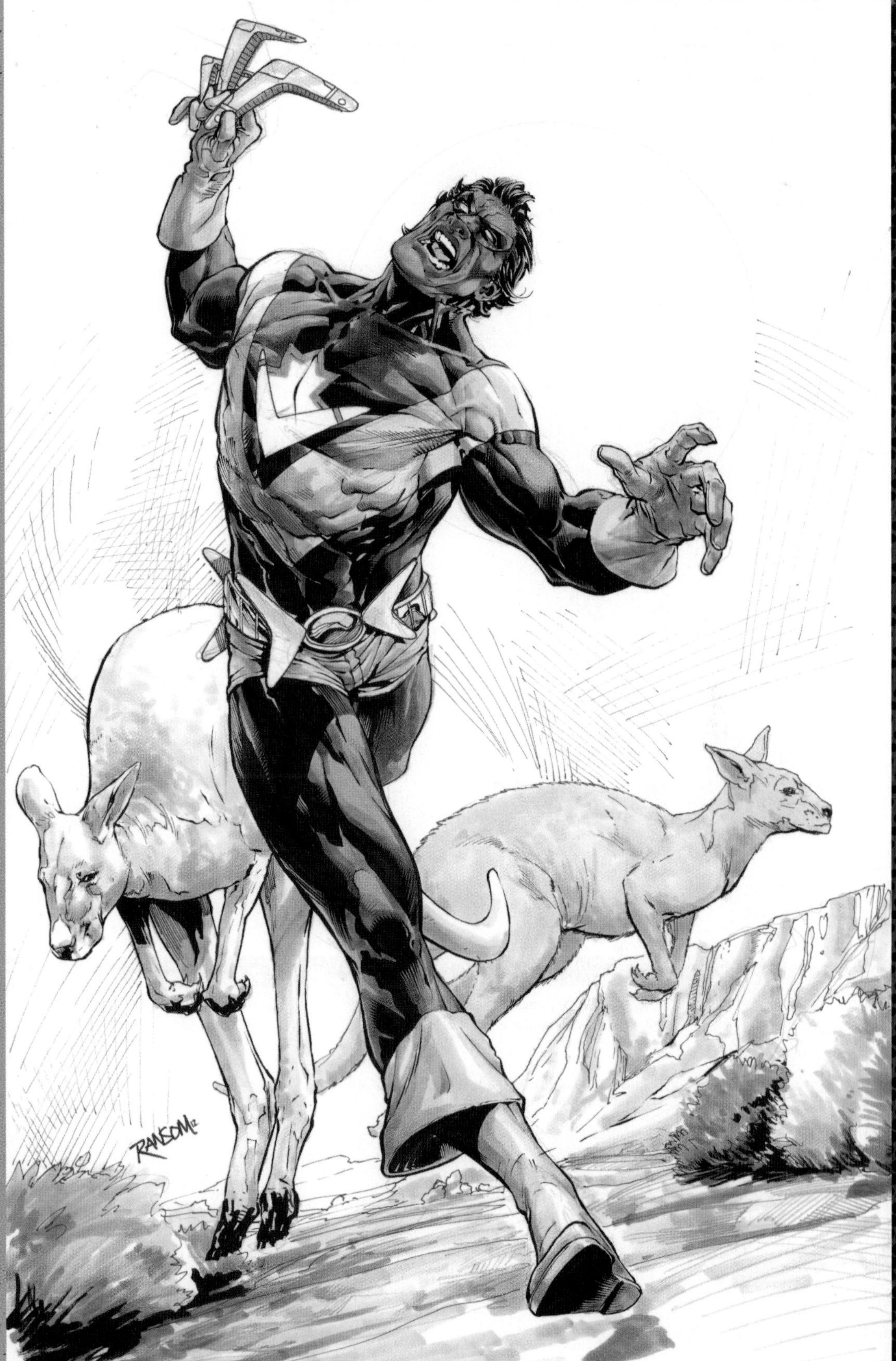
RANSOM'12

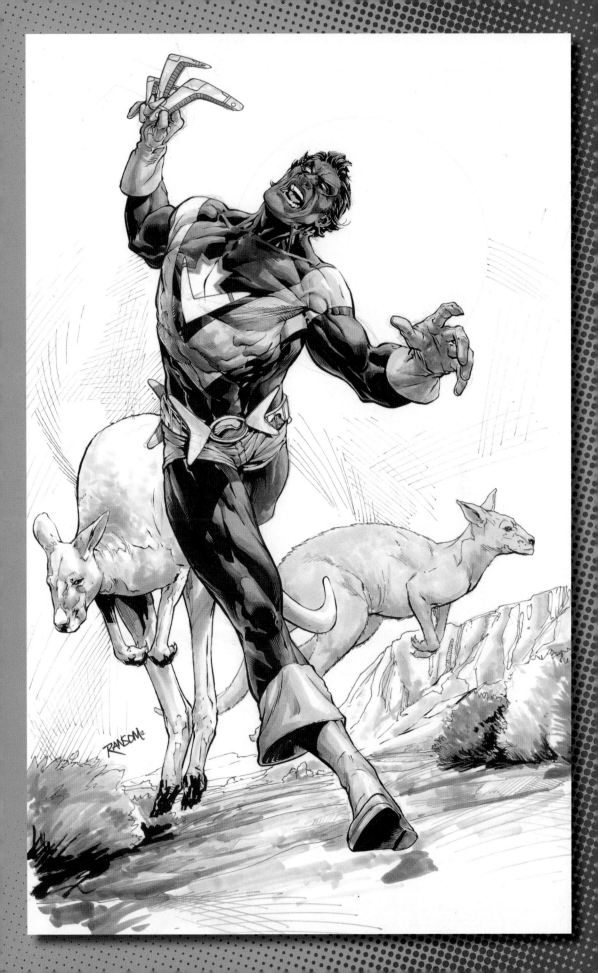

MORE GREAT BOOKS FROM ROBERT KIRKMAN & SKYBOUND!

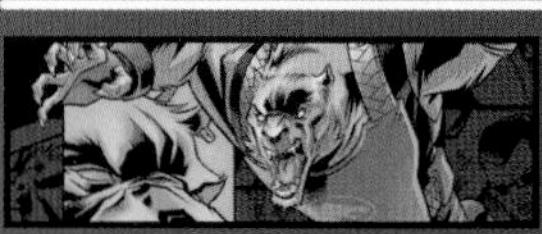

THE ASTOUNDING WOLF-MAN

VOL. 1 TP
ISBN: 978-1-58240-862-0
$14.99
VOL. 2 TP
ISBN: 978-1-60706-007-9
$14.99
VOL. 3 TP
ISBN: 978-1-60706-111-3
$16.99
VOL. 4 TP
ISBN: 978-1-60706-249-3
$16.99

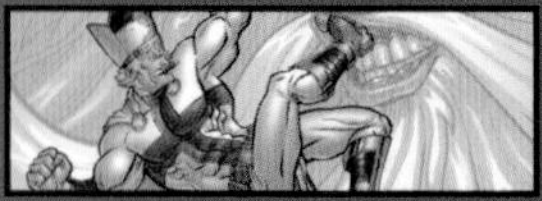

BATTLE POPE

VOL. 1: GENESIS TP
ISBN: 978-1-58240-572-8
$14.99
VOL. 2: MAYHEM TP
ISBN: 978-1-58240-529-2
$12.99
VOL. 3: PILLOW TALK TP
ISBN: 978-1-58240-677-0
$12.99
VOL. 4: WRATH OF GOD TP
ISBN: 978-1-58240-751-7
$9.99

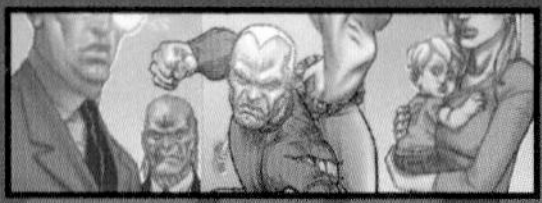

BRIT

VOL. 1: OLD SOLDIER TP
ISBN: 978-1-58240-678-7
$14.99
VOL. 2: AWOL
ISBN: 978-1-58240-864-4
$14.99
VOL. 3: FUBAR
ISBN: 978-1-60706-061-1
$16.99

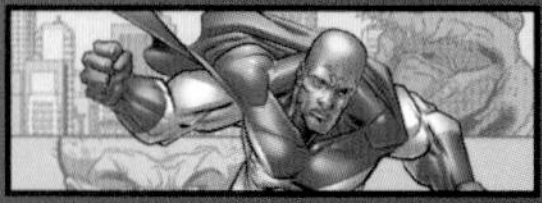

CAPES

VOL. 1: PUNCHING THE CLOCK TP
ISBN: 978-1-58240-756-2
$17.99

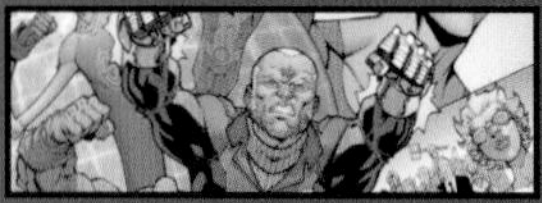

GUARDING THE GLOBE

VOL. 1: UNDER SIEGE TP
ISBN: 978-1-60706-356-8
$16.99

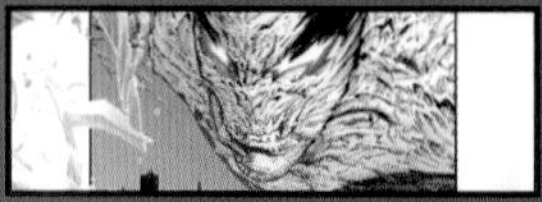

HAUNT

VOL. 1 TP
ISBN: 978-1-60706-154-0
$9.99
VOL. 2 TP
ISBN: 978-1-60706-229-5
$16.99
VOL. 3 TP
ISBN: 978-1-60706-552-4
$14.99
THE IMMORTAL EDITION, VOL. 1 HC
ISBN: 978-1-60706-241-7
$34.99

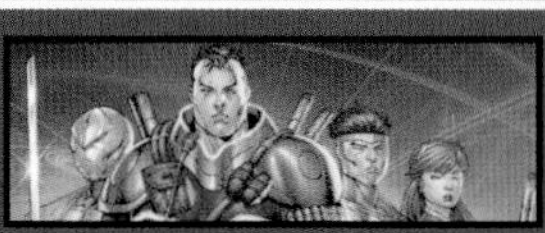

THE INFINITE

VOL. 1 TP
ISBN: 978-1-60706-475-6
$9.99

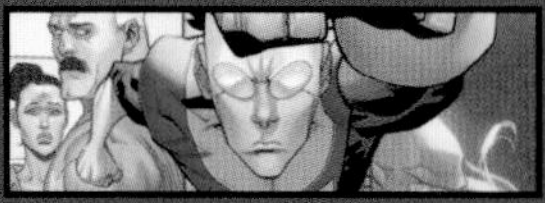

INVINCIBLE

VOL. 1: FAMILY MATTERS TP
ISBN: 978-1-58240-711-1
$12.99
VOL. 2: EIGHT IS ENOUGH TP
ISBN: 978-1-58240-347-2
$12.99
VOL. 3: PERFECT STRANGERS TP
ISBN: 978-1-58240-793-7
$12.99
VOL. 4: HEAD OF THE CLASS TP
ISBN: 978-1-58240-440-2
$14.95
VOL. 5: THE FACTS OF LIFE TP
ISBN: 978-1-58240-554-4
$14.99
VOL. 6: A DIFFERENT WORLD TP
ISBN: 978-1-58240-579-7
$14.99
VOL. 7: THREE'S COMPANY TP
ISBN: 978-1-58240-656-5
$14.99
VOL. 8: MY FAVORITE MARTIAN TP
ISBN: 978-1-58240-683-1
$14.99
VOL. 9: OUT OF THIS WORLD TP
ISBN: 978-1-58240-827-9
$14.99
VOL. 10: WHO'S THE BOSS TP
ISBN: 978-1-60706-013-0
$16.99
VOL. 11: HAPPY DAYS TP
ISBN: 978-1-60706-062-8
$16.99
VOL. 12: STILL STANDING TP
ISBN: 978-1-60706-166-3
$16.99
VOL. 13: GROWING PAINS TP
ISBN: 978-1-60706-251-6
$16.99
VOL. 14: THE VILTRUMITE WAR TP
ISBN: 978-1-60706-367-4
$19.99
VOL. 15: GET SMART TP
ISBN: 978-1-60706-498-5
$16.99
VOL. 16: FAMILY TIES TP
ISBN: 978-1-60706-579-1
$16.99
ULTIMATE COLLECTION, VOL. 1 HC
ISBN 978-1-58240-500-1
$34.95
ULTIMATE COLLECTION, VOL. 2 HC
ISBN: 978-1-58240-594-0
$34.99
ULTIMATE COLLECTION, VOL. 3 HC
ISBN: 978-1-58240-763-0
$34.99
ULTIMATE COLLECTION, VOL. 4 HC
ISBN: 978-1-58240-989-4
$34.99
ULTIMATE COLLECTION, VOL. 5 HC
ISBN: 978-1-60706-116-8
$34.99
ULTIMATE COLLECTION, VOL. 6 HC
ISBN: 978-1-60706-360-5
$34.99
ULTIMATE COLLECTION, VOL. 7 HC
ISBN: 978-1-60706-509-8
$39.99
THE OFFICIAL HANDBOOK OF THE INVINCIBLE UNIVERSE TP
ISBN: 978-1-58240-831-6
$12.99
INVINCIBLE PRESENTS, VOL. 1: ATOM EVE & REX SPLODE TP
ISBN: 978-1-60706-255-4
$14.99
THE COMPLETE INVINCIBLE LIBRARY, VOL. 2 HC
ISBN: 978-1-60706-112-0
$125.00
THE COMPLETE INVINCIBLE LIBRARY, VOL. 3 HC
ISBN: 978-1-60706-421-3
$125.00
INVINCIBLE COMPENDIUM VOL. 1
ISBN: 978-1-60706-411-4
$64.99

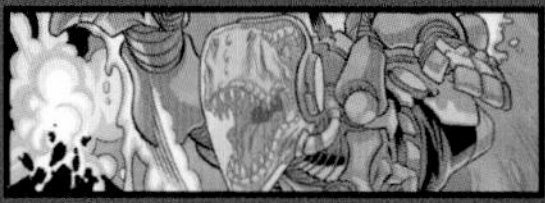

SUPER DINOSAUR

VOL. 1
ISBN: 978-1-60706-420-6
$9.99
VOL. 2
ISBN: 978-1-60706-568-5
$12.99
DELUXE COLORING BOOK
ISBN: 978-1-60706-481-7
$4.99

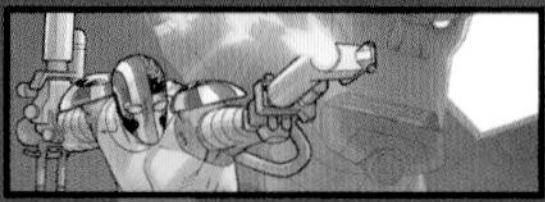

SUPERPATRIOT

AMERICA'S FIGHTING FORCE
ISBN: 978-1-58240-355-1
$14.99

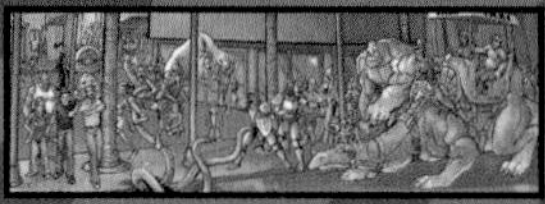

TALES OF THE REALM

HARDCOVER
ISBN: 978-1-58240-426-0
$34.95
TRADE PAPERBACK
ISBN: 978-1-58240-394-6
$14.95

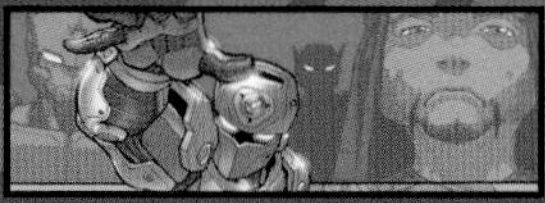

TECH JACKET

VOL. 1: THE BOY FROM EARTH TP
ISBN: 978-1-58240-771-5
$14.99

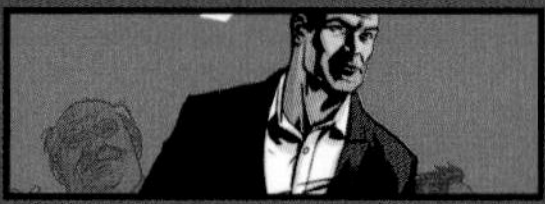

THIEF OF THIEVES

VOL. 1
ISBN: 978-1-60706-592-0
$14.99

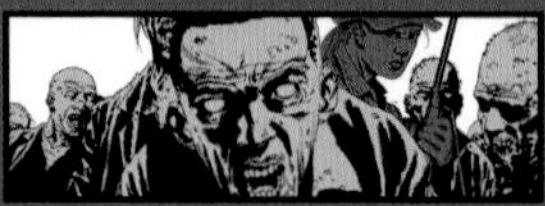

THE WALKING DEAD

VOL. 1: DAYS GONE BYE TP
ISBN: 978-1-58240-672-5
$9.99
VOL. 2: MILES BEHIND US TP
ISBN: 978-1-58240-775-3
$14.99
VOL. 3: SAFETY BEHIND BARS TP
ISBN: 978-1-58240-805-7
$14.99
VOL. 4: THE HEART'S DESIRE TP
ISBN: 978-1-58240-530-8
$14.99
VOL. 5: THE BEST DEFENSE TP
ISBN: 978-1-58240-612-1
$14.99
VOL. 6: THIS SORROWFUL LIFE TP
ISBN: 978-1-58240-684-8
$14.99
VOL. 7: THE CALM BEFORE TP
ISBN: 978-1-58240-828-6
$14.99
VOL. 8: MADE TO SUFFER TP
ISBN: 978-1-58240-883-5
$14.99
VOL. 9: HERE WE REMAIN TP
ISBN: 978-1-60706-022-2
$14.99
VOL. 10: WHAT WE BECOME TP
ISBN: 978-1-60706-075-8
$14.99
VOL. 11: FEAR THE HUNTERS TP
ISBN: 978-1-60706-181-6
$14.99
VOL. 12: LIFE AMONG THEM TP
ISBN: 978-1-60706-254-7
$14.99
VOL. 13: TOO FAR GONE TP
ISBN: 978-1-60706-329-2
$14.99
VOL. 14: NO WAY OUT TP
ISBN: 978-1-60706-392-6
$14.99
VOL. 15: WE FIND OURSELVES TP
ISBN: 978-1-60706-392-6
$14.99
BOOK ONE HC
ISBN: 978-1-58240-619-0
$34.99
BOOK TWO HC
ISBN: 978-1-58240-698-5
$34.99
BOOK THREE HC
ISBN: 978-1-58240-825-5
$34.99
BOOK FOUR HC
ISBN: 978-1-60706-000-0
$34.99
BOOK FIVE HC
ISBN: 978-1-60706-171-7
$34.99
BOOK SIX HC
ISBN: 978-1-60706-327-8
$34.99
BOOK SEVEN HC
ISBN: 978-1-60706-439-8
$34.99
BOOK EIGHT HC
ISBN: 978-1-60706-593-7
$34.99
DELUXE HARDCOVER, VOL. 1
ISBN: 978-1-58240-619-0
$100.00
DELUXE HARDCOVER, VOL. 2
ISBN: 978-1-60706-029-7
$100.00
DELUXE HARDCOVER, VOL. 3
ISBN: 978-1-60706-330-8
$100.00
THE WALKING DEAD: THE COVERS, VOL. 1 HC
ISBN: 978-1-60706-002-4
$24.99
THE WALKING DEAD SURVIVORS' GUIDE
ISBN: 978-1-60706-458-9
$12.99

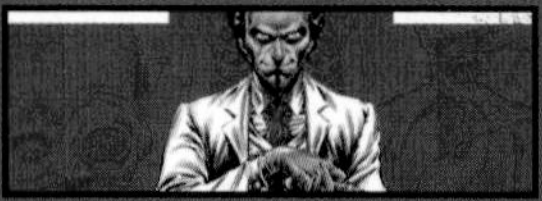

WITCH DOCTOR

VOL. 1: UNDER THE KNIFE TP
ISBN: 978-1-60706-441-1
$12.99

TO FIND YOUR NEAREST COMIC BOOK STORE, CALL:
1-888-COMIC-BOOK